SERVETUS, SW
AND THE NATU

Andrew M. T. Dibb

University Press of America,® Inc.
Lanham · Boulder · New York · Toronto · Oxford

Copyright © 2005 by
University Press of America,® Inc.
4501 Forbes Boulevard
Suite 200
Lanham, Maryland 20706
UPA Acquisitions Department (301) 459-3366

PO Box 317
Oxford
OX2 9RU, UK

Library of Congress Control Number: 2004118290
ISBN 0-7618-2975-X (paperback : alk. ppr.)

Table of Contents

Prologue

For some people researching and writing history is the height of joy and fulfilment. If that history is about the most sublime subjects, it becomes also a quest for personal growth and understanding. It is humbling to come into close contact, across the centuries, with great minds, with people who have dedicated their lives to understanding the nature of God. It is reassuring to know that learned scholars can go off the rails as easily as any one else. It is less gratifying to witness the intolerance so often engendered by heterodox beliefs, and the extremes to which anger and self-righteousness often carry people. Yet reflection on these things reminds one of one's own short-comings and one's own intolerance.

In many respects this thesis has been a personal spiritual journey, an examination of the labyrinthine concepts surrounding the nature of God. Who is the God we worship, and why do Christians understand him to be the God they think he is? How do we know that our own personal, denominational interpretation of the Bible is accurate and true?

A study of the history of theology down the ages gives many insights and answers to these questions. It should not surprise us if we find a firm friend in someone who died centuries ago, or perhaps discordance with a theologian, a scholar, who until a close examination of his work showed us a different side of him.

The study of history has convinced me of one thing: no one individual, church, era or movement has ever had the definitive understanding of who God is, of how he manifests himself or affects the people of this world, be they believers or unbelievers. The subject of God is too vast, too infinite, to be encapsulated by one person. History marks the changes of the understanding of God down the ages, from the simplicity of the Apostles to the complexities of the Schoolmen, to our modern ecumenical relativism. At any given time, who was right? Who was wrong?

The simple solution of backing one's argument with the phrase 'the Bible says', doesn't answer these questions. Throughout the ages people have had access to the Bible, have read, studied and interpreted it according to their best understanding, and in so doing have reflected some aspect of God. Yet the Bible is infinite. It can be read in an countless ways, as one sees people doing down the ages.

History brings all these varieties, complexities and divisions to the forefront of the mind, and there the presence of God becomes a living, vibrant force satisfying the needs of each age, allowing new and different ones to emerge.

Writing a Doctoral Thesis is, in many ways, a community effort. As the subjects become living, breathing people with thoughts and ideas of their own, even if they are only accessed in books, manuscripts and through the eyes of interpreters, so much of what they say becomes grist for the mill.

That grist, however, cannot be obtained without considerable outside help, for which I would like to thank the following people:

Firstly, many thanks to the staff of the Department of Church History at the University of South Africa. Their encouragement over the years, from undergraduate studies to the present, has been tremendous. Professor Gerald Pillay encouraged the first tentative steps towards this study. Dr. Joan Millard supervised my Master of Theology dissertation, and gave me the courage to undertake this Doctoral thesis. Professor Gary Frank, my first promoter, had a seminal influence on this study.

Special thanks, however, to Professor Jafta, current head of the Department Of Church History, who has patiently promoted this thesis to the end. His guidance and encouragement has been much appreciated. His willingness to wade through numerous drafts and offer both criticism and advice has made my task much easier, and his unfailing enthusiasm and support of this study bolstered my spirits.

Also at Unisa, many thanks to Mrs. Mary-Lyn Suttie for her help with research. Her computer searches have been most useful. Thanks also to the unknown members of the Library staff for providing photo-copies of countless articles and so saving me hundreds of hours of 'leg' work.

Outside of Unisa, I would like to thank the staff of the Swedenborg Library at the Academy of the New Church in Bryn Athyn, Pennsylvania. As one of the largest Swedenborgian research facilities in the world they made it possible for me to gain access to information and materials unavailable elsewhere, including information about Emanuel Swedenborg and copies of rare books about Servetus. In 1998 they allowed me to photocopy their entire collection of noncopyrighted material on Michael Servetus, which forms the back-bone of the Servetus information in this study. Photocopying took all day, and their support and good humour were much appreciated.

I'd like to thank the Rev. Erik E. Sandstrom for his help in researching Swedenborg, and Mrs. Rachel Longstaff for her help in finding some of the more obscure books on Michael Servetus.

In the non-scholastic field, thanks are also due to the General Church of the New Jerusalem, especially Rev. Philip Schnarr for his interest in this project. Similarly, many thanks to the people of my congregation, the New Church Buccleuch, for being willing to allow me the freedom to pursue this study. Their interest and fortitude in listening to thesis-related subjects has been phenomenal.

I also particularly want to thank Mrs. Virginia Stephens and Dr. Margo von Beck for proof-reading and correcting long stretches of this thesis, and also for giving valuable insight into Swedenborg's theology.

Finally, one cannot undertake a study of this sort without the full support of one's family. I would like to thank my wife, Cara, and my children, Malcolm, Meghan and Laird for their patience with me. Dad always had 'some work to do on his thesis', and while I made every effort not to allow it to unduly inconvenience the family, it did. I am grateful for their support and encouragement, and hope that some day they too will know the pleasure of research and writing.

Acknowledgments

The author and publisher gratefully acknowledge permission to quote material from the following publications:

Earl Morse Wilbur's translation *Two Treatises of Servetus on the Trinity.* © 1932. By permission of Harvard Theological Studies.

Maxwell Staniforth's volume, *Early Christian Writings.* © 1987. By permission of Penguin Books Ltd.

John Elliot's translation of Swedenborgs *Arcana Coelestia.* By permission of The Swedenborg Society.

William Dick's translation of Swedenborg's *True Christian Religion.* By permission of The Swedenborg Society.

Doris Harley's translation of Swedenborg's *Athanasian Creed.* By permission of The Swedenborg Society.

Cyriel Sigstedts volume, *Swedenborg Epic.* By permission of The Swedenborg Society.

Alfred Acton's two volume work, *Letters and Memorials of Emanuel Swedenborg* (1948 and 1955). By permission of the Swedenborg Scientific Association.

W.R. Woofenden's translation of Swedenborg's *Journal of Dreams.* By permission of the Swedenborg Foundation.

J.C. Ager's translation of Swedenborg's *Angelic Wisdom concerning the Divine Love and the Divine Wisdom.* By permission of The Swedenborg Foundation.

Introduction

The essence of Christianity is the belief that Jesus Christ was born into this world, lived among people, died on the cross and was resurrected. The very idea of Christ's birth begs the question of his parentage - was he God or man? His life amongst people stirs questions of the origin of his teaching and power. His death and resurrection complete the circle by recalling of his relationship with God and Mary, and pose the question 'how'. Attempts to balance understanding of the relationship within him between the divine and human exacerbate the friction among theologians. For two thousand years these issues exercised the minds of the greatest (and least) Christian scholars. Solutions and consensus have not come easily. They evolved over centuries, facing constant re-examination and discussion and often bitter debate. Gradually the concepts of the place of Christ within the Godhead took the form they have in Christianity today.

The story of the attempt to understand the nature of Christ has been told many times and viewed from countless angles. Each generation of theologians and historians has either added to or subtracted from the mosaic of thoughts, ideas and opinions of previous generations. Yet through it all an orthodox picture emerged that has remained sacrosanct, beyond question or doubt if one wished to retain the label of 'Christian'.

There would never have been any controversy about the nature of God if some people had not taken dissenting views. It could as easily be argued that without the ancient 'heretics' the commonly accepted explanations of the trinity and Christology would neither have evolved, nor taken such firm root in the thinking of the church. Dissent in itself is not harmful to theological development, often serving as a catalyst, as an opportunity to define and redefine issues. Acting in contradiction to orthodoxy, dissenting voices keep the orthodox alive and prevent it from becoming self-sufficiently moribund - although history shows that this opinion was not shared by those in the past who styled themselves as 'defenders of the faith'. Byzantine emperors and medieval Inquisitions shared similar powers to crush dissent to 'protect' the church from alternate views of the place and nature of Christ in the Godhead.

The result is a history littered with people who queried the orthodox understanding of the church. Men like Arius and Nestorius provide ancient examples, and the title of 'heretic' prefaces almost any treatment of their works. Two later examples are Michael Servetus and Emmanuel Swedenborg, who both - rightly or wrongly - share the 'heretic' epithet.

Servetus and Swedenborg re-examined the issues of Christology and came to conclusions far removed from that of orthodoxy. Servetus was burned at John Calvin's stake for his efforts, while Swedenborg has largely been relegated to obscurity for his. Yet their story is part of the history of God, and their challenges to orthodox theology ought to be met and examined, weighed in the balances so that their assumptions may be measured against centuries of history, and history measured against them.

Michael Servetus was a Spaniard born in Aragon in either 1509 or 1511. Beginning as a Catholic he converted to Protestantism and began his own studies in theology. He was tried for heresy by both the French Inquisition and John Calvin, and the latter burned him at the stake in Geneva in 1553. Servetus' departed from orthodoxy on the subject of the trinity. His examination and comparison of Biblical texts and commonly taught theology led him to believe that the church erred in its understanding of the trinity. He taught a oneness of God within the person of Jesus Christ in distinction to the three-ness of God according to the Nicene trinity.

Swedenborg was born in Stockholm, Sweden, in 1688. His religious pursuits began in 1743 after a series of mystical dreams. Many people find a caveat in Swedenborg's claims to have been permitted to enter the spiritual world, but this should not obscure his understanding of the nature of God. Through original thought he presents alternative answers to some of Christianity's most difficult questions.

Servetus, however, did not live long enough to carry his concept of the trinity into the major issues of Christology and expound the relationship of the human and divine within Christ. This work fell to Emmanuel Swedenborg.

Like Servetus, Swedenborg rejected the standard Nicene trinity and Chalcedonian duality. He taught that God is one in both substance and form, and that the visible Jesus Christ after the resurrection was a Divine Human in whom is the trinity as soul, body and operation. While his concept of the trinity is similar in many respects to that of Servetus, Swedenborg had a luxury not afforded to respects to that of Servetus, Swedenborg had a luxury not afforded to the earlier man - time. Over a period of nearly thirty years Swedenborg wrote copiously on the nature of God, describing a Christology in which the human and divine natures of God become one through a process he calls 'glorification'. The similarity in the teaching of these two men, in spite of Swedenborg's ignorance of Servetus, leads to the question of what sources they may have had in common. Servetus relied heavily on the Patristic writers, while Swedenborg claimed a divine revelation. Nevertheless, it can be argued that both find a degree of agreement with the writings of Tertullian, although neither adopt his theology without adaptation.

Abbreviations

AC	Arcana Coelestia (Swedenborg)
AE	Apocalypse Explained (Swedenborg)
AK	The Animal Kingdom (Swedenborg)
ANF	Ante Nicene Fathers
AR	Apocalypse Revealed (Swedenborg)
Ath. Cr.	The Athanasian Creed (Swedenborg)
BE	A Brief Exposition of the Doctrine of the New Church (Swedenborg)
Canons	The Canons of the New Church (Swedenborg)
CL	Conjugial Love (Swedenborg)
Coro	Coronis (Swedenborg)
De Verbo	The Word of the Lord, from Experience (Swedenborg)
Dia	Dialogues on the Trinity (Servetus)
DLW	Divine Love and Wisdom (Swedenborg)
DP	Divine Providence (Swedenborg)
EAK	The Economy of the Animal Kingdom (Swedenborg)
Ecc. Hist.	Ecclesiastical History (Swedenborg)
Ep. Ephesians	Epistle to the Ephesians (Ignatius)
Ep. Magnesians	Epistle to the Magnesians (Ignatius)
Ep. Philad	Epistle to the Philadelphians (Ignatius)
Ep. Polycarp	Epistle to Polycarp (Ignatius)
Ep. Romans	Epistle to the Romans (Ignatius)
Ep. Smyrnians	Epistle to the Smyrnians (Ignatius)
Ep. Trallians	Epistle to the Trallians (Ignatius)
Faith	The Doctrine of Faith (Swedenborg)
HH	Heaven and Hell (Swedenborg)
Hist. Cr.	The History of Creation (Swedenborg)
Infinite	The Infinite and Final Cause of Creation (Swedenborg)
LJ	The Last Judgement (Swedenborg)
LJP	The Last Judgement (Posthumous) (Swedenborg)
Lord	The Doctrine of the Lord (Swedenborg)
NCL	New Church Life

Principia	The Principia (Swedenborg)
RC	Restitution of Christianity (Servetus)
RP	Rational Psychology (Swedenborg)
SE	Spiritual Experiences or Spiritual Diary (Swedenborg)
SS	Doctrine of the Sacred Scripture (Swedenborg)
TCR	The True Christian Religion (Swedenborg)
Tr	Erroribus Trinitatus (Servetus)
WE	The Word Explained or Adversaria (Swedenborg)
9Q	Nine Questions (Swedenborg)

Chapter One

Christology

Christology is defined as 'a comprehensive term for the statement of the identity and significance of Jesus' (Keck 1986, 362). Into this definition one pours nearly two thousand years of debate beginning during Christ's life itself and continuing into the present, necessitating 'a narrowing of the complete wholeness of "the Christ event" - a reduction to mere words of much more than verbal impact of the historical figure and the risen Lord' (Dunn 1980, ix). The issues around Christology are so broad and encompassing that the effort to understand and criticize them entails understanding and criticizing the complete theological framework of the nature of God (Norris 1963, vii). Defining the identity and significance of Jesus means broaching the entire history of Christianity, for Christology is the bedrock upon which the church is build.

The study of Christology began as the leaders of the church tried to make sense of Jesus of Nazareth. He has consistently raised more questions than answers, and the answers themselves spawn new questions until one is led to the conclusion that to fully examine and explain the story of Jesus is an impossible dream (O'Collins 1995, 2).

However, in order to develop its theology the church has had to come to grips with Christological questions. These look both backwards and forwards in time, backwards to Jesus' antecedents in the history of Israel, the events of his life, death, resurrection and the response these evoked within his temporal context (O'Collins 1995, 2). One looks forwards from the point of his resurrection to the new community that grew up in the wake of his resurrection and which was founded upon his teachings (O'Collins 1995, 3). This community took their inspiration from Jesus' life and defined their concepts of God, their private and public prayer, their liturgy, art, literature, and philosophy of life from his example (cf. O'Collins 1995, 3).

As each generation since the resurrection has tried to come to grips with the issues surrounding Jesus, so they have looked to their own experience to make sense of theological complexities. Christianity did not arise fully developed from the experience of Pentecost, nor did a complete and universally accepted interpretation of its doctrine materialize from thin air. From the earliest days of the Christian Church communities developed different expressions and approaches to Jesus based upon their own historical, philosophical and linguistic backgrounds (O'Collins 1995, 1). Each of these played a tremendous role in forming the overall view of the church, including definitions which were orthodox and those which were heterodox.

Developmental Christology has been affected over the centuries in two ways. First was the growth in understanding the message and meaning of Christ's life as it was examined and interpreted by scholars according to the spiritual needs and practices of any particular time. The second was the impact of other philosophies, be they Hellenic, Roman or modern. These gave theologians new tools to prize from the Gospels an understanding of the nature of Christ and these have added to (or detracted from in some cases) the overall picture of Christ.

Part and parcel of Christological development is the tension between orthodox and heterodox opinions. Variations and differences of view have always categorized Christian theology, and continue to do so today. However, heterodox views should not be seen as detracting from the overall view, for in many cases they have stimulated the Church into making definitive statements which have come to bind the accepted formulas of those who wish to be considered 'mainstream'.

Servetus and Swedenborg are two very heterodox theologians. Their views of the nature of the Trinity and of Christology put them outside the accepted boundaries of orthodox Christianity. However, like many before them, their views and opinions should cause the Church to question and re-evaluate, update and redefine many issues that have not been seriously challenged for hundreds of years. Like many scholars before them, their personal loyalty to Jesus Christ led them to question the Christological formulations passed down the ages into their eras, while their primary loyalty to the Scriptures, rather than to historical interpretations, led to a rejection of those interpretations. Their Christologies need to be seen in the context of orthodox Christianity, and orthodoxy in the context of their new insights.

Underlying Principles in Christology

In order to evaluate Servetus and Swedenborg it is necessary to begin by examining the underlying principles of Christology. Like any study, Christology contains within it certain unspoken assumptions coloring the mind of the theologian. O'Collins (1995) breaks down the principles into three main categories, philosophy, language and the distinction between 'high' and 'low' Christology. Each of these three basic categories determines the product, and variations between them cause the diversity of understanding in the subject. Because of this it is useful to examine them briefly.

Philosophy

The basis of 'philosophy' in this context is thought from experiential knowledge of Jesus. It would not have been possible for the earliest theologians to come to any concept without a foundation in experience. The writers of the Gospels either had personal experience of Jesus, or access to people who did have such experience. Their interpretation of the history of Jesus was partly based on this experience and partly on their own interpretation of what He said. It is conceivable to speculate, for example, that if a hostile Pharisee had written a Gospel, based on his observations of Jesus, the outcome would have been very different from those in the Bible. There is, therefore, a close correlation between experience and philosophy that cannot be ignored.

O'Collins extends the questions about the relationship between philosophy and experiential knowledge. Does experience give us reliable information about Jesus, and whose experience counts? (O'Collins 1995, 4). In other words, was it enough to have known Jesus? There were those, like Doubting Thomas, for instance, who could say of Jesus, 'my Lord and my God' (John 20, 28). Others who also saw Jesus did not share this conviction. Herod and Pilate, for example, saw a man, the Pharisees a trouble-maker, the inhabitants of Galilee, one who had lived among them. The physical Jesus did not necessarily give any clue to the inner Jesus, not even the fact that he performed miracles. In the Gospel of Matthew the Pharisees, who had obviously heard of his works, came to him asking to be shown a sign (Matthew 16, 1).

Experiential knowledge of Jesus did not answer questions about his relationship to the Divine, but forced the issue. Thus Luke began his gospel with the Christmas story in which Jesus' conception explains the virgin birth. John equated Jesus with a pre-existent Logos, existing before creation and responsible for it. These statements, laying the primary basis for Christian belief in the divinity of Christ, anticipate many Christological questions that would be left for later generations to ponder over and attempt to answer.

As access to those who had direct experiential knowledge of Jesus declined with years, it became necessary to supplement experience with interpretation, and thus with 'philosophy'. To do this, early theologians looked to their own philosophic experience and understanding in an attempt to fit Christ into a cosmic whole. It was impossible for them to visualize a Galilean fisherman as the creator of the universe and a manifestation of God. Yet affix abstract terms to him, like substance, hypostasis, prosopon and so on, and the fisherman disappears in a whiff of philosophic smoke, to be replaced with an intellectual construct who can be simultaneously God and Man, Creator and Redeemer.

O'Collins (1995, 4) continues to comment that 'the whole Christian tradition about Jesus (and, for that matter, non-Christian traditions about him) can be seen as recording and interpreting various collective and individual experiences of Jesus'. One could add to these experiences beyond simply seeing or hearing him, the understanding and interpretation of what he did and said.

The interpretation of those experiences must, however, be seen in relation to the philosophy of the person recording them. To some degree one sees this in the use of the various names given to Jesus in early writings. The Apostle's experience, for example, showed them Christ's death and resurrection, and their philosophy (simple at first, but growing more complex) told them that these things were important. It was this sense of importance that led them to try to make sense of the events in philosophic terms.

Language

Closely related to the underlying philosophy of the earliest writers is the use of language. An observed event is an objective thing (providing one ignores the point of view of the observer), but the words with which one describes that event is subjective, betraying the basic philosophy of the writer. The belief in redemption through Jesus (which is the essential philosophy of the Gospel writers) is portrayed in the words chosen to express his life. Words like 'expiation,' 'love,' 'conquest' refer to Christ's redemptive work. As terms they are relatively easy to explain. Other words are more symbolic, he is the 'bread of life,' the 'shepherd, and 'the 'light' and the 'vine' (O'Collins 1995, 11). A great deal of theology involves exploring the meanings of these terms and coming to a deeper understanding of the redemptive process through them, although the question always remains as to how far our language can go in expressing Christ and God (O'Collins 1995, 12). Exploration of terms will, like the terms themselves, contain basic philosophic underpinnings that will color the interpretations themselves.

The primary difficulty in finding the right words to express the nature of God, of Christ, even of redemption, is that the subject is, by definition, above the human understanding. As God is infinite and people are finite, words used to describe him and his activities are at best 'indirect, analogical and symbolic' (O'Collins 1995, 13).

Frequently words applied to God only have meaning when compared with inadequate human equivalents. For example, it is frequently asserted that God is love, but God's love is infinite, containing the love of creating, of maintaining creation and of redemption. Human beings have no such loves. People see a dim image of infinite love by comparing it, for example, with their love of making and maintaining things, yet the things they build and maintain are very poor images of the work done by God, for they have no 'life' of their own. Even the rapidly evolving computer is clumsy by contrast with the human brain and mind.

For this reason finite humans grapple to express infinity in finite words. Certain terms and statements used are 'utterly inappropriate to God' (McGuckin 1994, 138) as they give an incorrect interpretation of his nature - unless they are explored and explained and shown to be in harmony with each other. One inappropriate pairing of terms used in connection with Christ is 'human' and 'divine'. Even at face value these terms are mutually exclusive. Divinity by definition is infinite and uncreate, while humanity is finite and created. How can such contradictory terms be applied to one individual? Yet in the case of Jesus Christ, this is precisely what happens (see McGuckin 1994, 138).

Theology comes back time and again to this very issue, for it is not possible to understand Jesus Christ unless and until one reaches a conclusion about the relationship of the divine and human within him. It is in this area that both Servetus and Swedenborg, especially the lattcr, find themselves expressing different explanations than those characteristic of the orthodox church.

Christology from above and below

A third element in Christology that draws from both the philosophic and linguistic assumptions implicit in the subject is that of the origin of Jesus' divinity. The style of writing of a person who believes that Jesus is inherently divine and became man is different from that of one who believes Jesus to be a man who became divine. These two points of view have colored (and continue to do so) the whole of Christology for they determine the direction in which the flow of divinity moves.

It is important to describe these two approaches quite fully if one is to make sense of later developments in Christology.

1.   *Christology from above* (or high Christology) begins with the Godhead. The principle point is that Christ existed before the incarnation, and as a divine being descended to earth, emptying himself of divinity in order to become human. The incarnation is the descent of divinity into the world (Reid 1990, 75).

2.   *Christology from below* (or low Christology) goes in the other direction. Low Christologies begin with the humanity of Jesus and work towards an expression of his divinity. At times in church history this approach to Christology skirted issues of adoptionism and Arianism, yet not all those who focused on the humanity of Christ denied his divinity. For many theologians of this school, divinity is a given, but the real emphasis is on the life and work of the historical (Reid 1990, 76).

Those who begin from above, begin with the idea that Jesus was divine before the incarnation, and so set the concept of the incarnation at the centre of their thought - as is taught in the Gospels of Luke and John (Smith 1974, 22). In this view Jesus is always divine - either because he is the 'Son of the Most High', or the 'Logos [who] was God'. Because of this, divinity is able to reach into human lives and save them. High Christology is especially developed in the prologue of the Gospel of John, where Jesus is the 'Logos' pre-existing creation and yet coming into the world to reveal the light to those in spiritual darkness (O'Collins 1995, 16). Opponents of this approach would argue that by stressing the divinity of Christ, the full-picture of Christ's humanity is often overlooked (O'Collins 1995, 18) - an issue that would erupt in the church in the fourth, fifth and sixth centuries.

Low Christology, on the other hand, focuses on the message, works, life, death and resurrection of Jesus, arriving at the concept of the incarnation (Smith 1974, 22). This is the presentation of Christ in Matthew and Mark (O'Collins 1995, 16). Just as high Christology has its detractors, so does the low. O'Collins (1995, 18) notes that

> ... a 'low' Christology emphasizes one-sidedly the human life of Christ and excludes anything like an appropriate recognition of his divinity. Historically low Christologies have taken the form of holding that the power of God came upon the man Jesus and adopted him at his baptism or resurrection.

In these words we see the basic principles of Arius and Theodore of Mopseustia echoed in general terms, and reaction to this point of view led to the councils of Nicaea and Ephesus.

A balanced view of Christ, however must take both his divinity and humanity into account. However different they may be, these two approaches complement each other (O'Collins 1995, 17), each highlighting a different aspect of Christ's life, and both are intimately connected with soteriology (Reid 1990, 84). Reid observes that 'Christology and soteriology are interwoven and in experience cannot be separated' (Reid 1990, 85). Because of this interrelationship the church has been greatly enriched over the centuries by both approaches. As Christology developed, so those who advocated a high Christology (for example, Athanasius, Cyril of Alexandria and more recently Karl Barth) have been greatly influenced by those who took a low Christology. The debates leading to the great ecumenical councils were frequently characterized by the two great sees of Antioch and Alexandria. The former generally followed the low, the latter a high Christology, and both have led the church's understanding of the ontological nature of Christ and soteriology.

With these thoughts in mind it is possible to explore the concepts of the nature of God prevailing in the Christian world. The basic assumptions outlined above are present in all theological thought, for one cannot write about God without having a philosophic concept of him which frames the words one uses. Similarly whilst the words themselves are drawn from the philosophy of the writers, they shape and add further levels of understanding and insight into the subject. The very choice of words underpins again the type of Christology one uses, and this, plays a central part in the development of ideas in Christology.

It also makes it possible to understand some of the basic philosophic approaches of both Michael Servetus and Emanuel Swedenborg. They too have a philosophic approach and use language most likely to express their underlying philosophy. They espouse a high Christology and tackle the implications of this on both the Trinity and the old question of how the humanity relates to the divinity in the Person of Jesus Christ, although the path they use to describe this relationship is distinctly different from the orthodoxy establish by the church.

Underlying Principles of Servetian and Swedenborgian Christology

The theology of Servetus and Swedenborg needs to be seen in the context of these Christological principles. Servetus never claimed any experiential knowledge of God, as Swedenborg did. His 'experience', no different from that of anyone after the Apostles, came from his reading of Scripture. Interestingly, Servetus, raised in Roman Catholic Spain and educated in Catholic France, felt free to question and reinterpret the accepted dogmas of the church. By the time the Reformation dawned in Western Europe, the orthodox Trinity was beyond question. None of the major reformers even questioned the validity of the first seven ecumenical councils. To them the Nicene Creed and its successors were as sacrosanct as the Bible itself.

Yet Servetus felt himself able to comment and criticize, to take on the might of Rome and the burgeoning reformist movements of the time. The urge to do so was the result of his 'experience', which, in this case was a philosophic and theological exploration of the Bible without the preconditions of orthodoxy. He simply set aside a millennium and a half of discussion and debate and read the Bible without any preconceived ideas, jettisoning the entire structure of Christian thought and scholarship in order to study the teaching of the Bible itself (Odhner 1910, 13). The result was an entirely new theology and new Christology. With the Bible as his basis he challenged the authorities to prove that the orthodox dogmas were indeed biblical.

Swedenborg, on the other hand, comes from a very different perspective for two reasons. As shall be shown in Chapter Seven, he claims to have been introduced into a spiritual world and to have experienced the presence of God. In a way not unlike those of many mystics his claim to knowledge of the nature of God has a basis in his own experience. It is not the purpose of this study to question the validity of Swedenborg's spiritual experience any more than one would question those of others who have had similar experiences. However, Swedenborg's experiences are continually in mind when reading his theology although that should not distract the reader from closely examining what he said as a challenge to orthodox Christianity in its own right.

The second reason is the historical times in which Swedenborg wrote. The Age of Enlightenment was characterized by enquiry into countless things which up to that point had been accepted without question. Astronomical and geographical discoveries from the late middle ages opened peoples' minds to the physical world around them. Progress in medical knowledge in the seventeenth century, and the philosophical crises of the early eighteenth led people to question their historical understanding of things. It was but a short jump to question theology, and, as the eighteenth century wore on, there was an increasing pressure to explain and justify the central tenets of Christianity, including the nature of God (Dunn 1980, 2).

Swedenborg was a man of his times and environment. As a philosopher, a scientist, an engineer, he wrote more prolifically than did Servetus, and, when he turned his mind to theology, he brought all his previous experience and knowledge, including the culture of his own times, to bear on the deepest subjects of the Church, the nature of God.

Both Servetus and Swedenborg espouse a high Christology. Both draw similar ideas that the prophecies of the Old Testament which speak of Jehovah descending and use that as a basis for the descent of Christ, which in turn is the basis of his soteriology, as is evident in his book, *The True Christian Religion,* that 'Jehovah God came down and took upon Himself human form, in order to redeem and save mankind (TCR 82).

For each, high Christology has ramifications in both their concepts of the Trinity - both taught that the Trinity is in the person of Jesus Christ as the soul is in and through the body. This concept has repercussions on their concept of the human and divine in Christ, a subject in which they both take issue with the Council of Chalcedon. These issues will be discussed fully in the appropriate places.

Chapter Two

The History of the Trinity

The history of the Trinity has been written many times. To put Servetus' and Swedenborg's concept of the nature of God into perspective, however, requires a brief summary of this history. Both believed that the Christian Church fell at the Council of Nicaea in 325 AD[1]. They believed that it progressed on a steady downhill path since then. Swedenborg, with a longer historical perspective than Servetus, held that the church recovered briefly and superficially at the time of the Reformation, until, in the mid-eighteenth century, in the last judgment he claimed to have witnessed that Church came to a full stop. The cause of the fall was a misunderstanding of the nature of God.

Although Servetus and Swedenborg had similar reservations about the development of the Trinity, they expressed them very differently in their writings. Servetus, the Reformation theologian, footnoted and annotated his sources. His books are filled with direct quotations from the patristic sources supporting his theses, and from the medieval scholars whom he rejected. Often his writing is full of invective against these men.

Swedenborg, the eighteenth century enlightenment scientist, takes a different tack. His books are filled with carefully reasoned rebuttals, he seldom mentions any earlier scholar by name. His writings are marked with an absence of invective.

This makes it easier to follow Servetus' references than Swedenborg's. In presenting this chapter, we shall look at and examine the sources directly mentioned in Servetus' work, believing that Swedenborg, through the inference of his writings, would generally concur. The outcome is a history of the Trinity as Servetus would have seen it, and with which Swedenborg would agree.

The Earliest Christology and Concepts of the Trinity

It is important to remember that the earliest adherents to Christianity were Jewish, and so were heavily influenced by Jewish thought. 'There is, of course, as yet no complete agreement on what is to be understood by the term "Jewish Christian theology"' (Grillmeier 1975, 38), except to say that there was a huge diversity within Judaism, especially on the subject of Christology (Nickelsburg 1993, 365).

Jewish response to Christianity can be characterized in several ways, ranging from ignoring it, to marginalizing Christians, to expelling them from the synagogue (Nickelsburg 1993, 366). The earliest Jewish Christians, however, drew their theology from their experiential knowledge of Christ, either through knowing him personally, as the Apostles did, or from others who knew him, as was the case with both Paul and Luke.

As Christology began to evolve in this earliest state of Christianity, it was as often less openly stated than inferred. For example, New Testament writers do not elaborate on what Jesus meant when He said, 'I and my Father are one' (John 10, 30). Nor is the Trinity explained when Christ commanded His disciples to baptize in the name of the 'Father, Son and Holy Spirit' (Matthew 28, 19). Historically, New Testament silence on these issues indicates that the Apostles were less concerned with the theological detail than with the message of salvation.

However, both Christology and the Trinity are present in their early writings. Identifying Jesus as the Christ, for example, indicates the fulfillment of Jewish expectations of the Messiah (Nickelsburg 1993, 369). Similarly the use of the term 'Lord' indicates the exalted status to one who, by natural birth and position, should not aspire to it (Nickelsburg 1993, 370).

This earliest Christology is called 'Name Christology', because it relies on the names given to Christ to link Him to the Father. This linking, is of course, the central fact that made Christianity different from all other religions. Yet even in the Name Christology there are tensions that had to be unraveled in later years. For example, Christ is often referred to as 'the Son of Man', linking Christ with the prophetic figure in Daniel. This title does not, of itself, carry messianic connotations, and could be seen as more closely tied to a 'Christology from below' image of Christ. At the same time, however, the term 'Son of God' is also used, especially in the Gospel of John, where it 'refers to the pre-existent heavenly being who becomes incarnate' (Nickelsburg 1993, 370). The name implies 'complete transcendence and pre-existence' (Grillmeier 1975, 42), and thus implies a high Christology.

Even in this earliest usage of names to describe Christ, there are the seeds for later discussion and dispute. The relationship of two seemingly incompatible concepts, humanity and divinity, finite and infinite, together in one person, is at this point only just beginning to dawn on Christian minds as a problem that will have to be solved.

In this era, before the issues of Christology and the Trinity became pressing, there was a sense of innocence in the doctrine, although as time passed by, it became increasingly necessary to articulate these matters. There appears to be a development of ideas, although, really the progress towards the Council of Nicaea was beginning which can be seen in the writings of three early Christians, frequently referred to by Servetus: Ignatius, Irenaeus and Tertullian.

The Christology of Ignatius

Ignatius became the Bishop of Antioch in about 69 AD - about forty years after Christ's resurrection. In about 107 AD he was sentenced to death in Rome, yet he welcomed the opportunity to be fed to the lions as a chance to express his faith in Christ. En route to Rome he wrote a series of Epistles to the Christians in the cities he passed. The Apostolic Church greatly loved these letters for they addressed two popular subjects, the glory of martyrdom and the need for congregations to stick together in times of trial by being loyal to their bishops.

However, a vague Christology shines through in his writings, supporting the contention held by Servetus and Swedenborg that indeed, the Apostolic Fathers had no notion of a divided Trinity, nor were they confused about the relationship of human and divine in Christ. For example, in the Epistle to the Ephesians, Ignatius states, 'There is one Physician, who is possessed both of flesh and spirit, both made and not made, God existing in flesh, true life in death...' (Ep. Ephesians 7).

Ignatius' Christology is closely related to that of the original Apostles themselves - only one bishop held the See of Antioch between the Apostle John and himself. He lived long before any of the Christological disputes erupted. The Ignatian Epistles describe Jesus Christ as God becoming visible, for he represents 'the mind of the

Father' (Ep. Ephesians 3). As such he is inseparably one with the Father, 'so constituting one single harmonious unity throughout' (Ep. Ephesians 5). As the mind of God, Christ gives knowledge of God (Ep. Ephesians 17). Although he does not specifically say so, it follows from other things Ignatius says, that this mind could not be known until Christ became a human being. To put it another way, 'Jesus Christ ... was with the Father from all eternity, and in these last days has been made manifest' (Ep. Magnesians 6).

Ignatius describes a progression from divinity to humanity. Speaking philosophically, he writes,

> Look for Christ, the Son of God; who was before time, yet appeared in time, who was invisible by nature, yet visible in the flesh; who was impalpable, and could not be touched, as being without a body, but for our sakes became such, might be touched and handled in the body; who was impassable as God, but became passable for our sakes as man (Ep. Polycarp 3).

In this passage, Christ is not depicted as a separate being, but as a part of the progression whereby God became man. A very similar concept is described in Tertullian's work, Adversus Praxean.

Ignatius' letters also describe the process of becoming man, for example,

> Under the Divine dispensation, Jesus Christ our God, was conceived by Mary of the seed of David and the Spirit of God. He was born, and He submitted to baptism, so that by His passion He might sanctify (Ep. Ephesians 18).

In this way the mind of God became flesh in Jesus Christ, who is God 'now appearing in human form to bring a new order, even life without end' (Ep. Ephesians 19). Christ came down from the Father, and returned to Him (Ep. Magnesians 8). In doing so, Christ became the 'doorway to the Father' (Ep. Philadelphians).

In Jesus Christ we have divinity and humanity, for he is both seed of David and Son of God. This point, which becomes a major issue of Christian doctrine, and which was codified at the Council of Chalcedon, presents in embryonic form the concept of a duality in Christ. Ignatius, in theological innocence, does not elaborate any further on the subject. For him it is sufficient that Christ is both human and divine, and this does not in any way interfere with the oneness and unity of God.

The fact that he is now in the flesh is a theme Ignatius repeats several times (Ep. Ephesians 18, 29). In several places Ignatius counters the docetic heresy[2], especially in the letter to the Smyrnians. He stresses the fullness of Christ's humanity, even to the point of suffering in the flesh, concluding that 'his passion was no unreal illusion' (Ep. Smyrnians 2). To him the representation of the mind of God was made true flesh. In the Epistle to the Trallians he writes,

> Christ was of David's line. He was the son of Mary; he was verily and truly born, and ate and drank; he was verily persecuted in the days of Pontius Pilate, and verily and indeed crucified, and gave up the ghost in sight of all heaven and earth and the powers of the nether world. He was also verily raised up again from the dead, for his Father raised him... (Ep. Trallians 9).

He repeats this theme in the Epistle to the Romans in connection with the Eucharist (Ep. Romans 7), calling it 'the firmest conviction' in his letter to the Smyrnians (Ep. Smyrnians 1). Ignatius, however, does not wander far from the principle that Christ was born of God. He 'was begotten before time began, and established all things according to the will of the Father' (Ep. Ephesians 7).

The unity of the Father and Son is implied in statements referring to the inseparable oneness of Father and Son. In the Epistle to the Magnesians, Ignatius declares openly that Christ 'was wholly one with the Father, and never acted independently of him...' (Ep. Magnesians 7).

In spite of the many passages indicating the oneness of God in Jesus Christ, so there are also passages inferring a separation. For example, Ignatius speaks of 'Jesus and the Father' (Ep. Magnesians 1). A further example is in the greeting in the Epistle to the Romans, where Ignatius calls Christ 'the Father's Son'. The implication of separateness, however, is slight compared to the overwhelming teaching that Father and Son are inseparably one. They seem to be more a statement of different points along the progression from invisible to visible, rather than one about different hypostases in God, or persons so distinct that they border on individual beings. Yet it is the thin end of the wedge, which, being hammered over generations would widen to the yawning gap of three Persons.

The Christology of Irenaeus

The second Patristic author that it is important to note is
Irenaeus. He was one of the earliest Christian writers. Living between
120 and 202 AD, his major work is estimated to have been written at
about 180 AD. Irenaeus served at Lyons as a presbyter to Polycarp.
During the persecution of Marcus Aurelius in 177, Irenaeus was sent to
Rome to protest the increase of heresy. At Rome he found that the
Montanist heresy was supported by the Bishop of Rome. He also found
the Valentinian heresy to be rife, and Gnosticism widely accepted. This
state of affairs so shocked him that he began a lifelong struggle against
heresy.

He was appointed bishop of Lyons on his return. It did not
take long for the heresies present in Rome and other parts of the Church
to penetrate to his see. In response, Irenaeus 'condescended to study
these diseases of the human mind like a wise physician' (AH –
Introduction). He approached the subject with a clinical detachment,
describing the error, and applying the antidote of Biblical truth to
counteract it.

Irenaeus viewed heresy as an opportunity for the faithful to
censure the faithless,

> ... the primitive truth was secured and recorded, the language of
> Catholic orthodoxy was developed and defined, and landmarks of
> faith were set up as a perpetual memorial to all generations (AH –
> Introduction).

The task Irenaeus set himself had a dual purpose. The first was to make
it impossible to confuse Gnosticism with Christianity, the second to
make it impossible for Gnosticism to survive, or even be revived again.
In addition to his fight against Gnosticism, Irenaeus was also involved
in the Easter Controversy, and although this issue was not resolved
until after the Council of Nicaea, his contribution was meaningful.

Irenaeus died with thousands of his flock in the persecution of
202, instituted by the Emperor Severus, but his great work remains as a
testimony to his loyalty to the clear teachings of the Bible. His *magnus
opus*, *Adversus Haeries*, or *Against Heretics*, is a monumental
exposition of the errors of Gnosticism, and the counteracting truth that
sets them to rights.

Adversus Haeries is divided into five books. The first of which
is a detailed illustration of the heresies current at that time. In the

second book, Irenaeus undertakes to demolish these heresies by refutations from the Old and New Testaments. The final three books set out Catholic orthodoxy, again drawing fully from the Bible for support. A reading of Irenaeus shows it to be clear that he firmly grasped the doctrines of the Bible, as taught at that time.

Irenaeus' point was not to establish the unity of God per se, but to describe the workings of the Supreme God in creation. However, in refuting the Gnostics, Irenaeus reveals his thought on the nature of God. To this end he explains that the Word, or Logos, in terms of the incarnation and of salvation without the complicated levels of intermediaries posited by the Gnostics. The implication of his writing is that the Word of God, incarnate as Christ, makes Christ God. Thus he affirms that God is one and unique in majesty and goodness, and supreme in his power (Norris 1966, 69)

In the opening book of the *Adversus Haeries*, Irenaeus establishes that the principle that there is only one God by quoting at length from the Apostolic Creed, stating that the church believes

> ... in one God, the Father almighty, Maker of Heaven and earth, and the sea, and all things that are in them, and in one Christ Jesus, the Son of God, who became incarnate for our salvation; and in the Holy Spirit (AH I.X.2).

Thus he declares that there is but one God, and Christ is the only begotten (AH I.IX.2). Setting his theology in opposition to that of the Gnostics, Irenaeus stressed that all things were made by this one God, as opposed to the complex series of beings that form part of the Gnostic teaching. He notes that 'the world was not formed by angels ... but was made by the Father through the Word' (AH II.II.1).

The Gnostics claimed that if God created the world, then God must be responsible for the evil in the world. Irenaeus rejects this. He accepts it as a given that God created the world, saying,

> [t]he rule of truth which we hold, is, that there is one God Almighty, who made all things by his Word, and fashioned and formed, out of that which had no existence, all things which exist (AH I.XXXII.1).

If God created the world, then it follows that he created by means of an agency, which is the Word, or Logos, which proceeds from God. He describes God, in the process of creation, as forming 'a conception in his mind that was also done which he had thus mentally conceived' (AH II.III.2).

This 'conception in his mind' is the Logos, for in early Christianity, the Logos was identified not only as the words proceeding from God's mouth, but also the thought and reason behind those words. God created by means of his words.

Irenaeus' view of God as he is in himself is somewhat abstract. For him

> ... the Father of all is at a vast distance from ... men. He is a simple, uncompounded being, without diverse members ... since he is wholly understanding and wholly spirit and wholly thought and wholly intelligence, an wholly hearing, and wholly seeing, and wholly light, and the whole source of all that is good (AH II.XIII.3).

In other words, God is indescribable. But his Logos can be known, for he created from the concepts of his mind, and his creation reveals the things of his mind. Thus one cannot see God, but one can see the Logos, or Word. It was this 'Word of the Father who descended' (AH I.IX.3).

Because of the interest at that time in Gnosticism, Irenaeus stresses that Christ was not a 'mere man, begotten of Joseph in the ordinary course of nature, but was very God ... and very man' (AH III.XIX). The thought and conception in God's mind, by which he had created, was born into this world as Jesus Christ, 'and he who was the Son of God became the Son of Man' (AH III.XIX.1).

When Christ was born, he took on actual flesh from the Virgin (AH III.XXII.1), and through that flesh underwent the passion of the cross. Irenaeus states that,

> [t]he Lord suffered that he might bring those who have wandered from the Father back to the knowledge and to his fellowship. The Lord suffered, and bestowing the knowledge of the Father, conferred on us salvation (AH II.XX.3).

As creation was effected through the Word of God, so salvation was achieved through the manifested Word in Jesus Christ. Christ is also the only way that one can come to have any knowledge of God (AH II.XXVI.1). Irenaeus' theology can be summed up as follows,

> [there is] one God, the Creator of heaven and earth, and all things therein, by means of Christ Jesus, the Son of God, who because of His surpassing love towards his creation, condescended to be born of the Virgin, he himself united man through himself to God, and

having suffered under Pontius Pilate, and rising again, and having been received up in splendor, shall come again in glory, the Savior of those who are saved, and Judge of those who are judged, and sending into eternal fire those who transform the truth, and despise his Father and his Advent (AH III.IV.2).

The Christology of Tertullian

The third seminal Apostolic Father in Servetus' thought is Tertullian, who died around 202 AD. Tertullian's book, *Against Praxean*, outlines his Christology. It was one of the earliest systematization's of the relationship of Father and Son. In many ways Tertullian bridged the divide between the earliest Apostolic Fathers and those who came later and whose questions and controversies led to the Council of Nicaea. He was the first theologian to use the term 'Person' to express different characteristics of God, and so introduced an idea that would mushroom into the problematic issues of the Church ever since.

In the treatise Tertullian makes the point that those who criticize Catholic doctrine fail to understand the divine economy, which he describes as being that the 'one only God has also a Son, His Word, who proceeded from himself, by whom all things were made, and without whom nothing was made' (Tertullian. Against Praxean II).

This sums up the entirety of Tertullian's thought, containing such key concepts that the Son is the Word, that it proceeds from God, and is the origin of all things. His understanding of how this economy came into being, however, is particularly important if one is to understand the primary sources in Trinitarian and Christological thought.

Tertullian elaborates his economy by bringing the Son into the world in the form of Jesus Christ. He entered the world through the Virgin, lived, suffered, died, and was resurrected. Further, the Holy Spirit is sent by the Father to sanctify those who believe in the Father, the Son and the Holy Spirit (Tertullian. Against Praxean II). His economy then rests on the Trinity, its inner dynamics and functions.

Tertullian's bases his concept of the Trinity in an idea of unity in trinity,

> ... placing in order the three Persons in the Father, the Son and the Holy Spirit, three, however, not in condition, but in spirit, yet of one substance, and of one condition, and of one power, inasmuch as He is

one God, from whom these degrees and forms are reckoned under the name of Father, and of the Son, and of the Holy Spirit (Tertullian. Against Praxean II).

Tertullian's use of the word 'Person' should not be misconstrued to mean 'individual'. The term 'Person' most properly means a mask, or a presentation, and this is the sense in which Tertullian uses it. To him a 'Person' is a recognition of the 'degrees and forms' of God. Later in his treatise, he speaks of persons in terms of the invisible and visible, thus the Father is the invisible face of God, while Christ is the visible. This line of thinking makes it possible to understand somewhat the complex nature of God without having to resort to the sophistry of the Scholastics, who, understanding a baser concept, reduced the three Persons to three Gods.

It cannot be stressed strongly enough that this Trinity is not a multiplication of Persons as individuals. Tertullian notes that people fall into error when they assume the numerical order of the Trinity 'to be a division of the unity' (Tertullian. Against Praxean III). The fact of the Trinity does not alter the sole government, or Monarchy, of God, because the Son does not divide the monarchy but shares in it, for in its origin it belongs equally to the Father, Son and Holy Spirit (Tertullian. Against Praxean III).

The unity in the Trinity is preserved by the relationship of the Son and the Father and so protects the entirety of God. Tertullian asks,

> As for me, who derive a Son from no other source but from the substance of the Father, and (represents him) as doing nothing without the Father's will, and as having received all power from the Father, how can I be possibly destroying the Monarchy? (Tertullian. Against Praxean IV).

In the same vein, the Holy Spirit does not destroy or divide the Trinity, for it proceeds 'from the Father through the Son' (Tertullian. Against Praxean IV). In addition to not dividing the Trinity, the Son is also the agent by which the monarchy is administered.

Moreover, this oneness does not allow a separation of beings. Tertullian is adamant that 'the Father and Son are two separate Persons' (Tertullian. Against Praxean IV), but they are not separate beings, rather two faces of one God. To explain his meaning here, Tertullian uses the term 'Divine Procession' (Tertullian. Against Praxean V).

In order to understand 'Divine Procession', one is taken back to the concept of God

... before the creation of the world, up to the generation of the Son, for before all things God was alone - being in himself, and for himself universe, and space, and all things. Moreover, he was alone, because there was nothing external to him but himself (Tertullian. Against Praxean V).

Yet even in that Divine aloneness, God had his own reason or thought, which is the Logos, or Word (Tertullian. Against Praxean V). In this initial phase, the Logos was reason, from which 'he silently planned and arranged within himself everything which he was afterwards about to utter through his Word' (Tertullian. Against Praxean V).

The Procession from invisible to visible God continues, for the process of planning from his Reason caused that Reason to become the Word (Tertullian. Against Praxean V). As speech is the interlocutor carrying reason into thought, so in a real way speech is secondary to thought. So too in God, the Word is a second Person to God's reason, and thus to God himself (Tertullian. Against Praxean V). Thus,

... even then before the creation of the universe, God was not alone, since he had within himself both reason, and inherent in reasons, his Word, which he made second to himself by agitating it within himself (Tertullian. Against Praxean V).

When God brought the objects of his reason into being, the first thing put forth was the Word itself, 'having within him his own inseparable reason and wisdom' (Tertullian. Against Praxean VI). In this way the Word came into being as a person, not a separate individual, but as an extension on a lower plane, so to speak, of God Himself, and through this Word, all things were created. The Word took upon him his own form (Tertullian. Against Praxean VI), which was the word of God's mouth proceeding from him. So, 'he became his first begotten Son, because begotten before all things, and his only begotten also, because alone begotten of God, in a way peculiar to himself' (Tertullian. Against Praxean VII).

The point that Tertullian makes here, is that the Son of God was only begotten when he proceeded from God. How does one then come to see the Son as a Person? Tertullian states that he has substance, but what makes him more than a mere verbal construct (Tertullian. Against Praxean VII)? The assumption behind this question is that sound in itself is really nothing, only emptiness. Yet Tertullian writes,

I ... contend that nothing empty and void could have come forth from God, seeing that it is not put forth from that which is empty and void; nor could that possibly be devoid of substance which had produced such mighty substances (Tertullian. Against Praxean VII).

God is substance itself, and all things flowing from him have substance. This substance is the Word, which Tertullian designates as 'a person', calls the Son, and places second in the procession to the Father (Tertullian. Against Praxean VII).

Heretics, and here Tertullian specifically mentions Valentinus, separate the progression of the Word from God, placing the progression at a distance from its origin. The effect is a destruction of God and the dissolution of the concept of his unity. The Word is not separated from its origin, for the Word does not come into being of and from itself, but from the Father, as an expression of the Father's reason. As a result there can never be a separation into two (Tertullian. Against Praxean VIII).

Put another way, one could say that the Son is an emanation of the Father. To illustrate the continuity and connection of Father and Son, Tertullian uses the example of a tree trunk inseparable from its root (Tertullian. Against Praxean VIII). Using this concept of a progression, Tertullian writes that he calls the Father and Son 'Two' as 'distinctly two things, but correlatively joined', for 'everything which proceeds from something else must needs be second to that from which it proceeds, without being on that account separated' (Tertullian. Against Praxean VIII).

The same relationship is true for the Holy Spirit who makes up the third Person of God, for where 'there is a third, there must be three' (Tertullian. Against Praxean VIII). The Holy Spirit is the third continuation from God, which Tertullian describes as being in the same sequence of a root, a tree and the fruit of a tree (Tertullian. Against Praxean VIII).

Thus the Trinity, 'flowing down from the Father, through the intertwined and connected steps', does not interfere with the Monarchy, the oneness and wholeness of God (Tertullian. Against Praxean VIII). There is no separation, therefore, between the Father, Son and Holy Spirit.

It is wrong, Tertullian asserts, to conceive of the Trinity as a separation of Father, Son and Holy Spirit. The identity of the Godhead did not come about by diversity, but by distribution and distinction, for the Son is the derivation of the Father's substance, 'for the Father is the entire substance, but the Son is a derivation and portion of the whole' (Tertullian. Against Praxean IX). Thus the concept of Monarchy does not demand that Father and Son be one and the same thing, for in that case neither is held nor acknowledged (Tertullian. Against Praxean X), but neither are they separate entities.

In defense of his argument for the distinction, not separation, of the Persons of the Trinity, Tertullian brings forth many Scriptural quotations - too many to be considered here. However, as he continues his exposition of the subject he poses this question,

> I ask you how it is possible for a Being who is merely and absolutely One and Singular, to speak in plural phrase, saying, 'let us make man in our own image'? (Tertullian. Against Praxean XII).

This question strikes in a Scriptural way to the heart of his discussion on the Trinity. He stresses a monarchy, allowing a differentiation within that monarchy into Persons, but not allowing a distinction into separate persons. Answering his question, Tertullian asserts that 'it was because he already had his Son close at his side, as a second Person... and [the Holy Spirit as] a third Person also' (Tertullian. Against Praxean XII). To him the use of the plural in no way detracts from the monarchy, but describes the order of Divine Progression existent within God at the time of creation, allowing for the concept that within the economy of God there is one who issues the command, one who exercises it, and one that brings it to fruit (Tertullian. Against Praxean XII). It is not Scripturally possible, then, to separate the Trinity.

Further, the distinction of God into Persons does not imply a plurality of God. Tertullian declares that 'two beings are God, even three ... in order that the Father may not ... have been born and have suffered, which it is not lawful to believe...' (Tertullian. Against Praxean XIII). Holding fast to the monarchical nature of God, Tertullian asserts 'that there are, however, two Gods or two Lords, is a statement which at no time proceeds out of our mouth' (Tertullian. Against Praxean XIII). The presentation of the Father and Son as two comes from the fact that God is invisible. It is not possible to see God. Before the advent people 'saw God according to the faculties of man, but not in accordance with the full glory of the Godhead' (Tertullian. Against Praxean XIV). It follows that when people are recorded in the scriptures as seeing Gods, 'he must be a different Being who was seen' (Tertullian. Against Praxean XIV).

However, the Son is visible, 'by reason of the dispensation of his derived existence' (Tertullian. Against Praxean XIV). The Son tempers the Father, making it possible for people to see him. Before the incarnation the Son was visible through prophets, in visions, and in the enigma of a glass (Tertullian. Against Praxean XIV). Tertullian thoroughly examines the Trinity in the pages of the Old Testament, and then turns to the New, where again both a visible and invisible God is shown (Tertullian. Against Praxean XV). The thrust of the New Testament is that the Son,

> ... was always seen from the beginning, who became visible at the end, and that he, (on the contrary) was not seen in the end who had never been visible from the beginning; and that accordingly there are two, the visible and the invisible (Tertullian. Against Praxean XV).

The point of this rather convoluted statement is that that part of God which had always been visible, who talked with people and did the will of his Father, became visible in the flesh of Jesus Christ, whilst the invisible Divine, remained invisible within him. The difference is not one of two separate beings, but of the invisible and visible aspects of one being, referred to as Father and Son. Even in the New Testament, where frequent mention is made of Father and Son, they are never two, but one,

> ... for the Father acts by mind and thought, whilst the Son, who is in the Father's mind, gives effect and form to what he sees. Thus all things were made by the Son, and without him was not anything made (Tertullian. Against Praxean XV).

God made all things. He laid the foundation of the course he meant to follow even to the last. Tertullian describes the Son's activities in the Old Testament as a learning experience 'in order to level for us the way of faith, that we might the more readily believe that the Son of God had come down into the world' (Tertullian. Against Praxean XVI). By means of his learning 'he knew full well what human feelings and affections were, intending as he always did to take upon him man's actual component substances, body and soul' (Tertullian. Against Praxean XVI).

Yet even so, the Son always acted in the Father's name. Even the titles proper to the Father are given to the Son. Some people balk at this idea, believing that the oneness of God spoken of in the prophets applies also to the Son, and prevents the distinction of God. However, the fact that there is only one God does not detract from the fact of the Son of God,

> But what hinders them from readily perceiving this community of the Father's titles in the Son, is the statement of Scripture, whenever it determines God to be but One; as if the self-same Scripture had not also set forth two, both as God and Lord (Tertullian. Against Praxean XVIII).

Scripture shows one God, but it also shows a duality in God of Father and Son, and yet remains consistent. The Father is the 'first person of God, while the Son is the second' (Tertullian. Against Praxean XVIII). To mention God as one, refers to the Father, but is not detrimental to the Son, for the Son is undivided and unseparated from the Father. The Son is not actually another, and 'should not be supposed to have come from another God' (Tertullian. Against Praxean XVIII).

Since the Son cannot be separated from the Father, Tertullian says, there is a union of co-operation in all things. God created by means of wisdom, and that wisdom was Christ, who is 'the wisdom and power of God' (Tertullian. Against Praxean XIX). Tertullian writes,

> Now this Word, the power of God and wisdom of God, must be the very Son of God. So that if [he did] all things by the Son, he must have stretched out the heavens by Christ...(Tertullian. Against Praxean XIX).

The fact of the existence of the Son does not, in Tertullian's mind, necessarily lead to the idea of three Gods. The distinction between Father and Son is not caused by a severance of their substance, but from its dispensation. They are neither divided nor separate, being distinct in degree, not in state (Tertullian. Against Praxean XIX). It follows, then, that while the Word does indeed speak of God as One, for example, 'I and my Father are one' (John 10, 30), there are many places which speak of Father and Son as distinct Persons. The distinction, however, is not of separation, but of different dispositions of God.

Having examined the relationship of Father and Son in great depth, with many quotations and explanations from both the Old and New Testaments, Tertullian turns to the subject of the Holy Spirit. Introducing the topic he notes that 'he is distinct from Father and Son as to their Personal existence, one and inseparable from them as to their Divine nature' (Tertullian. Against Praxean XXV). Father, Son and

Holy Spirit are distinct from one another, being one in essence, not in Person. However, as the same reasoning applies in dealing with the Holy Spirit as applied to the Son, it is not necessary to explore it further here.

Whenever one stresses the divine origin and nature of Christ, one is led to the question of how he became flesh and dwelt among us. Christ as the Word of God, as a progression of the Divine, can be understood on a higher, more spiritual level. But Christ lived on earth as an ordinary man. Tertullian, sensitive to issues of docetism and Gnosticism, stressed the real humanity of Christ. The incarnation, he writes, 'was by a real clothing of himself in flesh. For the rest, we must believe God to be unchangeable, and incapable of form' (Tertullian. Against Praxean XXVII).

God can only be seen then, in the flesh, which makes Christ the visible aspect of the invisible, the last in the series of Divine Procession. The incarnation did not change the Son; it transfigured him into someone who could live on earth. Normally transfiguration changes the thing transfigured, the old is lost and a new emerges, but God, however does not change. Taking on the flesh, being transfigured into a human being, could not change God, for Jesus was both God and man.

At this point, Tertullian wrestled with the paradox of Christology, of how God can be limited in a human form, or how a finite human could contain the infinity of God. The paradox is of such a nature, that one cannot be in the other and both survive. If Jesus is a man, then,

> Jesus, therefore, cannot at this rate be God for he has ceased to be in the Word, which was made flesh, nor can he be man incarnate, for he is not properly flesh, and it was flesh which the Word became. Being compounded, therefore, of both, He actually is neither, he is rather some third substance, quite different from either (Tertullian. Against Praxean XXVII).

Finally Tertullian comes to the conclusion that Jesus is both flesh and God, 'differing no doubt according to each substance in its own special property, inasmuch as the Word is nothing else but God, and the flesh nothing else but man' (Tertullian. Against Praxean XXVII). In Jesus, then, there is a two fold state of humanity and divinity, each wholly preserved, and yet subsisting upon each other. Thus Christ is anointed by the Father, while he died for the Father. At the resurrection, Christ is with God in heaven, having,

> ... received from the Father the promised gift and has shed it forth, even the holy Spirit - the third name in the Godhead, and the third degree of the Divine Majesty; the declarer of the one Monarchy of God, but at the same time the interpreter of the economy ... such is in the Father and the Son and the Holy Spirit, according to the mystery of the Doctrine of Christ (Tertullian. Against Praxean XXX).

Apostolic Christology laid the seeds for the beginnings of the Christological debates that would rage from the beginning of the fourth century onwards. Gradually it became apparent that the innocent and general concepts of God raised more questions than they answered. The introduction of the word 'Person' by Tertullian had a long-lasting effect on the Church, and the issue swung to how the 'Persons' of God could be one expression of God.

The Arian Controversy

The next major step in Christian History came at the beginning of the fourth century, when Constantine the Great was proclaimed emperor of the western half of the Roman Empire. Constantine had been proclaimed emperor at York in 306, became full emperor of the West in 312, and sole emperor of the entire Roman Empire in 323. A difficult man to understand, Constantine was motivated by religion all his life. Beginning as a pagan, he initially worshipped a solar god called 'Apollo'. This gave way to a monotheistic reverence for a divine spirit who governed the universe. The symbol of this spirit was the sun. When he underwent a religious experience of seeing a cross in the sky, he put a Christian emblem on his legions shields and conquered in the name of Christianity (Davis 1983, 29). He became a Christian, at least in name, and was finally baptized on his death-bed. Regardless of his personal adherence to Christianity, which is disputed, during Constantine's reign a monumental event took place in the history of the Church, an event as much shaped by the Emperor's interference as by anything else.

The roots of this event lay in the ordination in 311 of one Arius as a presbyter in Alexandria. Arius had been trained in the Antiochene school, and believed in a Christology from below, stressing the human nature of Christ, in his case, to the detriment of the Divinity. Arius was part of a succession of theologians who flourished in the third century, who questioned how the Divine and human could exist in one person.

We know a bit about Arius from history. Epiphanus notes that,

> [h]e was very tall in stature, with downcast countenance - counterfeited like a guileful serpent, and well able to deceive any unsuspecting heart through its cleverly designed appearance. For he was always garbed in a short coat and sleeveless tunic; he spoke gently, and people found him persuasive and flattering (Williams 1987, 32).

One can gather from this description that Epiphanus did not like Arius overly much. We also know, however, that he was a charming man, who greatly impressed the ladies.

Our concern with Arius, however, is not so much his looks, but his theology. Shortly after Arius became a deacon, Alexander was ordained Bishop of Alexandria. This is important because Alexander was schooled in the Alexandrian School. He believed in a Christology from on high, stressing the divinity of Christ, sometimes at the expense of his humanity. He saw Christ as the Word, distinguishable from the Father, but not separate from Him, so that very much in terms of earlier writers, he saw the Word as 'the Father's express image and likeness, not subject to change' (Davis 1983, 54).

Alexander, then, was much more in tune with the earlier Apostolic Fathers, while Arius was more closely associated with the separation of the Father and Son. Controversy between the two was inevitable, and came to a head in 319 when Arius was censured for his preaching.

We can get an idea of Arius' message from a letter he wrote to a fellow past student, Eusebius, Bishop of Nicomedia, where he sums up his concept of Christ. He writes that he cannot concur with Alexander's teaching that as God always existed, so did the Son, that 'the Son co-exists unbegotten with God'. He writes to Eusebius,

> We are persecuted, because we say that the Son has a beginning, but that God is without beginning. This is the cause of our persecution, and likewise, because we say that He is of the non-existent. And this we say, because He is neither part of God, nor of any essential being (Arius, Letter to Eusebius of Nicomedia).

Arius' Christology was a long way from that of Ignatius, Irenaeus and Tertullian, being more a radical Antiochene Christology from below. By 318, his ideas had crystallized into the teaching that Jesus Christ was not begotten of the Father, did not share in His divinity. The Son, he stressed, had a beginning, while God had no beginning (Young 1983, 59). Thus the Son was a creature, not substantially different from ordinary human beings - although He was the first and greatest of God's creatures (Young 1983, 61). He bolstered his argument by stating that the essence of God is 'transcendent, unique and indivisible, it cannot be shared' (Davis 1983, 52). A result of Christ being a creature, is that 'he was capable of evil as well as virtue' (Jedin and Dolan 1980, 17).

Arius' argument about the nature of God and Christ can be summarized as follows,

1. God alone is self-subsistent, uncreate, immaterial and therefore without any kind of plurality or composition; he is subject to no natural processes, no emanation or diffusion of his substance.
2. He is entirely free, rational and purposeful.
3. He initiates the creative process by freely bringing the Son into being, as a subsistent individual truly distinct from himself; he does this 'before all ages' yet there is a sense in which the Father exists prior to the Son, since the Son is not eternal, that is, not timelessly self-subsistent.
4. By the will of God, the Son is stably and unalterably what he is, a perfect creature, not just 'one among the others', he is the inheritor of all the gifts and glories God can give him, but, since this is the effect of God's sovereign will, the Father's glory and dignity is in no way lessened by such a gift (Williams 1987, 98).

It has been argued that Arius' primary interest was to uphold the Divinity of the Father (Stead 1994, 25). That he did so at the expense of the Son, was the cause of great controversy. The effect was swift censure by Alexander. In 319 the Bishop circulated a letter warning his readers not to fall into Arian heresy. The letter came too late for some, and was ignored by others; Arius' ideas were gaining purchase.

As the controversy spread across the Church, the Emperor Constantine became aware of it. He was distressed that his empire was being rent asunder by a religious matter (Davis 1989, 54), and entered the fray. Unfortunately, there is every indication that Constantine had no concept of the depth of the issues at hand, nor the overall effect it would have on the church. It has been argued that his ends were primarily to preserve the Empire.

In 325, he convened a Council at Nicaea to iron out this issue. Traditionally 318 Bishops were in attendance, and that the outcome became binding on the church. Unfortunately, no minutes were kept of that Council, but several vitally important things came out of it.

The Arian faction began by offering an Arian creed, stating that the Son was a Creature, that there was a time when He was not, and so on. This was rejected by the majority of the Bishops. An attempt was made to create a creed acceptable to all parties from Scripture, and this too was not possible. The result was a man-made creed, deliberate in its rejection of Arianism. It became known as the Nicene Creed, and is still binding on all Christians.

The Nicene Creed

The thrust of the Nicene Creed is to stress the unity of God, and the Divinity of the Son of God. Thus it begins with the affirmation of the Oneness of God,

> We believe in one God, father almighty, maker of all things, both visible and invisible.

This preamble is not that different from what Arius himself believed, and was a point of common ground. The essence and nature of God in himself, has never been under question. However, according to Christian doctrine, God revealed himself in some way in the Person of Jesus Christ. This is the point of departure for the orthodoxy and Arians. So the Creed continues,

> And in one Lord, Jesus Christ, the Son of God, begotten from the Father, only begotten, that is from the substance of the Father, God from God, light from light, true God from true God, begotten not made, one in substance with the Father, through whom all things came to be, both those in heaven and those on earth.

This statement tackles Arius head on, and establishes the divinity of Christ. The Creed confirms belief in the fact that Christ was begotten not made. Thus he was not a creature of God, but a proceeding from God, and so is God. This is strengthened by the statement that he is 'one in substance with the Father'.

The word 'substance' is an English translation of the Greek word, 'ousia', and 'one in substance' in Greek is 'homoousia' thus the same substance. If Jesus is of the same substance as the Father, then he also is completely Divine with all that that entails - a far cry from Arius' creature. It would seem that this Creed, then, achieved the purpose for which it was written.

However, instead of answering all questions about the relationship of Father, Son and Holy Spirit, it simply introduced more. The term substance or ousia, was partly to blame, for it was a difficult word to define, and could have at least three different meanings.

By closing their eyes and squinting a bit, the Arian followers could interpret this creed in many ways. The result was that instead of closing the door on Arianism, the Council of Nicaea actually made it possible for it to flourish, until eventually it took hold of almost the whole of the Eastern Empire - with a few notable exceptions.

If the purpose of the Nicene Creed was to lay to rest the notion that Christ was a creature of God, rather than God himself, then, because of the imprecision of the term homoousia, it failed. Accepting the fact that Father and Son are one and the same substance, does not explain how they came to be Father and Son, with all the connotations of unity and division built into those terms.

As the Arian controversy raged on, so another Alexandrian bishop began to shine. This was Athanasius, who took the reigns of that see at the death of Alexander in 328. Athanasius had been present at the Council of Nicaea as a deacon, and was an ardent supporter of the Nicene Creed.

Athanasius' theology rested in the firm conviction that the Word became flesh to redeem the human race (Davis 1989, 89). 'God,' he argued, 'can never be without his Word, as light can never cease to shine' (Davis 1989, 89). This shining light, who became the Redeemer of the human race, was Jesus Christ, not a creature as Arius would say, but the Word made flesh. Yet he struck a distinction between father and Son which is a matter of subsistence as person's or hypostases. Thus the theology of Nicaea took another step. The oneness of the Divine substance can be distinguished into three persons, each partaking fully of the Divinity, yet each distinct within themselves, the Father, Son and Holy Spirit. The issue of the relationship of substance and Person has formed the crux of Christology every since.

The Athanasian Creed

The Athanasian Creed is a fuller exposition of doctrine than the Nicene Creed. The latter deals with the sameness of the Divine substance in the Trinity, and establishes the divinity of Christ. The Athanasian Creed, however, deals far more fully with the expression of that Divine substance in the Person's or hypostases of the Father, Son and Holy Spirit. The Creed begins with an affirmation of one God,

> We worship one God in Trinity, and the Trinity in unity, neither confounding the Persons, nor dividing the substance...[3]

Thus the concept of Trinity is introduced almost immediately, deflecting the argument away from the Christological issues to the ontological ones of the nature of God. The thrust of Athanasius' Creed, which has become universally accepted in the Christian world, is that within the unity of God exists the diversity of Person - a separation within oneness, or a oneness formed from separation. In this vein the Creed continues,

> There is one person of the Father, another of the Son, and another of the Holy Spirit, but the Godhead of the Father, of the Son and of the Holy Spirit is all one, the glory equal, the majesty co-eternal.

In trying to protect and preserve the divinity of Christ, Athanasius falls into the trap of separating the three aspects of the Divinity. The term Persons or hypostases is crucial, yet just as ousia was a slippery and dangerous word in trying to describe the essence of God, so Persons is equally open to various meanings.

The idea of the Person is not distinct individuals, such as Tom, Dick and Harry, but rather states of rest that the Divine falls into in order to perform different aspects of the Divine work. For example, the Father is the appearance of the Divine in the process of creating the universe. The Son the appearance in redeeming and saving the human race within that created universe, and the Holy Spirit the means by which Father and Son act.

The difficulty in this creed is that of conceiving of a unity in this Trinity, for one can only think of either a Trinity or a unity. It is not possible to think of one and three simultaneously, and so the idea of threeness within God was firmly rooted in Christian theology by the use of the term Person. From this time onwards, the church would grow increasingly convinced that God was actually three persons. The idea of unity, whilst held as a matter of intellectual thought, began to loose ground as other doctrines sprang in the wake of this separation of God into three.

The Divine and Human in Christ

The settlement of the Trinitarian issues at Nicaea, and later in the Athanasian Creed, opened the door for further dispute around the nature of God. The resolution of the 'homoousios' and 'hypostasis' question led directly to speculation on the relationship of the divinity and humanity in Christ. If Jesus was indeed a part of God, sharing the same substance of the Father, begotten, not made, then how could he be human? How could he have been crucified, dead and buried, for the Divine is not passable.

As in every other issue in the church, this question percolated around for a long while before coming to a head. Different ideas were presented by the Alexandrian and Antiochene schools of thought, each holding to their historical positions of Christology from on high or from below respectively. In the years after Nicaea, a further development took place that would greatly influence Christian theology, the correlation between theology and Neo-platonism.

Plato saw two levels to creation, a higher, originating realm, and a lower realm of effects. The result is a dualism between spirit and matter, and became the paradigm around which much of the discussion of how Christ could be both divine and human revolved. According to this model, it became possible to see in Christ a higher aspect, the Divine, expressing itself in a lower plane, the human. Neo-platonism also played into the old rivalries between Alexandria and Antioch, with the former stressing the Divine, and the latter the human.

Responsibility for this stage in the development (or regression as Servetus and Swedenborg might think) of Christology, really falls to the Antiochene school. Stressing the humanity of Christ, they tended to strike a wedge between the Divine and the human in Christ. Diodore of Tarsus, is credited with creating a 'God-man' Christology, in which he distinguished two subjects within Christ's person, the Word of God (who is the Divine Son) and the man born from Mary (the human son) (Davis 1989, 143).

Although both these aspects existed within Christ, they were not the same thing. The Word, or Son from eternity, is unchanged and unchangeable. It could not be crucified, nor could it die. In contrast, the human was changing. Jesus increased in age and wisdom, he suffered as ordinary people do, and indeed, died on the cross. Thus the human of Christ was a temple, or vessel in which the Logos dwelt.

Pressed to its limits, this doctrine wore down and broke the bond of unity between the divine and the human, setting the two natures side by side in a parallel course within Christ, rather than in an interchange of human and divine characteristics. Eventually the idea evolved that there were actually two sons, one Divine and one human.

Although Diodore's theology was discredited in his own lifetime, is spawned other, similar ideas, the most important of which was espoused by Nestorius, whom the historian Socrates calls 'a proud and arrogant man' (Soctrates 7, 28, 32).

Nestorius

Nestorius rose to the centre of the growing dispute about the duality of natures in Christ in 428 when he was enthroned as archbishop of Constantinople (McGuckin 1994, 21). Most of his work is a regurgitation of earlier dualistic theology remodeled to suit the needs of his milieu (McGuckin 1994, 22). Much of the controversy that dogged his episcopal reign could have been avoided if he had been a different kind of man. Making enemies of the Empress, of the monks and indeed of ordinary people, Nestorius ensured that when his ideas were openly expressed, there were many who rejected them because they rejected him.

The dispute was initiated when Nestorius ruled against calling Mary the "mother of God" or '*Theotokos*', on the grounds that God could not have a mother. His alternative title of 'Mother of Man', *Anthropotokos*, was so widely rejected that he compromised, with a third title, "Mother of Christ" (*Christotokos*). These terms may seem strange to those who pay scant attention to Mary at all, but in the fifth century these were fighting words. Aside from denigrating the Virgin, they were also perceived, rightly, to deny that Jesus Christ was actually God. At the time a little jingle was sung in the streets of Constantinople, saying,

If Mary is not, strictly speaking, the Mother of God,
Then her son is not, strictly speaking, God (McGuckin 1980, 28).

Nestorius was an Antiochene, his theology began with the point that Christ was both fully human and fully divine. His Divine side was consubstantial with the Father, unchangeable, nor could it be made to suffer. It did not need the human side with all its impediments, except to save the human race.

On the other hand, the human side was akin to our own. Christ was not a body filled with the Divine, but an integral human being with every human characteristic except sin. This position necessitated a conclusion dealing with the relationship of the divine and human within Christ. He concluded that these two natures were 'distinct, unaltered and unconfused' (McGuckin 1994, 135). At no point was there any mixture of the two.

To explain this duality in one Person, Nestorius used the term 'prosopon' or face, which was the visible Jesus Christ who walked this world, and who was at the same time Logos and human. When one worships Christ, one worships both these two natures simultaneously.

Nestorius follows in the Tradition of the Athanasian Creed, saying one and speaking three, except he says that in Christ there is one and yet speaks two. All the protestations of unity in trinity and unity in duality aside, one is left at this point with one God sundered into pieces.

Cyril of Alexandria

It is not fair, however, to fully blame Nestorius for the next phase of Christological development. His views gained wide acceptance, particularly in the eastern half of the Roman Empire, and also among the Germanic tribes who at that time were pressing into the western side of the Empire. Yet there were those who ardently rejected his dualistic theology. Key amongst these was Cyril of Alexandria.

Modern Christians rank Cyril as one of the finest theologians of his day, and one of the greatest patristic writers of all generations (McGuckin 1994, 1). In his own time, however, his opposition regarded him as a rank heretic. He ardently rejected both Nestorius and his views.

Nestorian ideas began to reach Egypt in the early part of 429. Cyril concluded that Nestorius had abandoned the idea that Christ is the single subject of the divine and had embraced the discredited theory of Two Sons. He was deeply offended by this. He believed that 'the primary message of the incarnation was not about the discrete relationship of God and man, but nothing less than the complete reconciliation of God and man in Jesus' (McGuckin 1994, 34).

Cyril adamantly maintained that Mary is the Mother of God, for Christ is the Logos in human flesh (Cyril, LME 4). Drawing from the Nicene Creed and the works of Athanasius, Cyril stresses that Christ is God by nature. It is true that before the incarnation the two hypostases of Father and Son contained the Divine. When the Son took on the human flesh, that Divine became visible in Him. Mary, therefore, is not solely the mother of the flesh, but the mother of the human manifestation.

The lines were drawn between those who stressed a disconnection, so to speak, between the Divine and human, and those who blurred the distinction. Over time this controversy escalated with increasing hostility between Cyril and Nestorius. On three occasions Cyril wrote to Nestorius urging him to recant, each time Nestorius refused. Finally the matter became so heated that the Emperor, Theodosius, called for a council to meet at Ephesus in 431.

The Resolution of the Council of Ephesus

The Council of Ephesus was a fiasco. Nestorius refused to attend the meetings. His strong supporter, John of Jerusalem arrived after it was finished, and, when all was said and done, the sticky problem of the duality in Christ was not resolved. Further confusing events were imperial soldiers taking Nestorius' side, and the unprecedented event of the Bishop of Alexandria excommunicating the Archbishop of Constantinople.

The impasse and confusion became so great, that eventually the Emperor dissolved the Council, excommunicated both Cyril and Nestorius, and ordered them to hold private meetings to iron out their differences.

The outcome of this mess was that the gathering at Ephesus with all its attendant ill feelings contributed to a major advance in the church's understanding of the nature of Christ. It was a step that could only come in the wake of Nicaea and Constantinople. These earlier Councils marked the passage of thought from the early un-defined concept of the Trinity to a definitive explanation of the relationship of the divinity and humanity in Christ.

The solution that finally emerged from the debris of the Council of Ephesus is known as the *communicatio idiomatum*, or the sharing of qualities between the human and divine. This idea laid the foundation for the next major battle of Christology, whether Christ has one will or two. The concept of the *communicatio idiomatum* is simple, Christ has two natures, human and Divine, completely separate and distinct. However, to prevent the disintegration of the personality of Christ, it was agreed that these two natures shared properties. Thus there were divine attributes within the human, and vice versa. In this way, the Church could accept the essential Nestorian divisions of Christ and at the same time retain Cyril's insistence on the unity and oneness of Christ.

As in all cases of compromise, it was not unanimously accepted. In Egypt, especially, there were those who rejected this solution. It was held, and still is by the Coptic Churches of today, that Christ has only one nature, one will, one life. However, the majority of the Catholic Church was willing to accept the compromise.

The Council Of Chalcedon

The compromise did not heal the discrepancies in Christology between the Alexandrian and Antiochene schools of thought. By 450, less than twenty years later, controversy flared up again, this time stimulated by Eutyches, a priest in Constantinople. Schooled in Alexandrian theology, he refused to admit that there were 'two natures after the incarnation' (Garret 1974, 34). He could not accept that Christ was of one substance with the Father in matters of the spirit, and another substance in terms of the body. To recognize Christ as having the same substance as ourselves in his humanity meant that Christ was nothing more than a warmed over human being. He held that after the resurrection, Christ was divine both as to his divine and human, thus having one essence.

The Alexandrian School, led by Dioscorus, who had succeeded Cyril, rallied around Eutyches, and under his leadership the Pope of Rome, Leo, was approached to add to their weight against the *communicatio idiomatum*. Surprisingly Leo refused, and this refusal set the church irreversibly on the path to a fragmented Christology.

As controversy mounted, the Emperor, Marcian, called a council at the city of Chalcedon, outside Constantinople. More than five hundred bishops attended, making it one of the biggest ecumenical councils in history.

The overriding force at Chalcedon was the doctrinal statement
by Pope Leo in support of the Ephesian formula and the *communicatio
idiomatum*. The Tome of Leo became the standard by which
Christology was interpreted. In many ways it was a repetition of the
original creeds, dating back to the Nicene Creed. A brief overview of
the salient facts will help us to understand the importance this work has
had to the development of Christology,

> ... the whole body of the faithful acknowledge their belief in God the
> Father almighty, and in Jesus Christ, His only son our Lord, who was
> born of the Holy Ghost and the Virgin Mary...
> God is believed to be both Almighty and Father; it follows that the
> Son is shown to be co-eternal with him, differing in no respect from
> the Father....
> [The Son] was conceived of the Holy Spirit, in the womb of His
> Virgin Mother... that birth, uniquely marvelous and marvelously
> unique, ought not to be understood in such a way as to preclude the
> distinctive properties of the kind [i.e. humanity] through the new
> mode of creation. For it is true that the Holy Spirit gave fruitfulness
> to the Virgin, but the reality of His body was received from her
> body... (Leo II).

So far, so good. Up to this point Leo has not made any points that
anyone would dispute. However, Leo held to the idea of the
communicatio idiomatum, which becomes increasingly apparent as his
theology develops. In the third section of the Tome he deals with the
relationship between the divine derived from the Holy Spirit, and the
human from Mary,

> Thus the properties of each nature and substance were preserved
> entire, and came together to form one person... Thus there was born
> true God in the entire and perfect nature of true man, complete in his
> own properties, complete in ours (Leo III).

One should not imagine that Leo at this point meant that
Christ shared our sinful nature. He qualifies the human nature as being
that 'which the Creator formed in us from the beginning' thus before
the fall of man. Christ became human, but He never shared the
sinfulness of the human being,

> He did not become partaker of our sins because he entered into
> fellowship with human infirmities. He assumed the form of a servant

without the stain of sin, making the human properties greater, but not detracting from the divine (Leo III).

In taking on the human nature, Christ in no way diminished the divine within, which Leo stresses,

> Each nature preserves its own characteristics without diminution, so that the form of a servant does not detract from the form of God (Leo III).

> The Son of God, therefore, came down from his throne in heaven without withdrawing from his Father's glory, and entered this lower world, born after a new order, by a new mode of birth. After a new order, inasmuch as he is invisible in his own nature, and he became visible in ours (Leo IV).

Thus Leo paints the case of the incarnation, stressing at all times the unity yet distinction of the two natures of Christ.

The Tome of Leo was read in full at the Council of Chalcedon, and was held to be in complete accord with the Creeds of Nicaea (325) and Constantinople (381). Based on it the assembled Bishops, with the exception of thirteen from Egypt, and Dioscorus, who was stripped of his episcopal office and priestly dignity, composed a binding expression of faith in the duality of divine and human in the person of Christ. This document is known as the *Definitio Fidei*.

Thus the Council of Chalcedon codified and made mandatory for all Christians to believe the formula that

> Christ, Son, Lord, Only begotten [is] recognized IN TWO NATURES, WITHOUT CONFUSION, WITHOUT CHANGE, WITHOUT DIVISION AND WITH SEPARATION[4]... the distinction of natures being in no way annulled by the union, but rather the characteristics of each nature being preserved and coming together to form one person and subsistence [hypostasis], not as parted or separated into two persons, but one and the same Son... (Bettenson 1981, 51).

The separation of Christ into bits and pieces was complete. At Nicaea Christ was presented as being of one substance with the Father, and the idea of persons introduced, but not elaborated. Athanasius, however, stressed the role of the Persons, or hypostases in such a way that it became increasingly possible to divide the Trinity, and more difficult to see the unity in God. At Ephesus, to combat the Nestorian division of the human and divine in Christ, the idea of a *communicatio idiomatum* was mooted, and this in turn made possible the separation of two natures in Christ.

The Effect of Trinitarian Christology on Christian Theology

The Trinity became the defining quality of Christian doctrine. Once the dogma had been codified by the Ecumenical Councils, later Christian students were left to try to make sense of it. From the time of Augustine to the end of the medieval period, concepts about the Trinity went through three distinct phases, and in each of them it was recognized that both the Trinitarian and Christological concepts were neither Scripturally defensible, nor rationally evident.

Bainton (1953) describes three schools of thought resulting from the attempt to reconcile the doctrine of the Trinity with the Scriptures and with reason. He calls these the 'Illustrative', the 'Demonstrative' and the 'Fideist'.

The first phase of the development of discussion on the nature of God was the illustrative. Those falling into this school believed that while the Trinity could not be proved or demonstrated, it could be illustrated in the Scriptures (Bainton in Becker 1953, 32). This phase was initiated by Augustine, who held that while the doctrine is not directly taught, it can be deduced, and the deduction itself is a matter of revelation, since it would not occur to the unaided the human mind (Bainton in Becker 1953, 32).

Augustine describes the Trinity as three divine Persons, with the Father as the originating cause, the Son begotten from him, and the Holy Spirit proceeding from him. The Son bears the special relationship of being the Word begotten,

> The Word of God, then, the only begotten Son of the Father, in all things like and equal to the Father ... is altogether that which the Father is, yet is not the Father, because one is the Son, the other is Father (Augustine. De Trinitatus XV xiv 23).

Thus Father and Son are one, yet they are different, the difference arising in the begetting, which is God uttering his Word, producing for himself the Word that is equal in all things. Wrestling with this concept Augustine explains,

... the Father is not greater than the Son in the substance of truth, but that both together are not anything greater than the Holy Spirit alone, nor that any two at all in the same Trinity are anything greater than one, nor all three together greater than each severally (Augustine. De Trinitate III 5).

To illustrate this Trinity, Augustine turns to a comparison with a person made in the image of God, and retains a psychological Trinity[5], a person's ability to love, the act of loving and the object of the love, or in the mind in memory, intellect and will (Bainton in Becker 1953, 33). Thus the Trinity can be illustrated by a long line of similar relationships, which, since they all reflect God in one way or another, reflect the Trinity within him.

Augustine's illustrative approach to the Trinity influenced generations (Bainton in Becker 1953, 33). Peter Lombard, 'The Master of the Sentences' asserted that 'the doctrine could be found on every page of Holy Writ' (Bainton in Becker 1953, 33).

The illustrative theory of the Middle Ages continued from Augustine into the twelfth century when Richard of St. Victor 'affirmed that [the Trinity] may not only be illustrated but also demonstrated' (Bainton in Becker 1953, 32). By claiming this he brought a new twist to the Trinitarian question, leading to a new quest, to demonstrate the Trinity in the pages of Scripture.

This school of thought raised many questions, not the least of which was why God stopped elaborating at three persons and not indefinitely. Richard answered this question by drawing from Augustine's definition of love. Love he wrote demanded three persons: one to love, one to receive the love and a third to share it in order to prevent jealousy. Thus love demands a trinity (Bainton in Becker 1953, 35).

The long list of Medieval theologians who tried to illustrate and demonstrate the Trinity in Biblical terms attests to the concept that the Bible is not susceptible to philosophic manipulation. Rather than abandon philosophy, however, the Scholastics abandoned the Bible. In the fourteenth century a new approach to theological and philosophical issues arose - nominalism. Nominalism can be defined as 'the view that only particulars are real and that universals are but observable likenesses among the particulars of sense experience' (Jones 1968, 345).

Carried to its extremes, nominalists held that the universals are only names, or merely noise. True reality rested not in universal names, but in the object itself. The fourteenth century adherents of this school of thought, of whom William of Occam was the most important, were called 'the Moderni' - even in their own day (Bainton in Becker 1953, 37).

When nominalism was applied to the Trinity it undermined the traditionally held concept of three Persons united in one substance. Nominalists could reason that the reality of God lay in the three Persons, but that the substance, as a universal, did not exist. Under this system God was either one or three, but 'in either case, the Trinitarian godhead of orthodoxy, the notion that God is both one and three, is denied' (Jones 1969, 189). If the universal is perceived as a reality, then the Godhead would have to be extended to embrace a fourth aspect, and once again the concept of a quaternity raises its head (Bainton in Becker 1953, 37).

Nominalism tied Christology into knots. William of Occam 'held that neither God's existence nor his unity nor his infinity can be proved' (Jones 1969, 317). It is not possible to prove God's unity, because each person in the Trinity must needs be a reality in himself. There is no universal binding them together, and therefore each person is an absolute entity or being in its own right. Without a universal substance holding the Godhead together, the unity of the three Persons is sundered, with tritheism as a result (Bainton in Becker 1953, 39).

While Occam did not declare a tritheism,

> As a matter of fact, he did say that there is no relation distinct in any way from the absolutes. And if one concedes that God is in reality Father and Son and Spirit, then one must assume that in God there are three absolutes in reality distinct. Such a position is obviously indistinguishable from tritheism (Bainton in Becker 1953, 39).

Thus the doctrine of the Trinity is rendered incomprehensible and irrational. The acids of Scholasticism burned deeply, destroying the one factor making the Trinity theologically acceptable - the oneness and wholeness of God.

In the face of this dichotomy between faith and reason, many scholars suspended their reason in favor of faith. Gregory of Rimini delivered a series of Lectures on the Sentences[6] in Paris in 1344 (Bainton in Becker 1953, 42). He was unwilling to yield the faith because he failed to see intellectually how three could equal one. He believed that the faith must be held to under all circumstances, even in the face of rationality. Tied into a knot by his own reasoning, Gregory concludes, that people

> ... are driven, therefore, to admit that in this life, being what we are, the solution transcends our capacities because the derivation of the Son and the Spirit is ineffable and incomprehensible (Bainton in Becker 1953, 43).

Another example is Cardinal D'Ailly who was 'even less ready than Gregory of Rimini to surrender' (Bainton in Becker 1953, 43). He finally came to the conviction that it is impossible to either demonstrate or illustrate the Trinity, although did not stop him, however, for placing a form of divine sanction on both, and in doing so he placed an unsubstantiated personal revelation over the authority of the Bible, and held it to be binding on Catholics. For him truth was not a matter of reason but revelation, and where the two did not coincide, faith was the more important. In fact, the ability to believe in the face of reason is a gift from God (Bainton in Becker 1953, 43).

This attitude led Medieval Scholasticism into an abyss of irrationality in which reason, which could not fathom the mysteries of the Trinity, was held ransom to a faith declared and enforced by the church alone.

D'Ailly's irrationality found its final form in the works of the Scot, John Major and Erasmus. Unable to maintain a balance between faith and reason, with D'Ailly calling for the subjection of reason to faith, there were those who subjected faith to reason. Major's tentative effort was to declare it permissible

> ... to say that there are three Gods, provided the term God be construed according to the person (Bainton in Becker 1953, 44).

Finally Erasmus summed up the statements by saying,

> According to dialectical logic it is possible to say that there are three gods, but to announce this to the untutored would give great offence (Bainton in Becker 1953, 45).

The cycle was complete - from the attempt to ensure the recognition of the divinity of Christ, and preserve the unity of God at the Council of Nicaea, through the reasoning of Augustine, Lombard, and the Moderni when the Trinity was effectively divided into three Persons, and the understanding of God held to be a matter of faith only.

Notes:

---

[1] 'Of this [Christian] church there have been two epochs, one extending from Christ's time to the Council of Nice, and the other from that Council to the present day' (TCR 760). 'The church was different before the Council of Nice, as long as the Apostles Creed was in force. It became changed after the Council of Nice, and still more after the Athanasian Creed was composed.' (Ecc. Hist. 2).

[2] I.e. the heresy that Christ only appeared to have been born, but in reality His appearance on earth was only an appearance.

[3] This version of the Athanasian Creed, and in the rest of this paper, is from the version given in Lord 56. See Appendix A.

[4] Emphasis is Bettenson's.

[5] Augustine. De Trinitate IX and X.

[6] I.e. the Sentences of Peter Lombard.

Chapter Three

Michael Servetus

Few defenders have risen to champion the cause of Michael Servetus since his burning at the stake in 1553. Most have done so more from outrage at the lack of contemporary religious tolerance than because of his theological beliefs. Servetus represents an approach to theological study and inquiry inimical to the orthodoxy of the Reformation era, a theological conformity shared by Catholic and Protestant alike.

Those sympathetic to his cause describe him as 'a dreamer, an enthusiast, a mystic' (Osler 1909, 16), a 'valiant yet strangely neglected personality' (Beilby 1936, 210). There are few, however, who take a charitable view of the man. The truth remains that while in the theological eclecticism of this millennial era, his execution is recorded but his theology is almost unknown. To most people he is known only for his opposition to Calvin and his tragic death at the Reformer's hand (Beilby 1936, 211). Most treatises on the Reformation make very brief mention of his name and then usually in connection with John Calvin[1].

Aside from the general ignorance about him, Servetus has made a serious contribution to the history of theology. He challenged the understanding of Christology in a unique way. Seen in his own era, and often portrayed as such in our own, Servetus was a rank heretic, deserving of death (Osler 1909, 23). Nevertheless, he was an important link in the continuity of anti-Trinitarian speculation running through much of medieval scholastic theology (Bainton in Becker 1953, 29). He carried the raging questions of scholasticism to their conclusion, asserting that existing theology needed to be scrapped and an entirely new Christology, based solely on the Bible we worked out.

A nineteenth century biographer wrote, that in spite of the cold reception his works received,

> ...he seemed to have thought himself at as full liberty as the leaders of the great movement then afoot to give his own interpretation to the kind of reform which not only the Church, but its doctrine, required. For such an undertaking he was as well qualified by culture, as any of the Reformers - better qualified, in fact, than many among them, as in genius we believe he was surpassed, and in liberality and tolerance approached, by none (Willis 1877, 40).

Servetus 'out protested the Protestants of his time' (Beilby 1936, 211). He believed that if the doctrines of the church were reformed, the church would return to a primitive, simple Christianity (Osler 1909, 16). To achieve this, he took the position that anything in theology not directly sourced in the Bible itself should be discarded, and the Bible scoured for passages and inferences giving a true picture of God. Committed to this vision, he alienated many of his contemporary Reformers who were unwilling to move beyond the ecumenical creeds of Christianity. His sharp and often bitter tongue won him few friends and eventually contributed to his conviction and burning in 1553.

Since then, his name has been reduced to a mere footnote in history, and active memory of his work suppressed. In the Reformed Churches, at least into the eighteenth century, students, without ever studying Servetus, were bound to a subscription stating,

> [w]e detest all the heresies which have anciently disturbed the churches, especially the diabolical imaginations of Servetus, who attributes to the Lord Jesus Christ a fantastical divinity; forasmuch as he calls him the Idea and Pattern of all things, and names him personal or figurative Son of God, and finally, forges for him a body of three elements uncreated, and thus mixeth and destroyeth the two natures (Anon 1724, 214).

Early Years

There are several biographies of Servetus making it possible to establish an overview of his life, although the date and place of his birth are in doubt. *Miguel Serveto* was either born in Tudela, Navarre in 1511 (Beilby 1936, 212) or in 1509 at Villaneuva (Anon 1724, 26). The main indications, however, are that he was reared at Villaneuva, for that was the name he took as a pseudonym later in life. Also the family seat is in that town, and the local church still bears the family crest on the altar (Beilby 1936, 213, Osler 1909, 5).

Servetus seems to have belonged to a moderately well to do family who prized and could afford education (Osler 1909, 5). His academic life began in a monastery in his native province. His education, even at this early stage, laid the foundations of his later work. Possibly he was destined for the priesthood, for his early education indicates a gifted child who, at a very young age, read Latin, Greek and Hebrew, 'the last two very unusual accomplishments of the period' (Osler 1909, 5). Early indications were that he had both the mental and moral endowment for high placing in the church (Willis 1877, 6).

At twelve or fourteen years old Servetus entered the University of Saragossa, at that time the most celebrated in Spain (Willis 1877, 7). Here he made his first contacts with academia. He remained at Saragossa for four or five years, acquiring the considerable knowledge that forms the background to his books. At twenty he shows substantial knowledge of biblical language as well as the church fathers. It is obvious that during those years, he perfected he was broadly exposed to the classics as well as scholasticism. His scientific knowledge included mathematics, astronomy and geography (Willis 1877, 9).

His scholarly bent did not lead him to the church. Saragossa offered foundation studies for the priesthood, but young Servetus seemed more interested in law. At age seventeen, in 1528, he went to the University of Toulouse, over the French border, to study law as a profession. He never saw his native country again (Beilby 1936, 213).

He remained at Toulouse for two or three years, long enough to study the intricacies of both civil and canon law. In all probability, he continued to study theology and the other subjects which also interested him. Geography, astronomy and anatomy would later become the grist of his livelihood (Willis 1877, 10).

The outcome of Servetus' life shows that law as a subject never engaged his mind fully. His natural inclination was to theology, and while at Toulouse, ostensibly studying the law, he first encountered the Bible (Willis 1877, 10). It is fascinating to reflect that until this time, in 1528, Servetus had never seen a Bible (Beilby 1936, 214). He was eighteen years old, fully capable of reading the original languages, and schooled in the accepted interpretations of the time. His first encounter with the written Scriptures shocked his faith in Catholicism.

Most likely Servetus had no preconceived anti-Trinitarian ideas in his early reading. There do not appear to have been any anti-Trinitarians in France at that time (Anon 1724, 26). It is more conceivable that his attraction to the Bible lay in curiosity aroused by his earlier studies at Saragossa. At that time the Reformation was making itself felt in France, and he was exposed to some of its teachings (Anon 1724, 26, 27). The results of this exposure to Scripture itself, not indirectly through the church fathers as he had experienced before, had a profound effect on the young Servetus. The more he applied himself to the study of Scripture, the more convinced he was that the church needed to be reformed (Anon 1724, 27). By the age of twenty, Servetus felt 'moved by the divine impulse' to write about God, salvation and similar themes as he understood the Bible to teach them (Beilby 1936, 216). He thus set into motion a series of events leading ultimately to his death in Geneva.

The years at Saragossa and Toulouse had a marked effect on the development of his theological understanding, but they only laid the foundation of his thought. Servetus was a perennial student, perfecting his knowledge (Willis 1877, 17).

The interlude at Toulouse was followed by another fundamentally important phase in his life. The pull of the church was still strong, and the attraction of an academic role in the church a powerful force for a brilliant young man who had yet to blot his copy book. His university training made him proficient in the ancient languages and in a spectrum of theological subjects. Servetus' early promise as a rising star in the church reached its next level of development when he entered the service of Father Juan de Quintana (Beilby 1936, 214, Osler 1909, 5).

De Quintana, a Franciscan monk, was the confessor to Emperor Charles V (Beilby 1936, 214), and so one of the potentially most powerful priests in Europe at the time. It is not clear what position he served in, possibly as a private secretary (Willis 1877, 19). This brief interlude of between one and two years, proved to be a point of closure in the relationship between Servetus and the Roman Catholic Church - although he would maintain a semblance of being a good Catholic for years to come. Associated with the imperial court, Servetus saw aspects of the church that revolted him. One example of his disillusionment came in 1530, when, in the company of de Quintana he was present at the coronation of Charles V. The pageantry of the occasion made a lasting negative impression on the young man's mind (Beilby 1936, 214).

The worldliness and mercenary character of the Papacy reinforced his desire to reform the church. At Charles V's coronation, indulgences were for sale in the marketplace, making a mockery in Servetus' mind of the simple concepts of repentance taught in the Bible. His revulsion turned to an obsessive hatred (Osler 1909, 5).

However, Servetus remained in the employ of the Emperor's chaplain for a little longer. It was during this time that he attended the Diet of Augsburg, and the gathering of clerics, both Protestant and Catholic 'must have had a profound influence on the young student' (Osler 1909, 6). Concerning that time Servetus wrote,

> For my own part, I neither agree nor disagree in every particular with either Catholic or Reformer. Both of them seem to me to have something of truth and something of error in their views; and whilst each sees the other's shortcomings, neither sees his own. God in his goodness gives us all to understand our errors and inclines us to put them away. It would be easy enough, indeed, to judge dispassionately of everything, were we but suffered without molestation by the churches freely to speak our minds (Osler 1909, 6, see also Willis 1877, 25).

Servetus realized that his understanding and interpretation of the Scriptures was incompatible with both branches of the church. During his time at Augsburg it is quite likely that he spoke to Melancthon and other leading Reformers, and possibly even Luther himself (although there is no evidence of this) (Willis 1877, 26). How much contact he made with the Reformers at this point, however, is not known.

The accumulation of study and experience left him distinctly dissatisfied with the accepted Christianity of his day. His educated and fertile mind weighed up the theology taught at Saragossa and Toulouse, the worldliness of the Catholic Church and the newness, and sameness, of Protestantism. Into this mix he cast his own reading in the Scriptures themselves. The result was a view that all of Christianity needed to be reformed.

At about this point working for de Quintana became intolerable - probably because of his rejection of Catholicism. He left the chaplain's employ and traveled, visiting Lyons, Geneva and Basle (Beilby 1936, 214). He seems to have wanted to set himself up as a Reformer (Anon 1724, 27).

In Basle he met Oecolampadius, the Reformer (Anon 1724, 27). At first their association was friendly, but as Servetus' ideas began to take their distinctive form, and as Oecolampadius came to understand him more, so the relationship cooled. In 1530 at a meeting of Oecolampadius related to his fellow reformers, Bucer, Bullinger and Zwingli, that Servetus overflowed 'with Arian heresies and other objectionable opinions. He was advised to do 'everything possible that such dreadful blasphemy get no further wind to the detriment of Christianity' (Zwingli in Willis 1877, 33, 34). Even before Servetus had published his first book, the Reformers united in condemnation, this was a premonition of events to come.

What could have caused such heated accusations of Arianism and such determination to stamp out this theology? Servetus' Christology will be discussed in the next chapter, but even at this early stage, his anti-Trinitarianism was seen as destructive of Christian theology.

Oecolampadius was scandalized by Servetus' assertion that the church had misinterpreted the nature and role of Christ, and recognized that his statements would upset the whole of Christian doctrine, both Protestant and Catholic. He criticized Servetus' views on the nature of the human and divine in Christ as two natures in one divine Person (Willis 1877, 35) which he saw would undermine the church. He wrote to Servetus saying,

> You contend that the Church has been displaced from its true foundation of faith in Christ, and feign that we speak of his filiation in a sense which detracts from the honor that is due to him as the Son of God. But it is you who speak blasphemously; for I now understand the diabolical subterfuges you use.... I own that I am not possessed of the extreme amount of patience which would keep me silent when I see Christ dishonored... You do not admit that it was the Son of God who was to come as man; but that it was the man who came that was the Son of God; language which leads to the conclusion that the Son of God existed not eternally before the incarnation (Oecolampadius in Willis 1877, 35).

Servetus' presence in Basle was no longer tenable. If true Reformation was to happen, it had to begin anew and elsewhere. He was not attracted to Luther's system of salvation by faith alone as a panacea of all ills. Nor would he find Calvin's rejection of ritual a viable alternative to the ills of the church. In his mind, cosmetic reform was not enough; a corrupt tree could not bring forth good fruit (Beilby 1936, 216). True reform had to begin by correcting the Church's first departure from Biblical teaching, and, in his mind, that meant correcting the concept of the Trinity.

As he departed, he left a manuscript for a book he had written against the orthodox doctrine of the trinity in the hands of Conrad Rouss, a bookseller. Rouss sent it to Haguenau for printing. The year was 1531 (Anon 1724, 27). The book, Servetus' first published work, was entitled *'De Erroribus Trinitatus'* - On the Errors of the Trinity. In it, as will be shown in the next chapter, Servetus set out to restructure completely Trinitarian theology.

Critics stress that Servetus draws his interpretation of God from the Neo-Platonists and their doctrine of the Logos and an archetypal universe existing prior to Creation (Beilby 1936, 224). They also accuse him of leavening the work with a certain amount of pantheism (Beilby 1936, 225).

The Reformers of the day received *De Erroribus Trinitatus* negatively, and Servetus' reputation as a heretic was firmly established. Reformer after Reformer across Germany and Switzerland denounced the book. However, when one considers that Servetus at the time of its writing was only twenty years old, it is possible to gain insight into the mind of a young man who, Don Quixote-like tilted at the windmills of established religion. The enthusiasm and certainty of youth pursuing a cause shines from each page of the *Trinitatus*. Had they thought of it, the Reformers must have been maddened to have an intellect such as this in opposition rather than on their own side.

The year - 1532 - after publishing *De Trinitatus* Servetus published another book, also printed at Haguenau, titled *'Dialogorum de Trinitate libri duo'* - Two Books of Dialogues on the Trinity (Anon 1724, 29). This second book purports to be a retraction of everything in the *Trinitatus* on the grounds of being false and immature. In fact it ends up supporting the former's contentions (Bainton 1953, 62).

It seems that Servetus, caught up in the fervor of the Reformation believed himself as at liberty to reject the doctrine of the Trinity as other reformers rejected the teachings of the Catholic Church. His presumption was not correct. As he would discover twenty years later, sixteenth century Protestants were no more tolerant of heterodox views than their Roman Catholic contemporaries. Life in Germany became too dangerous to remain - although at his trial he gave as reasons for his return to France that 'he was poor and did not understand the German language' (Anon 1724, 36).

The Middle Years

Dropping the name Servetus, he began a new phase of life. Adopting the name of his home town, Michael Villeneuve, or Villanovanus, entered society as a student and lecturere, an author and editor. Yet his new identity could not quench the hope that someday he would be able to reform the world and lead the church back to the simple Christianity of the Apostles (Osler 1909, 8).

By signing his name to the *Trinitatus* and the *Dialogues* he had placed his life in danger. *Trinitatus* became available in the Catholic world in 1532 at the Diet of Ratisbon (Bainton 1953, 68). Servetus himself sent a copy to the Bishop of Saragossa. As in the Protestant world, it was not well received. A suggestion was made that Servetus be lured back to Spain to stand trial for heresy, and the heretic, no doubt hearing of this, 'longed rather to flee to the sea or to one of the New Isles' (Bainton 1953, 74).

As Michael Villeneuve he sought the anonymity of Paris and entered the Sorbonne at the College of Calvi. Later he transferred to the College of the Lombards and read mathematics (Bainton 1953, 218).

The year of 1534 was a watershed year for Servetus. While still in Paris he met John Calvin for the first time (Beilby 1936, 215). Calvin was also a young student, and while the details of their association are obscure, both were keen to change the church. The acquaintanceship was not friendly. Their basic theological premises, leading to tragedy twenty years later, began at this stage to solidifying in opposition. Because of his reputation as a heretic - although this would have been unknown to Calvin - Servetus was cautious in his dealings with the future Reformer. Challenged to a public debate over their differences, Servetus failed to attend. Years later, at the trial in Geneva, Calvin taunted him about this, saying, *'Vous avez fuy le luite'* [you fled the encounter] (Osler 1909, 9, cf. Anon 1724, 38).

Perhaps because of growing acrimony with Calvin, Servetus left Paris in 1534 and settled in Lyons. There, 'poor enough in pocket if rich in lore' (Willis 1877, 104), he worked for Trechsels, a firm of publishers. His university education and skill with Latin, Greek and Hebrew made him a valuable editor (Willis 1877, 87). In 1535 he produced 'a splendid folio of Ptolemy's Geography ... with commentaries on the different countries, which show a wide range of knowledge in so young a man' (Osler 1909, 9).

He was, in fact, going to keep contact with this firm for many years to come. In 1541 he undertook to produce an edition of Pagnini's Bible in six volumes, in 1542 a second edition of the Ptolemy, and in 1545 another version of the Bible in seven volumes (Bainton 1953, 219).

His time at Trechsels between 1534 and 1537 opened Servetus' range of contacts to other than religious court Chaplains and Reformers. During this time he met Symphonien Champier [Campreggius][2], 'one of the most interesting and distinguished of the medical humanists of the early part of the sixteenth century' (Osler 1909, 9). Servetus edited several of Champier's books[3]. It is possible that Champier even made a home for Servetus in Lyons (Willis 1877, 101).

Quite likely it was on the advice of Champier that Servetus returned to Paris and studied medicine in 1537 (Bainton 1953, 106). He did extremely well at his studies, and after two years was lecturing himself. As in his theology, however, his medicine was not orthodox. Influenced by Champier's astrology, Servetus gave lectures on judicial astrology, on the relationship of astrology and medicine in spite of this being forbidden by the church (Osler 1909, 11). Consequently he was condemned by the Doctors of the Faculty as a charlatan (Bainton 1953, 113). In response he wrote an 'apology' in which he attacked the doctors and defended astrology (Osler 1909, 12). In his mind he was simply follow the example of the ancient Greek philosophers (Bainton 1953, 113).

This controversy is important in Servetus' life as it shows his propensity to assume a position and defend it at all costs, convinced of his rightness and sources. The characteristic ran through his adult life, taking form in the *Trinitatus* and *Dialogues*, and later in his correspondence with Calvin and eventually in his final book, *Christianismi Restitutio.* Ultimately it would contribute to his death.

Servetus qualified as a medical doctor in 1538, and during the summer of that year took up residence in Charlieu, about twelve miles from Lyons (Willis 1877, 128). However, before leaving Paris he was fortunate to encounter a young student, Pierre Palmier, who became the Archbishop of Vienne (Osler 1909, 14)[4]. Palmier was taken with Servetus, and, when he discovered him practicing medicine at Charlieu, invited him to the archiepiscopal seat at Vienne as his personal physician (Willis 1877, 130). Servetus was to spend the next dozen years, living incognito as Michael Villeneuve, posing as a Roman Catholic in the court of the Archbishop.

During his trial in Geneva, Servetus maintained that he lived at Charlieu for three years (Bainton 1953, 219). During that time it is possible, that he put into practice one of the issues held against him by Calvin - his rejection of paedobaptism. In 1539 Michael Servetus turned thirty, the year he believed was the only year in which baptism could be rightly received. He defended his position to years later to Calvin, saying,

> Christ, as an infant was circumcised, but not baptized; and this is a great mystery; in his thirtieth year, however, he received baptism; thereby setting us the example, and teaching us that before this age no one is a fit recipient of the rite that gives the kingdom of heaven to man. It were fit

and proper in you, therefore, would you show the true faith in Christ, to submit yourself to baptism, and so receive the gift of the Holy Spirit promised through this means' (Servetus in Willis 1877, 129).

While it is not possible to know if Servetus was in fact rebaptised at age thirty, such an event was certainly within the bounds of possibility.

This interlude at Lyons was one of increasing wealth, prestige and the leisure to pursue his interests other than medicine. He retained his association with the Trechsel printing house (Osler 1909, 15). Two of his projects during this time were used as evidence against him during his trial in Geneva in 1553. The first of these was a new edition of Ptolemy in 1541 - dedicated to the Archbishop of Vienne (Osler 1909, 15). The contentious issue in this edition was his rejection of the commonly held belief that the land of Canaan was still 'flowing with milk and honey' as it was purported to have been in Old Testament times. Servetus accurately indicated that the Holy Land of the sixteenth century was little more than a dessert. During his trial Calvin labeled this as heresy and used it to indicate the level of theological depravity to which he had sunk.

The following year, 1542, he brought out an edition of Pagnini's Bible[5], indicating his continued interest in theological studies. His approach to commentary makes him one of the 'earliest and boldest of the higher critics' (Osler 1909, 15). While Servetus was oblivious of the future outcome of his work, the Pagnini Bible shows something of his concept of the nature of the Bible. He observes that the Hebrew language 'cannot be exactly kept up in our translations' (Servetus in Anon 1724, 42). His proficiency in Hebrew gave him the insight that too many people translate too literally, and, in doing so, lose the true meaning of the Hebrew. From this, they try to find a mystical sense in the Words of the Bible. His point of view is very clear as he writes,

They who are ignorant of the Hebrew language and history are only too apt to overlook the historical and literal sense of the Sacred Scriptures; the consequence of which is that they vainly and foolishly expend themselves in hunting after recondite and mystical meanings in the text where nothing of the kind exists (Servetus in Willis 1877, 141).

This attitude runs throughout Servetus' theology as we shall see in later chapters. He takes the literal sense of the Bible at face value while recognizing that while the Old Testament speaks particularly to and about its own times, it contains within predictions concerning Christ. The Bible then, has 'a two-fold face ... in like manner as one sword has two edges.

Thus the teachings about Christ in the Old Testament were hidden from the Jews, but revealed to Christians' (Servetus in Anon 1724, 43).

This approach formed the basis of the notes Servetus added to the text. He held that within the history of the Israelites are prophecies about the life and actions of Christ (Anon 1724, 45). He pointed out that it was not possible to read back into the history of the Jews the stories of Jesus, and the Jews did not look forward to Jesus when the prophecies were written. The history of the Old Testament while applicable to its time, contains, as a vessel, the prophecies, meaning that the Old Testament can be read either as history, or as prophecy, but not both simultaneously. Calvin held up this departure from contemporary biblical interpretation as proof of Servetus' heretical opinion. His ideas, however, were not completely original. Careful analysis of Servetus' edition and that of an earlier one by Melchoir Novesianus of Cologne, 1541, shows that Servetus actually followed the Novesianus edition very closely (Willis 1877, 143).

Satisfied with his work on the Bible, Servetus writes in the Preface to Pagnini's Bible,

> I may, therefore, venture to affirm that Pagnini's translation, as it now appears, approximates more closely to the meaning and spirit of the Hebrew than any former version. But the Church and those learned in the Hebrew tongue, must be the judges here - any others are incompetent (Servetus in Willis 1877, 142).

Servetus' boldness in his biblical interpretations did not go unnoticed. The version was condemned at Lyons, the notes were expunged in Madrid, and Rome placed the book on the *Index Prohibitorius* (Willis 1877, 154). Calvin, who saw the Old Testament as prophetical 'in the strictest sense of the word', brought up the commentary as evidence against Servetus during the trial of 1553 (Willis 1877, 155).

His editing work brought Servetus into close contact with the Huguenot publisher, John Frelon (Bainton 1953, 144). This association was to have further ramifications for Servetus. Frelon was acquainted with John Calvin, and, under his sponsorship, the two Reformers were introduced through correspondence (Willis 1877, 158). The introduction was made under Servetus' assumed name of Villeneuve. Calvin, almost maintaining a degree of secrecy, signed his letters Charles Despeville. The correspondence took place in 1546 and 1547, while Servetus lived in Vienne, the respectable physician to the Archbishop. No one, not even Calvin, suspected him of being Michael Servetus.

One can only speculate on what these two men hoped to achieve with this correspondence. In all probability, Calvin hoped to rectify Servetus' errors, and Servetus Calvin's. The correspondence was not a happy one. The confrontational characteristics in Servetus' character became increasingly pronounced as the interchange continued. His abusiveness towards the Reformer undid any possible good their communication could have had. The letters, which are extant, in tone and contents shocked and disgusted Calvin (Osler 1909, 16).

On at least one occasion, Calvin threatened Frelon he would break off the correspondence

> ... if he goes on writing to me in the style he has hitherto seen fit to use, however, you will only lose your time in soliciting me further in his behalf; for I have other business that concerns me more nearly, and I shall make it a matter of conscience to devote myself to it, not doubting that he is a Satan who would divert me from studies more profitable (Calvin - 13 Feb 1546 - in Willis 1877, 159).

The personal and theological antipathy between the two men was too deep to be bridged. All in all Servetus wrote 30 letters to Calvin, many of them contained in the *Restitutio* (Willis 1877, 166). The result was 'a mutual hatred and animosity, which proved very fatal to the latter' (Anon 1724, 61).

Part of the cause of this deep hostility lay in Calvin's injured feelings. At this time both were employed in setting down their theological interpretations, Calvin in his *Institutes of the Christian Religion*, and Servetus in the early drafts of *The Restitution of Christianity*. It is hard to imagine two more different books on Christianity.

As part of his drive to correct Servetus' theology, Calvin sent him a copy of the *Institutes*. Servetus read the work carefully. He took it to pieces citing both Scripture and Patristic authority to show where he though Calvin was wrong (Willis 1877, 167). He returned the book to Calvin with his own notes in the margins. Calvin was enraged. Writing to a friend he commented that 'there is hardly a page that is not defiled by his vomit' (Willis 1877, 168).

In response to the *Institutes*, Servetus sent Calvin a copy of his book. Calvin described it as 'a large book stuffed with idle fancies, and full of arrogance. He says I shall find in it admirable things, and such as have hitherto been unheard of' (Calvin in Anon 1724, 61). This is the first intimation that Servetus was writing a book of theology, the first draft of the *Restitutio* (Bainton 1953, 144). In spite of persistent requests from Servetus to return the manuscript, Calvin kept it. Later it would reappear amongst the documents furnished to the authorities at Vienne that led to Servetus' arrest (Willis 1877, 172).

The depth of the antipathy Calvin felt towards Servetus is indicated in his reaction to Servetus' offer to travel to Geneva to meet the Reformer. In response, in a letter, Calvin made a comment that would forever bring his name into question in relation to Servetus. He says,

> He offers to come hither if I like it; but I will not engage my word, for if he comes, and if any regard be had to my authority, I shall not suffer him to escape without losing his life (Calvin in Anon 1724, 61).

This threat was tragically carried out in 1553.

The Final Years

After 1547 Servetus' correspondence with Calvin slowed and ceased - although the mutual animosity simmered in the silence between them. Calvin knew, by this time, that his correspondent was Michael Servetus, the notorious heretic. Servetus, however, continued to live as Villeneuve in Vienne, as the personal Physician to Pierre Palmier, the Archbishop. To all appearances, these were quiet times for Servetus. In reality, the pressure to share his understanding of theology was building.

The manuscript he had sent to Calvin began to take definite form in his mind. In 1552 he completed an extensive book of 734 pages. He printed it privately in Vienne. Except for the initials M.S.V. it was anonymous (Beilby 1936, 222). He titled the work 'Christianity Restored'.

Every aspect of this enterprise was dangerous, for its theology was almost identical with that of the *Erroribus* and *Dialogues*, except that he extends his discussion to treatments of faith and regeneration, and several others. At the end he includes his correspondence with Calvin.

The *Restitutio* is an almost unread book. Both Protestant and Catholic authorities destroyed all but a handful of copies almost as soon as it was published. Further interest was turned aside by the reputation, persisting to this day, that 'it is a most difficult work to read, and, as theologians confess, a still more difficult one to understand' (Osler 1909, 22).

Servetus crossed the lines of tolerance with the publication of the *Restitutio*. Although he had been most careful in his publishing arrangements, news leaked to Calvin. It is speculated that John Frelon, who sent Calvin a monthly parcel of books, included a copy of the *Restitutio*. His motives in doing so were not hostile to Servetus, and in all likelihood Servetus knew and consented to this package - possibly as a compliment for the copy of the *Institutes* Calvin had sent him (Willis 1877, 232). In addition, Servetus seems to have been unaware of Calvin's reaction to the thirty or so letters that crossed between them. In all likelihood he expected Calvin to treat the *Restitutio* with the same confidentiality he had treated the letters (Anon 1724, 32).

What possibly neither Frelon nor Servetus anticipated, however, was Calvin's response. As he read the work he would have seen what to his mind were errors, heresies and blasphemies set out on 'the printed page and ready to be thrown broadcast on the world' (Willis 1877, 233).

It has been pointed out that

> The Christian Church early found out that there was only one safe way of dealing with heresy ... it was universally realized that only dead heretics ceased to be troublesome (Osler 1909, 23).

Calvin had other contacts in Vienne and Lyons than Frelon. One such man was a certain William Trie, a Protestant living in Geneva, who was in correspondence with a cousin, Arneys, who lived in Lyons. Arneys was a Catholic. Their letters focused on religion and the distinctions between Protestantism and Catholicism. Without doubt Calvin knew of this correspondence and used it to his own advantage in denouncing Servetus.

Under his guidance, Trie wrote to Arneys denouncing Servetus. The letter, dated 26th February 1553, begins with a discussion on heresy, and proceeds into a fulsome description of Servetus' variance from orthodoxy - particularly in relation to Jesus Christ and infant baptism. Relying on the shock value of his words to inflame the reader, Trie then writes,

> The man I refer to has been condemned in all the Churches you hold in such dislike, but is suffered to live unmolested among you, to the extent of even being permitted to print books full of such blasphemies as I must not speak of further. He is a Spanish-Portuguese, Michael Servetus by name, though he now calls himself Villeneuve, and practices as a physician (Trie in Willis 1877, 237).

The letter to Arneys included the title page, the index, and the first leaves of the book (Anon 1724, 72).

This denunciation could only have come from Calvin. It is highly unlikely that Trie could have had access to the technical knowledge of Servetus' first two books. Also how else would he have known that Servetus and Villeneuve were the same - something Calvin knew quite well. 'The letter from first to last is Calvin's' (Willis 1877, 238).

Two weeks later a second epistle arrived from Geneva, this time having copies of letters from Servetus to Calvin. Acting as Calvin knew he would, Arneys denounced Servetus to the French Inquisition. The material sent by Calvin was handed to Matthieu Ory, the Inquisitor. Events began to move quickly at this point. On March 16th 1553, the Inquisition summoned Servetus, he was confronted with the evidence, and denied that it was his writing (Bainton 1953, 155). A search was made of his apartment, but no evidence was found (Bainton 1953, 155). Further searches were made at the printers, and again no evidence was found. Archbishop Palmier felt the evidence against Servetus was very flimsy (Bainton 1953, 155).

At first, it seemed as if Calvin's evidence was not enough for Ory. Handwriting could be denied, and the scraps of printed work could not be proved to belong to Servetus nor printed by Arnoullet and Geroult (Willis 1877, 248). The Inquisitors asked Arneys to write to Trie and ask for evidence that the book referred to was indeed being printed (Willis 1877, 248). The reply led directly to arrest,

> With my last letter, indeed, you will find an acknowledgement by the man himself of his real name, which he had disguised, and the excuse he makes for calling himself Villeneuve, when his proper name is Servetus or Reves (Trie in Willis 1877, 249).

This information, however, could only have come for Calvin. It is not likely that he could ever have encountered either the name or books of Servetus - since they were both suppressed and abominated.

The evidence was before the Inquisition at this point comprised,

1. The letters of Trie
2. The printed pages of the *Restitutio*
3. More than twenty epistles from Servetus to Calvin (Willis 1877, 252).

The Inquisition examined each of these carefully. Exposed in this way, they arrested Servetus and the printer Arnoullet - interned separately to prevent collaboration (Willis 1877, 253).

The trial began on April 5th 1553 in the Criminal Court of the Palace in Vienne and continued the next day (Willis 1877, 254). During that time Servetus was confronted with his writing and asked to explain. There is evidence that his answers were not always honest - which could be interpreted as a desperate attempt to extricate himself from this situation. For example, on being shown leaves from Calvin's *Institutes* in which he had commented on passages entirely in accord with Catholic faith (Willis 1877, 258). He responded with 'tears in his eyes' saying,

> My Lords, I tell you in truth. When these letters were written at the time that I was in Germany about twenty-five years ago [they were written from Vienne], a book was printed in Germany by a certain Spaniard called Servetus. I do not know where he came from in Spain, nor where he lived in Germany, except that I have heard it was at Hagenau, where it is said his book was printed (Servetus in Bainton 1953, 160, Willis 1877, 258).

As for the comments themselves, he claimed to have written them without thinking, or perhaps as a subject of discussion (Willis 1877, 257).

On the second day of the trial, he admitted to writing to Calvin from curiosity. He claimed that when Calvin 'saw that my questions were those of Servetus he replied that I was Servetus' (Servetus in Bainton 1953, 161, see also Willis 1877, 259). Therefore to please Calvin he assumed the role or persona of Servetus for the sake of the argument. He stressed that this communication had ended ten years previously (Bainton 1953, 161).

The Inquisition was not convinced. He was incriminated by a series of letters to Calvin covering such topics as free-will, paedobaptism, and the Trinity (Willis 1877, 258 - 261). Servetus was warned that the court wanted very particular answers to each of their questions (Willis 1877, 261).

However, before the Inquisition could complete their examination, Servetus escaped. There have been many questions about whether others collaborated with him[6], but on the night after the second day of the trial, he arose at four in the morning, asked to be let into the prison garden. Climbing a tree, he escaped over the roof of a shed (Bainton 1953, 162 see also Willis 1877, 263).

In spite of his escape the Inquisition was not willing to let the matter rest. They could not ignore the possibility that the books Calvin claimed had been printed were in existence. The rest of April 1553 was spent searching Servetus' effects (Bainton 1953, 163, Willis 1877, 269).

Eventually they discovered that the printer, Arnoullet had three secret presses, and finally one of the workers confessed to printing a book called *Christianismi Restitutio* (Bainton 1953, 163). The also discovered that on January 13th 1553, five bales of books were sent to Pierre Martin of Lyons (Bainton 1953, 163) - he still had them, and they turned out to be the missing volumes (Willis 1877, 273).

On June 17th Servetus was judged guilty of heresy by the French Inquisition. He was to be fined a thousand pounds, and, together with his books, burned at the stake. In his absence the sentence was to be carried out in effigy (Bainton 1953, 164, Willis 1877, 274). Almost all copies of the *Restitutio* were included in the burning (Beilby 1936, 229).

Capture in Switzerland

Fleeing from the French Inquisition, Servetus headed first towards Spain, then changed his mind and headed towards Naples. He must have remained hidden in France for about three months, however. By some perverse twist of logic he decided to travel to Italy by way of Geneva (Beilby 1936, 229). His reasons for taking this route have been a topic of much discussion. One theory is that he knew that the Libertine[7] party in Geneva expected to defeat Calvin. It is possible that he hoped these men would vindicate him in the Protestant world, and they hoped he would help them overcome Calvin. If this theory is true, the it is possible that he was in Geneva for nearly a month before being caught, during which time he plotted with the Libertines (Osler 1909, 18). This argument is challenged as often as it is put forward, and in truth no one really knows why Servetus went to Geneva.

During his trial Servetus stated that

> ... he had lodged the night before his arrival at Louyset and entered alone on foot. His plan was not to stop but to go to Naples and there to practice medicine. With this intent he lodged at the Inn of the Rose and had already requested the host and hostess to engage a boat to take him further up the lake where he could pick up the road for Zurich. He had concealed himself as much as he could that he might be able to go on without recognition (Servetus in Bainton 1953, 169).

Whatever reason brought him to Geneva, it was there that he was apprehended. On August 13th 1553 he attended worship, was seen, reported and cast into prison (Beilby 1936, 230). At this point in the story of Michael Servetus those opposed to John Calvin become increasingly hostile. Those who favor him tend to ameliorate his actions with reasons. Thus Bainton quotes him as saying

> ... [t]hose who would spare heretics and blasphemers are themselves blasphemers. Here we follow not the authority of men but we hear God speaking as in no obscure terms He commands His church forever. ... Why is such implacable severity demanded unless that devotion to God's honor should be preferred to all human concerns and as often as His glory is at stake we should expunge from memory our mutual humanity (Calvin in Bainton 1953, 171).

Calvin's actions over the following months are seen as an expression of obedience to God's word. His intolerance is determined by his concept of God, his concept of the role of the elect, and so of double pre-destination, and the way the Scriptures are interpreted to support his position (Wadkins 1983, 432).

The heresy trial following Servetus' arrest is too long and complex to be dealt with here. Thirty-eight charges were preferred against him (Beilby 1936, 231), all related to his theology - although the charges changed from time to time. The trial itself involved five phases,

1.   First came a series of examinations on the basis of charges supplied by Calvin.
2.   Further oral examinations by the public prosecutor followed.
3.   The trial continued in the form of a running debate between Calvin and Servetus, who took advantage of his ink and paper to address several pleas to the Genevan Council.
4.   The Swiss cities were consulted and their replies submitted to the Council.
5.   On the basis of this material, the court deliberated and passed judgment (Bainton 1953, 182).

Neither Servetus nor Calvin acquitted themselves well during the trial. Both engaged in hostile and defamatory interchange. While Calvin's intransigence hastened a verdict of guilty, Servetus' consistent abrasiveness and abusive language contributed to the outcome.

The trial stretched out over the course of many weeks, until on the morning of 27th October 1553, the tribunal of judges gathered to read the prisoner his formal condemnation. He was found guilty under ten separate headings, the two most important dealing with the doctrine of the

Trinity and infant baptism (Osler 1909, 19). Their final words announced the penalty of death:

> Having God and His holy Scripture before our eyes, in the name of the Father, and of the Son, and of the Holy Ghost, by this our definitive sentence, which we here give in writing, we condemn thee, Michael Servetus, to be bound, and carried to the stake, and burned alive with thy book, written with thine own hand and printed, till thy body is reduced to ashes; and thus shalt thou end thy days, to serve as a warning to others who are disposed to act in the same manner (Beilby 1936, 231).

Calvin tells how Servetus received the news,

> At first he was stunned and then sighed so as to be heard throughout the room; then he moaned like a madman and had no more composure than a demoniac. At length his cries so increased that he continually beat his breast and bellowed in Spanish, "Misericordia, misericordia!" (Calvin in Bainton 1953, 209).

There was, however, to be no appeal. In the sixteenth century, as in many before and since, those who challenge the orthodoxy of the church die defending their faith. By twenty-first century standards Servetus was fully in his rights to believe as he wished. Fully free to write and disseminate his beliefs. But he did not live in the twenty-first century. His milieu demanded death for disagreement, and he was willing to pay the price. His final speech before being burned at the stake, written under obvious duress, is an outline of his theology. In the face of death he was unwilling to change his beliefs.

He was burned in effigy in France, and in reality in Geneva. On 27th October 1553 the sentence was carried out. He was led from his cell in Geneva to Champel 'a small eminence about a musket shot from Geneva' (Anon 1724, 212). There, amid the mocking shouts of the crowd he was tied to a stake, and the green wood stacked around him was set on fire. As the flames climbed higher his last words rang out, 'Jesu, Thou Son of the Eternal God, have compassion upon me! (Willis 1877, 487).

The point of Servetus' life and death is more than simply religious intolerance. The issues he raised concerned the nature of God and His relationship to the individual human being. By challenging the ancient and unchanged Christological formulas of the Reformation era, and by being willing to die for it, he requires that people give his opinions sober thought. His life and death beg people to judge his theology apart from the heat of Calvin's insecurities in the light of rational thought - and in the freedom of knowing that a spiritual and intellectual freedom makes such thought possible.

Notes:

---

[1] For example, Estepp (1986) dedicates two pages to him. While giving a useful summary of his life, the overall article focuses mostly on Calvin. Bruce Shelley (1982) also mentions Servetus only in context of Calvin, describing his appearance in world history as 'one low point in Calvin's influence'. Even K.S. Latourette (1975) gives a scant two references to him, both times with reference to Calvin. Not all those who study Calvin are concerned with Servetus, William J. Bouswma (1988) mentions him once, in the context of Calvin's having to explain the execution.

[2] Champier was one of the more ebullient figures of the Renaissance (Bainton 1953, 101). He was an astrologer (Willis 1877, 102), an ardent Galenist, an historian, the founder of the hospital and of the medical school (Osler 1909, 10). He was deterred by no inhibitions from essaying war and theology, patristics and the poetry of passion, chivalric biography and the pursuit of medicine. He was one of the disseminators in France of the Florentine Neo-Platonism and an ardent reconciler of discrepancies in the classical tradition (Bainton 1953, 101).

[3] These works included his 'Hortus Gallicus' (1533)'Pentaharmacum Gallicum' (1534), Cribratio Medicamentorum with the Medulla Philosophae appended and Prognosticum perpetuum Astrologorum, Meicorum et Prophetarum (Willis 1877, 101).

[4] Archbishop Pierre Palmier, inducted into his see in 1528. A man of cultivated tastes and expensive interests, a patron of letters, a more liberal prelate than Palmier one would scarcely find (Bainton 1953, 83, 84). Palmier had the reputation, well deserved as it appears, of being a lover of learning for its own sake, and fond of the society of men learned like himself (Willis 1877, 130). He renovated the diocese, scrutinizing the education, attire and demeanor of his clergy. He did not condone heresy if flagrant instances were brought to his attention (Bainton 1953, 83).

[5] Pope Leo X was a primary patron of Santes Pagnini. When he heard that Pagnini was translating the Old Testament from the original Hebrew into Latin, he asked to see a specimen, liked it, and undertook at once the expense of the labourious enterprise (Durant 1953, 486). The work took twenty five years to complete. It is said to be the first edition of the Bible to be divided into chapters (Willis 1877, 139).

[6] 'In the town of Vienne it was generally thought that the Vibailly De le Cour had been the active party in favoring the evasion of Villeneuve. He was known to be intimate with the doctor, who had lately carried his daughter successfully through a long and dangerous illness...' (Willis 1877, 265). Osler notes that the jailer was 'his friend' (Osler 1909, 17). In all likelihood he acted with the

assistance of his immediate associates in the Vienne department of justice (Willis 1877, 267).

[7] Libertines, so called 'from their zealous defense of the immunities and privileges of the citizens against the old tyranny of the Roman Catholic Bishops and recently introduced consistorial rules and regulations of the Reformer' (Willis 1877, 318).

Chapter Four

On the Errors of the Trinity in Seven Books

Fewer books have stirred up such wrath as Servetus' first published work, *De Erroribus Trinitatus, Septem Librum*. It was a 'veritable bombshell in the theological world' (Beilby 1936, 216). Servetus, at age twenty, tackled the cornerstone doctrine of Christianity, the doctrine of the trinity. 'The book was in many ways an impressive achievement' (Pettegree 1990, 40), when one considers his age when he wrote it and managed to get the book printed and distributed.

It is doubtful that Servetus had any realistic idea of the impact his study would make. Fresh from university and angered at the state of Christianity from his time with Quintana, Servetus focused his learning and intellect on this study. His training in theology shines through in abundant patristic references including Aristotle, Clement of Rome, Clement of Alexandria, Cyprian, Basil, Hilary, Ignatius, Irenaeus, Tertullian and many others. He used no fewer than forty church fathers, and a wide range of non-patristic sources (Pettegree 1990, 40). His references to the Old and New Testaments show a thorough-going knowledge of the Bible and his analyses of Greek and Hebrew words and form a sound working knowledge of both Biblical languages.

The Trinitatus is not an easy book to master. Although liberally annotated with Biblical and Patristic references, Servetus makes it difficult for a reader to follow his argument. It seems to have little cohesion and the outline of his argument is difficult to follow. However, although it is often obscure, there is a progression of ideas in the Trinitatus that can be roughly illustrated under the paradigm that Christ is a man, Christ is the Son of God, Christ is God. While articulating this in the first book, Servetus follows the basic argument without mentioning in those terms again.

Aside from the looseness of construction, the sheer volume of references and excursions into Biblical usage hides his main points. This, however, does not mean that they are not there, and, after careful sifting it is possible to come up with an understanding of what he was trying to say.

His aim in writing the Trinitatus was to point out, and correct, erroneous ideas of the Trinity deeply rooted in Christian theology. He believed that the idea of the existence of three persons or entities in the Godhead 'is an impossibility, and so a fundamental religious error' (Willis 1877, 55). To him the concept of Trinity was anathema, and, does not use the word 'Trinity' except in the title as it is not used in the Scriptures (Beilby 1936, 218).

To explain his understanding of Biblical Christology, Servetus takes his reader on an excursion through the idea that God, who is one and indivisible, was made known to the human race in the person of Jesus Christ, who was not a Son from eternity, but a man who became the Son of God. His point of view, however, should not be confused with mere adoptionism.

'Trinitatus' is written in seven books, each dealing with a different aspect of Servetus' case against orthodox Trinitarianism. Each deals with a general 'Argument', outlining Servetus' theology. Following the argument is a lengthy 'synopsis' describing the development of the subject. Finally the argument is explained in detail, replete with Biblical quotes and references.

If Servetus had followed the argument and synopsis more closely in his general discussion of the points he raises, the whole book would be easier to read.

Book I

Argument

Any discussion of the Trinity should start with the man. That Jesus, surnamed Christ, was not a hypostasis but a human being is taught both by the early fathers and in the Scriptures... He, and not the Word, is also miraculously born Son of God in fleshly form, as the Scriptures teach, not a hypostasis, but an actual son. He is God, showing God's divinity in full; and the theory of a comunicatio idiomatum is a confusing sophistical quibble...

The first section of the first book outlines Servetus' opposition to the principles arrived at by the first three ecumenical councils. The Council of Nicaea (325) established the concept of God in a common substance but distinct hypostases. On that point the Nicaean Creed states,

> [We believe] in one Lord Jesus Christ, the only-begotten Son of God, Begotten of the Father before all ages, Light from Light, true God from true God, begotten not made, of one substance with the Father...
> (Bettenson 1981, 26)

The Nicene Creed, establishing the relationship of the Father and Son, does not address the issue of how a Divine being, the Word, was made flesh and became a man. Divinity and humanity are mutually distinct qualities, incompatible even (McGuckin 1994, 138) if one considers that there is no ratio between the infinite and the finite. The Council of Nicaea left open the question of how these related in Jesus Christ.

Those who taught a 'high Christology' underplayed the role of the human in Christ. He was the Word made flesh dwelling amongst us, the humanity being simply an addendum to be cast off when necessary.

This high Christology, espoused by the Alexandrian School, raised many issues. For example, if Christ was already divine, how could he be tempted, suffer and die. Charges of Patripassianism[1] were common.

In counterpoint to this view were those who followed a low Christology, stressing the humanity of Christ rather than his inner Divinity. Mostly taught by the Antiochene School of thought, those who followed these ideas to their logical conclusions flirted with the concept of the 'Two Sons', one divine, one human. Others, like Nestorius, toned the rhetoric down considerably, but still strove to depict a humanity bordering on adoptionism.

At the Council of Ephesus (431), called to settle the dispute between Cyril of Alexandria and Nestorius, and in the years following, a compromise was reached. The idea of a COMMUNICATIO IDIOMATUM came into being. This principle states that in Christ there is both a human and divine nature, both complete but distinct. To avoid difficulties raised by the thought of Two Sons, the theory arose that the distinction between human and divine was overcome by a 'sharing of qualities' - the 'communicatio idiomatum'.

According to this doctrine the two natures in Christ could affect each other without being commingled. Thus Christ saved the human race from his divine power, but suffered and died in his human.

The issue came to a head at the Council of Chalcedon in 451. Pope Leo outlined the process of the virgin birth, stating that Christ was 'conceived of the Holy Spirit, in the womb of his Virgin Mother, whose virginity remained entire in his birth as in his conception' (Leo in Bettenson 1981, 49).

> The properties of each nature and substance were preserved entire, and came together to form one person... Thus there was born true God in the entire and perfect nature of true man, complete in his own properties, complete in ours [totus in suis, totus in nostris] (Leo in Bettenson 1981, 50).

Leo's Tome was accepted in completeness at the Council of Chalcedon, 451. Christ was pronounced to be 'complete in the Godhead and complete in manhood' (Bettenson 1981, 51). This completeness is vested in two natures in Christ. The Chalcedonian formula is very definite in stating this,

> ... one and the same Christ, Son, Lord, Only begotten, recognized IN TWO NATURES, WITHOUT CONFUSION, WITHOUT CHANGE, WITHOUT DIVISION, WITHOUT SEPARATION (Bettenson 1981, 51 - emphasis Bettenson's).

The union of Father and Son in substance does not remove the distinctions, but they come together to form 'one person and hypostasis, not as parted or separated into two persons, but one and the same Son' (Chalcedon in Bettenson 1981, 51).

Servetus rejects these Christological constructs in the first section of the 'Trinitatus'. He reiterates that Jesus Christ is a man, the Son of God, and God himself, and is therefore categorically not a hypostasis. The very term 'hypostasis' was anathema to him, for it depicted a lesser or lower form of God and was confused with the tri-personal presentation of the Divine Substance. In his theology, Christ is not a manifestation of the Divine, but the divine itself in human form. Because of this there is no need for communication between the human and divine, as understood in orthodox terms. Thus the idea of a 'communicatio idiomatum' is, he writes, a 'confusing sophistical quibble' (Tr. 1 Argument).

The second part of the initial argument in this first book deals with the role of the Holy Spirit. Christologically, the Nicene Council concerned itself almost exclusively with the relationship of Father and

Son. As the Arian revival died down, and as theologians began to assess the Nicene Creed in a less contentious light, it became obvious that the role of the Holy Spirit had yet to be elucidated.

The Council of Constantinople explored the role of the Holy Spirit in relation to the Trinity (Davis 1990, 124). The conclusion came in the statement that the Holy Spirit was of one substance with the Father and Son, and as they are hypostases in their own right, so the Holy Spirit is also.

Servetus devotes the second half of the first book, or chapter, of the Trinitatus to voice his opposition to this theory. His rejection is categorical,

> The doctrine of the Holy Spirit as a third separate being lands us in practical tritheism no better than atheism, even though the unity of God be insisted on ... The Holy Spirit as a third person of the Godhead is unknown in Scripture (Tr. 1 Argument).

Servetus does not reject the orthodox trinity without offering an alternative. Beginning by defining the Holy Spirit as 'an activity of God himself' (Tr. 1 Argument) he asserts that 'the doctrine of the trinity can be neither established by logic nor proved from Scripture and is in fact inconceivable' (Tr. 1 Argument).

Turning to medieval scholarship[2], Servetus illustrates how, in his mind, philosophic terms introduced to explain the nature of the trinity have obscured and obliterated it. His final contention illustrates the point that the doctrine of the Trinity

> ... arose out of Greek philosophy rather than from a belief that Jesus Christ is the Son of God; and he will be with the church only if it keeps his teachings (Tr. 1 Argument).

Book II

Argument

Having torn into shreds the orthodox and ecumenically held concept of the Trinity, Servetus is now ready to rebuild the understanding of God. The foundation for this is laid in the second book of the Trinitatus, the argument of which reads,

> *Christ, the Son of man, who descended from heaven, was the Word by uttering which God created the world. He became flesh as God's first-born, and was the Son of God. He was both human and divine...*

This second argument follows on from the first, for, if 'any discussion of the Trinity should start with the man' (Tr. 1 Argument), then it becomes necessary to explain how that man ends up being God.

He begins with the idea of who Christ is, saying, 'Christ, the Son of man who descended for heaven, was the Word by uttering which God created the world' (Tr. 2 Argument). The idea that Christ is the Word of God is not new to theology, but as Servetus unravels his concept of this matter, it will become possible to understand his radical new interpretation of that idea.

In orthodox theology, the Word is as it were the soul of Christ, one step removed from the man who walked the earth. In Servetian thought, however, the Word and Christ are not a discrete step apart, but are one and the same being, with the Word becoming Christ by descending from heaven. 'Heaven', he says, should not be taken literally. Quoting the Gospels[3] and the Epistles[4], he shows that heaven is not a place but a state of being. Christ was 'born from above' (Tr. 2.1) and 'heaven was to him the light unapproachable in which the Father dwells' (Tr.2.1).

In coming down from heaven, Christ is the Word (Tr. 2.3). Quoting the preface to John's Gospel, Servetus defines the Logos as 'not a philosophical being, but an oracle, a saying, a speech, a discourse, a declaration of God' (Tr. 2.4). His interpretation of the Word, or Logos in this way closely parallels Jaruslav Pelikan's treatment in his book 'Christ through the Ages' (Pelikan 1985). Pelikan defines the Logos as 'reason or structure or purpose' of God, which can be interpreted as being the activity of God's mind (Pelikan 1985, 58).

This rationality can be seen in the rationality of creation, in the laws of physics and nature, which, becoming more easily illustrated each year as scientific understanding grows, will indicate that even in current chaos theory there is still an underlying order. Could this be the rationality of God? Could it be the Logos or power of God's mind that Servetus envisioned as becoming incarnate in the flesh of Jesus?

Following this train of thought, Servetus points out that the Word 'is God speaking' (Tr. 2.5). This word, this speech, became flesh in the man Jesus,

> And after the Word became man, we understand by the Word, Christ himself, who is the Word of God, and the voice of God; for like a voice, it is uttered from the mouth of God (Tr. 2.5)

Thus the descent of Christ into the world was not the incarnation of a second person in the Trinity - or a hypostasis in its own right - but the enfleshment of the voice of God.

Christ was born in two ways. From the Father he received his divine and everlasting life. From Mary he received the flesh. These two make one in him (Tr. 2.9), 'for the begetting of the Son of God was made like the begetting of ourselves' (Tr.2.9). Servetus admits that trying to understand this is difficult, for

> ...neither the prophets nor the angels in heaven know, nor do I know, how to explain this kind of begetting (Tr. 2, 10).

The difficulty in understanding arises because people think in terms of the flesh (Tr. 2.10). However, if one could rise above worldly concepts of conception, pregnancy and physical birth, one could consider God uttering his Word at the dawn of creation, and, in so doing, 'begot the Son, namely him who was manifested in later days' (Tr. 2.11). Because God has no time, and because the past and future are both present to him, his utterance brings the Son into being and eventually into the physical body itself.

Thus Christ was begotten as the use of God's voice, his Logos. He was not begotten as a different hypostasis, as a second person in the Trinity, but is the active, creative Word of God. So Servetus writes,

> they ask me whether I assume two Natures as hypostatically united in Christ ... they are off the track in this matter by taking the name of the Word as meaning its Nature, and how great is their profane abuse of this hypostatic union (Tr. 2.16).

In his mind the 'whole Nature and essence of God is in Christ' (Tr. 2.16), and this forms the cornerstone of his treatment of the Trinity. If the Word of God contains all things of God, and if that Logos is incarnated in the man Jesus, then it follows, according to Servetus' thought, that Jesus was indeed God. He was not some hypostasis or persona of God with an inter-sharing of Divine and human attributes, but is the full manifestation of God.

> And do not speak to me, he writes, of one substance, or one Person, after you clearly see that these inventions are not derived from the Scriptures (Tr. 2.16).

The blame for foisting onto the church the misunderstanding about the true Nature of Christ is first laid at the feet of the Ebionites[5], then of the philosophers, who 'despoil the Christ of all but his bare human nature' (Tr. 2.17). Yet Christ has revealed himself down the ages as the voice that spoke to Abraham, as the Word given to Moses on Mount Sinai, and through the prophets (Tr. 2.17).

> Hence it is spiritually to be understood that Christ is God for as He is not called Man without having flesh, so he is not called God without having the spirit of God (Tr. 2.18).

The communicatio idiomatum describes the theory of a sharing of human and divine attributes in Christ. Servetus, on the other hand, sees these attributes as completely interconnected, just as in an ordinary human being it is not the spirit alone nor the flesh alone that makes one human, but the two working together as one. The divine and the human cannot be separated any more than 'the voice from him that utters it' (Tr. 2.28).

> For it is a wonderful mystery that thus joins God to man and man to God, and wonderfully has God made the body of Christ his own, that it might be the tabernacle for him to dwell in (Tr. 2.18).

Having dealt with the interrelationship of the Father and Son, Servetus again turns his mind to the third part of the Trinity, the Holy Spirit. The second half of the argument in this chapter reads,

> *God's spirit, moving all things, operates within us as the Holy Spirit, which is a person of the Godhead. It proceeds from the Son, not as a separate being, but as a ministering spirit. It is holy, one of the three persons of the Godhead, and sanctifies us by dwelling within us (Tr. 2 Argument).*

Servetus makes no personal distinction between Father, Son and Holy Spirit. They are not manifestations of one God, but different functions of God. This is the foundation of his treatment of the Trinity. The Holy Spirit is, by his definition, 'the breath of life' (Tr. 2.19, cp. Tr. 1.43). In Servetus' view the understanding of the Holy Spirit, like that of the Son, has been warped by 'the philosophers' (Tr. 2.20).

The unity in the Trinity is demonstrated in the relationship of the Holy Spirit to Father and Son. As he has said before, the Holy Spirit is the activity of God and it 'proceeds from the Son' (Tr. 2.27),

> ...for as the Word sets out from God, when he speaks, in order that a thing might be done anywhere, so his Spirit sets out from him anywhither when he intends [a] result anywhere (Tr. 2.28).

The relationship of God, the Word and the Holy Spirit, can most easily be compared to end, cause and effect. God proposes or intends. The utterance of that intention is the Word, or, when in the flesh, the Son, which is the means, and the intention, carried out by the means is the Holy Spirit. The interrelationship between them is one of distinction but also of unity. Servetus declares,

> I shall not admit that the comforting Spirit is something other than Christ. On the contrary, they are one (Tr. 2.30).

The oneness leads Servetus back to the issue of the Trinity. He is willing to accede to the point that there is indeed a 'person of the Father, of the Son and of the Holy Spirit, and thus to a Trinity of "Three persons in one Godhead"' (Tr. 2.31). However, he uses the term 'person' in distinction to the term 'being'. His understanding seems to draw on Tertullian's concept of 'person' in the sense of being a legal entity, rather than an individual being in its own right[6]. Three beings in God denote tritheism and atheism, while three 'persons' in God can be seen as one in unity.

Book III

Argument

The pre-existent Word, first uttered by God in Creation, was afterwards incarnate in Jesus as the Son of God. Christ's

*spirit manifested the power of God's Word in Creation in the
world, and he deserves our holy service...*

Although loosely structured, Servetus' argument on the nature
of God begins to take form. He established in book one that Christ is
man, Son of God, and God himself, and in book two that the trinity is a
oneness proceeding from God. The focus of Book III is to illustrate the
manifestation of God in Christ as an extension of himself.

Perhaps the most important biblical verses on the subject of
Christology are those in the Prelude to John's Gospel. Servetus uses the
words 'the Word became flesh' (John 1, 14) to introduce the chapter
dealing with the elaboration of the relationship of the Father and the
Son in the Trinity (Tr. 3, 1).

Drawing on his previous definition of the Son as the
'utterance' of God's Word, Servetus shows that the Son existed from
the beginning. This should not be interpreted temporally 'because his
existence depends essentially upon his Father's utterance, which took
place at the 'beginning' (Tr. 3.1). There was never a time, then, to
interject the invalid concept of time into the eternal nature of God,
when God did not have the 'Word', for if one uses the analogy of God
as intention, that intention will always take some form, which is the
utterance, and hence the Word.

This utterance 'by which all things were made',

... became the Son of Man because, though eternally born of God, he
is afterwards born of man in time, although he is only one being (Tr.
3.1).

The incarnation was essentially Christ 'putting on a garment' (Tr. 3.1).
This does not detract from the humanity of Christ, for although Christ is
the Son of God, he was born a man (Tr. 3.2), and all the actions of
Christ are the actions of God in man (Tr. 3.5).

This concept marks a giant stride away from orthodox
Christology. In terms of Nicaea and Chalcedon, Christ is the Son born
from eternity - co-existing side by side with the Father. The Logos is
the soul within him. Trinitarian theology, however, demands a
separation, at least conceptually between Father and Son, and with that
separation the unity of God can at times be lost.

Servetus' point is that this separation never occurred. The Son
was not begotten as a 'Son' in the physical sense, but is the utterance of

the Father's mouth. He is the Divine truth by means of which all things were created. He is not, however, a person in the sense of either hypostasis or personality, but the logical extension of God's activity . At the moment of incarnation this Logos, or divine utterance, took the form of a man for the first time as the Divine Word in the flesh. Thus Jesus had the power of the Divine

> to lay down his life and take it up again, for since divinity is joined with man, all the Father's authority is in me and is mine (John 5, 26, Tr. 3.10).

Servetus was aware that this would lead to charges of Patripassianism - the concept that the Divinity of the Father suffered on the cross. Classical Patripassianism was espoused by Praxean and Sabellius (Davis 1984, 41ff). The notion was early rejected by the fathers of the church, especially by Tertullian who wrote the 'Epistle Against Praxean'.

Servetus rejects possible charges of Patripassianism by labeling it a product of thinking according to the communicatio idiomatum. He wrote,

> If the sophistical communicatio idiomatum were effaced from the minds of men, this difficulty would easily vanish; for when I say Son, I refer to the flesh, and I do not say that he who was in the Son suffered, but that the Son suffered (Tr. 3.12).

Here Servetus' Christology takes another step. The Son of God was not born from eternity, but is the utterance of God's Word incarnate. The incarnation, however, is as a man, a being of flesh and bone, who was born, lived and died in the flesh.

> Just as it is an affair of the flesh to be born, he wrote, so it is an affair of the flesh to suffer, to be scourged, to be crucified, to die and to rise up again; nor do these things in any wise pertain to the spirit (Tr. 3.12).

These words seem to carry Servetus backwards to the very questions giving rise to the doctrine of the communicatio idiomatum. He espouses a difference between spirit and flesh, one impassible, the other passable, which begs the question of how two such incongruous elements could be united in one being.

Orthodox Christianity could only resolve this issue by the declaration of two distinct natures in Christ, which nevertheless share qualities. Servetus skates towards this point of view, but avoids it first by heaping scorn on Patripassians - he calls them 'Deipassians' (Tr.3.12). Their error was that they were merely philosophers, and not truly theologians (Tr. 3.12).

His solution is to describe the unity of the Father and Son, as spirit and flesh, or thought and word. He means that there is no sharing of attributes, but complete unity,

> ... in Christ is all the wisdom of the Father, in his mouth the new law and the interpretation of the old law, the Word of God, which gives knowledge to the Father (Tr. 3.14).

Christ came forth from the Father in a sequence of one thing to another. To illustrate this, Servetus describes the process of how a spark of fire comes from a stone. The spark, always in potential in a stone, only comes into being when the stone is struck. It is therefore an extension, a product of the stone. The same can be said of Christ, who was personally in God, 'but now is really among men, and that is pre-eminently his coming forth from God' (Tr. 3.14). Christ in the flesh, then, carried the fullness of the Godhead to humanity in much the same way that a spark carries all the potential of the stone.

The Nicene and Chalcedonian Councils arrived at the conclusion that Christ is the human manifestation of the Word of God, and that he is a hypostasis of the Divine in his own right. Servetus posits, however, that the Word is the speech of God. This Word did not become the son, but infilled Christ, and the man Christ, so infilled, was the Son. Quoting Biblical passage after passage, Servetus challenges the reader to produce 'one iota in which Scripture called this Word the Son' (Tr. 3.16).

Servetus finished the third chapter by exhorting his reader 'to tremble when you deny Jesus Christ' (Tr. 3.20). Christ is the giver of eternal life. Belief in him is the foundation of faith.

> Some admit in words that he is called the Son of God, since they add that he is called Son in a dependant sense, and conjointly with another invisible Son, and all this is one aggregate , and one Son. Others confess that Jesus Christ is the name of his human nature, yet they refuse [to believe] the man had the relation of a Son ... I simply and candidly admit and believe that this Jesus is the Christ, and is the

Son of God, and that he that does not thus believed hath been judged already (Tr. 3.22).

Book IV

Argument

God has manifested himself in three different dispositions. Of these, the Holy Spirit is his activity in the spirit of Man, and is the minister of his Word. God is seen in the Person of Christ, represented in the Scripture under the imagery of angels; but the real image of God is Christ. The term Nature is appropriate only to God, the Word no longer exists, Person means a representation of another being; Christ incarnated is the image of a substance, but not of the Nature of God.

Having dealt with the coming forth of Christ from the Father, Servetus turns to Christ's manifestation, extending the discussion to include the Holy Spirit. Servetus' concept of how God manifests himself in the person of Christ and the activity he called 'the Holy Spirit', gets to the heart of his treatment of the nature of God.

Notice Servetus' consistency when he refers to the manifestation of God 'in three dispositions'. At no point is he willing to use the terms of orthodoxy, 'person' or 'hypostasis', for these are not Biblical terms. However, the very idea of a Trinity indicates a threefold revelation of God, although this triple manifestation of God does not imply the trinity as it is usually understood.

To demonstrate this, Servetus begins with ways God has manifested himself in the past, 'now under the appearance of a breath, now under the Person of the Word' (Tr. 4.1). He uses Tertullian's term 'disposition' to describe these manifestations. Prior to the incarnation, he argues, the manifestations of God were 'dispositions' which took 'the appearance of Persons' (Tr.4.1).

Servetus' concept of a 'disposition', which he first broaches in Book I, is drawn from Tertullian's use of the word in his *Epistle Against Praxean*. Also this idea will be explored more fully in a later chapter, at the moment it is enough to know that it contains the concept of 'economy, management, disposition, dispensation, distribution, division, arrangement, modification' (Tr.1.29). Translator Earl Morse Wilbur sums up the concept saying,

> The idea is that God disposes or manages himself in three different
> ways for three different forms of his activity (Wilbur 1932, 45)

Thus, 'disposition' as Servetus uses it is a catchall phrase describing the activity of God ranging from the utterance of his mouth, or the Word, to the activity resulting from that utterance, which is the Holy Spirit.

However, the idea of the dispositions of God as his manifestations takes form in Book IV of the Trinitatus. Servetus describes the succession of manifestations, or dispositions of the Divine both generally and in terms of the Trinity, as

> ... one Person, that is, with the aspect of Deity, appearing in the son,
> another in the Holy Spirit. And the absolute and distinct beings in
> which the Persons have appeared are God the Father, a man the Son,
> and an angel the Holy Spirit (Tr.4.1).

This manifestation of God in person does not indicate a difference of persons. In Servetus' mind there is no room for a 'three in one' Trinity. He stresses this point in his explanation,

> ... when I speak of the man Christ Jesus, I do not separate from him
> the divinity of the Father; so when I speak of a messenger or a
> ministering spirit, I do not separate from it the character of the
> divinity, that there may be in the Persons one divinity of the Father
> (Tr. 4.1).

The 'Persons' are simply ways in which God appears. The disposition of God is determined by the recipient. The Holy Spirit, for example, may be spoken of in bodily forms, but really is the activity of God in human beings (Tr.4.2). When, however, Christ was born, 'Person' became 'being' (Tr.4.8). This is a far cry from the Athanasian concept of the Holy Spirit as a person of the God-head, existing in his own right, co-equal and co-eternal with God.

While Servetus' argument on the manifestation of the disposition of God is hard to follow, he makes it more complex by striking a distinction between things what would logically seem to stand together. One example is his statement that the Word and the Holy Spirit are distinctly different. Both are dispositions of God, the Word being God's utterance and the Holy Spirit the resulting activity (Tr.4.3). He writes,

> I call the Holy Spirit, as Ignatius does[7], a minister of the Word just as angels are ministers of Christ (Tr. 4.3).

The Holy Spirit as an activity fits into the emerging picture of Servetus' concept of God. First there is God, who can be called the Father. The utterance of his voice is the Word, which, incarnated in the man Jesus is the Son. The activity of God is the Holy Spirit. This could be compared to a person intending something, thinking or speaking that intention and finally doing it. In this paradigm each aspect, or disposition, is distinct, for one can speak of intention, thought and action as if they were distinct things, yet if they proceed from one source, they are one. Thus Servetus maintains his point, that the division of the Trinity into three distinct persons is not tenable.

The final manifestation of God is in a man. Servetus uses the term 'prosopon' meaning the face or mask, and thus a person (Wilbur 1932, 134). Christ is the mask of the divine and is presented as such in the Bible where prophetic portrayals of Christ are images of him who was to come, and so images of the Divine itself (Tr.4.4).

The process of how the Word became man rests, in Servetus' mind on the phrase in John that 'the Word became flesh'. This, he argues, indicates change from person (or disposition) into being. The change does not imply that Christ became a separate or distinct entity from God, for the human

> ... did not really withdraw from God, but Christ ascended to God, and Christ is now just as really in God as the Word was in God before (Tr. 4.8).

The 'being', Christ, is a withdrawal from the Divine making the physical birth of Christ possible. There is then an 'ascent' back to God as Christ the man, who is the Son of God, becomes God himself. Servetus offers no clue as to how this ascent took place, except perhaps that since all things of the Old Testament pre-figured Christ, so his life fulfilled those things[8], and so became one with the Divine Itself.

Because Christ has ascended to God, God is not manifested 'in any hypostasis or form but the man Christ himself' (Tr.4.8). The Word, being the utterance of the Divine, now ceases to exist, for the utterance is visible as Jesus Christ (Tr. 4.8) - the creative Word and the object of Creation becoming one in Christ.

It is, therefore, Servetus asserts, a 'gross misuse' to speak of the Person of Christ as two natures united into one (Tr.4.9). Since the incarnation, there is a full manifestation of the Divine in the man Jesus Christ, who, in coming down from God, was not a prophet, but the Word made flesh (Tr.4.10).

Book V

Argument

Examination of the Old Testament usage of the words for God - Elohim and Jehovah - shows that both refer to Christ, as centre of all, and essence of all things.

The relationship of Father and Son is shown in the ascent of Christ from man to God. Having established this point in the previous book, Servetus now turns back to the Old Testament to illustrate this relationship in the usage of names for God. The two most common names, Elohim and Jehovah, refer to the Father and Son respectively (Tr. 5.1).

> I have interpreted Elohim as meaning God and His Word, and I say more plainly that Elohim was in person man, and in nature God (Tr. 5.1).

It is possible to see this duality in the term 'Elohim', for it is plural in form, but used in a singular construction (Tr. 5.2). The plurality comes from the combination of nature and person, for these two are distinct in concept. Yet the term is used as if it were singular, illustrating the unity of Divine and man in Jesus Christ. Without stating it in so many terms, Servetus stresses the unity of the Father and son that is the hall-mark of his theology.

Thus when the name 'Elohim' is used, it indicates a prophecy about Christ (Tr. 5.2), and indeed, Servetus asserts that Elohim is Christ (Tr. 5.2). He defends this by arguing that the soteriological attributes of Christ are attached to 'Elohim' but never to Jehovah, who was the source of all things, and who saves through Jesus Christ (Tr. 5.3).

At this point in the Trinitatus, Servetus uses Biblical analysis to show the relationship between Father and Son in the use of the two names, for example, Elohim is never put before Jehovah, 'but on the contrary, it always says Jehovah Elohim' (Tr. 5.4). This positioning of names indicates to Servetus that Jehovah, who is the essence, gives essence to Elohim, thus to Christ himself (Tr. 5.4). This is a subtle way of indicating once again that the man Jesus Christ draws his nature from the higher essence, or Jehovah, and therefore is the Divine in human form.

Finished with exploring the term 'Elohim', Servetus turns his attention to 'Jehovah',

> The other name, most holy of all, Jehovah, some say means Essence, others begetting. Yet it includes both, and can be interpreted thus, Jehovah, that is, source of being, parent of beings, one who causes to be, gives being, cause of being (Tr.5.6).

The very name of God, therefore, is an indication or a prophecy of Christ, for Jehovah caused Christ to be and makes all things through him (Tr.5.6).

The name 'Jehovah' is also a vehicle for other meanings. For example in Genesis 17, 1, 28, 3, 35, 11, the name 'Shaddai' is added to Jehovah. 'Shaddai' is derived from a word meaning 'desolation', thus one who lays waste (Tr.5.7). By pointing this out, Servetus ties together the point of his argument even more closely together, for God is in all things. By the utterance of his mouth he both creates and saves. That utterance, the Word, is Christ, and his activity is the Holy Spirit. In his interpretation of the Scriptures of the Old Testament, even the use of the names of God attests to this unity.

Book VI

Argument

The incomprehensible God is known through Christ, by faith, rather than by philosophic speculations. He manifests God to us, being the expression of his very being, and through him alone God can be known. The Scriptures reveal him to those who have faith, and thus we come to know the Holy Spirit as the divine impulse working in us.

The Erroribus Trinitatus is drawing to a close. Servetus has laid down the fundamental principles of his Christology. In this penultimate chapter he stresses the oneness and unity of god. Christ is indeed the son of God, not as a hypostasis, however, but as the very image of God. The power of his argument rests in the concept that in Christ alone 'God exists and can be known' (Tr.6.Synopsis).

God in himself is incomprehensible. He can be neither imagined, nor understood, nor discovered by thinking, unless one contemplates some aspect of him. 'The likeness of Christ and the person of the Word are just this' (Tr.6.1). In contemplating Christ, one comes to a truer understanding of God, for as Servetus has noted many times before, Christ is God in Person, and by him it is possible to understand God (Tr. 6.1). Thus Christ lifts, as it were, the veil of God, making him visible as never before (Tr.6.1).

The major obscurantist cause in Christianity, Servetus believed, was the philosophic movement which reduced Christ to a phantasy by hiding his true nature and his relationship with the Divine Tr.6.1). In particularly vehement words Servetus accuses 'the accursed philosophers' who wrest the meaning of words to make 'their own prejudged notions while ignoring the plain teachings of Scripture' (Tr. 6.2).

The result, Servetus says, is that 'Christ is improperly called the image of God' (Tr.6.4). He asserts that Christ is not an image, for Christ is

... the face of God, and God himself was the likeness or a kind of form containing the very being of God (Tr. 6.4).

At this point words fail Servetus, and, grappling with the concept of how Christ is the image engraved or stamped upon God he returns to his point that by seeing Christ one is able to see God, 'for the very vision of his face is a vision of God' (Tr. 6.4).

The philosophers, therefore, 'are strangely deceived when they speak of the hypostasis of the Father and not a hypostasis of God' (Tr. 6.5). Christ is not an image of the Father but the 'character' or impress of God. Suddenly Servetus' words flow out in a flood of passion,

Christ, therefore, is called an aspect, a fact, a likeness, a sign, a character, a seal, a distinguishing mark, a kind of engraving, of the hypostasis, that is, of the being of God, because in him alone God exists, nor can God be known through anyone else (Tr.6.6)

The result of this is that Christ is God and is the only way people can see God. In him the invisible God is made visible (Tr. 6.6). Christ, then, not only sets God forth, but leads the way to him (Tr.6.8). Thus the whole point of the incarnation was missed by the philosophers who,

> ... if they admit this very plain way of seeing God, they will better understand what the spirit of God, and the Holy Spirit, is, for all depends upon knowledge of Christ, and if we are ignorant of this, we are ignorant of everything (Tr.6.9)

Book VII

Argument

The eternally begotten Son was a spoken word by which God made himself known. The Hebrew shows that the whole nature of God abode in Christ as Elohim, man being blended with God. The Word was a disposition of God, who begot the Son, a visible being. The Holy Spirit also is a real being, as Christ was. The Word was an actual being, creating all things, manifesting God in bodily form.

In this final chapter Servetus pulls his whole argument together. Much of what has been stated before was merely a series of building blocks leading upwards to his final declaration of faith.

Servetus begins his summation with the point that there has always been a distinction in God between what is 'real' and what is 'personal'. By 'real' he means something having existence in itself. In the orthodox concept of the relationship of the Father and the Son, the Father begets the Son from eternity, who then is a 'Person' in his own right. He co-exists with the Father, and so could be considered 'real'.

However, Servetus' point is that the Son, and so the Holy Spirit, is not 'real' - there is not Son co-existent with the Father. The relationship instead is 'personal', taking its meaning from the Latin 'persona' meaning 'mask'. Thus the Son is a mask, or a presentation of the Father, a visible face to an invisible deity.

Although Christ was a persona of the Divine, he is not simply an emanation, for God has no emanations within himself as the ancient Gnostics claimed (Tr.71.). Christ is a manifestation of the likeness of God. As the Logos, Christ is God speaking. He is the oracle of God (Tr. 7.1).

The unity this causes between Father and Son leads Servetus to say of Christ 'he really is the Father now' (Tr.7.4). For Christ is so fully at one with the Father, as the manifestation of his voice, as his image, that they are one. Quoting the Gospel of John he reminds his readers that 'he that seeth me seeth the Father' (John 14, 9, Tr.7.4).

> In him is the whole deity of the Father, in so much that even the angels marvel at this. And not only is God present in him, but the whole authority of God has been given him ... he is God and the Lord of the Word (Tr.7.5).

The only way, Servetus writes, to dim the vision of the completeness is to think of Christ as a second being in union with the Father (Tr. 7.5). He was the Word that became flesh, and thus was 'man blended, rather than united, with God' (Tr.7.5). To support his view, he calls upon Irenaeus and Tertullian, who, he says,

> Say that the change was made from the Word to flesh, and that alone with this a kind of Deity was blended and united with the man, because God is Christ in just this (Tr.7.5).

The concept of blending the Divine and human is contrary to the Chalcedonian formula of a co-existent, yet separate duality within Christ. In explaining and defending the concept of a blended nature, Servetus writes in his marginalia that Christ, or Elohim, is 'in person man and in nature God, which,' he emphasizes, 'you should properly keep in mind' (Tr.7.6)

To support this he goes back to his argument that God is being in itself, and the Word is the dispensation of God, thus containing the fullness of God's quality. This in turn is passed over to man. The man, then, has the same qualities as God, 'and with this the being itself is altogether united and blended because God was in Christ, reconciling the world' (Tr.7.6).

All this comes together in Christ, for

The likeness of God is now a body. This was the same as God, and this is now the same as man, and remains God, and is in God as heretofore (Tr.7.11).

Thus the Divine Logos is 'now in the form of man, like us, the form of God shining in man' (Tr. 7.11). Christ, then, is

... the visible God who created the world, and appeared to Abraham, Isaac and Jacob. He is the God of the Law and the Prophets (Tr. 7, 14).

There is no contradiction in the fact that this same God is also the Father of Christ, for Christ is the oracle, the voice of God, the doer and the means by which the deed is done, one and indistinguishable.

* * *

Servetus' Christology, can be summed up in the statement that Jesus was a man, Son of God and God himself. Thus the trinity does not exist as a series of ontological persons in the Godhead. The Trinitatus follows this pattern of development.

In Servetus' mind it was clear that Jesus was a man, and that the Scriptures refer to him at all times as a man (Tr.1.4). This humanity, however, does not require a demarcation from the Divine, for the human is designed to contain the divine - to defend this he quotes many passages showing human beings to be the 'sons of God' (cf. Tr. 1.15). Christ, therefore is 'complete in divinity' (Tr. 1.16).

The further definition comes in Jesus as the 'Son of God'. Servetus illustrates that this term is not used in the Scriptures other than as applied to Jesus (Willis 1877, 60, Tr. 1.8,9). As the Son of God, Christ is the manifestation in the flesh of the Word of God (Bainton 1953, 48).

This 'Word of God' is not a Son from eternity, but is the utterance from the mouth of God, which at first manifested in the Elohim of the Old Testament, came to earth as Jesus Christ - who was born a man, and remains a man in filled with the Divine presence. He is God in human form.

Finally, Servetus' paradigm leads to the activity of God, which is the Holy Spirit moving in peoples' hearts and on the face of the earth. It is not a distinct entity in itself, but part of the overall whole of God, manifested to us in human perceptions of God.

The three aspects, or dispositions of God, therefore, are not three individual parts of God, as hypostases of one substance, but three activities of God, ranging from the invisible motivation, through the visible expression of God, to the activity of God in human lives. In Servetus' mind the error of the orthodox Trinity lies in the failure to see this interrelationship of dispositions of God.

Thus Michael Servetus published his first work at age twenty, in an era not noted for its public acceptance of diversity in the fundamentals of Christianity. Even the most cursory of readings prompted the German and Swiss reformers to react with a most condemnatory awe.

The Protestant leaders were incensed as they began to realize the general tenor of the book. Melancthon, at first, was sympathetic, and expressed pleasure in the work, but, as he read further, his 'criticism changed its tone and became intensely hostile' (Beilby 1936, 217).

Most bitter in his attack, however, was Oecolampadius who wrote to Brucer saying,

> Our church will be very ill spoken of, unless our divines make it their business to cry him down. I beseech you in particular to keep a watchful eye over it and to make and apology for our church ... We know not how that beast came to creep in among us. He wrests all the passages of the Scripture to prove that the son is not co-eternal and consubstantial with the Father. And that the man Christ is the Son of God (Oecolampadius August 5th 1531 in Anon 1724, 35).

Taking the matter to heart, Oecolampadius also wrote two letters to Servetus, begging him to renounce his errors and accusing him of putting greater trust in Tertullian than in the Fathers of the Church (Anon 1724, 36). Other reformers were no more sympathetic to Servetus' ideas. At a conference attended by Oecolampadius, Brucer, Capito, Zwingli and Bullinger, Zwingli advised that the utmost vigilance should be kept, to prevent the whole of Christianity from being undermined (Bainton 1953, 53).

With the tolerance level so low, Servetus left Basel at that point. Traveling to Strasburg, under the leadership of Brucer, he expected a milder regime. On an earlier occasion Brucer had formed a favorable opinion of Servetus, and was known to allow private gatherings of heterodox believers 'so long as they did not disturb the peace or attack the established church' (Bainton 1953, 54). However, the outcry was so great that Servetus could not remain there either and moved on.

As a result Servetus fell into genuine danger, which would eventually catch up to him in 1553 when first Jean Calvin denounced him to the French inquisition and later burned him at the stake in Geneva.

What are the merits of Servetus' approach to the trinity if one set aside the hysteria generated by the Reformers (and Inquisition)? Certainly Servetus' took a stance that was totally unpopular in his day, and has remained so since. However, it cannot be argued that he built his concept out of thin air. His examination led him to question and reject the orthodoxy built upon the ecumenical councils. He underpinned his argument with both the authority of Scripture and the Patristic fathers. It could be argued that he did not move out of the realm of Christian theology, he simply removed what he considered distortions imposed upon theology by the councils, especially Nicaea and Chalcedon. Without those councils to guide his thinking, he felt free to interpret the Scriptures as he read them, bringing to bear his encyclopedic knowledge of the Old and New Testaments, and his excellent grasp of Hebrew and Greek. The result was a completely unorthodox view of God which he was willing to die defending.

Notes:

[1] That is, the concept that the Father and the Son are one and the same, thus the Father suffered in Jesus Christ (cf. Chadwick 1977, 87).
[2] For a list of Servetus references in the Trinitatus, see Appendix A
[3] Lk 17, 21, Matt 11, 11
[4] Phil. 3, 20, Eph. 2, 6
[5] The Ebionites were Jewish Christians [who] considered Jesus to be no more than the human son of Mary and Joseph (O'Collins 1995, 14). They saw Jesus as the elect of God and a true Prophet. Denied the virgin birth. Believed that Jesus was created as an archangel which descended on Jesus the man (Davis 1983, 34) The man Jesus was never more than a man like other men; so that when the Spirit forsook him, only a common man suffered on the cross, and shall come again hereafter to reign a thousand years on earth (Gwatkin 1927, 11).
[6] `In persona Tertullian seemed to have in mind the use of that word in Roman law, where it mean a party in a legal action. These personae, or parties, have their place in the economy, or administrative activity of God. They are seen in the government through which the monarchia, the rule of one God operates.

Here is unity of substantia, but a unity distributed in a trinity in form an in aspect' (Latourette 1975, 145)

[7] Ignatius. Ep. Ad Philad ix ANF 1, 84

[8] Jesus said, 'Do not think that I came to destroy the Law or the Prophets. I did not come to destroy but to fulfil.' (Matt 5, 17)

Chapter Five

Dialogues on the Trinity In Two Books

After the less than enthusiastic response to the *Trinitatus* by the Protestant Reformers, Servetus turned his energies to again explain his concept of the Trinity. The second book, more a booklet, is a different approach to the same subject. Writing merely a year after the *Trinitatus* was finished, Servetus feels secure enough in the Reformation environment to publish the book under his own name. Servetus leaves out the extensive Biblical, Patristic and scholarly references, arguing more from reason. The result is the *Dialogues on the Trinity*, with the first book concentrating on Christ as the manifestation of God, and the second on Christ's relationship to God.

Servetus' attitude towards the response of the Reformers, is captured in his opening. He begins the *Dialogues* with a short greeting, in which he claims the book is a retraction of the *Trinitatus*, 'not because it is untrue, but because it is incomplete and written as though by a child for children' (Dia. Greeting).

It is clear that in Servetus' mind the errors of the *Erroribus Trinitatus* lie less in the subject matter, than in the presentation. Admittedly a difficult book to grasp - especially for the twenty-first century reader - Servetus himself labels it a 'barbarous, confused and incorrect book' (Dia. Greeting). He lays the blame on his own lack of experience and the 'printer's carelessness'. His nineteenth century biographer, Willis, tartly remarks that

> [t]he printer ... is not to be blamed for any shortcomings of the kind
> referred to by the author - if there be defect it is his own, and it was the
> matter not the manner that had been found fault with (Willis 1877, 75).

This indicates Servetus' frustration, for he clearly had an idea in his
mind of how the traditionally accepted understanding of God was
wrong. He believed he could correct it. One needs to remember that he
was still a very young man, filled with the enthusiasm of youth. The
first attempt to articulate his views seemed clumsy, over-burdened with
references and quotations, hiding his logic.

The second attempt to articulate his theology of the Trinity,
tcok the form of a classical dialogue between the characters, Michael
and Petrucius. The book differs in overall style from the *Trinitatus*,
although each book is introduced by a synopsis outlining the arguement
Servetus intents to present.

Book One

The introduction to *Book One* lays the foundation for the
discussion between Michael and Petrucius. As Michael, Servetus
outlines and describes his principles. It is interesting to note that
something of Servetus' concern for those caught in what he thought of
as the grip of falsity about God, is stated as his motivation for
continuing his attempt to set forth a new understanding of the nature of
God. Michael's first words sum up Servetus' concern, 'I am greatly
tormented in mind when I see that the minds of Christians are so
estranged from any knowledge of the Son of God' (Dia. 1.1).

He begins the *Dialogues* with the concept of Christ as the
manifestation of God prior to the advent, linking him, as he did in the
Trinitatus, to God's creative activity. He starts by repeating an assertion
made in the *Trinitatus* that Christ was foreshadowed in the Genesis
creation story and refered to specifically in the Gospel of John. He lays
out his principle by linking the two references to creation.

> Necessarily, according to Scriptures, these three ought to agree, the
> Logos, Elohim, and Christ, as is proved by a mere comparison of the
> beginning of Genesis with the beginning of the Gospel of John (Dia.
> 1.1)

In Christ the Logos and Elohim now have body and substance. They were initially the Word, but now they are the Word made flesh, and the glory of God, hidden in pre-incarnation time, is revealed and shown in the person of Jesus Christ. Before the incarnation the Word, which was also the Logos and Elohim, were in shadow, barely understood by people. Now it is visible.

To explain how Christ makes the invisible visible, and indeed how the whole Trinity came into being, Servetus begins at the point of the invisible God,

> ... as he was before the creation of the world ... altogether incomprehensible and unimaginable to us, and by mere good pleasure of his will he determined to create the world and to manifest himself to us (Dia. 1.3).

God could not remain invisible, he needed to show himself. The manifestation of God to people began in creation, for before that time there was no one to manifest himself to. Yet even so, the initial manifestation took place in shadow, which could only be dispelled in the final act of revelation, which took place in Christ as a man.

To understand how Christ reveals and brings God to the human presence, Servetus asks his readers to compare the opening verses of Genesis with John. Both begin with the words 'in the beginning'. Moses, writing Genesis uses the name 'Elohim' while John uses 'Logos'. It is Servetus' contention that both refer to Christ (Dia.1.3). Both describe the creative force of God, and, since they refer to Christ, specifically in John, they show that Christ is the Word, the Oracle of God.

There is a logical progression in this line of thought. In Genesis God reveals himself as the creator. In John he reveals that he created by means of the Word, or Logos. Finally, also in John, he shows that this Logos became flesh and 'dwelt among us'. Creation took place by the spoken word, for God said 'Let there be...' The spoken word of Genesis, the Logos of John, and Christ, are all one and the same.

The Logos and Elohim, however, are only shadowy visions of God. The true face of God is Christ the man. For Servetus 'if God was manifested in the flesh, it must be that in seeing the flesh you see God...' (Dia.1.4).

Elohim and the Logos was the light referred to in the opening verses of Genesis and John, and from the light all things were made.

Yet according to John, that light came down and dwelt among us as Christ. Not it is no longer an indirect presence of God, but a direct presence, on the human level (Dia.1.4).

This argument takes care of the relationship before the incarnation of the invisible God and the visible Christ. The first two building blocks of Servetus' concept of the Trinity are in place. To complete the structure he turns to the Holy Spirit to show that the same relationship is true.

Like Christ, the spirit comes directly from God. Servetus evidently ties the idea of 'Spirit' closely to breath[1]. The spirit came into being with God's breathing and speaking. This links up with the concept put forward in the *Trinitatus* that the spirit is the activity of God and ties it in very closely with Christ.

The interrelationship of God, his manifestaion in Christ and his activity in the Holy Spirit comes to its fulness in Christ,

> For as God founded the world, and determined to be manifested by the Word, he at the same time also communicated his Spirit to the world. And this order was also observed in Christ; and when Christ had been manifested, his spirit was given which once was the spirit of Elohim (Dia.1.5)

Thus the Holy Spirit communicates itself to people inwardly (Dia.1.5). Before Christ was born, people only had a shadowy concept of the spirit for it was not yet fully revealed in Christ (Dia.1.5). In a similar way, people before the advent could not truly worship God, because they worshipped an invisible God. True worship only began when God was revealed in Christ (Dia.1.5). Servetus writes,

> I affirm that God is seen and worshipped in Christ alone; and in general I say that every way of coming to God is in Christ, even as he himself testified hat he was the way, and he that worships Me worships the Father[2] (Dia.1.5).

Worship is predicated, then, on seeing God, 'for worship presupposes seeing, and what is worshipped in spirit, ought to be seen in spirit' (Dia.1.5). The 'philosophers' – Servetus' dismissive term for certain patristic fathers and medieval schoolmen alike - obscure this vision by pressing 'visions of God upon us' (Dia.1.5) - visions which lead to disunity and division in God.

Having stressed that all pre-incarnation manifestations of God are shadowy, Servetus anticipates the question of how Christ was manifested before the incarnation. After correlating Elohim, the Logos and Christ, he has Petrucius ask Michael the leading question addressing this point, 'How was the light hidden, and manifested through angels?' (Dia.1.6).

The plain teaching of Scripture, Servetus writes, is that no one could see God and live. Before the advent, in which God is revealed in Jesus Christ, God manifested himself in the form of an angel who was 'a figure, and as it were the shadow of the true manifestation to come' (Dia.1.6). This also explains the existence of angels, who 'were created for our sakes, and minister unto us, and good angels guard us, even as bad ones tempt us' (Dia. 1.6). Part of their use prior to the incarnation was to reveal the invisible God to people.

God thus dwelt in the angel so that it 'was God himself who then manifested himself through the angels' (Dia.1.6). The angels who appeared were not the creators, but agents of creation, who made it possible for God to create and be active on the earthly plane.

Angels provide the means Servetus needs to establish his point that Christ is God. After describing in detail the angelic ministry, he concludes that 'God, and the angel, and Christ, were the same thing' (Dia.1.6), although this statement must be limited to the times when the angel was indwelt by God. Yet in Christ is the fulness of all the things that God, acting by means of angels, did before the incarnation (Dia.1.6). Christ is able to do all the things the angels had done on his behalf, and since there is no longer an intermediary between God and people, he can accomplish them more fully and more perfectly.

This still, however, does not complete Servetus' contention that Christ was a man. In fact, in the face of things, there seems to be a contradiction between the assertion of manhood and angelic agency, for angels themselves are not people. This contradiction, however, is unravelled in Servetus' mind by a proposition and its answer.

> If you believe, Petrucius asks, that the Godhead has a habitation anywhere, do you expose that it dwells elsewhere than with men? (Dia.1.7).

The concept of Christ as a man, rather than a hypostasis of the Divine substance is central to Servetus' thought. This was his first point in the *Trinitatus*, and the aim of the *Dialogues* is to express it again, albeit in slightly differnt terms. Having established so far that God has always manifested himself as Elohim, the Logos and Christ, initially in an angel indwelt by God, Servetus can now stress that the fulness of God can only be revealed in a man. All previous manifestations were preliminary, preparing the way, so to speak, for the fulness of manifestation in Christ.

Quoting Paul, Servetus assents that 'in Christ dwells the fulness of the Godhead bodily' (Col.2.9). Christ had to be a man because he is the body of the Godhead (Dia.1.7). All the shadows of previous manifestations become clear in Christ (Dia.1.7). The reason people fail to see the fulness of Deity in Christ is because the 'philosophers' have interfered with and distorted the concept of Christ by referring to him as a second person in the Trinity (Dia.1.7). By considering Christ as a man, however, in whom is the Godhead,

> ... you will clearly see that there is substantial Godhead in the body of Christ, and that he is himself really of the same essence and consubstantial with the Father (Dia.1.7).

This argument still does not, however, prove that Christ 'alone was Elohim and the Logos' (Dia.1.9), so Servetus turns his mind to exploring the relationship in much more detail.

The answer is somewhat convoluted. Christ exists in the same nature or substance that once formed Elohim and the Logos. Yet all things done by God as Elohim or Logos were a preparation for Christ (Dia.1.8). When the Word became flesh, the manifestation of God in Elohim and Logos was incarnated in Christ himself. There is, therefore, no difference between what went before the incarnation and what came afterwards, the substance being the same. Thus Christ is the same, only from being prefigured in Elohim and Logos, he became actual in the man Jesus Christ (Dia.1.8).

If one accepts this proposition, Servetus states, it explains how all things were made through Christ, for this is the implication of his being both Elohim and Logos. In him the substance of God came down into the world

> ... and he assumed flesh, who made the carnal substance partaker of the Divine substance, so that the one man is partaker of both Subtances (Dia.1.9).

This partaking of divine and human substance is, Servetus asserts, 'the true incarnation' (Dia.1.9). However,

> [i]t is not to be imagined that the Word of God is turned into flesh by a change of elements, but to the Substance of the Word there was added a partaking of the flesh, so as to make one hypostasis ... The substance of the Word and the substance of the flesh are one substance (Dia.1.9).

In this way the Word became flesh, and the flesh came down from heaven as a man (Dia.1.9). Thus in Christ the fulness of God exists. He is the creator of all things, for the creative substance of God exists in him as 'he now exists both as flesh and spirit' (Dia.1.9).

The result, then, is that people can have faith in Christ as a man in whom the fulness of God exists (Dia.1.10). This is the saving faith and the only path to salvation.

> I declare that you cannot get saved by another faith, if you do not believe that he is the Son of God, who was given for your salvation, and suffered to extirpate your sins (Dia.1.10).

It is not possible, Servetus reasons, to truly believe in God if one does not believe that Christ is in fact God. He stresses that Paul always speaks of faith in God 'in Christ', for one cannot know, see or believe in God except in the person of Jesus Christ (Dia.1.10).

However, if this is true, how is it that 'the schools'[3] have not believed that Jesus is the Christ, the Son of God? Servetus' answer goes to the root of the concept of the *communicatio idiomatum*, that Christ is both Son of God and Son of Mary, simultaneously divine and human. The elements of divinity and humanity remaining separate, and yet sharing properties. Some

> ... would prove from this that there are two sons, or some pretend, two kinds of Sonship, a natural and an adoptive (Dia.1.9).

The scholastics, Servetus implies, believe that the divine side of Jesus Christ is the natural son, whilst the human side is merely adopted. This would mean that whilst people believe in the divine sonship, they cannot truly believe that the humanity of Christ is truly 'Son of God', but is only an adopted child. The only way to truly believe in Christ is to recognise that he is fully the Son of God.

Book Two

Having dealt in *Book One* with the concepts around Christ
prior to his incarnation, particularly the relationship of Christ to Elohim
and the Logos, Servetus turns to incarnation of Christ and his
relationship to God. The Synopsis introducing *Book Two* of the
Dialogues is perhaps his clearest definition on this subject, certainly
clearer than any formula given in the *Trinitatus*. It deserves careful
attention before turning to the arguments outlined in the discussion
between Petrucius and Michael.

Servetus begins the synopsis with the assertion that 'Christ is
not a creature, but the creator, begotten of God's substance as the
Word, in fleshly form.' These opening words build from the previous
contention that Christ is both Elohim and Logos. Thus he is not a
creature, but the creator. John's prologue echoes behind these words,
'through him were all things made... and the Word came down and
dwelt among us'. They also draw a distinct line through any argument
that Servetus was essentially Arian in his doctrine. Servetus admits that
there was a 'time when Christ was not', in other words, a time before
the incarnation when the man Jesus did not yet exist. However, if Christ
was both Elohim and Logos, then it follows that he always existed. The
comparisons with Arius, therefore, does not stand up, and no such
comparison can properly be made.

Since Christ is the creator, it follows that he is one and the
same as God, and so Servetus asserts that he is 'begotten of God's
substance as the word, in fleshly form'. Remember that Servetus held
that the Word was the creative utterance of God. Coming from God,
this utterance cannot be separated from him. The word of God is God.
Christ, who is the Word made flesh, then, is the Word in human form,
and so is God. He is of the same substance as God.

This is Servetus' strongest statement rejecting the orthodox
Trinity. The idea of Trinity is contained in his second point, that while
the early fathers admitted that Christ 'was begotten of God's substance,
in human flesh - after all, the Nicene Creed clearly states that he is 'of
the substance of the Father' - they insert the idea of Trinity by insisting
that Christ is the 'disposition of God's substance'.

There is a distinct difference between being God's substance
and being a 'disposition of God's substance'. The first implies complete
unity with the substance, the second a derivation from the substance.
The disposition held by the early fathers, he maintains, is explained as

the mingling of man with God. The idea indicates that it is not possible for the divine to be present in human flesh.

However, in his next point, Servetus rejects this assumption. He states that '[t]his [mingling] does not involve a confusion of Natures, for this term does not apply to God' (Dia.2.Synopsis). In the *Trinitatus* he argued that only God has nature (Tr. 4.arg), for the very term, derived from *natus* implies birth. God cannot be born, therefore in the literalistic meaning of the word, cannot have *nature*. Instead Christ, begotten of the Divine substance, is this nature for he alone is born of God. The human nature is not at variance with the Divine, but fully supportive of it. There is not the confusion of two mutually exclusive natures, therefore, but the harmony of Divinity being repesented in the human as its nature.

In the next two points Servetus defends this assertion. First he argues that 'without the incarnation the divinity of Christ cannot be maintained'. According to Servetus' thought, this proposition rests on the force of the word 'incarnation.' Literally the incarnation is God taking on human flesh. It presupposes the idea that God pre-existed the birth of Christ. Without this presupposition, Christ would be an ordinary man, and charges of adoptionism or Arianism could be levelled against him. But, by stating that Christ's incarnation is the grounds of his divinity, Servetus correlates the human Jesus with the divine itself.

Then, he says, for this reason, Christ shows both divine and human nature, born of God and Mary. The mingling mentioned earlier, lasts only until the resurrection, when Christ laid aside the flesh and 'became equal to God in glory' (Dia.2.Synopsis).

God, therefore, was made man in Christ. Humanity and divinity exist in him, not as dual natures, but as one nature. Since the resurrection, 'Christ is in every respect an infinite being dwelling in the highest heaven with God' (Dia.2.Synopsis), able from his humanity to 'join us in the spirit', and so save people from their sins.

This grand view of Christ does not permit any entry point for the traditional trinity. The complete unity of God is seamless - he makes no allowances for the idea of three Persons or hypostases, for these can, and have at times, led to the idea of separations and distinctions in God. Similarly, as noted before in the *Trinitatus*, there is no separation of functions and uses of God, played out in the activities of the Father, Son and Holy Spirit. There is only a unity of purpose focusing on the salvation of the human race.

Servetus' synopsis of *Book Two* gives an important view into his concept of the nature of God. The short, suscinct points have behind them a wealth of thoughts and questions garnered from Biblical, patristic and scholarly research. Each point of the Synopsis is dealt with at length in the *Dialogues* following - although much of the clarity is lost in the process. Beginning with the idea of Christ as a creature, Servetus describes how

> ... with great blasphemy they despise him as a creature. On the contrary, I shall easily persuade you that he is the creator, if with faith you hold the whole order of the dispensation of Christ's kingdom, namely the Word of God, and its going forth into the world through the incarnation, and its return to the Father through resurrection (Dia.2.1).

Notice the sequence of Servetus' thought. Christ, who is the Word came into the world through the incarnation, and returns to the Father through the resurrection. This is hardly revolutionary theology, but it becomes so in his next statement that 'God himself was the Word.' This means that the Word was not a hypostasis, nor a second person, but was God himself. Christ, being the substance of God in flesh, therefore is God. Thus the Word was made flesh, or, put another way, in Christ, God took on flesh.

Servetus does not try to explain in physical terms how this incarnation took place, but with great eloquence he admits that,

> [g]reat and ineffable is the mystery, that how that flesh is of the same substance as our own, and that by its own nature it has a divine substance; that it was conceived in the womb of a virgin and born from the substance of God, that it brougth forth after a likeness of us, coming forth from God even from everlasting; that Christ was made from a woman, born of Mary, and was at the same time begotten of the substance of the Father (Dia.2.2).

Such is the mystery of the incarnation in Servetus' eyes. It does not answer how Christ had something in common with Father and mother, except perhaps in the same way that human beings draw characteristics from both parents, yet it forms the basis of his theology. Divine and human elements in Christ inform his being, and, contrary to the terms of Chalcedon, they are neither distinct nor separate.

In keeping with his earlier statements about the mingling of divine and human, Servetus states that it is an 'hallucination' to believe that 'the substance of God can not be mingled with the substance of man'. Servetus calls this 'pitiable madness' (Dia.2.2), yet this is the very cornerstone of the Chalcedonian formula and the communicatio idiomatum. 'What else is the mystery of the incarnation but a mingling of man with God' (Dia.2.). The point of Chalcedon was to prevent a confusion of natures. Servetus rejects the idea that a mingling of Divine and human necessarily implies confusion.

He begins his argument by stating that the term 'nature' cannot be properly applied to God - a point he stressed at length in the *Trinitatus*. God has no 'nature' as such because the very etymology of the word implies birth, and, since God was not born, he cannot be said to have anything associated with birth (Dia.2.3). Christ, however, does have 'nature'. Since he was born of God, his nature is divine, drawn from the Divine itself (Dia.2.3). It follows, then, that since God has no nature per se, and Christ as a human does, 'that those things which are God's' were in fact 'given to some creature by his natural origin and birth, and be in him' (Dia.2.3). This is no cause for blasphemy, but rather an 'admiration for the works of God' (Dia.2.3).

The greatest harm done to the divinity of Christ, Servetus continues, comes from the unwillingness to 'admit that Christ's flesh is of one substance of God' (Dia.2.3). The flesh itself was 'exalted unto God' (Dia.2.4), during the process of which there is no '...confusion or plurality of beings, but one sole being, one hypostasis or one substance, one thing formed of heavenly seed planted in the earth and coalescing into one substance' (Dia.2.4). Thus the idea of two natures in Christ deprives people of the knowledge of Christ 'for in that way there will be confusion in every generation' (Dia.2.4). In Christ the mingling of God and man does not cause confusion, for the nature of God, or rather those things that come from God, remain in Christ, and the nature of man, or those things in man born from God, remain in the Divine substance (Dia.2.4). From this, Servetus writes, 'it appears that Christ has participation in God and man, so that he cannot be abstractly called a creature, but one fairly partaking with creatures' (Dia.2.5).

Christ and man, Servetus says, 'come from the same mold' (Dia.2.5), and he makes people sons of God. The difference between Christ as the 'Son of God' and a human being as a 'Son of God' through repentence, is that Christ has within him the flesh of God, the

Divine substance itself, while people are still limited, finite and merely human.

The process of incarnation made it possible for Christ to take on human nature, to descend to our level and redeem the human race. However, putting on flesh only makes sense when seen in the context of the resurrection, for therein lies the victory or salvation.

> This dispensation of the incarnation was followed by another admirable one in the resurrection, in which the existence of the creature, which he acquired through his incarnation, was laid aside just as if it were an accidental thing. There is nothing now in Christ which is animal (Dia.2.6).

Just as Servetus does not describe how Christ took on the flesh, so neither does he elaborate on how Christ 'laid aside' the heavenly nature from Mary. The process, however, results in his being 'wholly perfected and glorified by his resurrection'. Thus Christ, after an interlude in the flesh of this world, returns to the state of the Word as it was before the resurrection (Dia.2.6). 'The return from man to God took place in the same way as the proceeding from the word into the flesh took place before' (Dia.2.6). Thus the resurrected Christ is one and the same with God, for by taking on flesh Christ brought the shadowy vision of God into the clarity of full sight, and in laying aside the flesh he made it possible for that vision to remain fixed in the person of Jesus Christ. Christ, then, is no longer less than the Father, as the case had been while he was in the world. Nor is the Father greater than him, for they are one and the same.

Servetus sees Christ as being infinitely present in all things. With his resurrection any merely human limitation fell away, so that 'he fills heaven and earth' (Dia. 2.7). The temptation to locate Christ in a particular part of heaven, Servetus says, comes from a 'carnal mind'. In thinking of him filling all heaven, Servetus envisions a supra-heavenly existence, for 'Christ is in that heaven to which the angels do not attain' (Dia.2.7). From this highest of heavens, above all living creatures, Christ can be present in all spiritual things in both heaven and on earth (Dia.2.7). 'Thence his spirit comes to us, as if to a new sphere, not by moving nearer in space, because Christ is no more absent in space than God is, nor is God elsewhere than is Christ' (Dia.2.7).

The resurrected Christ is present with people in spiritual things, one example of which is the Holy Supper. In the sacrament 'the body of Christ is mystically eaten in the mystical bread' (Dia. 2.8) and Christ both gives the Holy Spirit and makes his abode with people. In Servetus' mind these two things would be closely connected, for the way Christ would make his abode in the human heart would be through his activity, which is the definition of the Holy Spirit given in the *Trinitatus*. Thus Christ's presence in his activity in human life is communicated by means of the sacrament and, in this example, by the Holy Spirit.

The unity of the Trinity, therefore is complete as Father, Son and Holy Spirit act completely as one. 'The greatest blasphemy,' Servetus says, 'is that of those who say that God is, or acts, somewhere out of Christ' (Dia.2.9).

God is one because the Father is in Christ (John 14, 10). Thus Christ is not finite, for 'his power is now as great as it ever was, because he it is that then existed, not only in power and person, but also in substance' (Dia.2.9). This oneness of God is revealed in the man, the person, of Jesus Christ, a vision lost by those who separate Christ from the Father. Servetus writes,

> We, to repeat, worship him as the Apostles and many others did; indeed, all the angels worship him (Heb. 1.6) ... We worship him who received the glory, and created all things (Rev. 4.9). We worship him who is living, and was dead, and is now alive forevermore (Rev. 1.18). We say that this man is to be honoured with all the honour with which the Father is honoured, indeed the Father cannot be honoured save through him (John 5, 23, Dia.2.9).

* * *

In many ways the *Dialogues* on the Trinity is a much simpler and easier book to follow. By leaving out much of the detail of the *Trinitatus*, Servetus presents a far clearer and more coherent account of what he is trying to say. The difference, however, between the two books is largely cosmetic. Servetus is still unwilling to concede any point that would take away from the absolute oneness of God.

The picture clearly emerging from the *Dialogues* is very much in harmony with the *Trinitatus*, that God created by uttering the Word. That Word, the words of his lips, does not constitute a separate person any more than human words make a second person. The creative power of the Word is also God's manifestation of himself. At first, as described Biblically as Elohim and the Logos, this Word was almost invisible, at best shadow.

Christ is the incarnation of this Word, and as such is born of the Father, not as a separate being, but as a man begotten by God and filled with his presence. At the resurrection he is reunited to the Father. The difference between the manifestation of God before the incarnation and afterwards is not one of substance, but of degree, for now the shadowy, almost invisible Word of God is clearly visible in Jesus Christ, who, as the creative Word proceeding from the mouth of God, is active in human lives. This activity Servetus calls the Holy Spirit. Again, it is not a separate entity, but a manifestation of God's creatitivity, especially in leading people to salvation.

The Trinity, therefore, as it emerged from Servetus' pen in 1531 and 1532, is radically different from that adhered to by both the Protestant and Catholic worlds. God is one, in whom is a Trinity, but that Trinity is one of proceeding, of activity, not of person. The substance of God is not divided either in actuality or in thought, but maintained whole.

In both books Servetus defends his logic with copious scriptural references. His unwillingness to use the term 'Trinity' lies in the fact that it does not appear in the Bible. Nor does person or hypostasis in reference to God. By rejecting these terms, he was pressed to come up with an idea of God which could be defended in purely Biblical terms.

The response to this work was just as unfavourable as the response to the *Trinitatus*. Protestant Germany and Switzerland became too hostile for Servetus, and, taking the pseudonym, Michael de Villeneuve, he fled to France, first to Lyon and then to Paris to continue his studies. His pen was to lie quiet for the next twenty-one years, at least in matters of Christology.

Notes:

---

[1] Spiritus = both spirit and breath.
[2] John 4, 23.
[3] I.e. the medieval scholastics.

Chapter Six

The Sources for Servetus' Christology

Where did Michael Servetus' Christology originate? He had encountered Protestant reformers, and been revolted by Catholic excesses, but neither of these could have been responsible for his rejection of orthodox Trinitarianism. Neither the Catholic Church nor the Protestant even so much as questioned the Christological formulas. The answer must lie in Servetus' own reading of theological sources at university, and his own reading of the Bible.

Mid-twentieth century biographer, Roland Bainton, speculates that Servetus could not possibly have come to his position based on study originating in a study of scholastics. He characterizes Servetus as a religious man, but not a speculative thinker (Bainton in Becker 1953, 29). He further suggests that because Servetus had been exposed to Judaism and Islam, in an attempt to understand their rejection of the Trinity, he rejected it himself (Bainton in Becker 1953, 30, see also Bainton 1953, 14). There may be an element of truth in this, for Servetus himself notes in the *Trinitatus*,

> [f]urthermore, and worse than all this, how much this tradition of the Trinity has, alas! been a laughing stock to the Mohammedans (sic), only God knows. The Jews also shrink from giving adherence to this fancy of ours, and laugh at our foolishness about the Trinity... And not only the Mohammedans and Hebrews, but the very beasts of the field, would make fun of us did they grasp our fantastical notion, for all the works of the Lord bless the one God (Tr. 1, 59).

It would appear from Servetus' study that while he may not be a speculative thinker - for Servetus never speculates but pronounces his ideas with an absolute certainty - he thought in a different pattern from the traditional Christian. If his concern about Moslem and Jewish thought was a major concern, he would have mentioned it earlier in his works, and possibly cited it more clearly as a reason for his writing. The reference is more incidental than causal. The source of Servetus' Christology must have lain elsewhere, and been simply confirmed by his references to the monotheistic religions.

Any reading of Servetus' material shows a broad exposure to both patristic and scholastic sources. The groundwork of this knowledge was laid in the early days of his education. Possibly destined for the priesthood, the young Servetus began his education in a monastery, where it became apparent that he was 'an intellectual prodigy' soon mastering Latin, Greek, Hebrew,[1] and Arabic[2] (Odhner 1910, 12). His intellect and family standing made it possible for him to progress beyond the monastery to the University of Saragossa, 'then the most celebrated in Spain' (Willis 1877, 7) at age twelve or fourteen. Here he was exposed to some of the greatest minds of his day, including Peter Martyr de Angleria[3].

During his term at Saragossa, Servetus was exposed to both the patristic and scholastic thought that was to become influential in his theology. This was followed by a two-year study of law at the University of Toulouse, where studying the Code of Justinian, he would have discovered that denying the Trinity carried the death penalty (Bainton 1953, 130). The *Trinitatus* was written two or three years after he left university, and in all likelihood his interest in theology continued during his time with de Quintana, when he would have had access to books (Bainton 1953, 21).

It seems that Servetus came to his theological position for reasons other than not wanting to offend Moslems and Jews. Could it be that his broad reading at university created in his mind a cauldron of conflicting and contrasting ideas which was ignited when, finally, at twenty years of age, he read the New Testament only to discover that the central theological principle of Christianity, with its supporting terminology and concepts totally absent from Scripture (Bainton in Becker 1953, 30)?

The result was that Servetus came to question the orthodoxy he had been taught. If it was not in the Bible, where did it originate and what was the belief before it? His studies of theology would have led him back to the Council of Nicaea in 325, or more precisely immediately before it when the relationship of Father and Son was seriously challenged by Arius (Odhner 1912, 68, see also Restitutio 22). Servetus dated the fall of Christianity at the Council of Nicaea

(Bainton in Becker 1953, 31), 'when the Son of God was snatched away from us, when the church was banished from the earth, and all abominations established by laws'[4] (Restitutio 666).

His quoted sources, especially in the *Trinitatus*, reflect this before and after syndrome. Sources before the Council of Nicaea form the basis of much of his theology, everything after the Council he discarded as corruption (Bainton in Becker 1953, 31). Thus, Servetus' sources can be divided into two broad categories - those he refers to in defense of his argument and those opposed to it. In addition, they range from classical Aristotle to the Patristic Fathers to Medieval scholastics.

In analyzing Servetus' use of his sources, recognizing his rejection of orthodox Trinitarian thought, it would be most useful to begin with an examination of what he found offensive about the medieval scholastics. Then, looking at his use of the Patristic Fathers, it becomes possible to reconstruct his understanding of how the Trinity was construed in the pre-Arian/Nicaean age.

Servetus' Rejection of Scholasticism

Bainton describes the speculations of the Scholastics as 'acids' (Bainton in Becker 1953, 29), eating away at, undermining, and eventually destroying the doctrine of the Trinity. He sees Servetus as the final acid, completely destroying the traditional concept of the Trinity. In his theory, Servetus simply carries Medieval Scholasticism to its conclusion. Whether this is true or not is debatable. Servetus not only rejects, but also ridicules the Scholastics and all they stood for. However, they form part of his general source material, and he was knowledgeable of the path of theological thought forming the basis of these 'acids'.

The formulation of the Trinity at Nicaea, reinforced at the following councils, entrenched the belief in three Persons in one substance in Christianity. It meant that subsequent scholars were tied to it and were thus compelled, unless they wished to be labeled as heretics, to interpreting both Scripture and their environment in Trinitarian terms. However, the Nicene Trinity is not Biblical, and the key terminology cannot be found in the pages of the Bible. Nor are the basic assumptions of Nicaea clearly taught. This set scholars in a difficult position, for they could not deny the Trinity, under a penalty of death imposed by Justinian's code of law. On the other hand, they also could not prove it either.

In Servetus' mind the product of Trinitarian speculation was a 'monstrosity ... since this philosophy about three beings entered into the world [the philosophers[5]] have said that there are three Gods' (Tr. 1.55). The root of the Trinitarian dilemma lay in the ancient heresiarchs, Arius[6], Macedonius[7], Aetius[8], and Eunomeus[9]. The common factor amongst these is the separation of Father and Son in one way or another (Tr. 1.55), and this was the problem the Council of Nicaea tried to solve. The solution, however, raised other questions, about the dual human and divine natures in Christ. Servetus charges that while rejecting the duality of Nestorius, the church itself became Nestorian in saying that Jesus is Son of God and son of man (Tr. 1.55).

For Servetus the Christological formulas muddied the scriptural teachings of God. The one God of the Old Testament was redefined with the result that

> ... since this philosophy about three beings entered into the world, [scholars] have said that there are three Gods; because although they deny it with the mouth, our brethren confess it in fact (Tr. 1.55).

Compounding this error, in Servetus' mind, was the separation of the humanity and divinity in Christ. One example of this is Nestorius, who never actually admitted 'two sons', but used what Servetus calls 'sophistry' to defend himself. Nor are these things simply matters of the early church, for Nestorius' tricks are 'quite in the manner of men today' (Tr. 1.55).

For Servetus, then, scholastic theology carried the ideas of the ancient heresiarchs a step further. Peter Lombard, for example, added to the Trinity an essence, 'a kind of nature, not begetting like the Father, nor begotten, like the Son, nor *proceeding*, like the Holy Spirit, but is a kind of supreme being' (Tr. 1.55). Thus Scholasticism, at least in Lombard, created a Quaternity.

As seen earlier, from the time of Augustine to the end of the Medieval period, concepts about the Trinity went through three distinct phases. While it is unlikely that Servetus categorised the subject in this way, labelling these phases makes it possible to examine how he used authors as ammunition to reject the submerging of the concept of God into a Trinity of persons. Since he refers to scholars in each of these phases, the next section will examine briefly the focus of each, and Servetus' specific rejections.

The Illustrative

This first phase of the development of discussion on the nature of God 'claimed that the doctrine of the Trinity, though incapable of demonstration can at least be illustrated' (Bainton in Becker 1953, 32). This phase was initiated by Augustine, who held that while the doctrine is not directly taught, it can be deduced, and the deduction itself is a matter of revelation, since unaided the human mind 'would never arrive at it' (Bainton in Becker 1953, 32).

The roots of Servetus' brief comments on Augustine[10] lie in his overall rejection of the doctrine of the Trinity. Some of Servetus' references to Augustine are very brief and passing, however, examination of the Augustinian sources at those places show both that Servetus had a clear knowledge of what the ancient Bishop was saying, how it related to the subject, and how to reject it.

To Servetus, who saw God as one being, the idea of three, severally identifiable Persons in the Godhead was repugnant. He did not feel bound to accept any of Augustine's illustrations of the Trinity in Scripture. One such example of his rejection of Augustine's psychological construction is illustrated in the verse 'One God and Father of all, who is above all, through all, and in you all' (Eph. 4.6). In the passage in Augustine's De Trinitate relating to this reference, Augustine writes,

> [f]or if [the verse speaks] of the Father, and of the Son, and of the Holy Spirit, so as to assign each clause severally to each Person, *of him*, that is to say, of the Father, *through him*, that is to say, through the Son; *in Him*, that is to say, in the Holy Spirit - it is manifest that the Father and the Son and the Holy Spirit, is one God, inasmuch as the words continue in the singular number, 'to whom be glory for ever' (Augustine. De Trinitate I vi 12)[11].

Servetus claims that Augustine, in describing Ephesians 4, 6 'explains this as referring to the three beings, *of him*, referring to the first, *through him*, to the second, *in him* to the third' (Tr. 1.38)[12]. On the surface, Augustine does seem to be talking about three Persons, for the term 'each Person' implies a separation into three. However, he does not say 'three beings', but speaks of the phrase applying 'severally to each person'. Webster's Dictionary defines 'severally' as 'separately, distinctly'. For Servetus this distinction described a divided Trinity,

which Augustine believed could be demonstrated Scripturally, while
Servetus maintained it could not. He writes,

> But I do not believe that Paul, had he been questioned about this,
> would philosophize thus; for this would be contrary to his wont; and
> it would be irrelevant for him to treat of these things in that
> connection (Tr. 1.38).

Augustine might well have responded that the identification of several
persons in God does not in the least imply a Trinity of separate beings.
His argument is that the terms Father, Son, and Holy Spirit apply to
relational differences within God, and God is one in substance
(Augustine. De Trinitate V vi). The relationship of the Son to the
Father hinges on the terms begotten and unbegotten. The Father is
unbegotten, the Son begotten.

The Nicaean formula raises more questions than its answers.
One such question, which is addressed by Augustine, relates to the
difference between *proceeding* and being begotten. If Father, Son and
Holy Spirit are all persons, why is the Son begotten while the Holy
Spirit Proceeds? 'Augustine[13], Servetus says, 'has a great horror of this
question' (Tr. 1.56). Servetus charges that he dodges this question in
his section of De Trinitate by saying that '[t]he question why the Holy
Spirit is not begotten and how he proceeds from the Father and Son
will only be understood when we are in bliss' (Augustine. De Trinitate
XV xxv 45).

Death, according to Augustine, frees the body from its
limitations, making it possible to know things hidden in this world.
Thus after death, he promises, 'we shall see the truth without any
difficulty, and shall enjoy it to the full, most clear and most certain'
(Augustine XV.xxv.45). In the state of bliss, people will not enquire
into the question of why the Holy Spirit is not a Son, although it
proceeds from the Father, but shall experience it instead.

Servetus, however, has no horror of the issue. To him the
question of why the Holy Spirit is not a Son, although begotten of the
Father is simple,

> I dispatch the matter in a very few words, and say that the flesh is
> begotten in the natural way, but the spirit is not begotten at all; or to
> say that the Word is begotten is a mere dream, and a great misuse of
> words (Tr. 1.56).

In his discussion of how the Holy Spirit proceeds, Servetus
demonstrates his knowledge of Tertullian's Adversus Valentinian and

Irenaeus' *Adversus Haeres* by comparing the scholastic concept of the Holy Spirit *proceeding* from the Father with Gnosticism in the creation by Valentinian's Demiurge. Thus in Servetus' mind the connection between the 'philosophers' of Medieval theology and the ancient Gnostics is very real.

Augustine's illustrative approach to the Trinity influenced generations of theologians (Bainton in Becker 1953, 33). The one who attracted most reference from Servetus was Peter Lombard, 'The Master of the Sentences' who asserted that 'the doctrine could be found on every page of Holy Writ' (Bainton in Becker 1953, 33). To this Servetus replied what while Lombard wrote

> ... that almost every separate syllable of the New Testament agrees in suggesting the Trinity. But to me not merely the syllables, but all the letters, and the mouths of babes and sucklings, nay the very stones, cry out, One God the Father, and his Christ the Lord Jesus; *for there is one God, and one mediator between God and men, the man Christ Jesus[14]*; and, *To us there is one God, who is the Father ... and one Lord, Jesus Christ[15]* (Tr. 1.4).

Again Servetus refers to Ephesians 4, 6 with the terse comment that 'a second authority which, according to Peter Lombard very evidently supports the Trinity is, *Of him through him and in him are all things*'[16] (Tr. 1.38). Servetus does not reply directly to Lombard, but mentions Augustine's response to the same verse, with the comment that Paul did not mean Persons in God, but rather three phases of God (Tr. 1.38).

He takes issue however, with Lombard's assertion that every detail of the Trinity can be found on the pages of Scripture, noting that

> In the Scriptures there is frequent mention of the existence of God the Father, and of the Son, and of seeing and praying to them; but of the Holy Spirit no mention is made, except where it speaks about doing something, but as a sort of casual statement; which is noteworthy, as though the Holy Spirit denoted not a separate being, but an activity of God, a kind of in-working or in-breathing of the power of God (Tr. 1.40).

However, the Trinity of Person's does not, in his view, appear in Scripture at all. Those who try to illustrate the Trinity scripturally, strayed so far from the teaching of the Bible that they completely lost sight of what was taught of God there. Again, Lombard acts as his example, for Lombard, interpreted the Trinity in distinctly non-biblical terms. If the Trinity can be seen illustrated on each page of Scripture, then how does one understand the distinctions within the Trinity? In scriptural silence, Lombard declared that there must be more than one substance that neither generates nor is generated (Bainton in Becker 1953, 34). Lombard teaches that the substance of 'the Father is said to love with the love that proceeds from him' (Tr. 1.58). Yet that substance is different from the Son, who, as the Word is wisdom. Thus the Father cannot be wise. Sarcastically Servetus notes that under such circumstances, the Father, not knowing how to act from his love, 'wavers and knows not whither he goes' (Tr. 1.58).

This, to Servetus is non-sense, and non-Biblical. His language of rejection clearly indicates his feelings as he calls his readers to 'hear the sound reasoning of Lombard the Rabbi...' (Tr. 1.58), warning,

> At present we have grown accustomed to them (i.e. illustrative reasoning), but future generations will judge these things amazing, more so than the things that Irenaeus relates of Valentinus; nor is there in the whole Bible one letter which leads to these fancies[17] (Tr. 1.58).

From the way Servetus referred to both Augustine and the Lombard, it is convincing that he had read and understood their works. His rejection of their teachings indicates that while thinking their propositions through, he weighed them up both Scripturally and against other authors and found them wanting. To him the Trinity as understood by the Christian world could not be illustrated in the Bible because it did not exist. The basic error to him was that there were not three Persons in the Trinity, as the scholars understood them. Failure to recognize that left the theological world scrambling to prove something improvable, resulting in teachings further and further away from the truth.

The Demonstrative

The illustrative theory of the Middle Ages continued from Augustine into the twelfth century when Richard of St. Victor 'affirmed that it [the Trinity] may not only be illustrated but also demonstrated' (Bainton in Becker 1953, 32). By claiming this he brought a new twist to the Trinitarian question, leading to a new quest, to demonstrate the Trinity in the pages of Scripture.

Servetus again shows his knowledge of this line of speculative thought. He briefly outlines the argument put forward by Richard and Henry of Ghent with the dismissive comment that

> [c]ountless other arguments of this sort I deliberately pass by; and instead of solving all the things that might be brought up by philosophers at this point, you may observe this rule, which is that of the lawyer; namely, that those things which deserve special mention are, unless they are specially mentioned, understood to be disregarded (Tr. 1.44).

He concludes his treatment of Richard and Henry by stressing that 'not one word is found in the whole Bible about the Trinity' (Tr. 1.44). His rejection of the scholastics is more than sheer arrogance - it is based on the rejection of the first principles of Trinitarian doctrine. If the Trinity does not exist, it cannot be seen in the pages of the Bible, which Servetus holds as the unerring Word of God, and the complete revelation of God's being. Anything not found in the Bible, therefore, does not exist. Since the Bible is silent about the Trinity, Persons or an Essence, then he is not going to spend time trying to explain or rectify the writings of those who claim they do (Tr. 1.44).

The Fideist

When it became apparent that the Trinity could be neither illustrated by nor demonstrated in the Bible, the Scholastics abandoned the Bible in favour of nominalism. Nominalism can be defined as 'the view that only particulars are real and that universals are but observable likenesses among the particulars of sense experience' (Jones 1968, 345). Servetus cites five authors from this school. A brief examination of their theology and Servetus' rejection of it will highlight both his reading and understanding of scholastic thought, and sum up his overall rejection of scholastic theology.

William of Occam

Occam 'held that neither God's existence nor his unity nor his infinity can be proved' (Jones 1969, 317), because each person in the Trinity must needs be a reality in himself. There is no universal binding them together, and therefore each person is an absolute entity or being in its own right. Without a universal substance holding the Godhead together, the unity of the three Persons is sundered, with tritheism as a result (Bainton in Becker 1953, 39).

Occam did not declare a tritheism, although to Servetus he seems to have. Servetus dismisses the Moderni in general, commenting that Occam insists that people 'lay the foundations of our faith upon certain notions, relations, formalities, quiddities, and filiations of which Paul never thought' (Tr. 1.58). Their doctrines 'are founded upon the sand, and not upon the solid rock; and regarding the majesty of the faith as not firm, they seem to make a game of it' (Tr. 1.58).

In nominalism Occam had moved beyond the Bible, a move Servetus could not countenance. He held nominalism as even less tenable than Tri-theism.

Gregory of Rimini

The Moderni would not concede to the great contradiction between their philosophic formulas in explaining the Trinity and their faith of the Church. Gregory of Rimini was unwilling to yield the faith because he failed to see intellectually how three could equal one. He believed that the faith must be held to under all circumstances, even in the face of rationality.

The test issue for Gregory comes from Lombard's Sentences - which in turn had its roots in Augustinian speculation, on why the Son is generated while the Holy Spirit proceeds. If there is a universal, then that would be the origin of both generation and *proceeding*. But nominalists denied a universal in God. Thus each takes on his own being.

> If it be suggested that the Son comes from one and the Spirit from two, this explanation does not suffice because the origin of the fire is no different if it be kindled from two flames rather than from one (Bainton in Becker 1953, 42).

Tied into a knot by his own reasoning, Gregory concludes, that it is impossible to understand how the Son and Spirit are derived differently from the source (Bainton in Becker 1953, 43). Servetus has no sympathy for this problem. Labeling it one of the 'countless monstrosities ... countless questions, not only doubtful, insoluble, and knotty, but also most absurd' (Tr. 1.56), he takes Gregory's willingness to believe in the face of this doubt to task,

Gregory says that it is not possible for him to know, although he confesses that he believes; but God knows what sort of faith he had, when placed in such a difficult situation (Tr. 1.56).

For Servetus there is no conflict between generation and *proceeding*. In both the *Trinitatus* and *Restitutio* he outlines how the Son is the divine Word in human form, thus the visible presentation of God. The Holy Spirit is the activity of that Word. By removing the concept of individual Persons, who, in Medieval theology, were increasingly taking on a tritheistic connotation, Servetus rises above the need for scholastic speculation. Thus he does not feel called upon to agonise between inconsistencies of reason and revelation, and the need to believe contrary to his understanding.

Pierre D'Ailly

Cardinal D'Ailly was another who could not give up his faith in the orthodox concept of the Trinity even in the face of his own reasonable doubts (Bainton in Becker 1953, 43). He typified the attitude which led medieval Scholasticism into an abyss of irrationality. The result was that reason, which could not fathom the mysteries of the Trinity, was held ransom to a faith declared and enforced by the church alone. Thus he stopped trying to explain how the Trinity could be explained as one God in three Persons, and remain one, while maintaining the integrity of the Person. In response to this dilemma he placed his faith on the pronouncements of the church, shutting off his reasoning about the matter.

John Major and Erasmus

Unable to maintain a balance between faith and reason, with D'Ailly calling for the subjection of reason to faith, there were those who subjected faith to reason and set into motion the idea that reasoning about the Trinity was not permissible. John Major led the way, saying that while one could

... say that there are three Gods, provided the term God be construed according to the person... to prevent unbelievers from believing in a plurality of Gods, nevertheless, that is what is understood among experts (Bainton in Becker 1953, 44).

Finally Erasmus summed up the statements by saying,

> According to dialectical logic it is possible to say that there are three gods, but to announce this to the untutored would give great offence (Bainton in Becker 1953, 45).

The Scholastics had reached the point most abominable to Servetus. They had completely sundered the Trinity into a Tri-theism. As a result he rejected the Moderni outright. The point of much of their speculation is to show that three beings cannot exist in one being and remain one. Nor can one being be three and remain one. As the theologians foundered in these rocks, so Servetus gives his response.

His rejection of Scholasticism is entire. The basic premise is the conviction of a Trinitarian concept of God, dating back to Nicaea, which, carried into formalistic and philosophic reasoning, becomes impossible to maintain. The error is not that of the individual theologian, but the creed itself. Thus he sets out to 'prove not only that three beings can not exist in one God, but that they can not even be imagined, and it is wholly impossible to have any notion of them' (Tr. 1.45).

Servetus' rejection and denunciation of these Scholastics offers a far more credible reason for his anti-Trinitarian stance than simply placating monotheistic Jews and Moslems. At the beginning of this chapter it was noted that Roland Bainton, speculates that Servetus could not possibly have come to his position based on study originating in a study of scholastics, or from the New Testament because he was no 'primarily a speculative thinker' (Bainton in Becker 1953, 29).

It is quite plausible, however, that Servetus came to his position precisely because of the scholastics. His education would have led him to drink deeply in these authors long before he was exposed to the Bible itself. Being a logical person, he would have followed the development of thought from illustrative, to demonstrative to fideist/Moderni and noted not only the change in schools of thought, but also the reason why each school failed. If at the same time he was exposed, as there is every reason to believe that he was, to the patristic fathers, with their emphasis on the oneness and unity of God appearing in Christ and active in the Holy Spirit (as Irenaeus would have put it), he would have noted the discrepancies between the ancient and the medieval. Reading the Bible at about age twenty - within a year or so of the *Trinitatus* being written, confirmed for him the fact that scholastic speculation has little basis in Scripture, leaving him free, at least in his own mind, to seek out his understanding of the Trinity.

Servetus and the Church Fathers

It is likely that Servetus could not have rejected Scholastic Trinitarianism without some prior input that was confirmed by Scriptural reading at the University of Toulouse. While it is possible that, as Bainton says, his primary motivation may have been to allay the criticisms of Jews and Muslims, it is more likely that Servetus himself discovered what he thought were discrepancies between the earliest Church fathers, the Scholastics and the Bible. In his mind the agreement between the Church Fathers and the Bible outweighed the speculations of the Scholastics. In rejecting them, it was necessary to reject their underlying principles, especially the dual divisive statements put forward at Nicaea and Chalcedon. The roots of his rejection of the ecumenically held Trinity, therefore, lay in the writings of the earliest Christians.

Judging by the many references in the *Trinitatus*[18] one finds the greatest influences on his thinking in his doctrine of the Trinity, coming from Irenaeus, Tertullian, and to a lesser degree from Ignatius. In addition to these are Clement of Rome, Cyprian, and a number of Fathers meriting only a single reference[19]. While references to these earliest Christian theologians are scattered through the *Trinitatus*, their theology as a whole influenced Servetus' thought.

The Christology of Tertullian

Probably the single most important source in Servetus' thinking was Tertullian. Although his references to the Apostolic Father are no greater than anyone else in the *Trinitatus*, it is Tertullian's thought process that is so closely copied by Servetus. Here we see the outline of the Servetus' argument. The clearest example of this is contained in the work *Against Praxean*.

Tertullian's Christology was far more palatable to Servetus than anything the Scholastics could have written. Apart from basing much of his Christological formulas on Tertullian, especially on the idea of *divine progression*, Servetus uses him extensively to support his principles. One example is in the third book of the *Trinitatus*, where

Servetus quotes Tertullian as saying that 'the manifestation of speech, which led to the begetting of the Son, was from the beginning made before the beginning' (Tr. 3, 19).

Here we see Tertullian's *divine progression* forming the basis of Servetus' thought. The Divine speaks the Word, and from the Word all things were made. This was the Word that became flesh and dwelt among us. It carries quite a different connotation of a Son created from eternity co-existing with the Father. In Servetus' theology, the Son is the Word uttered by the Father's mouth in the same way that Tertullian describes a stream arising from its source.

For Servetus this *divine progression* was scripturally defensible, especially in the prologue to John, although tracing backwards from the incarnate Christ to God, for 'he who is now flesh was formerly the logos, and that the logos was even from the beginning, and the Word was with God, that is, the second being was with the first' (Tr. 2.6).

This set Tertullian apart from the scrabbling Scholastics who looked for and tried to prove a Trinity of Persons in Biblical terms. Their failure, he reasoned, his thoughts based on Tertullian's writing, were that the scholastics assumed that the Word 'was a kind of being distinct from God, and from that they might fairly have deduced a plurality of Gods' (Tr. 2.6). Yet the *divine progression* as defined by Tertullian gave a different emphasis to the relationship between Father and Son.

Closely linked to this is the term 'Person'. Both Tertullian and Servetus use the word, but again Servetus uses it in the way of Tertullian. Tertullian conceived of the Persons in the Trinity as being 'dispositions', a term that Servetus adopts and uses with fervor to demonstrate that 'Persons' does not mean individual Gods, as the nominalists would understand it, but faces of God making possible the revelation of invisible Father in visible Son (see also Tr. 1.5).

Clinging closely to this definition of a Person, Servetus reminds his readers that 'Person' does not mean an integral human being, but 'the outward form or appearance' (Tr. 1.51). Thus the human being is defined by his or her 'person' meaning their gender, their status, their religion. The same is true of God. The Persons of the Trinity are not a mathematical number of beings, but manifestations, or dispositions of God,

> [f]or in Christ shone forth one Person of the Deity; and in the appearances or utterances of God the Father, another; and in the

sending of the Spirit another; and thus in the Gospel we know three Persons, that is to say, by a divine manifestation (Tr. 1.51).

In support of this, Servetus calls on Tertullian's concept that the Person, or disposition, does not represent the substance, but the manifestation of that substance, thus the disposition (Tr. 1.51). Or, to put it another way, 'he himself is the face of the Father, nor is there any other Person of God but Christ; there is no other hypostasis of God but him' (Tr. 7.5).

Servetus also turns to Tertullian for an explanation of that knottiest of Christological problems, of how Christ could be both God and man. That Christ is God is a theological given, he is the Word uttered by God's mouth. That he is man is equally given, since he was born of the Virgin Mary. How the two co-exist in one being, however has been an issue with the Church for a long time. Servetus' answer is to turn to the early Church Fathers, including Tertullian. He writes,

> The older writers say that man as blended rather than united with God ... this, however, is not the way of filiation, for this peculiar quality or kind of filiation is in man alone ... And this is the view of Irenaeus and Tertullian, who say that the change was made from the Word to flesh, and that along with this a kind of Deity was blended and united with the man because God in Christ is just this (Tr. 7.5).

Thus Tertullian provides part of Servetus' answer to the Chalcedonian formula. Christ was God in the flesh, and, in the flesh he was a man. The *divine progression* has taken its final step, from God to God's reason, to the Logos, to Christ, a man born on earth.

In Servetus' mind, Christ was a man, who is the Son of God, who is God. Servetus may stress the divinity of Christ, but he never loses sight of his humanity. He refers to Tertullian's work, *Against Praxean*, to establish that Jesus was a man, was seen by his contemporaries as a man, and carried the name Jesus, which Tertullian noted was a man's proper name. Also those who knew him disputed that Jesus was anything but an ordinary man (Tertullian. *Against Praxean* XXVII, Tr. 1.2).

Interestingly, Servetus also draws from Tertullian to stress that 'the term Christ is a word belonging to a human nature' (Tertullian. *Against Praxean* XXVIII, Tr. 1.3). He notes that while the name 'Christ' has been invested with divine connotations, originally it was a word belonging to human nature' (Tertullian. *Against Praxean*

XXVII)[20]. In Old Testament times, Christ was the title of a king, and therefore 'the title Christ is suitable as a name for the Creator's Son' (Tertullian. Against Marcion XXVIII).

Thus Servetus relies heavily on Tertullian to demonstrate his basic point, that the uttered Word of God was flesh in Jesus Christ, a man living in this world, in whom was the fullness of the Godhead bodily.

The Christology of Irenaeus

The second Apostolic Father to influence Servetus was Irenaeus, citing him approximately the same number of times as he does Tertullian and Ignatius. His work 'Against Heretics', the only book of his quoted by Servetus.

The pattern of thought most clearly visible in Servetus' writing comes from Tertullian's work, Against Praxean. However, in the *Trinitatus* he refers almost as frequently to Irenaeus' book, *Adversus Haeres*. Mostly references to Irenaeus stand as confirmation to Tertullian's theology of one God, and the *divine progression* from him of the Son and Holy Spirit. However, Servetus also finds many opportunities to heap scorn on the Scholastics (see especially Tr. 1.58 and Tr. 2.5). By often referring to Irenaeus in this context, it is as if Servetus drew from Irenaeus' example of rejecting the Gnostics to give himself permission to reject the Scholastics and indeed the entire structure of Christian theology.

If this is the case, then it explains why Servetus draws special attention to those places where 'Irenaeus especially derides all those who say that the Word of God is a kind of philosophical being' (Tr. 2.5). He saw the development of Christian theology as leading to precisely that point, especially as it is articulated by the Moderni. He associates Irenaeus' scorn for the Gnostics with his own thoughts on the authors of medieval scholasticism, who like the Gnostics before them, 'endeavor, by violently drawing away their proper connection, words, expressions and parables wherever found, to adapt the oracles of God to their baseless fictions' (Adv. Haeres I.viii.1).

Another passage from Irenaeus that Servetus may have had in mind when writing about the Schoolmen is as follows,

> You see, my friend, the method which these men employ to deceive themselves while they abuse the scriptures to support their own system out of them. For this reason, I have brought forward their

modes of expression themselves, that thus thou mightest understand the deceitfulness of their procedure and the wickedness of their error (Adv. Haeres I.ix.1).

Servetus' sense of common purpose with Irenaeus extended beyond rejecting others to a similar view of the nature of God. The theology informing the background of Servetus' thought was from Tertullian, but he found many passages to support him. Primary of these is the concept of one God, revealed as Jesus Christ. Thus Irenaeus wrote that,

> ... there was but one God announced by the Law and the Prophets, whom Christ confesses as his Father, and who, through his Word, one Living God with him, made himself known to men in both covenants (Adv. Haeres IV.v).

God and Christ, therefore, are the same (Adv. Haeres IV.v.1), for they are from the same substance (Adv. Haeres IV.ix.1). Irenaeus' theology coincides with that of Tertullian when he describes how this Son was initially the speech of God, which was born in the flesh. Yet the God in the flesh was the same God who created all things. Irenaeus asserts that there 'is but one God, who made heaven and earth' (Adv. Haeres II.1). All things were made by means of the Word, or Logos, which was 'both suitable and sufficient for the formation of all things' (Adv. Haeres II.ii.5). Servetus follows this argument very closely. *Trinitatus* 2.7 is simply a paraphrase of Irenaeus.

Servetus, therefore, not only draws permission from Irenaeus to embark on a rejection of orthodox theology, he uses his writings to form and bolster his own work.

The Christology of Ignatius

Servetus' use of the Ignatian epistles is more of confirmatory interest than core material. Drawing his main theology from the writings of Tertullian, he referred to Ignatius as an indirect source. Clearly he was familiar with Ignatius' Christology, which, because it was derived from the teachings of John the Evangelist, the beloved disciple, Servetus would have held it to have been pure from its proximity to the Source.

The bulk of Servetus' references to Ignatius lie in one passage, dealing with his key concept that Christ is the visible body of the invisible God. He writes,

> The likeness of God is now a body. This was the same as God, and this is now the same as man, and remains God, and is in God as heretofore. It was hitherto a certain kind of divine reason, hence a Logos, but it is now a form as a man, like unto us, the form of God shining forth in man; it has put on flesh, as it were, although this is the same as man mingled with the divinity. Likewise if you read Ignatius, the disciple of John the Evangelist, you will find the same expression as in Irenaeus; and I beg you to observe this and not to depart from the ancient tradition in a single point, and then you will easily reject all the new inventions, blasphemies, and follies of our age (Tr. 7.11).

Servetus uses these epistles to defend his position that the divine and human are 'mingled' in Christ - a concept directly contradictory to the separation maintained by the Chalcedonian formula. One such reference is the statement in the Epistle to the Ephesians, where Ignatius states, 'There is one Physician, who is possessed both of flesh and spirit, both made and not made, God existing in flesh, true life in death...' (Ep. Ephesians 7). In Servetus' mind, this statement stood in complete contradiction to the Definition of Chalcedon in which the two natures of Christ exist 'without confusion, without change, without division and with separation' (see Bettenson 1981, 51). Thus Servetus' rejection of Chalcedon finds support in the ancient letters of Ignatius. For Servetus, this non-mixing meant that at least some part of Christ is not God, and therefore it is not possible for one to accept Christ as fully God whilst having reservations about his human nature. The only way that Christ could be fully God, was if the divinity and humanity were mingled in him.

It is interesting to note that while referring to this 'mingling' of divinity and humanity, Servetus, without saying so, sides with Ignatius in the contention that there are many who do not accept that Christ is both man and God, thus humanity mingled with divinity. Servetus shares in the opprobrium Ignatius heaps on heretics in language that would not have been out of place in the *Trinitatus* or Restitutio. Those who do not accept both humanity and divinity in Christ are 'dumb dogs that cannot bark, raving mad and biting secretly, against whom ye must be on guard, since they labor under an incurable disease' (Ep. Ephesians 7).

Because Servetus refers to all of Ignatius' letters, it is important to take note of the unwritten, unspoken Christology shining through. It is captured in a word, a phrase, and on two occasions, poems[21]. Ignatius' Christology is closely related to that of the original Apostles themselves - only one bishop held the See of Antioch between John and himself. He lived long before any of the Christological disputes erupted. His view of Christ, in Servetus' view, typified the 'ancient tradition' (Tr. 7.11).

Ignatius describes a progression from divinity to human which must have resonated with Servetus. Speaking philosophically he writes,

> Look for Christ, the Son of God; who was before time, yet appeared in time, who was invisible by nature, yet visible in the flesh; who was impalpable, and could not be touched, as being without a body, but for our sakes became such, might be touched and handled in the body; who was impassable as God, but became passable for our sakes as man (Ep. Polycarp 3).

In this passage, Christ is not depicted as a separate being, but as a part of the progression whereby God became man. This ties in with Servetus' belief that Christ was the Word of God which took a human form. It is also very similar to the progression described in Tertullian's work, *Adversus Praxean*.

Islamic and Jewish Sources

In addition to the broad spectrum of Christian sources that form the basis of Servetus' thought, there are also a number of references to both Islamic and Jewish authorities, indicating, as has been noted before, that Servetus was familiar with concepts of God beyond those of Christianity. Servetus mastered both Arabic and Hebrew during his university years, and held that Muslims and Jews hold Christianity in low esteem because of the teachings concerning the Trinity.

His non-Christian sources range from the relatively well known authorities, such as Maimonides, Rashi and David Kimchi (Friedman 1978, 18), to a series of lesser known writers. In all he cites over a dozen Jewish sources, indicating a familiarity with Judaism beyond the scope of most of his contemporaries (Friedman 1978, 121).

In his study on Servetus, Jerome Friedman (1978), asserts that many of the sources quoted in Servetus were only available in manuscript form within the Jewish community. There is no clear explanation as to how Servetus came into contact with them, and one can only speculate that either there was a repository of such literature either as Saragossa or Toulouse, or that Servetus had contacts within the Jewish world. Since less than forty years before, Isabella and Ferdinand had decreed, in 1492, that Jews were either to convert to Christianity or leave the country (Estep 1986, 98), it is more probable that Servetus' contact with Jewish sources would have been covert. The same is true for his contacts with Islamic sources.

One of the charges most often leveled at Servetus was that he was a 'judaizer', and 'exhibited an inappropriate tendency towards Judaism which he attempted to pass on to his readers' (Friedman 1978, 121). However, Friedman notes that,

> Servetus' interest in Judaica centered almost entirely upon his search for adequate means to express his views of the Godhead. ... those concepts and tendencies absent in his own day were found in the patristic literature so important to him. Similarly, many concepts, ideas and more importantly, terms, absent from all Christian tradition were discovered in rabbinic Judaism (Friedman 1978, 121).

Reading Servetus' works, it appears that his interest in Judaica increased over the years, since he makes far greater use of Jewish thought in the *Restitutio* than in the *Erroribus*.

Servetus demonstrates a wide and eclectic knowledge of religion. His reading at university must have been widely supplemented over the years as he sought to explain the nature of God in terms more acceptable to himself. His references reveal his willingness to explain the oneness of God in terms that could be acceptable to Christians, Jews and Muslims alike, an approach seldom attempted by any Christian theologian.

Notes:

---

[1] Most of Servetus' use of Hebrew was in connection with reading and translating the Old Testament, and his proficiency was excellent - so much so that he was engaged to revise Pagnini's Bible. However, at least twice in the Trinitate he refers to Moses Maimonides, indicating that he had been exposed to some aspects of Jewish thought.

[2] Could his exposure to the monotheistic beliefs of Islam have come through study of the Koran? While making a few passing references to it, Servetus never refers to the Koran as a source for his thought, which is primarily based in the Scriptures.

[3] 'A scholar, diplomat, teacher and writer' (Willis 1877, 8). The issues around the Trinity, Judaism and Islam way well have been awakened in Servetus by Angleria, for 'an Italian by birth, it was no part of Angleria's religion to hate Jews and Saracens...' (Willis 1877, 9).

[4] ...mox oecumenico concilio a nobis ereptus filius dei, fugata ecclesia, et abominationes omnes legibus decretae (Restitutio 666).

[5] Servetus uses the term 'philosophers' to describe those who before Nicaea introduced Hellenic philosophy to Christian theology, and those after Nicaea, who embrace a Hellenized Christianity - especially as reflected in the doctrine of the Trinity.

[6] Arius preached adoptionism. He denied that Father and Son were of the same substance.

[7] Macedonius taught that the Holy Spirit was a ministering angel (Davis 1983, 107).

[8] Aetius elaborated on the Arian teaching. He believed that the Son was unlike (anomoios) the Father (Davis 1983, 94).

[9] Eunomius' doctrine was similar to that of Aetius (Davis 1983, 94).

[10] refer to Appendix B.

[11] Emphasis mine.

[12] Emphasis Servetus'.

[13] Along with John of Damascus (Tr. 1.56).

[14] I Timothy 2, 5.

[15] I Cor. 8, 6. Italics Servetus'.

[16] Italics Servetus'.

[17] The views of Lombard became the authoritative position of the Catholic Church after being enshrined in Canon Law by the Fourth Lateran Council in 1215 (Bainton in Becker 1953, 34).

[18] The Dialogues, written in a different style, are remarkably devoid of sources.

[19] See Appendix B for references to Classical, Patristic and Scholastic sources in the *Trinitatus*.

[20] 'For Christ means "anointed," and to be anointed is certainly an affair of the body. He who had not a body, could not by any possibility have been anointed, could not in anywise have been called Christ' (Tertullian. Against Marcion XXVIII).

[21] The poetry is inferred from the rhythmic nature of passages, leading commentators to see them as early Christian hymns. Staniforth (1980) sets these passages out in poetic form.

Chapter Seven

Emanuel Swedenborg

Few people were willing to question orthodoxy after the Servetus episode. The traditional, Nicene concept of God seemed to have no further challengers. Catholic and Protestant stood in solid unity over the question of the nature of God. The ecumenical church had defined God, and even though the subjection of reason to faith began to lose ground in the seventeenth century, still few questioned his essential nature. The focus of theology swung away from speculative thought to practice. Churches began to focus more on missionary work as the world opened up to European commerce. In intellectual circles people questioned the existence of God, or the validity of Christianity, but the interrelationship of the essence and Persons in God was no longer a central theme.

The issues of Christology, however, are endlessly fascinating to people. Every generation has those who challenge the accepted understanding, exploring new ways of understanding the Trinity. After Servetus another person rose to champion a concept of God similar to his. Comparison of their theologies shows a remarkable similarity of thought, as if Servetus started an idea, and two hundred years later, this man finished it. He was Emanuel Swedenborg.

Calvin branded Servetus a heretic, and his works, almost entirely lost at inception, have made little impact on theology. Swedenborg, however, initially attracted great attention, and, through the latter part of the eighteenth and the first half of the nineteenth century influenced a substantial number of writers, religious thinkers, philosophers, artists and poets. Fascination with him lies partly in his theology, and partly in the man himself, for he was one of the last of the great Renaissance men, knowledgeable and skilled in vast areas of Enlightenment science, recognized and respected as an expert in his own field, and in several others beside.

Swedenborg's life has attracted so much interest that a vast accumulation of 'Swedenborgiana' has been collected since his death. His letters, memorials, diaries, travel journals, books and articles give the modern researcher a wealth of information about him. His biography has been written many times, and scholars are planning yet another[1]. At least two substantial volumes of articles on the impact of his philosophy and theology have appeared since his Tri-centenary in 1988. There is very little about Emanuel Swedenborg not available to the general public.

In spite of this, he is relatively unknown. Part of the reason is his claim to have been commissioned by God and part of it his claim, supported by detailed descriptions, that he entered the realm of spirits. These claims alone, however, are not sufficient to relegate Swedenborg to the obscurity he currently enjoys. Christian history is littered with countless people, many of them saints, who make very similar claims. What set Swedenborg apart from those others is his rejection of the orthodox Trinity, and his espousal of a Trinity in the Person of Jesus Christ. Because of this he could not be embraced as a mystic by the Church, but was branded a heretic with the result that his works remain largely unread.

Swedenborg's theology is worthy of exploration on its own merits, for while challenging traditional concepts, he offers alternative expressions. These are closely reasoned, supported with Biblical quotations and often with scientific facts and observations as he tries to free Christian doctrine from the weight of faith and subject it to rational thought. He was, first and foremost, a product of the Enlightenment, he believed in reason, but not at the expense of faith. He also believed in faith, tried and tested by reason. The result is a theology based on Biblical and scientific logic.

Without understanding Swedenborg's spiritual journey, it is not possible to understand either his theology or his science. His scientific background provides the form for his teachings, while his mystical experiences provide the subject matter. Combined they present a new set of teachings covering the spectrum of Christian theology. In this thesis, however, it is only possible to examine his thoughts on Christology.

The Early Years

He was born Emanuel Swedberg, in Stockholm on Sunday, January 29th, 1688. His parents were Jesper and Sara[2] Swedberg. The Swedberg family originally came from the Dalekarlia area of Sweden which is peopled by many 'famous for their honesty, courage, patriotism and powerful love for freedom' (Stroh 1909, 690), qualities that would become synonymous with Swedenborg in his own lifetime. The Swedberg family homestead, 'Sweden'[3] was purchased by Jesper Swedberg's father, and many of the buildings are still extant (Stroh 1909, 690).

Jesper Swedberg, well known in his own right, was a clergyman, beginning his career as a chaplain to the King's Horse Guards. He found favor with the king, Charles XI of Sweden, and was promoted many times over the years, spending some years as a Professor of Theology at Uppsala University, and finishing his life as a Bishop (Sigstedt 1952, 4). Emanuel's mother, 'gentle, sweet faced Sara Behm', inherited family wealth, which in later years would make it possible for Swedenborg to publish his books at his own expense (Sigstedt 1952, 3). She died when Swedenborg was eight years old, leaving five children behind. Ten days after her death, the oldest child, Albert, also died. Some years later, Jesper Swedberg married Sarah Bergia, who became a much-loved stepmother.

Young Emanuel's home life was greatly enriched by his parent's personality and their circumstances. A primary thread in his early life age was his awareness of the presence of God. Growing up in an episcopal home, young Emanuel was thoroughly exposed to the Lutheranism of his time. 'Sundays and holidays were entirely taken up with church going and religious observances, [which] must have deeply affected the growing mind of the boy' (Sigstedt 1952, 5). Certainly, Swedenborg never moved far from the concept of God, as will be shown in the next chapter.

Young Swedenborg's spiritual experiences were not purely ritualistic. He relates that

> ... from my youth to my tenth year I was constantly engaged in thought upon God, salvation and the spiritual diseases of men, and several times I revealed things at which my father and mother wondered (Acton 1955, 696).

A tradition also tells that as a child he had unseen playmates who were the source of the things his parents wondered about – they opted to believe that these were angels speaking through his mouth (Toksvig 1948, 22). At about the same time, Emanuel found himself able to hold his breath for long periods, especially during the family prayers. Experimenting on coordinating his breathing with his heart beat, he found that his thoughts became almost dormant. 'As he looked back on his early life, Swedenborg regarded such practices as indispensable preparation for those profound abstractions of the mind beyond corporeal planes' (Sigstedt 1952, 5).

Religion, however, was not the only force shaping young Emanuel's mind. Patriotic influences also played their part. He came from a part of Sweden that had been wrested from Denmark a few generations before his birth, and his own maternal ancestors had played an important role in (Stroh 1909, 690). This patriotic background forms the second of the threads running through Swedenborg's life. As an adult he worked tirelessly in service of his country, and later, in his theology, he held that service to the country was out-ranked only by service to God and the Church, saying that 'men ought to do good to their country for a love for it, according to its needs, some of which are natural and some spiritual' (TCR 414).

A third thread, woven into his life in childhood, is his academic interest. In 1693 the Swedberg family moved to the university town of Uppsala, where his father was appointed a professor of Theology (Sigstedt 1952, 4). This brought young Swedenborg into the rich intellectual environment of higher education. Years later he would write to a friend saying that 'from my sixth to my twelfth year I used to delight in conversing with clergymen about faith' (Swedenborg. 1769. Letter to Dr. Beyer).

For ten years Uppsala was his home. When the Bishop was moved to another posting as Bishop of Skara in 1703, Emanuel remained there, living with his sister Anna and her husband Eric Benzelius, whom he saw as a second father (Sigstedt 1952, 11). Benzelius 'carried on a lengthy correspondence with the most promising men of his day, and was constantly in touch with the newest trends of thought' (Sigstedt 1952, 12). These he passed on to Emanuel.

One such new 'trend of thought' was the works of René Decartes. Uppsala University had been rent by a fierce controversy in the last years of the seventeenth century between Aristotelians and Cartesians. This controversy threaded its way from academia to the court of Charles XI. Final victory went to the Cartesians, leading to the establishment of a new scientific and philosophical status at Uppsala (Stroh 1907, 348). Prior to this dispute, students at Uppsala were primarily destined for the priesthood. Afterwards, however, a more secular curriculum accommodated the needs of those whose interests were not primarily religious (Hubener 1988, 288).

Emanuel Swedenborg grew up in the midst of this environment. It penetrated into his own home. He was exposed to academic thought from his earliest years, nurtured in the most modern theories possible by Benzelius, who was 'convinced that the future of learning lay in the realm of sciences' (Sigstedt 1952, 12). Evidence shows that he was a quick and responsive learner, who, developing an interest in science and scientific method, never lost it – lists of his library made after his death, showed that he was still buying scientific books long after his theological period began (Stroh 1907, 347).

On June 15th, 1699, at the age of eleven, Swedenborg was enrolled at the University of Uppsala (Sigstedt 1952, 9). A great deal of information about Emanuel's years at Uppsala has been gleaned from the records of that institution. In those days students were organized into fraternities, or 'Nations' according to the province of their origin. Young Swedenborg was made a member of the 'Vastman Dala Nation' where his father held the honorary post of inspector (Hubener 1988, 288). These 'Nations'

> ... existed not only to enliven the student's life but for mutual encouragement to advance in studies. At the instance of their inspectors, they held exercises and orations to which were added disputations of two-hour length. The language used was usually Latin, and the disputations were appointed by the inspector (Acton 1958, 9).

Evidence shows that Swedenborg took an eager part in these discussions and disputations (Toskvig 1948, 34). Perhaps it is from this early experience that his theological writings are so filled with disputations and discussions in the Spiritual World.   Records also show that newcomers to the Nation experienced severe hazing, although Swedenborg never makes any mention of this (Acton 1958, 9).

Perhaps more under the influence of his scientific brother-in-law than his theological father, Swedenborg avoided the theology department and enrolled in the Faculty of Philosophy. In many ways this was the faculty of science which offered a broad spectrum of subjects including history (Greek, Roman and Swedish), metaphysics and logic, ethics and government, mathematics – which included arithmetic, geometry, trigonometry, statistics – mechanics, optics, astronomy and 'eloquence' or the study of the ancient Roman writers, Cicero, Virgil Horace and so on (Acton 1958, 12). In addition to these, he studied Hebrew and Chaldee, French, Italian, German and Spanish. It was, all said, as broad a philosophical, scientific and liberal an education as one could get in the first decade of the eighteenth century, and it prepared Swedenborg well for his life.

He graduated at twenty-one years old, on June 1st 1709, when, in the presence of his father, he stood up to read his dissertation. Those who listened to him read noticed that his words 'were impeded by a noticeable stutter' (Sigstedt 1952, 12). This stutter is the final thread from his boyhood that affected Swedenborg as an adult. Throughout his adult life, in all his years as a member of the Swedish Diet, or Parliament, Swedenborg never made a public speech. His friend, Carl Robsahm[4], who left memoirs on Swedenborg, notes that

> ... it was difficult for him to talk quickly, for he then stuttered, especially when he was obliged to talk in a foreign tongue... He spoke slowly and it was always a pleasure to be with him at table, for whenever Swedenborg spoke, all other talk was hushed; and the slowness with which he spoke has the effect of restraining frivolous remarks of the curious in the assembly (Robsahm. Tafel I.34).

After graduating from Uppsala, Emanuel planned to travel across Europe on his *Grand Tour*. His initial departure was delayed for a year due to war between Sweden and Denmark. He chafed at the bit at his family home in Brunsbo, hoping to be able to study with the great Christopher Polhem, 'the leading machine inventor in Sweden' (Sigstedt 1952, 17). Under pressure from Bishop Swedberg and Benzelius, Polhem agreed to house and teach Emanuel, but for various reasons the visit did not take place at that time. Instead, Emanuel passed his time trying to find ways to exercise his fertile mind, writing and publishing poetry. He was also interested in the more manual arts of book binding and organ playing (Sigstedt 1952, 16).

His wait at Brunsbo came to an end in May 1710 when travel was possible once again and he embarked for England. The details of this trip and his later tour of the continent are drawn from letters and his journal.

Arriving in London in 1710, wherever he lodged he tried to take advantage of an available opportunity. He lived first with a watchmaker, then a cabinetmaker, and later a maker of precision instruments. He reportedly said, 'I steal their arts, which some day will be of use to me' (Sigstedt 1952, 20). England fascinated Swedenborg, and perhaps more than the skills of the people, he was intrigued with their individual freedom of speech which at that point of history was far greater than any other country in Europe. Years later he noted that the English are in the centre of heaven,

> ...because they have interior intellectual light. This light, although it is not apparent to the natural world, is quite evident in the spiritual world. The English derive it from their liberty of speaking and writing, and thus of thinking (TCR 807).

His time in London was spent in perpetual pursuit of matters scientific. He bought as many instruments as he could afford, he visited the best mathematicians in the city, and spent a considerable part of his first year with the astronomer, John Flamsteed (Sigstedt 1952, 21). In January 1712 he went to Oxford to continue his study of mathematics, and met Edmund Halley, the astronomer. His studies occupied so much of his time that he almost retired from social activity altogether. In August 1712 he wrote to his brother-in-law, Eric Benzelius,

> Since my speculations have made me, for a time, not so sociable as was serviceable and useful for me, and my liveliness has become somewhat exhausted, I have, therefore, for a little time taken up *studium poeticum* in order therefore to freshen myself ... Yet I think to take up *mathesis* again, after some time, though I also pursue it now, and if I become encouraged therein, I mean to make more *inventiones* therein than any one in our *aetate* [age]; but without encouragement, this is to torment oneself *et non profecturis litora busu arare*[5] (Acton 1948, 40).

Swedenborg seems to have enjoyed his excursion into English literature, finding the major poets 'well worth reading for the sake of their imagination alone' (Sigstedt 1952, 6).

From England, his *Grand Tour* took him to Holland, where he attended a conference on inter-European affairs. Here his love of disputation and discussion came to the fore, and he was often found in lively discussion on the affairs of the day (Sigstedt 1952, 25). He did not fail, however, to continue to extend his practical knowledge while in Holland, and there he learned the art of lens grinding.

From Holland he went to France, in the heyday of Louis XV. In Paris he repeated his London activities looking up the men of learning in that city. He found a patron in the Abbé Bignon, who in turn introduced him to 'the celebrated mathematician Professor Paul Varignon and the astronomer, De La Hire' (Sigstedt 1952, 26). Thus his education continued.

As the years passed, he began to think increasingly of the use to which he could set this knowledge in Sweden. He began to draw up machines that would lighten the workload of laborers and make life more efficient[6]. He also began to think of Christopher Polhem, commenting to Benzelius in a letter that,

> I have now a great desire to go home to Sweden, and take all Polhem's inventions in hand, making drawings of them and giving descriptions, also *conferera* them with physics, mechanics, hydrostatics, and hydraulics, and likewise with algebraic calculations; and to give them out in Sweden rather than in other places, and set up for ourselves a beginning of the Society in *Mathesis*, for which one has so find a fundament in Polhem's *inventioner*. I wish that mine also could serve thereto (Acton 1948, 59).

It is with these thoughts in mind that Swedenborg began his trip homewards with a burning ambition to serve his country in some constructive way (Toksvig 1948, 59). He was about to enter a period leading to prominence in Swedish history. Even before his arrival, his father, the Bishop, had recommended him to King Charles XII (Sigstedt 1952, 32). Opportunities lay before him, the most promising of which was professorship at the University of Uppsala, although finally this was a post he was not to take up.

Emanuel Swedberg's fertile mind began to produce fruit almost as soon as he arrived back in Sweden. First of his efforts went into the publication of a scientific magazine, the *Daedalus Hyperboreus*, or *Northern Daedalus*[7], written in Swedish with the express object of bringing scientific matters within the reach of ordinary Swedes. 'The first number of the *Daedalus Hyperboreus* was published in January 1716, the chief feature being the description of an ear trumpet invented by Polhem' (Toksvig 1948, 60).

At the same time, Swedenborg began working on a book of arithmetic, since none existed at all in Sweden. Again, he enlisted Polhem's support, and, using money from a personal inheritance, he published both the magazine and the book, which had the wonderful title of *'Glorious in Youth, Useful in Manhood, Pleasant in Old Age'* (Toksvig 1948, 60).

By this time, Polhem having almost met Swedenborg several years earlier, before the young man's journey to Europe, and having read the first copy of the *Daedalus*, developed a great desire to meet Emanuel Swedenborg. They met for the first time in February 1716 (Sigstedt 1952, 36).

> During the talks ... Polhem and Swedenborg developed the idea that when peace came they would establish a mechanical institute at Uppsala. This institute would undertake to supply the people with useful machines (Sigstedt 1952, 38).

Swedenborg was fixated on mechanics and machinery, and he found a mentor in Polhem. In September 1716, Polhem introduced him to Charles XII, King of Sweden, initiating a friendship that would last the king's lifetime. Swedenborg presented Charles with a bound copy of the *Daedalus*, and Charles read it avidly. Considering Swedenborg's mechanical bent, and on Polhem's advice (Toksvig 1948, 61), Charles offered him a job as an Extraordinary Assessor (or associate official) of the Royal Board of Mines. 'This Swedberg accepted, and, on December 10th 1716, received a royal warrant for his appointment, involving his acting as Polhem's assistant' (Sigstedt 1952, 41).

Thus Swedenborg's relationship with Christopher Polhem greatly advanced his position, especially in relation to the King. The partnership, however, soured slightly, as the King suggested that Swedenborg marry Polhem's daughter. The woman in question, however, was in love with another man, and Swedenborg, discreetly, withdrew from pressing his case (Sigstedt 1952, 47). He never married.

Charles XII was killed during the siege of Frederikshall on 30th December 1718, while Sweden was at war with Russia. The king's death somewhat changed Swedenborg's prospects for the future. For a year they had been in almost daily contact, but Charles' death meant that the projects he was working on were suspended. He had run out of money to print the *Daedalus*, and the rift with Polhem, although not permanent, seemed wide enough at the time. His biographer, Cyriel Odhner Sigstedt speculates that the period after Charles' death left Swedenborg in a depressed state,

Prospects indeed must have looked rather hopeless to Swedenborg and perhaps his dejected attitude was reflected in a little work printed at this time on 'The Motion and Position of the Earth and the Planets'. In this treatise proofs are cited from physics, geometry and astronomy to prove that the earth now revolves more slowly around the sun than in former times, and that at the end of it all will be total desolation. The earth, by slowing down on its course, will gradually become unserviceable as a home for mankind and the human race will be destroyed by cold and famine (Sigstedt 1952, 52).

Perhaps his gloomy outlook reflected a deeper malaise. The decline in his prospects was real, for although Charles had appointed him to a position on the Board of Mines, that Board, without the King's motivating presence, was disinclined to accept him. Swedenborg attended one meeting, but it was pointed out to him that he had neither position, nor was entitled to a salary – clearly he was not wanted (Sigstedt 1952, 52).

The Middle Years

No throne is left vacant for long. Charles XII's younger sister, Ulrika Eleonora, who was accepted as Queen on the condition that she recognized the right of the Diet to limit her monarchy. She inherited a country wracked by war, with a worthless, debased currency, and a demoralized populace. In spite of this, she ushered in 'a period of great cultural development' (Sigstedt 1952, 57).

One of the beneficiaries of this new era was Emanuel Swedenborg. It was the custom in Sweden at that day for the newly crowned monarch to elevate certain citizens to the status of nobility. The families of Bishops were among that number, and so, on May 26th, 1719, the Swedberg family was ennobled. Their family name was changed from 'Swedberg' to 'Swedenborg', reflecting their origins on the homestead 'Sweden' in the region of Dalekarlia. In his new nobility, Swedenborg 'took his seat on the velvet cushioned, but far from luxurious bench in the House of Nobles' – one of the four houses comprising the Swedish Diet (Sigstedt 1952, 58).

Swedenborg took his role in government extremely seriously, playing an active role in Swedish politics into his extreme old age. His first contribution, however, was a proposal to reform the currency debased by Charles XII. He proposed changing the money gradually over a period of years. Those who wanted the full value of their money, could receive it in twenty-five annual installments, but those who wanted their money more quickly would sacrifice a portion of its value (Sigstedt 1925, 57).

In submitting this proposal to the Diet, Swedenborg also began another practice that he would follow throughout the course of his life – working anonymously (Sigstedt 1952, 58). Many of his books and articles were published without him appending his name to them. Swedenborg, for all the fertility of his mind, eschewed the limelight.

One could speculate that if he had been a good public speaker, Swedenborg 'might have become a political leader' (Sigstedt 1952, 85). As it is there is no record of him ever making a published speech, he preferred to submit memorials to the Diet on certain subjects. All indications are that these were favorably received. Count von Hopken, Swedenborg's friend, and three times Prime Minister of Sweden remarked that

> ... he possessed a sound judgment on all occasions, he saw everything clearly and expressed himself well on every subject. The most solid memorials on finances and the best penned at the Diet of 1761 were presented by him (Toksvig 1948, 165).

It was also at this time, in the early 1720's, that Swedenborg began his prodigious output of scientific works. Whilst studying the geography in Sweden, he made certain discoveries which led him to conclude that at one time the entire country had been covered by water. He presented his theory to the Queen at the time of her coronation in a little book titled, *The Height of Water*. As an early scientific thesis, the *Height of Water* shows a trend in Swedenborg's thought that would become increasingly clear in later years, the combination of Scripture and Science. Observation showed him clearly that water had once covered Sweden[8]. He assumed that this must have been Noah's Flood, and working from these twin bases he developed his theory, placing Scripture and science side by side as co-expressions of God's will. This book 'shows a glimmering of the idea that the Word of God was not to be taken entirely literally' (Sigstedt 1952, 61).

The year 1721 found Swedenborg back in Amsterdam where he witnessed the signing of the peace treaty between Sweden and Russia. Twenty-one years of war were ended, and peace ruled once again. He had come to Amsterdam to publish a series of articles on scientific subjects under the title of '*Miscellaneous Observations*', and this work catapulted him to recognition by the European scientific community. Scientific journals carried

> ... in its pages one review after another of the published treatises, reviews by no means brief and highly appreciative of Swedenborg's theory of applying geometry to determine the causes of natural phenomena (Sigstedt 1952, 73).

In this early philosophical period, Swedenborg tried to cross the bridge between Newton and Descartes, and one finds him picking and choosing what he considered the best elements of both, synthesizing them into something unique. This individual thinking led to the publication of a treatise, published on the same trip in 1721, popularly called the 'Chemistry' in which he posited a theory that the properties of matter are determined by the shapes and sizes 'of the different particles of which matter is composed' (Sigstedt 1952, 77). These characteristics, along with the motion of the particles lead to the creation of substances.

For all his philosophy and study, Swedenborg was a frustrated man. His appointment to the Board of Mines by Charles XII had never been ratified. He was, essentially, without a job. For a man who believed in the need to express his intellectual ideas in solid, useful practicality, this situation was intolerable.   His frustration was exacerbated when, twice in 1720, vacancies occurred, and he was passed over (Toksvig 1948, 65).

By 1723, as a noble and a participating member of the Diet, Swedenborg threatened to bring a civil action against the Board. They responded by recognizing him as an Extraordinary Assessor, without pay. He was welcome to attend their meetings, and the understanding existed that he would be appointed to the next available position (Sigstedt 1952, 92). Thus began a long relationship with the Board. By the end of his time at the Board, they were pressing him to accept the position chairman.

The reason for Swedenborg's success on the Board was his keen interest in mining, machinery and people. He traveled the length and breadth of Sweden, visiting mines, descending into mine shafts, proposing changes, and settling disputes. He firmly believed that through this activity he promoted the health and welfare of Sweden. Thus he labored with a principle that would later find expression in his theological works, that true charity is to do one's job honestly, justly and faithfully. He held this to be the highest human virtue after loving God and eschewing evil.

Swedenborg was one of those rare men who could maintain several interests simultaneously. During the 1720's while deeply involved in Sweden's mining industry, he pursued, in his spare time, the study of philosophy. The early quest in *Height of Water* of balancing revelation and science, lead him on a ten year programmed of trying to understand the causes of things. The quest found fruition in 1734 when he published his first truly great philosophical treatise, *The Principia.*

Chapter Eight of this thesis explores the theological issues raised in the *Principia*, the philosophic content is too long and complex to be presented in this study. His philosophic argument deals with the Infinite and the finite, 'the Infinite is identified with God, and the finite with things of space and time' (Sigstedt 1952, 133). As a Christian, Swedenborg never questioned the existence of the Infinite, and the *Principia* is an exploration of how that Infinite created finite substances. In doing this, Swedenborg showed once again the remarkable ability to straddle two seemingly opposing points of view, for he is neither an idealist, who, crediting God with creation, ignores the physical universe, nor a materialist who ignores God. His conception of a logical God, based on a logical universe, meant that God could be understood in terms of creation.

The *Principia* is interesting for the several theories Swedenborg advances as part of his explanation of creation. The first of these is 'a nebular theory', in which he represents the creation of the planets of the solar system as bodies thrown out of the sun, and, cooling, formed the planets. This theory was later adopted by Immanuel Kant and the French astronomer and mathematician Pierre Simon de Laplace[9], who is best known for his nebular hypothesis of the origin of the solar system. Laplace 'informs us that he had received ideas on this from Buffon[10], and Buffon ... had Swedenborg's work in his library' (Retzius 1903, 569). Thus, although he is not credited with it, Swedenborg's ideas may have had more influence in scientific development than is generally known.

Swedenborg finished writing the *Principia* in 1733, and applied for leave of absence from the Board of Mines to travel abroad to have it published (Sigstedt 1952, 118). In 1734 he traveled to Leipzig, where he remained for the better part of a year while the book was in process. When finally it was published it received 'high praise from the learned press' (Sigstedt 1952, 121).

The *Principia* concerned itself with the question of how an Infinite God could create a finite universe. After it was finished, Swedenborg turned his mind to the connection between the two. In one month in 1734, while in Leipzig, he wrote a second philosophical book, a sequel to the *Principia*, to address this subject. He titled it *The Infinite*. In this work he 'endeavors to prove the immortality of man's soul' (Sigstedt 1952, 133).

The *Infinite* marks a transition in Swedenborg's thought. While still passionately interested in machinery and mining, and deeply fascinated by abstract philosophy, he begins at this point to explore the relationship between *The Infinite* and people, for while the universe forms a macrocosm, the human being is a microcosm, the reason and focus for all creation. The human being, however, whilst in the image of God is still finite, and this relationship intrigued Swedenborg.

He returned to Sweden and the Board of Mines after the *Principia* was published. He is now one of Sweden's most prominent men, a recognized scholar and philosopher across Europe. Yet his mind continued to explore the interaction of divine and human. In about 1735 he wrote, but did not publish a short work titled, *The Mechanism of Soul and Body* (Sigstedt 1952, 139). This study, a logical sequence from the *Principia* and *The Infinite*, was not satisfactory. His personal knowledge had too many gaps, mostly in the area of anatomy, the structure and function of the parts of the body.

In 1736, therefore, he applied for leave once again, to travel south to study anatomy further. It is a reflection of his position in society that before leaving Sweden he took 'formal leave of Their Majesties, who received him very graciously and accepted his thanks for granting him leave of absence' (Sigstedt 1952, 142). His journey, carrying him to Holland, France and Italy, gave him the opportunity of studying anatomy not available in Sweden.

The product of this time was a major work, *The Economy of the Animal Kingdom*. As in the case of the *Principia*, some of the theological aspects of this book will be dealt with in Chapter Eight and the philosophy and anatomical insights are beyond the scope of this thesis. However, of great importance is that during this journey Swedenborg began to have the very first of his spiritual experiences that led, a decade later, to his theological period.

It could be that the onset of his spiritual experiences was caused by the subject at hand, for the purpose of his studies in anatomy was to find the seat of the human soul. In the *Principia* he had satisfied himself that the Infinite had created the finite, and in *The Infinite*, he then argued that the reason for creation was the human being. Since human beings are the receptacles of life, the source of which is God himself, then, he reasoned that there must be some point, some organ or vessel, that is the primary receptor of this life. He reasoned that anatomical study would lead him to this vessel, and, over the next few years studied the human body in as much detail as the science of his day would allow.

The *Economy of the Animal Kingdom* begins with a volume dealing primarily with the heart and the blood. Initially he thought that in order for the soul to be present throughout the body, it would need to be in the blood, as the common element to the entire body (Sigstedt 1952, 149). He contended further, however, that 'the study of the blood, being so profound a subject, requires a knowledge of the whole of anatomy, medicine, chemistry and physics' (Sigstedt 1952, 150), and he set himself to this task, in the performance of which he

> ... made a series of important discoveries, particularly in respect to the motion of the brain, the seat of the physical phenomena and the localization of the motor centers ... Emanuel Swedenborg, therefore, according to the standpoint of his time, not only had a thorough knowledge of the construction of the brain, but had also gone far ahead of his contemporaries in fundamental questions (Retzius 1903, 566).

In this study, Swedenborg showed himself to be 'a learned anatomist and a sharp eyed observer' (Retzius 1903, 577), which is important when one considers the other, hidden events of his life at that time. Following his habitual pattern, he published the *Economy of the Animal Kingdom* anonymously and it was well received. The first edition sold out, and it was followed by a second and a third. His authorship was discovered, and the 1742 edition carried his name on the title page.

Spiritual Experiences

Throughout the process of researching, writing and publishing the *Economy of the Animal Kingdom* Swedenborg was having experiences of a different kind.

> In Amsterdam, about the 18th August 1736, Swedenborg commenced his work on the *Economy of the Animal Kingdom*. Its initiation was accompanied by his first supernatural experience of which there is

any record. He was staying at an inn called 'The Golden Lion", and had entered into a state of profound meditation, when he experienced a swoon that lasted for some time. Upon later reflection he noted that this swoon had served the purpose of clearing his brain and ordering his thoughts so as to give him greater power of penetration (Sigstedt 1952, 143).

The experience was sufficiently interesting for Swedenborg to note it in his journal, and it marks the onset of a steady progression towards the spiritual experiences that caused him to abandon scientific and philosophical study and focus entirely on theology.

While writing the *Economy of the Animal Kingdom*, he noted another phenomenon that was missing from his earlier life. As he wrote about the soul, he felt an inner sense of comfort and an assurance that his insights were true. At the end of his manuscript which summed up his theory of an orderly creation he wrote, 'These things are true because I have the sign[11] (Sigstedt 1952, 144). In the first volume of the *Economy of the Animal Kingdom*, he revealed that the sign was a light that he describes as follows,

> When, after a long course of reasoning, they make a discovery of the truth, straightway there is a cheering light, and joyful confirmatory brightness that plays around the sphere of their mind, and a kind of mysterious radiation – I know not whence it proceeds – that darts through some sacred temple in the brain (EAK I.19).

It is obvious that Swedenborg is not speaking of a physical light, observable by the senses, but an inner confirmation leading to confidence that he was on the correct path in his thoughts. The experience of this confirmatory light would remain with him for many years to come, and in later years he tried to explain it, for example in the *Word Explained*, where he wrote,

> Confirmation is also represented by a flame ... by the divine mercy of God such a flame appeared to me and often, and indeed, in different sizes with a diversity of color and splendor, that during some months when I was writing a certain work [*The Economy of the Animal Kingdom*], hardly a day passed in which a flame did not appear as vividly as the flame on a household hearth. It was then a sign of approval, and this was prior to the time when spirits began to speak to me *viva voce* (WE 6905).

It would be tempting at this point to paint Swedenborg as a mystic. However, in the late 1730's there was little mystical about him. He was a practicing Christian, but also a scholar and scientist. There is no indication that he set out deliberately to cultivate or manufacture a spiritual experience. To the contrary, it seems to have come upon him unawares.

Writing the *Economy of the Animal Kingdom*, however, brought him into states of deep concentration, and while in that state, either from habit or cultivation, we do not know, he fell into patterns of breathing that he had had as a child at times of worship. This type of breathing has been compared by many to the breathing exercises done by eastern yogis who use it to induce profound meditation. It has the ability to change bodily states and brings on visions and insights. Swedenborg refers to this as 'internal respiration'. In the *Economy of the Animal Kingdom* he describes internal respiration as follows,

> ... whenever the human brain is pondering reasons, and directing the rational mind to them, it desires to be at rest, and to draw breath quietly, as is usual with intense thinkers; it also, in order that it may be left to itself, deprives all the organs of their acumen, and consequently also the olfactory organ; lest anything should disturb its own process of analysis and provoke a greater influx of blood than such a state of the brain then requires. Power therefore is given it to draw in air through a shorter passage, without it coming into contact with the sensory fibrils, namely, through the mouth, differently from what we find to be the case with other animals (EAK II.42).

Thus in the intensity of his thought while writing, he began to breath in this way, although he says that ' the breathing was so directed unawares to me' (SD 3317). It was by means of this internal respiration that he would develop the mystical experiences that categorize his later life (Caldwell 1925, 41).

These inner experiences served to intensify his ability to concentrate, and enhanced the clarity of his thought. The *Economy of the Animal Kingdom* was followed by yet another anatomical book, *The Fiber*, published in Holland in 1740, a continuation of his search for the human soul.

In 1740, after an absence of four years, he returned to Sweden and resumed his duties at the Board of Mines. 'We find him testing ores, serving on commissions, settling disputes in mining courts and spending his spare time on his study' (Sigstedt 1952, 160). There was no external sign of any mystical experience.

Transition

Swedenborg makes no more mention of his spiritual experiences while writing the *Economy of the Animal Kingdom*, and the next three years find him at work in Sweden. He came into daily contact with the most advanced thinkers of the day, and they likewise give no indication of anything different or unusual about him. In June, 1743, he again applied to the Board of Mines for an extended leave of absence in order to publish another work, the *Animal Kingdom*, which is 'in fact a continuation of the *Economy of the Animal Kingdom*, just as that work was a continuation of the *Principia*' (Sigstedt 1952, 166). He published it at The Hague in 1744 in two parts, with a third issued later in London (Sigstedt 1952, 171).

The *Animal Kingdom* was the last of his purely anatomical studies (Sigstedt 1952, 172), and, unlike its predecessors, it was not well received, partly because it reflects a change in style from purely scientific to a more intuitive approach. He had searched for the human soul for ten years, reaching the point where he knew as much about human anatomy, indeed more, than anyone else did alive at that time, and still the soul eluded him.

> Swedenborg now seems to have come to realize the limitations of the reasoning faculty. Rational arguments, clear as crystal to one mind, had not the slightest effect on another. The truth seems to have dawned upon him that, as a path to faith, arguments were insufficient (Sigstedt 1952, 175).

He realized that the spirituality of the soul required him to transcend material substance. True knowledge of the soul could not come from observation, but from the soul itself (Sigstedt 1952, 182). In a sequel to the *Animal Kingdom*, his posthumously published work, *De Anima*, he 'acknowledges that he must treat the soul, not from experience or effect, but from first principles' (Sigstedt 1952, 175). His approach over the past decade had been back to front, and he stopped searching for the soul as an organ, and began to search out the effects of the soul in mind and body.

The years 1743 to 1745 were years of inner or spiritual crisis in Swedenborg's life. It was during this transition that Swedenborg began to have renewed spiritual experiences. He continued internal breathing when in states of deep concentration, and it appears that he still had confirmatory lights when his thoughts were on the right path.

The Journal of Dreams

The Royal Library in Stockholm purchased in October 1858 an original manuscript that had been unknown for many years (JD – Preface). It was a pocket-sized book of about sixty-nine pages. The opening page read like a travel itinerary, but as the reader continues, the subject changes, and it becomes a collection of dreams. This document provides a profound insight into the spiritual experiences and changes that overtook Swedenborg during 1743 and 1744.

While Swedenborg was preparing the *Animal Kingdom*, he began to have intense, unsought after, spiritual experiences in the form of vivid dreams. His scientific training led him to record them with the same kind of precision as reflected in his other work. His notes were, of course, not intended for anyone but himself, jotted down in disjointed and abbreviated forms, which makes them hard to decipher, although they show the struggles he passed through at this time (Sigstedt 1952, 182).

It is possible that the dreams were triggered by the conflict he was experiencing in writing *The Animal Kingdom* and *De Anima* in which he had to consciously acknowledge that scientific method would not reveal the seat of the soul. Intuitive research had not, until this point, been a part of his vocabulary; it represented a negation of the scientific principle he had fostered from childhood onwards. The effort to disengage his mind from a dependence on reasoning and refocus on 'the conscious reception of light through the soul' (Sigstedt 1952, 183), was no easy matter. He did, however, find that it led to a clearness of thought and an awareness of an inner leading that he had not noticed before.

This psychological battle manifested itself in his intense dreams. Swedenborg soon came to realize that they were symbolic of things in his own life. He noticed that during this time things that he considered essential elements of his personality began to change, for example the motive of working for his own honor subsided, and was replaced with a desire to find the truth because it is true (Sigstedt 1952, 183).

The struggle that engaged him at this point led him into alternating states of depression and exhilaration (Sigstedt 1952, 184). At times he was rebellious, looking back to his old, habitual pursuits and ways of thinking. At other times he experienced the clearest insight into issues and questions that had long eluded him.

In this diary there are many accounts of dreams, by which he was instructed about the work he was then doing, as for instance, about the state of the lungs in the embryo. He was also instructed that the key to the lungs is the pulmonary artery; that he should not make the notes to the *Animal Kingdom* so long, that he must not complete the *Economy of the Animal Kingdom*, that he should proceed to work on the *Brain*, that he had not properly arranged and carried out a certain subject etc. (Pendleton 1906, 36).

Thus the dreams had an instructive quality to them, although this was secondary to the psychological insights he gained into his own spiritual state. Swedenborg looked back at these dreams a part of his preparation for the later spiritual work he was to do (Sigstedt 1952, 183), for while he was in this state of spiritual crises, Swedenborg had an experience that would profoundly change his life. He had a vision of God.

Swedenborg's Visions of God

Amongst the entries for April, 1744, Swedenborg notes that he had seen God, not in a dream, but in a wakeful vision. What is interesting is that while this is recorded in the *Journal of Dreams* it is the middle of three visions of God that he had during a three-year period. The first, of which almost nothing is known, took place, presumably in a dream. Swedenborg had started his dream activity in 1743, and it is assumed that this first vision took place at about that time (Odhner 1900, 3).

It was a first approach of the Lord in person, and must necessarily have been tempered to the state of Swedenborg, whose spiritual sight was not yet fully opened. During this dream, then, the sleeper first received the divine 'call' to the 'holy office', which awaited him, and it would seem responded to this call by a promise. And this call was twice repeated, each time more clearly, as Swedenborg gradually became more actually consciously awake in the spiritual world (Odhner 1900, 3).

However, Swedenborg hardly refers to this dream visitation at all. It is quite different, however, with the entry at Easter, 5th April 1744. Swedenborg was in Holland. He had been to Church and taken the Holy Communion. That night his mind was filled with temptations and battles, such as he had been experiencing for a while. In the midst of this disquiet, he perceived a change,

> I had in my mind and body the feeling of indescribable delight, so that had it been in any higher degree the whole would have been, as it were dissolved in pure joy. In a word, I was in heaven and heard speech which no human tongue can utter, with the life that is there, with the glory and inmost delight that flow from it (JD 48; see also Sigstedt 1952, 184).

This inner state of peace stayed with Swedenborg for a while, but afterwards was replaced with his inner conflicts. On the next day, April 6th 1744, he traveled from The Hague to Delft where he experienced 'the most climactic event of his life' (Sigstedt 1952, 185). The entry from his diary tells the full story,

> In the evening I came into another sort of temptation, namely, between eight and nine o'clock in the evening when I read God's miracles performed through Moses, it seemed to me that somewhat of my understanding mixed itself therein; so that I could never have the strong faith that I ought to have ...In thoughts like those I passed the first hour or hour and a half ...At ten o'clock I went to bed and was somewhat better. I thought that the tempter was then going away. Straightway there came over me a shuddering, so strong from the head downwards and over the whole body, with a noise of thunder, and this happened several times. I found that something holy was upon me; I then fell into a sleep, and about 12, 00, 1, 00 or 2, 00 in the night, there came over me a strong shuddering from head to foot, with a thundering noise as if many winds beat together, which shook me; it was indescribable and prostrated me on my face. Then, at the time I was prostrated, at the very moment I was wide awake, and saw that I was cast down. Wondered what it meant. And I spoke as if I was awake; but found nevertheless that the words were put into my mouth. 'And oh! Almighty Jesus Christ, that Thou, of Thy so great mercy, deignest to come to so great a sinner. Make me worthy of Thy grace.' I held together my hands, and prayed, and then came forth a hand, which squeezed my hand hard. Straightway thereupon I continued my prayer, and said, 'Thou has promised to take to grace all sinners; Thou canst nothing else than keep Thy word.' At that same moment, I sat in his bosom, and saw him face to face; it was the face of holy mien, and in all it was indescribable, and he smiled so that I believe that his face had indeed been like this when he lived on earth. He spoke to me and asked if I had a clear bill of health. I answered 'Lord, Thou knowest better than I,' 'Well, do so,' said he;

that is as I found it in my mind to signify; love me in reality; or do
what Thou hast promised. God give me grace thereunto; I found that
it was not in my power. Wakened with shudderings (JD 49-54).

When Swedenborg recovered from this experience, his mind
was full of questions,

What can this be? Is it Christ, God's son, I have seen? But it is a sin
that I doubt thereof ... So I found that it was God's own son, who
came down with this thunder, and prostrated me to the ground, from
himself, and made the prayer, and so, said I, it was Jesus himself (JD
55).

He concluded that the vision he had had was of Christ himself. This
vision, apparently taking place in a dream, changed Swedenborg's life.
His doubts about the validity of intuition versus scientific method
vanished. At this point he did not yet know how this experience would
affect his life, nor what path he would now tread, but he had faith that
Christ was with him and would lead him, if he was willing to follow.

About a year later, Swedenborg had another vision of Christ.
This one is not described in the *Journal of Dreams*, but is related by his
friend, Carl Robsahm, who asked him about his visions of God. The
third manifestation of Christ apparently took place in London, in the
middle of 1745, about a year after the second appearance. Robsahm
quotes Swedenborg as saying,

I was in London and dined rather late at the inn where I was in the
habit of dining, and where I had my own room. My thoughts were
engaged on the subjects we have been discussing. I was hungry and
ate with a good appetite. Towards the close of the meal I noticed a
sort of dimness before my eyes; this became dense, and I then saw
the floor covered with the most horrid crawling reptiles, such as
snakes, frogs and similar creatures. I was amazed; for I was perfectly
conscious, and my thoughts were clear. At last the darkness
increased still more; but it disappeared all at once, and I then saw a
man sitting in the corner of the room; as I was then alone, I was very
much frightened by his words, for he said, 'Eat not so much'. All
became black again before my eyes, but immediately it cleared away,
and I found myself alone in the room. Such an unexpected terror
hastened my return home; I did not let the landlord notice anything;
but I considered well what had happened, and could not look back
upon it as a mere matter of chance, or as if it had been produced by a
physical cause. I went home and during the night the same man

revealed himself to me again, but I was not frightened now. He then said that he was the Lord God, the Creator of the world, and the Redeemer, and that He had chosen me to explain to men the spiritual sense of the Scripture, and that He Himself would explain to me what I should write on this subject; that same night also were opened to me, so that I became thoroughly convinced of their reality, the worlds of spirits, heaven and hell, and I recognized there many acquaintances of every condition in life. From that day I gave up the study of all worldly science, and labored in spiritual things, according as the Lord had commanded me to write. Afterwards the Lord opened, daily very often, by bodily eyes, so that in the middle of the day I could see into the other world, and in a state of perfect wakefulness converse with angels and spirits (Robsahm 15. Tafel I, 35).

Swedenborg, therefore, had three visions of God in a period of three years. His life was changed, in that his purpose, which had been to serve science, was redirected to the service of God. Externally his daily life continued unchanged. None of his friends or associates noted anything different or unusual about him, and he did not divulge any hint of the experiences he was going through – although he meticulously noted them down in his *Journal of Dreams*, thus providing insight to later generations of his hidden experiences.

Later on, in his theological works, Swedenborg referred back to these manifestations of God, without explaining them in detail. Some of his statements are simple, for example in *The Doctrine of the Lord*, he writes, 'Now by command of the Lord, who has been revealed to me ...' (Lord Preface). He also notes similar things in several places, for example,

Since the Lord cannot show Himself in person, as has just been demonstrated, and yet He predicted that He would come and found a new church, which is the New Jerusalem, it follows that He will do this by means of a man, who can not only receive intellectually the doctrines of this church, but also publish them in print. I bear true witness that the Lord has shown Himself in the presence of me, His servant, and sent me to perform this function. After this He opened the sight of my spirit, thus admitting me to the spiritual world, and allowing me to see the heavens and the hells, and also to talk with angels and spirits; and this I have now been doing for many years without a break. Equally I assert that from the first day of my calling I have not received any instruction concerning the doctrines of that church from any angel, but only from the Lord, while I was reading the Word (TCR 779).

Swedenborg did not only attest in his published books that God had appeared to him, but also in his private correspondence. For example in a letter to Oetinger he wrote,

> I can solemnly bear witness that the Lord Himself has appeared to me, and has sent me to do what I am doing, and for this end has opened the interiors of my mind, being the interiors of my spirit, that I might see the things which are in the spiritual world, and might hear those who are there, and this now for twenty two years (Acton 1955, 621).

Biblical Studies

Swedenborg returned to Sweden in mid-1745, and, in spite of the vivid spiritual experiences that had taken place on his journey, he returned to his position at the Board of Mines. In his private time he embarked on his personal preparation to fulfill the commission put before him by Christ (Sigstedt 1952, 203). Instead of studying philosophy and anatomy as before, he now turned his attention to an exhaustive study of Scripture which fully occupied him for the next three years (Sigstedt 1952, 203).

He set about his new studies in the same methodical attitude with which he had approached his other studies. He began by constructing a comprehensive index to the Old and New Testaments, although he does not try to interpret the Bible at this point (Sigstedt 1952, 207). He also started to restudy Hebrew in order to understand the original texts more accurately.

His index grew, and with it his knowledge of the Bible – which was probably not inconsiderable, if one remembers his background as a Bishop's son and a practicing Christian – so he began to gather collections of passages by subject (Sigstedt 1952, 208). Two interesting collections came out of this period. The first has been published under the title, *A Philosopher's Notebook*, in which Swedenborg correlates some of the subject titles from his index with extracts from the works of other authors, scientists, philosophers, theologians and so on. These notes were an aid to understanding the broad topics of the Bible.

A second interesting work is a notebook in which he tried to correlate the meaning of the Bible with a higher spiritual meaning. Here he was looking for immaterial ideas contained within the pages of the Bible. In this work, called *The Hieroglyphic Key*, Swedenborg attempts to apply 'his learned accomplishments to the elucidation of sacred texts' (Sigstedt 1952, 208). He declares that now 'it is allowable thus to interpret the Sacred Scripture, for the spirit speaks naturally and spiritually' (Sigstedt 1952, 208).

The concept of the Bible that evolved at this time was that the Scriptures are simply a natural expression of higher spiritual ideas, each reflected in its own speech. The difference between natural and angelic speech can be compared to two languages, both expressing the same idea, but in two different forms. In his studies of the Bible, Swedenborg endeavored to translate the natural ideas of the Bible, the histories and prophecies, into spiritual ideas. By doing this he hoped to lay open a higher, inner meaning of the Bible, so that from being a history of the Jews, it takes on a higher, more universal meaning.

In the autumn of 1745, Swedenborg began his first attempt at a consecutive study of the Bible, a short paper called *The Story of Creation as Related by Moses*. In this he makes a verse by verse account of the story of Creation. However, the work was not satisfactory to him.

In November of the same year, after a fervent prayer he began again. This work, which he originally intended to publish (Sigstedt 1952, 212), but which was only published posthumously is titled *The Word Explained*. It would keep him busy until 1747. His object in this study is given in the introductory paragraph,

> But let us examine the Scriptures, especially with the purpose of searching the kingdom of God, that is to say, its future quality, and many things appertaining to it. The Scriptures treat of the kingdom of God, not here and there, but everywhere; for this kingdom was the end in creation and of all things both of heaven and earth (WE 1).

Studying the Bible and understanding its meaning would mean the completion of Swedenborg's entire life's work. He had spent his life trying to understand natural phenomena, and had accomplished a vast spectrum of understanding in both science and anatomy. Yet he believed that none of this is of value without knowledge of its source. As he wrote *The Word Explained*, so he became increasingly convinced that the second coming of the Messiah was at hand, and that it would be effected by an unlocking of the secrets of the Bible (Sigstedt 1952, 210).

To make it possible for this Second Coming to take place, he needed to be led and taught the inner meaning of the Bible. He did not believe this could be achieved by rational thought, but from a deeper intuition caused by a revelation of the spiritual world. He came to this conclusion because of his spiritual experiences while studying and writing *The Word Explained.*

It is in this study, therefore, that many of the clearest statement of the process of his developing awareness of the spiritual world are given. In the text of *The Word Explained*, Swedenborg indented these notes as he did not intent them to be published in the final copy.

His experiences in writing *The Word Explained* take several forms. Firstly he was convinced that his thoughts were being led by a spiritual agency, and that ideas were 'dictated into his thought' (WE 7006). He came to realize that the source of this dictation was a series of spiritual associates who influenced his thoughts. Once he became aware of this general presence of spirits, he then experienced their direct impact on him in the form of automatic writing. He describes this in *The Word Explained,*

> Thus, this revelation was effected sensibly ... and sometimes so sensibly that the finger was led to the writing by a superior force, so that if it wished to write something else it could never do so. And this was done not only with an adjoined perception of the subject, nay, and also – and this has happened once or twice with some variety – without perception, so that I did not know the series of things until after it had been written (WE 7006).

He mentions this experience in several other places in *The Word Explained*, saying once, 'I have written entire pages, and the spirits did not dictate the words, but absolutely guided my hand, so that it was they who were doing the writing' (WE 1150, see also WE 1892). The point of this automatic writing was not to allow the spirits to communicate their message to Swedenborg, but to illustrate to him that his thoughts came to him from a source outside of himself. The phenomenon was quite rare, and the things written down in this way 'were deleted, because God Messiah did not will that it be done in this way' (WE 7006). In later years he insisted that he was not instructed by the angels or spirits, but by Christ alone, as he records in his *Spiritual Diary* passage number 1647,

> Thus have I been instructed consequently by no spirit, nor by any angel, but by the Lord alone, from whom is all truth and good; yea, when they wished to instruct me concerning various things, there was scarcely anything but what was false, wherefore I was prohibited

from believing anything that they spoke; nor was I permitted to infer any such thing as was proper to them. Besides, when they wished to persuade me, I perceived an interior or intimate persuasion that the thing was so and so, and not as they wished; which also they wondered at; the perception was manifest, but cannot be easily described to the apprehension of men.

As Swedenborg studied the five books of Moses, so he became aware of a deeper meaning, a deeper symbolism in the words that was not apparent to others. He still struggled to understand this (Sigstedt 1952, 212), but increasingly his life became one of intense spiritual study. All the time that he was doing this study, Swedenborg continued to live a perfectly normal life. He was one of Sweden's leading men, active in the Diet and on the Board of Mines, seldom absent from his post at the Board of Mines, and continuing to perform the work involved (Sigstedt 1952, 213).

> The Board, which had spurned his application twenty-five years before, wished to elevate him to its key position. This was in recognition of Swedenborg's brilliance and talents in the mining field, as well as of the esteem in which he was held. However, Swedenborg felt himself called by Christ to perform a specific task. In response to the invitation to become Councilor, he wrote to the King and asked permission to retire, a request the King reluctantly granted (Sigstedt 1952, 214).

Later Swedenborg was to describe this period of study and research as a transitional time, when his awareness of the spiritual world was not yet full. He wrote,

> At the time I did not perceive what the acts of my life involved, but afterwards, I was instructed concerning some of them, nay, concerning a number; and from these I could at last plainly see that the tenor of Divine Providence has ruled the acts of my life from my very youth, and has so governed them that I might finally come to the present end; and thus, by means of the knowledge of natural things, I might be able to understand those things which lie more interiorly within the Word of God Messiah, and so, of the divine mercy of God Messiah, might serve as an instrument for opening them. Thus those things now become clear, which up to the present have not been clear (WE 2532).

Full Contact with the Spiritual World

After taking leave of the Board of Mines, Swedenborg
traveled to Holland in 1747 to continue work on *The Word Explained*
and see it through the press. However, as once before in 1743, he came
to Holland with one purpose and found it changed. He never finished
The Word Explained, and the manuscript remained locked away for
another century (Sigstedt 1952, 215).

In Holland he realized that his work on *The Word Explained*
was insufficient and unsatisfactory. What he had been writing had too
much of himself in it. This realization came when he became fully
aware of the spiritual world around him. He found that in this new
state, not only could he see and converse with angels face to face, in
precisely the same way as one speaks to another person in this world,
but that he could do this in a state of full wakefulness. His dreams and
visions had changed into direct and open contact with the spiritual
world. His work at this point took on a different quality and character,
for now he no longer wrote tentatively, but with confidence and
assurance.

In this state Swedenborg started his studies anew, beginning
with a serial exposition of the Books of Genesis and Exodus, in which
he describes the inner sense verse by verse, and some times word by
word (Sigstedt 1952, 226). He asserted in the opening paragraphs that

> [t]he Word of the old Testament contains heavenly arcana[12], with
> every single detail focusing on the Lord, His heaven, the Church,
> faith and what belongs to faith; but no human being grasps this from
> the letter... [Therefore] unless he has it from the Lord no human
> being can possibly know that this is the situation. By way of
> introductory remarks therefore it can be disclosed that in the Lord's
> Divine Mercy I have been allowed constantly and without
> interruption for several years now to share the experiences of spirits
> and angels, to listen to them speaking and to speak to them myself. I
> have been allowed therefore to hear and see astounding things in the
> next life which have never come to any man's knowledge, nor even
> entered this imagination. In that world I have learned about different
> kinds of spirits, about the state of souls after death, about hell (the
> miserable state of people who do not have faith) and heaven (the very
> happy state of people who do have faith), and above all else about the
> doctrine of the faith that is acknowledged in the whole of heaven (AC
> 1, 5).

What then follows are twelve volumes of theology, reasoned and exposited with painstaking and scientific attention to detail, of the same kind Swedenborg had demonstrated in his philosophical and anatomical works. Swedenborg published the first volume of the *Arcana Coelestia* in London in 1749. It did not create much of a stir, and very few copies were sold.

The effort began to take its toll on Swedenborg's health. In 1749, after the publication of the first volume of the *Arcana Coelestia*, Swedenborg's doctors in London recommended that he take a rest. He spent the rest of the year at the rather fashionable resort of Aix-la-Chapelle in France (Sigstedt 1952, 236). While he was there, however, he continued work on the rest of the *Arcana Coelestia*. The rest of the volumes were published almost one annually until 1756.

Once Swedenborg's spiritual sight was opened, he never ceased writing. In 1758 he had five manuscripts that needed to be published. Much of the material in them was drawn from the *Arcana Coelestia* and rearranged into more accessible for in individual volumes[13]. The subjects range from a description of the spiritual world, doctrinal thesis on the nature of God, an outline of the doctrine of the 'New Jerusalem' as he called his new body of writings. In addition he had begun a serial exposition of the Apocalypse in which he sets out to give the inner meaning of that book of the Bible, much as he had done for Genesis and Exodus in the *Arcana Coelestia*.

All these writings, Swedenborg claimed, were written under the direct guidance of God, and resulted from an understanding of the nature of truth as it exists in the spiritual world. He believed that since people described spiritual things in natural terms, it is possible, from the realm of the spirit, to restate those natural things in spiritual terms. He saw this as his primary task.

'Proofs' of Swedenborg's Clairvoyance

It is interesting to note that in publishing his theological books, Swedenborg resumed his old pattern of publishing anonymously. By 1760 his books were beginning to draw the attention of those in Europe who would read Latin, but their authorship was a closely guarded secret. The reason for this secrecy can only be speculated at. A fear of ridicule is not consonant with his firm belief that he had been commissioned by God to write these books (Acton 1939, 196). Another is that Swedenborg

... profoundly acknowledged and perceived (perhaps this may be interpreted as being the same as a command by the Lord), that unlike his previous works, his theological writings were an immediate revelation[14] (HH 1), and that for this reason they were not to be published or to be read as the works or speculations of a man – especially of a man so prominent (Acton 1939, 198).

However, in 1761 three events happened that destroyed his anonymity. These can be referred to as 'proofs' of his clairvoyance, for they brought his ability to see into the spiritual world and his association with angels and spirits into public view. A brief examination of the incidents surrounding this exposure gives some view not only of Swedenborg's ability, but also of his character.

The first incident occurred in Gothenburg, on July 19, 1761, when Swedenborg, en route to Stockholm attended a dinner with fifteen other guests. Part way through the evening he became ashen faced, and restless. When asked the matter, he responded that a fire had broken out in Stockholm, three hundred miles distant, and that the fire was out of control. He feared for his own home. Later, he cried out in relief, 'Thank God, the fire is extinguished, the third door from my house' (Sigstedt 1952, 269).

This incident alarmed the other diners, who had property or relatives in Stockholm. Three days later a messenger arrived in Gothenburg with news of the fire, it was exactly as Swedenborg had described it, and it had, indeed, been contained three doors from his own house.

Such a public display of clairvoyance could hardly be kept form public knowledge. News of Swedenborg's extraordinary vision spread around Gothenburg and it did not take long to reach Stockholm. When he arrived home shortly after, he found himself in great demand by people curious about his abilities. However, at this point few people associated himself with his publications (Sigstedt 1952, 270).

> [However] a single copy of Heaven and Hell had ... found its way into Stockholm during the winter, as is proved by a sheet of paper in the handwriting of Swedenborg's friend, Count Gustaf Bonde, dated January 5th 1759. Bonde seems to have been the first person to guess or in some way find out, that Swedenborg was the author of the five London treatises (Sigstedt 1952, 271).

Most people, at this point, however, were more interested in his clairvoyance than his theology.

The second famous incident to raise awareness of Swedenborg's psychic powers is the well-known story of Madam De Martreville, widow of the Dutch Ambassador to Stockholm. The Ambassador had died, and some months later a goldsmith presented the widow with a bill for purchases made by the Ambassador. The bill was substantial, and the Madam De Martreville was unable to pay it. She approached Swedenborg and asked him if he could find out from her husband in the spiritual world what she should do. Swedenborg agreed to try.

Eight days later, Madam De Martreville dreamed of a secret drawer in a desk. When she awoke, she examined the desk, found the drawer, and in it was a receipt from the goldsmith for the full amount. The next morning, Swedenborg arrived at her residence, to explain that he had seen her husband in the spiritual world, but he would not speak to Swedenborg as he had something to tell his wife (Sigstedt 1952, 278).

This story became common knowledge in Stockholm at the time, and increased public curiosity about Swedenborg's powers. It did nothing to diminish his role and position in society. He was frequently invited to social events and attended the Diet.

The third incident drew a great deal of attention because it involved no less a person than the Queen herself. Later in 1761, the Queen invited Swedenborg to Court. When he appeared, she asked him if he could converse with the dead, to which Swedenborg responded that he could, and that it was a gift from the Lord to be able to do so. When she heard this, the Queen asked him if he would be willing to undertake a commission from her to speak to her deceased brother, Augustus William of Prussia, who had died on June 12 1758. Being willing, the Queen gave Swedenborg her commission in secret.

About three weeks later, Swedenborg again presented himself to the Queen, and asked to speak to her in private. Together they walked a short distance until they could not be heard by anyone.

> He then told Her Majesty something privately which he was bound to keep secret from everyone else ... Thereupon the Queen turned pale and took a few steps backward, as if she were about to faint, but shortly afterwards, she exclaimed excitedly, 'that is something which no one else could have known, except my brother' (Sigstedt 1952, 280).

The incident of the Queen's secret spread rapidly, and Swedenborg's ability to see into the spiritual world became generally known. He saw these three incidents as incontestable proof of his ability, although he was willing to give further proof to anyone who wanted it. One such example is of a German merchant to challenged Swedenborg to find out the subject of a discussion the merchant had had with a deceased friend,

> Some days afterward he [the merchant] went again to Swedenborg, full of expectation. The old gentleman met him with a smile and said, 'I have spoken with your friend. The subject of your discourse was the restitution of all things.' He then related to the merchant, with the greatest precision, what he and his deceased friend had discussed. The merchant turned pale, for this proof was powerful and convincing ... (Smithson, 1841, 135).

As his abilities became generally known, the task of remaining anonymous became increasingly difficult. By 1768, however, Swedenborg gave up, and his book on marriage, *Conjugial Love*, 'bore on its title page the name of the author, Emanuel Swedenborg' (Acton 1939, 194).

It was the publication of this particular work, however, that led directly to charges of heresy. These were laid by the Consistory of Gothenburg. As these charges will be examined in more detail in the conclusion, we shall defer them until then.

Last Journey

In 1770 Swedenborg was eighty two years old. He set out in the spring of that year with the manuscript of his last major work, the *True Christian Religion*. This would be his eleventh and last foreign journey (Sigstedt 1952, 410). It is reported that when he arrived in Amsterdam he was more cheerful than usual (Sigstedt 1952, 414). His time in Amsterdam, as was the case many times before, was fully occupied with seeing his latest book through the press. His reputation had preceded him, and while people there were cordial, even his friend, Cuno noted, 'I readily acknowledge that I do not know what to make of him. To me he remains an unsolvable enigma' (Sigstedt 1952, 415).

By August 1771 the *True Christian Religion* was published, and Swedenborg set out for London, arriving in September of that year. He stayed in his customary lodgings with his old friends, the Shearsmiths, in Great Bath Street (Sigstedt 1952, 426). Reports are

that he spent his time quietly, admitting fewer visitors than usual. He spent most of his time working on English translations of his books (Sigstedt 1952, 428).
In the last few months of 1771 his health declined. In December he suffered a stroke, and was confined to his bed, unable to speak (Sigstedt 1952, 429), although he rallied somewhat. He died on 29th March 1772, at 5, 00 p.m. and was buried in the Swedish Ulrika Eleanora Church on Princes Square, London. At a funeral dinner in his honor, the group who gathered was a tableau of the regard with which people held him, 'to many [he] was a benign and harmless visionary. To a few he stood out as a dangerous menace to the established church' (Sigstedt 1952, 434).

What does one make of Swedenborg?

Swedenborg's life is so well documented that very little is left to the imagination. His writings, far from showing the ravings of a madman, reveal in inner methodical, meticulous attention to his subject which, in spite of his claims of visions, are couched in rational and even scientific terms. He claimed twenty-seven years of contact with the spiritual realm, translating into thirty volumes in English, leave the reader of Swedenborg with the question of how one man, even a man of his genius, could have written with such consistency on such profound subjects. Like his friend Cuno in Amsterdam, many find him 'an unsolvable enigma' (Sigstedt 415).
Those who knew Swedenborg, whether they were for him or against him, lost no time in writing down their impressions of the man, and of his ideas. One contemporary, Professor Clemm, of Tubingen, in 1767 – five years before his death, offered three explanations of his writings,

1.   They were mere fantasies.
2.   They were the delusions of an evil spirit.
3.   They were the truth (Sigstedt 1952, 419).

Professor Clemm's alternatives have to be considered by anyone who comes into contact with Swedenborgian ideas. Cuno was unable to believe that he was a deceiver, but was willing to believe that 'he may have been influenced by his imagination' (Sigstedt 1952, 420). Others who studied his works in detail were less certain.

Beginning shortly after his death was a series of rumours, largely perpetrated by John Wesley, that he was insane. Wesley's dealings with Swedenborg were brief, and took place right at the end of his life. Wesley relates that one day he received a note from Swedenborg, saying that he understood from the Spiritual World that Wesley wished to meet him. He admitted that this was so. However, the itinerant preacher was about to leave for a six month tour across England, and wrote back to Swedenborg that he would gladly visit him on his return. Swedenborg responded that that would be too late, for he was to die at 5, 00 p.m. on March 29th, 1772. Wesley set out on his journey, and when he returned, Swedenborg had died at the time on the date he indicated (Sigstedt 1952, 425). The two men never met.

It seems that initially Wesley was favorable to Swedenborg and his ideas, but afterwards stood implacably against him (Noble 1886, 214). The reason for his change of mind was the rumor that Swedenborg was insane.

Allegations that Swedenborg was insane go back to 1743, when, in the midst of his initial spiritual experiences he traveled from Holland to England. In London he initially lodged with a man name John Paul Brockmer, a Moravian (Sigstedt 1952, 189). Brockmer understandably was curious about his guest, and while Swedenborg seemed interested in the Moravian Church, he showed no inclination to joining it. This may have been a source of friction between them.

The friction, however, came to a head when Swedenborg was robbed of his watch while unconscious in his room. When he demanded the return of the watch, Brockmer claimed that he had been robbed while lying unconscious in the street. Swedenborg denied that that had ever happened (Sigstedt 1952, 190). On another occasion, Brockmer claimed that Swedenborg, proclaiming himself the Messiah, had undressed and rolled in the mud, throwing handfuls of money to the crowd (Sigstedt 1952, 437).

These claims by Brockmer that Swedenborg was insane were, years later, communicated to a Pastor Mathesius, a Swede himself, who later told them to Wesley, and on the strength of that hearsay, Wesley firmly believed, and published that Swedenborg was insane. The Swedenborgian scholar, Carl Theophilus Odhner, speculates on how these stories may have come about. He suggests that Brockmer and his maid, who were known for meddling in Swedenborg's papers, found his *Journal of Dreams*. Curious to know what it said, they found someone who could translate Swedish. One entry could be the source of the story of him being naked in the street,

Afterwards, one night I was found in the Church, but I was naked, having nothing on but the shirt, so that I did not dare to come forward. This may mean that I am not yet [spiritually] clothed and prepared as I need to be (JD 206).

A description of a dream like this could, Odhner reasons, be misinterpreted as a real event, and elaborated on each time it was passed to another person (Odhner 1914, 235).

Close inspection of Swedenborg's life in the transitional period of 1743 – 1745, shows that while far from being deranged, he was involved in intricate scientific and philosophic thought. His writings from that period indicate clarity of mind, rather than the confusion one would expect from the kind of insanity described by Brockmer.

It would be convenient, however, to dismiss Swedenborg's theology as the workings of an insane mind, but that would be facile. Far too many people down the ages have had experiences similar to his. If every mystic, psychic or clairvoyant was dismissed from the history of theology, there would be precious little theology left. Instead one needs to set the circumstances of how Swedenborg came to have the insights he had, and to examine them in their own light, for, as with any other theologian, they are founded upon the Old and New Testaments.

The next three chapters deal with an overview of Swedenborg's theology as it relates to the Christology and the Trinity. As his spiritual associations and experiences are not germane to the subject, these have been set aside and his theology presented as if he had no such concepts. The point in this thesis is not the validate or invalidate Swedenborg's experience, but to examine the essence of his theology, for it is on this that one must judge him heretic, or recognize him as an inheritor of pre-Nicene thought.

Notes:

1 This work is being undertaken by the Bryn Athyn College of the New Church.

2 Maiden name: Behm (Sigstedt 1952:3).

3 The co-incidence of the name 'Sweden' in both the family homestead and later in the name 'Swedenborg' with the name of the country 'Sweden' exists only in English. In Sweden, the county is called 'Sverige', therefore preventing the common confusion in English between the family name and the country.

4 Carl Robsahm, treasurer of the Bank of Stockholm. 'He seems to have been intimately acquainted with Swedenborg during the latter part of his life and to have had great respect for him' (Tafel I:620).

5 'and to plough the shore with stationary oxen' (Ovid, Heriod. V. 116. Acton 1948:40).

6 In 1714 he sent drawings for fourteen machines home. Unfortunately the Bishop lost them (Sigstedt 1952:32).

7 Greek mythology tells of Daedalus and his son, Icarus, who built artificial wings of wax in order to escape from the Cretian labyrinth with its monster, Minotaur. Icarus was killed when he flew too close to the sun and the wax melted. However, this represents ingenuity and to some degree technology – although the story contains a sobering caveat.

8 Later, scientists amended this to glacial action, but since the principle was very similar, Swedenborg is usually given the credit for this discovery (Sigstedt 1952:63).

9 Born on Mar. 28, 1749, died on Mar. 5, 1827.

10 Georges Louis Leclerc Comte de Buffon , born Sept. 7, 1707, died Apr. 16, 1788, author of one of the most widely read scientific works of the 18th century.

11 Haec vera sunt quia signum habeo.

12 Secrets, mysteries.

13 For a listing of Swedenborg's writings see Appendix C.

14 That is, a direct revelation without some intermediate means.

Chapter Eight

Swedenborg's Rejection of the Traditional Trinity

Swedenborg's theology is noted for its rejection of orthodox Trinitarianism. He could not accept a Trinity of Persons, preferring to express the Godhead as a Trinity of Person. However, Swedenborg grew up in a Christian home – his father was a bishop of the Swedish Lutheran Church, and as such, he was exposed to Lutheran doctrine, which teaches quite clearly a Trinity of Persons in accordance with the Nicene and Athanasian Creeds. Prior to concentrating solely on theological matters, Swedenborg was a scientist, an anatomist and a philosopher, amongst other things. His basic religious up-bringing had firmly grounded him in a belief in God, which runs like a red-cord through his pre-theological work, hinting at the direction he would take in later years.

Swedenborg's Philosophic and Anatomical Stage

Throughout his life, Swedenborg never wandered far from the idea of God. His pre-theological works lead back over and over to this issue. In 1734 he published his first great scientific opus, *The Principia*, an attempt to make sense of the natural world, of which he was a great scholar[1]. He begins with a chapter titled 'On the means which conduce to true Philosophy and the true Philosopher' where he outlines the process of trying to arrive at a natural philosophy. A philosopher is faced with 'an arduous attempt to explain philosophically the hitherto secret operations of elemental nature' (Principia I, 3), which he does by experience and investigation (Principia I, 9), which in turn leads to wisdom (Principia I, 14) and rational thought (Principia I, 29). The philosopher's study will not only lead to an understanding of nature, but to an insight of God, which, for a true philosopher, is the end in view. Prophetically he writes,

> The philosopher sees, indeed, that God governs his creation by rules and mechanical laws, and that the soul governs the body in a similar manner; he may even know what those rules and mechanical laws are; but to know that the nature of that Infinite Being from whom, as from their fountain, all things in the world derive their existence and subsistence, - to know, I say, the nature of that Supreme Intelligence with its infinite arcana, - this is an attainment beyond the sphere of his limited capacity. When, therefore, the philosopher has arrived at the end of his studies, even supposing him to have acquired so complete a knowledge of all mundane things that nothing more remains for him to learn, he must there stop; for he can never know the nature of the Infinite Being, of his Supreme Intelligence, Supreme Providence, Supreme Love, Supreme Justice, and other infinite attributes (Principia I, 35).

In this pre-theological era, Swedenborg appears to accept the basic tenets of Christianity without question. His interest is less in the theological explanation of the nature of God, rather than of God as the primary creator and mover of the universe. Aspiring to be a true philosopher himself, and one of great learning in his context, he comes to the conclusion that a 'true Philosopher'

> ... will acknowledge that, in respect to this supremely intelligent and wise Being, his knowledge is nothing; he will hence most profoundly venerate Him with the utmost devotion of soul; so that at the mere thought of Him, his whole frame, or membranous and sensitive system, will awfully, yet sweetly tremble, from the inmost to the outermost principles of its being (Principia I, 35).

All nature, he asserts, is 'the work of God' (Principia I, 36), displaying his infinite wisdom, holding the Philosopher enthralled by the Divine, reflected in the miracle of the world (Principia I, 37).

The Principia led Swedenborg to 'come to see that the existence of the finite depends on the Infinite' (Infinite v). Swedenborg the Philosopher saw the universe as a finite expression of the infinite, each part dependent on the one before it, until, philosophically he arrived at the need to express ideas on the Infinite itself. The only answer to the questions of the universe is God. He was not, however, of the deistic mould of the eighteenth century, which posited a distant, dispassionate and mechanical God. His Christian upbringing had provided him with the powerful idea of a loving, wise and present God. Even in his philosophical writings, 'he still maintains his religious attitude, and makes it his chief purpose to use the philosophy of the Infinite to promote the worship and love of God' (Infinite vii). In the Preface to the *Infinite and Final Cause of Creation* (1734) he declares that

> [p]hilosophy, if it be truly rational, can never be contrary to revelation...The end of reason can be no other, than that man may perceive what things are revealed, and what are created; thus the rational cannot be contrary to the Divine; since the end for which reason is given us, is, that we may be empowered to perceive that there is a God, and to know that He is to be worshipped (Infinite 5, 6).

This seminal idea is the basic tone of the whole of his study of both scientific and philosophical subjects. All study leads inexorably back to the Infinite, which, to the senses is 'utterly unknown and inexplicable' (Infinite 9), for philosophers see and reason from finite things, and there is no relationship between the finite and the Infinite (Infinite 10). All created things, he reasons, are natural, which in turn springs from the Divine. Therefore, he writes,

> ... nothing exists, subsists, or is made, but derives its origin and cause from the Infinite, without whom nothing can exist, nothing can subsist, nothing in the universe can be, or can be made... In this respect, God is all in all, and there is nothing conceivable without a beginning and cause in the Infinite, provided always it be not repugnant to Him, no matter how low it stands in the finite series (Infinite 136).

Thus there is a cause and effect relationship between God and creation. Throughout the *Infinite and the Final Cause of Creation*, Swedenborg refers back to this causal relationship with the Divine. At no point, however, does he ever describe God in theological terms. There is no reference to any sort of Trinity or Christology. Of course, at this point Swedenborg had no need to make this kind of statement, for he is not seeking to be a theologian, but a philosopher. His aim is not to express the nature of God per se, but to show the presence of God in creation.

However, one does not study the effects of God in nature without, at some point, beginning to question the nature of God himself. In 1741 he addressed some of these issues in another

substantial study, *The Economy of the Animal Kingdom*[2]. At the time
Swedenborg wrote this, he was deeply immersed in anatomy, involved
in a search for the human soul and the 'principle of life'. Thus he
suggests one must seek the answer

> ... from the First *Esse*[3] (or being) or Deity of the universe, who is
> essential life, and essential perfection of life, or wisdom. Unless this
> First *Esse* were life and wisdom, nothing whatever in nature could
> live, much less have wisdom; nor yet be capable of motion (EAK
> 238).

The 'First *Esse*' in the *Economy of the Animal Kingdom* is a
more theological expression of the concept of the causal Infinite in the
Infinite and the Final Cause of Creation. Both are philosophical
expressions of God as the creator of all things and both imply that the
natural universe acts in reaction to the Divine Presence. The difference
is, however, that in the *Economy of the Animal Kingdom* Swedenborg
is filling out the earlier picture. Here one sees God as 'life and
wisdom', the forerunner of his later teachings on love and wisdom, and
since he asserts that 'love is the life of man' (Life 1), one sees how
much closer he is moving to his theological concepts of the nature of
God. There is therefore a steady progression in his understanding of
God as the creator to the nature of God.

He has not yet, however, begun to define God in any way
other than philosophically. He prefers to quote Aristotle in support of
his explanations, although he does not 'mean to derogate from the just
merit of Christian philosophers, highly instructed as they are out of the
Holy Scriptures' (EAK 239[4]), a practice he would relinquish once he
began a systematic study of theology for himself. This is indicative of
his state of development, for while concentrating on scientific and
philosophic things, he has not yet begun to systematically study the
theology of the 'Christian philosophers'.

Still, his interest in God is primarily philosophical. In a
preview of his later theology, he compares God to a sun, flowing, into
all things, and constantly giving them life (EAK 255) – in fact the
ground of much of Swedenborg's later theology on God's appearance
in heaven as a sun (HH 116ff) is outlined in this section. Although God
is an ever-present force in the *Economy of the Animal Kingdom*,
presenting him is not the primary objective of the book.

His philosophical studies at this point begin to have
theological overtones when seen in the context of his later work. One
such example in the *Economy of the Animal Kingdom* is his teaching

about series and degrees. In terms similar to those he will later use to describe the nature of the Trinity, he writes that 'we are led into the inmost knowledge of natural things by the doctrine of series and degrees conjoined with experience' (EAK 628). In time this observation would become the doctrine of discrete and continuous degrees, explained in a later chapter, by which one can understand how the Trinity exists within the Person of Christ, and yet remains a distinctive Trinity. Thus although Swedenborg does not make theological statements about the nature of God, his pattern of thought that would later govern his teaching, is being progressively laid down.

After publishing the *Economy of the Animal Kingdom* in 1741, Swedenborg turned his mind back to the search for the soul. His earlier work had pursued the soul in the physical body, and Swedenborg exhaustively searched the sources of his day – making a few medical discoveries in his own right while doing so. However, the soul was not to be found in the body, and so, in 1742 he turned to psychology to examine the functions of the mind in an effort to locate the soul there. In that year he finished a manuscript, which was published posthumously, titled *Rational Psychology*. In it he attempts to catalogue the human psyche, through the five senses, the emotions, and knowledge. Yet, as in his previous work, he turns back at the end to the Divine.

Following essentially the same principle outlined in the *Infinite and the Final Cause of Creation,* that created things take their being from higher things, he comes to the same conclusion about human psychology,

> From love, to wit, spiritual and corporeal loves, when compared together, it is plainly apparent that spiritual loves are the founts of all corporeal loves; consequently, that no corporeal love can exist without the pre-existence of a spiritual love, and that no spiritual love can exist unless there be actually a heaven (RP 457).

Followed to its conclusion, this line of thought takes one back to Swedenborg's point, 'The most universal fount of love is the Deity above oneself, and after this the comrade as oneself' (RP 459). Once again, Swedenborg finds that the only key to understanding the human being is to understand God. In the succeeding pages of the *Rational Psychology*, he returns to his theme of God as the *Esse,* or being, of all things, continuing to say,

[t]hus, in him we live, we have our being, we move. And, in that God is the very *esse* in everything spiritual, he is love itself, and this love must necessarily be within that esse which is from itself and yet distinct from itself (RP 460).

This early identification of the being of God as love is crucial to Swedenborg's later concepts of God, and as will be shown in a later chapter, is part of the key to his explanation of the Trinity existing in the Person of Jesus Christ. Still, however, Swedenborg makes no theological pronouncements on the nature of God, although in a further section on Divine Providence, he outlines the interaction of God and people, noting that it is the nature of God to pull all things to himself as can be seen in the goal or 'end of creation' which 'can be no other than the existence of a universal society of souls, or a heaven, that is, the kingdom of God' (RP 553). True to his philosophic quest, Swedenborg did not, at this point either move beyond or explore God other than as a creator.

Nor is God the primary focus of his next major book, *The Animal Kingdom* (1744), 'the consistent purpose in Swedenborg's physiological works was to demonstrate the existence of the soul in the body and the intercourse between them' (AK – Preface). The *Animal Kingdom* was the last of Swedenborg's works before he turned to theology, completing his long series of works, beginning with the *Principia* (AK – Translator's Preface). Up to this point, Swedenborg could be described as a Christian philosopher and scientist, struggling to explore and understand the mechanics of the universe, with especial regard to the dimension of human spirituality. In doing so he makes many interesting observations and a real, if generally unrecognized, contribution to the scientific knowledge of his day.

Swedenborg's Early Theological Stage

From 1743 to 1745 Swedenborg began to undergo his spiritual experiences. His focus shifted from philosophy and anatomy to theology. It is as if the pressure to understand had become sharply focused on the source of all things, God, and from that time onwards he put the entire effort of his life into exploring the nature of God. One of the earliest casualties was the orthodox Trinity.

In the autumn of 1745, Swedenborg began a seriatim study of the Old Testament, titled, *The History of Creation, as given by Moses.* At this point, he still had not yet turned aside from the theology of his upbringing. Describing the sixth day of Creation, he notes, 'it is said,

Let us make in the plural, and from this it is evident that all the persons of the Divinity, who were three, namely, Father, Son and Holy Spirit, concurred in the work of creation' (Hist. Cr. 4). Later on, describing how Adam became like God, knowing good and evil, Swedenborg explains that Adam 'came to the knowledge of both, and in this was like the Persons of the Divinity' (Hist. Cr. 39).

On November 17th 1745, Swedenborg, convinced that he had been called by God, turned his huge intellectual arsenal on a study of the Bible – a task that would carry him until 1747 when he began writing the *Arcana Coelestia* (Sigstedt 1981, 210). The result was a massive eight volumes of Biblical exegesis, the *Word Explained*. His opening words to the *Word Explained* capture his purpose,

> But let us examine the Scriptures, especially with the purpose of searching the kingdom of God; that is to say, its future quality, and many things appertaining to it. The Scriptures treat of the kingdom of God, not here and there, but everywhere; for this kingdom was the end in the creation of all things both of heaven and earth (WE 1).

Leaving behind his philosophical and scientific studies, Swedenborg now turns to examine the nature of God. His first pronouncements were not dissimilar to what he would have learned growing up in a Lutheran bishop's home, 'Heaven and earth were created and produced by God the Father, Son and Holy Spirit' (WE 1). At this point he had not yet begun to challenge the orthodox beliefs with which he had been brought up. This early concept led Swedenborg to use the terminology of Trinitarian doctrine.

Throughout *The Word Explained*, Swedenborg takes careful note of the names used for God in the Hebrew text. He relates these to the Trinity, and so explains the terms 'Jehovah', 'God' and 'Jehovah God'. 'God the Parent is expressed by Jehovah, his only begotten or the Messiah by God, and the triune person of the Divinity, that is, God the Parent, Son and Holy Spirit, by Jehovah God' (WE 122). God, therefore, was present in three Persons. This is clear in the creation story, where Swedenborg notes that 'many Persons of the Divinity concurred to the work of creation' (WE 4). In a much later passage he refers to Jehovah God, 'that is to say, all three persons of the Divinity, God the Parent, Son and Holy Spirit' (WE 499[5]).

The entire Trinity is expressed in the term 'Jehovah God' (WE 4299[6]). Using this principle in his exegesis, Swedenborg refers to God as 'Jehovah God', whenever there is a reference to a Trinity. One example of this is when the angel appears to Abram and changes his name to 'Abraham' (Genesis 17, 1-9). In his explanation of this verse, Swedenborg uses the terminology of the orthodox belief in the Trinity. Referring to the covenant entered into between God and Abraham he writes, 'this solemn covenant is entered into, dictated, and sealed by the most holy Trinity, that is, by Jehovah God, Parent, Son and Holy Spirit' (WE 188[7]).

He then explains that Jehovah as parent, called 'Jehovah Shaddai' in that passage, admonished and justified Abram, and could now enter into a covenant with him. The covenant 'is then entered into and dictated by the Son, the only begotten of God, who is here called not Jehovah Shaddai, but God' (WE 189). Then, after this, 'the Holy Spirit ratifies this covenant and confirms it' (WE 190). This exposition shows how close Swedenborg's thought was at that point to the traditional view of the Trinity.

Not only does Swedenborg use the terminology of the Trinity, but he also uses the ideas associated with it. For example, in a section dealing with Genesis 8, 1-9, he speaks of 'Jehovah, at the intercession of the Messiah his only begotten Son' (WE 118), implying a separation of Persons within the Trinity, and showing a clear grasp of Christian theology. In another passage he writes,

> That by the God of Joseph's father (Genesis 49, 25) ... are meant all three persons of the Divinity ... After the fall, Jehovah, the Father of God Messiah, is not the God of the human race without his only begotten Son, it being solely by his only begotten Son that he regards the human race and is their God. Without the only begotten Son, he is separated from the human race and is the God of the universe that he created. Therefore, his becoming the God of the human race is effected solely by his only begotten Son, by whom he looks upon the human race. From his justice, he has rejected men from himself, but by his only begotten Son, he receives them by mercy and pardons them (WE 3028).

These words carry the distinct flavor of the doctrine of the atonement, although Swedenborg does not enter into that teaching. In his later, theological works, he will reject these genera of thought completely. Even though Swedenborg uses Trinitarian terminology in *The Word Explained*, evidence of his later concepts of a Trinity in one Person shines through, indicating the path he would later tread with more confidence. Early in his exposition of Genesis, he notes how in the relationship of the Trinity, 'the Creator or Parent of all, his Only Begotten or Son, and the Holy Spirit, proceeding from both, are ONE, and, taken together, one God' (WE 26[8]). Later he explains the relationship of the three Persons to one God,

> That Jehovah God is one in Essence, but trine in Persons; that is to say, the Parent of all, of whom is predicated creation; his Only Begotten or Son, of whom is predicated salvation; and the Holy Spirit proceeding from both of whom is predicated sanctification, is here declared by God himself by mouth and Scripture; for, from himself as One, and at the same time from Many, he speaks in these words, *Jehovah God said, behold the man is become as one of us (Gen.3, 22)* (WE 80[9]).

Swedenborg's theology in his early theological stage can easily be seen as orthodox, yet by 1748, he moved away completely from traditional terminology, and, in the *Arcana Coelestia*, expressed himself unequivocally on the side of a Trinity in one Person in Jesus Christ, whom he called 'the Lord'. Beginning his exposition of Genesis, the third since 1745 he writes,

> In all that follows the name THE LORD is used exclusively to mean the Savior of the world, Jesus Christ, and He is called the Lord without the addition of the rest of his names. Throughout heaven he is acknowledged and worshipped as Lord, since he has all power in heaven and on earth (AC 14).

What could account for this turn around in Swedenborg's thought? Countless Christian theologians and scholars across the ages, with a few notable exceptions, have studied the Scriptures without abandoning the cornerstone of Christian doctrine. Why did Swedenborg do so?

Part of the answer lies in his own testimony about the way he read the Bible. Swedenborg used the terminology of his day, both scientifically and theologically. In the absence of any other ideas, he simply expressed his concept of God in familiar terms. However, later in life he indicates in several places that he never really accepted the ideas of the tri-personal Trinity. In the *True Christian Religion* he writes, how from his 'earliest years I have not been able to admit into my mind any idea of God except as One' (TCR 16). In a letter to an earlier reader, Dr. Beyer, Swedenborg noted that

> [f]rom my fourth year to my tenth year I was constantly engaged in thought upon God ... From my sixth to my twelfth year I used to delight in conversing with clergymen about faith ... I knew nothing at that time of that learned faith which teaches that God the Father

imputes the righteousness of his Son to whomsoever he chooses
(Acton 1955, 696).

In another letter to Dr. Beyer, he testifies that he

> ... was forbidden to read writers on dogmatic and systematic
> theology, before heaven was opened to me; because unfounded
> opinions and inventions might thereby have easily insinuated
> themselves, which afterwards could only have been removed with
> difficulty (Acton 1955, 630).

Retrospectively it would seem that Swedenborg simply used
the terminology of the Trinity without really assessing all the
connotations involved. Once he began to explore more deeply into the
Scriptures, especially after his spiritual experiences, and his
intromission into the Spiritual World, so he became increasingly
convinced as to the nature of God. By 1747 when he was writing the
first volume of the *Arcana Coelestia*, all doubts had left him. From that
point onwards, he only recognized a Trinity in the Person of Christ.
This led him to reject orthodox Christianity as based on the Nicene
Creed, and seek understanding of how the Trinity could be expressed in
Christ. In time he would formulate the doctrinal underpinning to
support a Trinity in one Person.

Swedenborg's Reflections on the traditional Trinity

Swedenborg's spiritual experiences wholly changed his view
of God. While he retained some of his philosophical ideas about God as
creator and prime mover, he could no longer accept the traditional
doctrines of the Trinity. Getting the matter accurately defined was of
paramount importance. For,

> ... the idea of God enters into all things of the church, religion, and
> worship; and theological matters have their residence above all others
> in the human mind, and the idea of God is in the supreme place there;
> wherefore if this be false, all beneath it, in consequence of the
> principle from whence they flow, must likewise be false or falsified;
> for that which is supreme, being also the inmost, constitutes the very
> essence of all that is derived from it, and the essence, like a soul,
> forms them into a body, after its own image; and when in its descent
> it lights upon truths, it even infects them with its own blemish and
> error (BE 40).

In Swedenborg's view the church's fundamental blemish and error lies in the concept of God. He notes that 'the divine Trinity is known, and yet unknown in the Christian world' (TCR 163, AC 2149). It is known from the fact that the Church declares that there is a Trinity of Father, Son and Holy Spirit, but cannot explain how they make a one (AC 9030). The result is that the Church is 'at this day founded on an idea of three Gods' (BE 35), which in turn has given rise to the teachings about justification, the vicarious atonement and faith alone.

The division of God into three distinct persons is equivalent to dividing God into three, for while the church teaches one God, it treats the Persons of the Trinity as if they were three separate and individual Gods. He writes that 'it is the faith of the present day church that God the Father imputes the righteousness of his Son, and sends the Holy Spirit to bring about its effects' (TCR 626, Faith 38). Like Servetus before him, Swedenborg did not believe that the Church came to this conclusion immediately. The doctrine of God, the Trinity and Christology evolved over a period of centuries to reach the state he refers to as 'the church at this day'. When he reviews the history of the Christian Church, he notes two epochs, 'one extending from the Lord's time to the Council of Nice, and the other from that Council to the present day; but in its progress it has been divided into three – the Greek, the Roman Catholic and the Reformed' (TCR 760).

The First Epoch – the Apostolic Church

Swedenborg describes the Apostolic Church as the era beginning at the time of the Apostles and 'for two or three centuries later' (TCR 174, TCR 636). He refers to the same state as 'the Primitive Church' (AC 4772, AC 4706, AC 2986, and AC 477). He spoke highly of this initial time of the Church, and, as it were looked for goodness and truth within it, based upon a general principle that he applied to the several dispensations[10]. He believed that when a Church 'is raised up by the Lord it is faultless to begin with. At that time one person loves another as his brother, as is well known from the Primitive Church after the Lord's Coming' (AC 1834).

The mutual love, or charity, between the people of the church in its earliest days, led to charity in understanding the doctrines of the Church, for love binds people together, while differences in doctrine have a tendency to divide them. As long as charity remains, people look to a common understanding, thus schism and heresy are avoided (AC 1834[11]). In particular Swedenborg has great respect for the concept of God expressed in those times. He describes their belief as one in 'a Trinity of God in one Person, the Lord God the Savior, is of Christ himself, and was thence in the Apostolic Church, and should therefore be called the Christian Trinity' (Canons 43).

The best expression of this is the Apostles' Creed, of which Swedenborg speaks highly. Its pure simplicity appealed to Swedenborg. Predating the Nicene Creed, Swedenborg notes that there is no mention of Persons or a Trinity of Persons, and certainly no Trinity from eternity (TCR 175). Rather it is a simple summation of the Biblical truths of the Gospel, focusing on Jesus Christ born from the Virgin Mary (TCR 175), and as a presentation of God, rather than of a Son from Eternity (TCR 636). Swedenborg contends that belief in a Son from Eternity, or a Trinity before creation, removes the importance and even the divinity of the Son born from Mary – which later became apparent in the disputes of the relationship of the human and divine natures of Christ. The end result is a steady evolution to a belief in three Gods. The Apostolic Creed avoids this by referring to the Son 'conceived by the Holy Spirit and born of the Virgin Mary', who thus is the manifestation of God on earth. This he adamantly maintains is the Son referred to in this Creed (Canons 43).

However, this ideal state of the Church could not last indefinitely, and in the fourth century the first epoch gave way to the second.

The Second Epoch – the Trinitarian Church

Swedenborg's account of the transition of the Christian Church from Apostolic to Trinitarian takes a different approach to the usual. He held that the early church was characterized by charity between its members, and a willingness to explore the Bible from the standpoint of charity. He writes,

> In the course of time, however, charity faded and passed away, and as it passed away evils took its place, and along with the evils falsities too wormed their way in. From this schisms and heresies resulted, which would never have existed if charity had continued to reign and live (AC 1834).

The primary heresy, the one that went to the very heart of the Apostolic Church, concerned the nature of God. Swedenborg asserts that 'the primitive or Apostolic Church never could have divined that a church was to follow which would worship several Gods in heart, and one with the lips' (TCR 638). The root of the heresy eventually giving rise to idea of a Trinity of Persons is Arius, to whom Swedenborg refers as committing the 'crime' and 'pernicious heresy' of denying the divinity of Jesus Christ (TCR 174). This came about when people began to think of Christ as the son of Mary, rather than the Son of God, and thus the idea of Christ as a merely natural man entered into the thought of the Church.

The response of the Church was to devise a Creed to protect the divinity of Christ, which they accomplished by 'inventing the dogma of a Son born from eternity' (TCR 94).

> By this means indeed the human of the Lord was exalted to divinity at that time, and still is with man, but it is not so exalted with those who regard the consequent union as hypostatic, like that between two persons, one of whom is superior to the other. What results from this but that the whole Christian Church should perish? (TCR 94).

The outcome of the Council of Nicaea, in Swedenborg's eyes, marked the end of the Apostolic Church, and the purity of belief in the Trinity. He writes that 'the cardinal point of doctrine respecting the Triune God... was subverted in the Church' (Ecc. Hist. 1). The bishops at Nicaea 'devised, decided upon and established by decree, that there have been three Divine Persons from eternity... to each of whom, by himself and in himself belonged personality, existence and subsistence' (TCR 174).

The Tri-personal Trinity is taught in the Nicene and Athanasian Creeds. In the Nicene Creed, the Son is 'begotten of the Father, born before all ages' and is consubstantial with the Father, as is the Holy Spirit. To Swedenborg this more than implied a separation of God into three Persons. The Athanasian Creed continues the idea even further,

> The Catholic Faith is this, that we worship one God in a Trinity, and the Trinity in unity, neither confounding the Persons nor separating the substance. But as we are compelled by the Christian verity to confess each Person singly to be God and Lord, so we are forbidden by the Catholic religion to say three Gods and three Lords (TCR 632).

This was a paradox for Swedenborg. In denying Arius the Church split the Godhead into three Persons. It is only the force of religion that prevents people from saying three Gods and Lord, while the power of

Creed, as it expresses it, makes it possible for a person to confess three Gods and Lords (TCR 632). The Creed left Swedenborg shaking his head in disbelief, for as a scientist he believed in the power of reason, as a Christian he believed in the power of the truth, as a scientist who was a Christian, he simply could not accept that they needed to be in opposition to each other. Reason should be able to be measured against religious truth, and vice verse. If a dichotomy appears, it must indicate false reasoning somewhere. The paradox expressed in the Athanasian Creed could only lead him to conclude that human reason had failed.

The Athanasian Creed

Swedenborg's attitude towards the Athanasian Creed may at first seem contradictory. On the one hand he expresses the dissent at the separation of the Father, Son and Holy Spirit, and on the other, as will be shown in a later chapter; he indicates that this Creed is essentially accurate as long as the Trinity of Persons is restated as a Trinity in one Person. The root of this contradiction in his attitude is two fold.

First, basic analysis of the Athanasian Creed, which Swedenborg does in detail in several places in his theological writings, indicates to him that this Creed was developed cautiously to favor three Persons in the Godhead. He believed that the framers of the creed 'saw that God is one, although they assumed three Persons in favor of their principle' (Ath. Cr. 8).

He indicates that they 'saw that the soul and body are one' (Ath. Cr. 9). At the same time they noted that the Divine assumed the Human (Ath. Cr. 10), and yet instead of uniting these two as a one, as soul and body, they separated them into two, adding the Holy Spirit which they made 'absolutely the same with the two other divines' (Ath. Cr. 11). The end result is a Trinity of three Divines, and most of the rest of the Creed is spent explaining and defending that proposition.

As this presentation stood directly opposed to Swedenborg's assertion of a Trinity in one Person, he takes a critical attitude towards most of the theology of the Athanasian Creed. However, Swedenborg wrote from another viewpoint that affected his treatment of this Creed considerably.

Swedenborg recognized that the Nicene and subsequently the Athanasian Creed came about in rejection of Arius, with the express purpose of defending the divinity of Jesus Christ. In his mind, it was a lesser of two evils to think of Christ as a divine second Person in the Trinity than simply as an adopted son was, with no intrinsic divinity.

The Arian heresy would have totally destroyed the basis of Christianity. With this in mind he writes,

> From all this it is evident that it was of Divine permission[12] that Christians at first received the doctrine of three Persons, provided that they at the same time received the idea that the Lord [i.e. Jesus Christ] is God, infinite, Almighty and Jehovah. For unless they had received this too, it would have been all over with the church, because the church is the church from the Lord; and the eternal life of all is from the Lord and from no other (Lord 55).

He further excuses the Athanasian Creed on the grounds that those who wrote it read three Persons into the statements of the New Testament where the terms Father, Son and Holy Spirit are used, 'because they did not understand the sense of the letter of the Word' (Ath. Cr. 13, 15). By mistaking these three attributes of God as Persons, rather than comparing them to soul, body and operation, they came to the idea of the Trinity, and yet in doing so they retained and protected the divinity of Christ (cf. Lord 55).

The Creed, however, is the major error of Christian thought, for while Swedenborg recognizes that the object of the Creed is not to divide the Persons of the Trinity into three distinct Gods, he maintains that this is a logical result for two reasons. First,

> [t]he reason why the idea of three Gods has principally arisen from the Athanasian Creed, where a Trinity of Persons is taught, is, because the word Person begets such an idea, which is further implanted in the mind by the following words in the same Creed, "There is one Person of the Father, another of the Son, and another of the Holy Spirit" (BE 33).

Thus the Creed itself leads the mind in that direction. The second reason is the confusion over the substance of God (ousios) divided amongst the Persons (or hypostases). Noting that

> ... whereas the authors and favorers of this creed clearly saw that an idea of three Gods would unavoidably result from the expressions therein used, therefore, in order to remedy this, they asserted that one substance, or essence, belongs to the three; but still there arises from thence no other idea, than that there are three Gods unanimous and agreeing together, for when it is said of the three that their substance or essence is one and indivisible, it does not remove the idea of three, but confounds it, because the expression is a metaphysical one, and

the science of metaphysics, with all its ingenuity, cannot of three Persons each whereof is God, make one; it may indeed make them one in the mouth, but never in the idea (BE 34).

In his works, Swedenborg explores the results of the Tritheistic aspects of the Athanasian Creed, indicating that they gave rise to other ideas he finds heretical. These include the belief that God the Father was alienated from the human race, only being reconciled through the blood of the Son (Ath. Cr. 53). This he holds is inimical to the very nature of God, which, being love itself, can never be alienated, but loves all, even the worst of devils, and seeks their reconciliation.

He also holds that the idea of Christ evolving from this Creed can not be intellectually understood, for 'who knows what is meant by his being born from eternal and being born yet co-eternal with the Father' (Ath. Cr. 55). Swedenborg cannot accept that Christ can be born and be co-eternal, and this sort of contradiction in terms was alien to his scientific nature that wished to both understand and order the things around him. For him this kind of statement required a distinction between intellect and faith, and he was unwilling to make such a distinction.

One of his major issues with this Creed, however, was that it led people to think materially, for the very terms used evoke material thought (TCR 623). To reduce the nature of God to a 'Person' is, for Swedenborg, materialism, for one thinks of the attributes and activities of God as being done by some 'Person' in the Trinity, rather than by God himself. He expresses his reasoning on this matter in the following passage,

> Everyone who thinks of God only from Person, makes three Gods, saying that one God is the Creator and Preserver, another Savior and Redeemer, and the third the Enlightener and Instructor. But everyone, who thinks of God from essence, makes one God, saying, God created and preserves us, redeems and saves us, enlightens and instructs us (AR 611).

The Persons in the Trinity may have solved the Arian problem, but gave rise to a series of others. Swedenborg, who was not a church historian, pays no attention to the Christological disputes of the early medieval period, except in the case of Chalcedon, which he saw as resulting directly from the Athanasian Creed, and which impacted severely on the Person of Christ.

The Council of Chalcedon (451) met to solve the issue of Christ's humanity and divinity. As was shown earlier, this council resolved that these two should forever be distinct within Christ, so that he has a dual nature, one side divine, of the same essence with the Father, the other human and co-essential with humanity. In Swedenborg's mind, this was a further sundering of the Godhead,

> If there is no acceptance of this divine truth, that the Lord's human is divine, then of necessity it follows that a triad and not a single entity should be worshipped, and only half the Lord, that is, his divine, but not his human for is there anyone who worships that which is not divine? (AC 4766).

Swedenborg's ambivalence towards the Athanasian Creed, therefore, rests on its basic premise of three Persons in the Trinity, and the resultant idea of three Gods. While he has other reservations about the Creed, they are subsidiary to these. One of the greatest problems with the Creed, for him, is that it closes the mind by presenting a paradoxical idea of God who is simultaneously one and three, and although the ideas lead towards a separation of the Persons, still, faith prevents it. For any acceptance of this Creed, he writes, 'the intellect has to be continually fettered under the guise of faith' (Ath. Cr. 128).

However, Swedenborg is willing to admit that with some adjustment the Athanasian Creed contains many truths. His adjustment, which will be explored in Chapter Ten, is to express the Trinity of Persons as a Trinity in one Person (Lord 55). For him,

> The whole creed of Athanasius can be reconciled when it is acknowledged that there is one, one only Divine, and if it is acknowledged that the one only Divine is his Divine which the Lord calls his Father (Ath. Cr. 19).

And in another place he advises his readers to

> ... take the idea that there is one Person, with a trinity in that person, and you will see that the Creed of Athanasius will coincide and agree from beginning to end without any paradoxes or things that must be of faith although not understood (Ath. Cr. 110).

Swedenborg's Rejection of Scholasticism

Apart from his few dismissive statements about the Council of Chalcedon, Swedenborg pays scant attention to the development of theology in the wake of the Athanasian Creed[13]. Accepting that human nature is more likely to identify with and stress the three ness of God, rather than the oneness, he expresses little surprise that many in the church took that path, for few could even begin to think apart from the faith, for as noted before, the paradoxes of the Creed require that 'the understanding should be fettered, bound in obedience to faith, and that this must hereafter be established as a law of Christian order in the Christian Church' (TCR 165, TCR 338).

Swedenborg does make some direct, though un-footnoted references to scholasticism and its trends, especially to the paradox of three Persons in the Trinity who must be seen as one person, a point that church discipline made impossible to dispute. One area in particular would have bothered Swedenborg, although he makes no reference to it, and that is nominalism. This philosophic approach led scholars to believe that each aspect of the Trinity was an entity in its own right, and, if each Person is an absolute in reality, distinct from the other persons, then such 'a position is obviously indistinguishable from Tritheism' (Bainton in Becker 1953, 39). Yet to express a belief in three Gods was unacceptable according to the Christian monotheistic ethic. The scholars found themselves caught between their reason and their faith.

As shown earlier, certain medieval scholastics followed this train of thought. Occam reached this point, and reached the conclusion that the doctrine of the Trinity could only be retained on the basis of faith (Bainton in Becker 1953, 28). Similarly, Swedenborg's assertion that the history of theology shows how the understanding is bound by faith ties in well with Gregory of Rimini's point that faith in three in one is irrational, and yet remains the object of faith none the less (cf. Bainton in Becker 1953, 42). For Swedenborg, who was so much a product of the Enlightenment, and who prized free and unfettered thought, this was the paralyzing result of not reading Scripture under God's guidance, but from one's own intelligence (TCR 165, 2). Swedenborg dismisses the binding of faith, saying,

> It is a fallacy that the understanding must be held bound under
> obedience to faith, and that faith seen by the understanding is not
> spiritual faith; when yet it is the understanding that is enlightened in
> the things of faith when the Word is read; and when enlightenment is

excluded the understanding does not know whether a thing is true or false; and in that case faith does not become a man's own faith but the faith of another in him, and this is a historical faith, and when it is confirmed it becomes a persuasive faith, which can see falsities as truths and truths as falsities (AE 781).

In the final analysis, his rejection of the orthodox Trinity is less a rejection of the Trinity itself, but of the disjointed, paradoxical and fallacious pass to which it had come. He could never accept the idea that something as important as the Trinity should be believed simply because the church deems it necessary, especially if the subject of that belief is an affront to his scientific and rationalistic sense of order. To him the idea of three Gods in the mind, and one on the lips was anathema, leading to spiritual insanity and the destruction of the church.

The Destruction of the Church

Swedenborg minced no words in describing the effect of dividing the Trinity on the life of the Church. In the *True Christian Religion* he asks, 'what results from this but that the whole Christian Church should perish?' (TCR 94). He held that all churches are founded on their belief in God, and if that belief is an accurate reflection of God, then the church will flourish. If, however, the belief has been warped, then the church will suffer. He maintained that the Christian Church had so completely falsified the idea of God by dividing the essence of God into three distinct Persons, and the Person of Christ into a human and divine, that the true nature of God was completely obscured, and the Church destroyed. The result is that an 'insanity has pervaded the whole of theology, and also the Christian Church' (TCR 4).

> The term 'insanity' is used because it rendered people's minds so confused that they do not know whether there is one God or three; one is on their lips, but three in their minds, so that their minds and lips, or their thought and their speech, are at variance. The result of this confusion is the denial that there is a God. This is the source of the materialism prevalent today (TCR 4).

Swedenborg believed that dividing God into three persons led to a denial of God (TCR 15), and the church cannot be sustained on such a denial, for the 'faith of the church respecting God is like the soul in the body' (TCR 177), and if that soul is denied, or dead, then the body drawing life from it will perish also. The end result is a misrepresentation of the nature of God in the teachings of the Church. Swedenborg gives two examples of how this happens. He writes,

> It has been declared that God could beget a Son from eternity, and then cause a third God to proceed from Himself and the Son. Also that he could be angry with the human race, put them under a curse, and then be willing to show them mercy through the son, by the Son's intercession and the remembrance of the cross (TCR 90).

For Swedenborg this belief is fallacious. He begs the question of how a Son could be begotten from eternity and still is co-eternal with God. He rejects the idea that God, whom he defines as pure love, can be angry with people or ever put them under a curse. Similarly, how could the Son intercede with the Father to save humanity, for then would not the Son be acting at variance with the Father, for if the Father curses humanity, and if the Son is of the same essence with the Father, then he would also curse people. Thus for Swedenborg the separation of the Godhead into three Persons creates an 'insanity' in the theology flowing from it. His words capture this theme,

> ... how foolish those are who think, and more so who believe, and still more so who teach that God can condemn, curse, and cast out any one into hell; that he can predestine the soul to any eternal death, avenge injuries, be angry and punish. The fact is that he cannot turn himself away from any man, nor look upon him with a stern countenance. Such things as these are contrary to his essence, and what is contrary to this is contrary to him (TCR 56).

The second example he gives touches on the effects in human life of the division of God into a Trinity of Persons. Swedenborg is referring to some of the teachings prevalent in some parts of the church that people have no free will, and are saved purely as an act of mercy from God. This belief springs from the irrationality in thinking about God, for he asserts that it is irrational to believe that regardless of a person's spiritual state, that God can,

> ... as by a Papal Bull, remit sin to whomsoever he will, or cleanse the most impious sinner from his dark evils, making a person who is as black as a devil, as white as an angel of light, and this while he remains as inert as a stone, or inactive as a statue or idol (TCR 90).

The only path to spiritual cleanliness and so salvation is to walk the same path as Christ himself.

The end result of centuries of reasoning about the nature of the Trinity has led to the whole of Christian theology being shot through with falsities and fallacies. Like a house built upon a faulty foundation, the entire edifice would come tumbling down. He writes, 'from a Trinity of Persons, each of whom is separately God, according to the Athanasian Creed, have arisen many discordant and incongruous ideas concerning god, which are delusive and monstrous' (TCR 183).

There is a Divine Trinity

He concludes that the entire doctrine of a Trinity of Persons should be swept away, with all the subsidiary teachings under it. On the strength of his rejection of the orthodox Trinity, Swedenborg is sometimes labeled as a 'Unitarian' or even anti-Trinitarian. His theological writings, however, show that his rejection of the Trinity is a rejection of the irrationality he saw in development of Trinitarian thought, because it lead to the paradox of one God in three Persons. In his mind, the fact of the Trinity and its explanation is very simple, 'there is in the Lord a trine, or trinity, for there is the divine called the Father, the Divine Human called the Son, and the proceeding divine, called the Holy Spirit (Lord 46).

The interrelationship of the parts of this Trinity may be compared 'with an angel, who has a soul and a body and thus also a proceeding' (Lord 46). Thus the three 'Persons' are three attributes or qualities of one God (TCR 165). The result is a Trinity of Person, in the Person of Jesus Christ. The mechanism of how this Trinity works can be most clearly seen in an overall view of his theology on the nature of God. Since he believed that a church should be founded on an accurate view of God, his theological writing spends a great deal of time dealing with this subject. The next two chapters will outline briefly how he understands God, and how that understanding impacts his belief in the Trinity.

Notes,

---

[1] Previous to the Principia 'he had devoted himself to scientific studies in the special branches of mathematics, physics, chemistry, geology, metallurgy, and kindred topics' (Infinite v).

[2] The term 'Animal' is drawn from the Latin, 'Oeconomia Regni Animalis', and should more properly translated 'mind', thus 'the Economy of the Mind'

[3] Swedenborg uses the term *esse*, meaning 'to be' to describe the 'being of God'. The term becomes important in his theological explanation of the nature of God, as will be seen in the following chapter.

[4] One such example could be his beloved brother-in-law, 'Eric Benzelius, Counselor to his sacred majesty the King of Sweden, Doctor of Theology and Bishop of East Gothland' – such is Swedenborg's dedication of his 1734 work, *The Infinite and Final Cause of Creation.*

[5] See also WE 526, 515.

[6] See also WE 4324.

[7] See also WE 134, 137.

[8] Swedenborg's emphasis added

[9] See also WE 5363.

[10] Swedenborg taught that five churches have or will exist on earth. The Most Ancient, Ancient and Jewish Churches all served the spiritual needs of the human race at different times before the advent. After the birth of Christ, the Christian Church fulfilled this need, and eventually the New Church, being a restoration of fallen Christianity. The way God presents himself to each of the pre-advent Churches will be discussed in Chapter Nine.

[11] Confer AC 2417, AC 2371

[12] Swedenborg uses the term 'permission' as something allowed by God, but which in its own life, is evil. 'It is said that God permits, this does not mean that he wills, but that he cannot avert on account of the end, which is salvation' (DP 234).

[13] The catalogue of Swedenborg's library at the time of his death indicates that he had no volumes of scholastic or medieval theology, indeed, apart from Bibles and encyclopedias, 'he possessed only two minor works of the Fathers' (NCL 1883, 183).

Chapter Nine

Swedenborg's Concept of God

The *essence* of Swedenborg's rejection of the traditional understanding of the Trinity and the dual natures in Christ rests in his understanding of God. Although his teachings about God are systematized in two books, *The Doctrine of the Lord* and *The True Christian Religion*, the bulk of his teachings about God are scattered across all the volumes. Most notable is the *Arcana Coelestia*, published between 1748 and 1756. Expounding the spiritual meaning of the books of Genesis and Exodus, the *Arcana Coelestia* lays before the reader the essential elements that God is one. Particularly, however, the *Arcana Coelestia* relates how Jesus Christ, this God in human form, developed from infancy to maturity reaching full unition with the divinity as the 'Divine Human'. The process of development is more technically described as the process of glorification, by which Swedenborg meant that the human taken on from Mary became divine through a process of progressively emptying himself of the more limiting aspects of humanity. The 'vacuum'then filled with the Divine, making it possible for the Divine to descend to human level. The twelve volumes of the *Arcana Coelestia* in English[1] give the reader highly detailed description of this process symbolically told in the story of the Patriarchs.

The *Doctrine of the Lord* was originally published in Amsterdam in 1763 and gives a brief overview of His entire teaching. Key points raised are that every detail of the Bible is about Christ. His advent is soteriological, for as Swedenborg writes,

> The Lord came into the world to subjugate the hells and glorify his human; and the passion of the cross was the final combat, whereby he fully conquered the hells, and fully glorified his human (Lord 12).

Quoting extensively from the Old and New Testaments, Swedenborg shows how this proposition is Biblically based. Much of the content of the *Doctrine of the Lord* is a condensation of the teachings given in the *Arcana Coelestia*, but without the detailed analysis of the process outlined in the *Arcana Coelestia*. In the *Doctrine of the Lord*, Swedenborg develops his theme in a steady progression, elaborating on each point of his argument before proceeding to the next.

The treatment of Christology in the *True Christian Religion* is fuller than in the *Doctrine of the Lord*. Published in Amsterdam in 1771, Swedenborg intended the *True Christian Religion* to be a final collation and summation of all his theology. Thus the sub-title of the book is 'The universal theology of the New Church, foretold in Daniel 7:13, 14 and in the Revelation 21:1, 2)'.

In the *True Christian Religion* Swedenborg dedicates the first three chapters to the subject of God and Christ. The first chapter outlines the teachings of God the Creator, the second those about Christ the Redeemer, and finally the Holy Spirit. In each of these chapters he examines the subject in depth, following a similar systematic style to that in the *Doctrine of the Lord*, but in a far fuller form. In this book, Swedenborg also high-lights the differences between his understanding of the nature of God and that of the orthodox theologians, touching as well as the naturalists and deists of the eighteenth century. Included in these chapters are also sections dealing with the creation of the universe and redemption.

The sequence of these chapters finishes with a treatment of the Trinity in which Swedenborg pulls together the concepts of Father, Son and Holy Spirit to demonstrate his understanding that they are not a Trinity of Persons, but of Person, which is his solution to the problem of how one God can subsist in three Persons. This concept will be explored in more detail in Chapter Ten.

There are other places in his Writings where Swedenborg also systematically addresses the Trinity and Christology. The little book, *The New Jerusalem and its Heavenly Doctrine*, is mainly a series of very short summaries of doctrine, followed by references to the *Arcana Coelestia*, giving a very full guide to the scattered references contained in the original work. This guide is essential to the researcher of Swedenborg's thought.

Two other places of interest in Swedenborg's Writings are the two treatments of the Athanasian Creed, both published posthumously and both contained at the end of Volume Six of the *Apocalypse Explained*. The first of these is simply titled, *The Athanasian Creed*, found at the very end of the *Apocalypse Explained*. It is an outline of Swedenborg's thought on the subject of that Creed, and is rather haphazardly put together. Notes and reminders to himself indicate that Swedenborg was collecting his thoughts on the subject. However, it is useful in that it gives insights into his understanding of the Creed.

The second treatment of the Athanasian Creed is a far more polished series entered into the script of the *Apocalypse Explained* itself, beginning at passage number 1091. This treatment takes the reader into concepts about the nature of God, extending these to include providence and the nature of people themselves.

While noting these particular treatments on the subject of nature of God, it should be mentioned that there are other, smaller groupings in Swedenborg's Writings on the subject. However, the titles listed above are the main entries.

Any attempt to pull together the entirety of Swedenborg's treatment of the nature of God, with emphasis on the Trinity and Christology is a massive undertaking. There are few, if any details in the thirty volumes comprising his theological writings that do not have some bearing, in one way or another, on the subject. This chapter is an attempt to provide a systematic overview of Swedenborg's teachings on this subject.

God is One

Like the ancient Hebrew prophets, Swedenborg asserts over and over, either directly or indirectly, that God is one. He writes that 'the recognition and acknowledgment that God is One is the highest and innermost, consequently the universal, of all the doctrinal things of the Church (Canons 4). Swedenborg does not deny that orthodoxy worships one God; his complaint is that in doing so they divide the unity of God into three persons, resulting in the loss of focus on the *esse*ntial oneness of God. For him the 'recognition and acknowledgment that God is one' is the starting point of all theology, and should be the end point as well. The thrust of the Old Testament is that there is only one God, who would, in time, come to earth, redeeming and saving the human race. This unequivocal emphasis on one God is the hall mark of Swedenborg's theology.

In exploring the idea of the one God, Swedenborg never leaves the touchstone of the Old and New Testaments. He believed that 'the doctrine of the Church is to be drawn from the sense of the letter[2] of the Word, and is to be confirmed thereby' (SS 50). In order to draw doctrine, or teaching, from the literal meaning of the Bible, one must be guided by certain principles, especially by concepts and teachings that are so clear as to have no other possible meaning, which Swedenborg calls 'the doctrine of genuine truth'. One such example of this doctrine is the concept that God is one, for it is the foundation of Israelitish monotheism, which was not changed by the advent of Christ or by the assumption of a human from Mary. Rather, these latter must be understood and interpreted in terms of the overarching monotheism.

Swedenborg believed that the Old and New Testaments were the infallible Word of God. He also believed that the Word speaks of nothing other than God. 'The whole of the Sacred Scripture, and all the doctrines thence derived of the churches in the Christian world, teach that there is a God, and that he is one' (TCR 6, see also Lord 1). If a person reads the Scriptures from this point of view then that oneness becomes more and more apparent (TCR 6).

It could be argued that all religions, not only in the Christian world, but including Judaism, Islam and Hinduism, look to one God (cf. TCR 9). The many 'gods' of Hinduism are really a depiction 'the several attributes or functions of divinity manifested in a multiplicity of forms' (Beaver, Bergman and Langley et al., 1982). Swedenborg says the same is true in the pantheons of the Ancient Greeks, for 'wise men ... as Plato and Aristotle, declared that these were not gods, but were so many properties, qualities and attributes of the one God, and were called gods because something of the Divine entered into them' (TCR 8). Thus the monotheism of the Christian Scriptures resonates with all major world religions. For Swedenborg this is not surprising. Since the oneness of God is the 'most universal' of teachings about God, it follows that its echoes will be found in any religion in which people sincerely seek to understand the nature of God[3].

Swedenborg goes further in this assertion, however. All people, when they think about God, tend to think of him as one. The reason, he says, is that 'there is a universal influx from God into the souls of people that there is a God, and that he is one' (TCR 8). This universal influx, or inflowing from God comes to all people with as an interior aspect of life as an 'internal dictate that there is a God and that he is one' (TCR 8). If God is life itself, and human life is derived from his, then the quality of human life must, at least on its purest levels reflect his quality. Since the quality of God is one, then human life, at the point at which it is communicated to human beings, must necessarily convey to the lower, more conscious human mind that God is one. This explains the instinctual acceptance of one God and the difficulty the church has had in explaining how Father, Son and Holy Spirit are one.

The fact that there are those who either divide God into a tritheism, or even into polytheism, does not alter this. The influx of the concept of one God is often above consciousness. It can be affected or altered by the things people have been taught. The recognition of one God in three Persons obscures the inflowing divine information of oneness by diffusing it into a Trinity. Thus the Medieval Scholastics, for example, found themselves trapped between belief in one God and doctrinal assertions of a Trinity.

The influx from God that he exists and is one does not interfere with human freedom to choose or reject either point. As Swedenborg points out,

> ... still, there are some who deny that there is a God, and who acknowledge nature as God. There are, moreover, those who worship several gods, and those who set up images for gods. The reason for this is that they have closed up the interiors of their reason or understanding with worldly and bodily things, and have thereby obliterated the primitive idea of God which was there in infancy (TCR 9).

The problem of the one God does not rest in his oneness, but rather in people's inability to express it. No amount of human reason can ever lead to a full understanding of the nature of God, and God, knowing this, has revealed himself to the human race in order to foster understanding. People, however, immersed in 'worldly and bodily things', perverted the revelation, 'with the result that there arose disputes, dissension, heresies and schisms in religion' (TCR 11).

Under the guidance of revelation the human mind can be led to perceive and conclude that there is a God, and that he is one (TCR 12). One such example is the physical universe, the theatre of God, reflecting his wisdom. Swedenborg writes that,

> [t]he unity of God may be inferred from the creation of the universe, because it is a work coherent as a unity from first to last, and

dependent upon one God as the body depends upon its soul. The universe was so created that God may be present everywhere, keep every part under his own direction, and maintain its unity for ever, that is, preserve it (TCR 13)[4].

The physical order of the universe could not exist unless it had been created and maintained by one God. Belief in one God, then, is the core of Swedenborg's theology. In a very rare case of intolerance – reflected from the Old Testament, he writes that 'no principle of the church remains' with the person who does not acknowledge one God' (TCR 15).

This basic principle forms the framework of all Swedenborg's theology concerning the nature of God, of Christ and of the Trinity. It is a point of view he never compromises. Being his starting point, he also works backwards towards this principle at all times. There is never any separation between the Father, Son and Holy Spirit, and the distinction between human and divine in Christ, while there for a reason, is soteriologically necessary to bring this one God down to human level in order for people to know and follow him.

The Nature of the One God

Swedenborg adopts a high Christology, the one God of heaven and earth descended in Jesus Christ. Prior to exploring this Christology it is necessary to come to some understanding of the nature of God as he exists in his oneness. Most of the concepts Swedenborg uses to describe this nature are highly technical, but not impossible to grasp.

The two most important aspects of the nature of God himself are that he is, and that he appears. To describe these aspects Swedenborg uses two Latin terms, *esse*, meaning 'to be' and *existere*, or 'to manifest'. The simplest thing one can say about God is that he is and he manifests himself. This does not advance us far along the path of understanding, for what is the quality of God's being, and how does he manifest himself? Swedenborg pays a great deal of attention to these questions, partly for their theological and philosophical value, but mainly because of their soteriological implications.

The Esse and Existere

One thing Christians can say for sure about God is that he is. The term *esse* – to be – describes God's condition, but it does not say a great deal more. The term is closely linked with the name given to Moses 'I Am'. Both 'I Am' and 'to be' describe states of being (TCR 19). Normally they are associated with some sort of qualifier, for example, 'I am cold', or 'to be cold is...' When the qualifier is left out, one is left with an absolute. God is not qualified by anything. He alone IS in the grandest sense of the word. If we add a predicate to the infinite *esse*, the implications are of limiting God in some way, and God cannot be limited. What then can be said of the divine *esse*? In the *True Christian Religion* Swedenborg wrote,

> The being of God (*esse*) cannot be described for it transcends every idea of human thought; and nothing enters human thought but the created and finite, not the uncreate and infinite, thus not the Divine Being (*esse*) (TCR 18).

This is the equivalent of saying that no one has ever seen Jehovah, except Jesus who has made him known (AC 1990). People cannot grasp the idea of God as he is in himself because human ideas are limited by this world (DLW 17), and if people could grasp anything of the infinity of God, they would impose their own worldly ideas onto the thought, until they created many anthropomorphic images of God, obscuring instead of reflecting him (AR 961).

Yet, according to Swedenborg, and as we have seen earlier when discussing the influx of God into human souls, God has no wish to be invisible, and so reveals himself to humanity, in human form, so that people may know of him, respond to him, and be drawn into his presence. Yet people can have no idea of divinity from their own reason which is limited by their finite nature. Thus everything people know about God has been revealed to them, from which revelation they can have at least an intellectual idea of the nature of God's being.

From revelation, therefore, one may know that God is *esse* or 'being itself', and that there is no prior source. All things are derived from God's being[5] (TCR 19) as the primary substance. Swedenborg asserts that since

> ... God is Being (*esse*), he is also substance, for unless being is substance it is only a figment of the mind. For substance is an entity

192   Swedenborg's Concept of God

that subsists; and who is a substance is also a form, for unless a substance is also a form, it is only a figment of the mind (TCR 20).

Divine substance, like any other attribute of the Divine, is a hard concept to grasp. Philosophically, substance is the stuff from which the universe is made. Material substance can be circumscribed and limited by time and space, it has certain characteristics making it identifiable, and qualities, either accidental or intrinsic, giving its nature. Divine substance, however, needs to be understood according to a different paradigm. People cannot experience divine substance, nor can they qualify or quantify it. The only picture available is through a comparison with natural substance, and like all analogies, this breaks down.

Divine substance is the 'stuff' of God, it is infinite, eternal and above human comprehension. Yet it is the very being of God himself, from which and by means of which he created the universe. Swedenborg understood this divine substance to be the divine love, the *esse* or God, manifesting itself in his *existere*.

The logic follows a progression, God is being, not an ethereal being, but one of divine substance. That substance must take a form is as true of divinity as of anything created from it. Wood, for example, cannot exist outside of the form that it takes. Similarly, because the Divine is substance, it also has a form. This form should not, at this point, be confused with shape, but rather the divine form is what makes it possible for the Divine to become practical.

Swedenborg uses the Latin term *existere* to define the form of God. The term is defined as 'standing forth; coming into *existence*; presence, taking form' (Rose 1985, 16). The divine manifestation is the manifestation of the divine Being, or *esse*, bearing the same relationship as substance and form in physical objects. Since the *esse* continually manifests itself, it follows that 'both substance and form' can be spoken of in connection with God (TCR 20).

It is possible, on paper, to speak of *esse* and *existere* as though they are distinct, as one speaks of substance and form as though they were two. In reality, however, they cannot be separated in the same way as one cannot abstract the substance of an object from its form, or vice versa and still keep the object intact. Swedenborg describes this interrelationship as being 'one distinctly' (DLW 14, 17), saying,

> *Esse* and *existere* in God-Man are one distinctly like soul and body. There can be no soul apart from its body, or body apart from its

soul... *Esse* is not *esse* unless it exists, because until then it is not in a form, and if not in a form it has no quality; and what has no quality is not anything (DLW 14, 15).

These highly philosophical explanations of God's nature lay the foundation for Swedenborg's understanding of God. Speaking of God as he is in himself is tantamount to speaking of the human soul, hidden as the life force within the body, revealed in the speech and actions of a living person. The same is true for God. By explaining the nature of God above the heavens, so to speak, Swedenborg lays the foundation for the explanation of Jesus Christ and the Trinity.

From describing the nature of God in this way, Swedenborg is then able to infill the description. From understanding that God has being and manifestation, substance and form, it becomes necessary to understand what the divine substance is, and how it is manifested.

The *esse* of God is love, pure, divine love, and high above human concept except in generalized and philosophic terms. This love is uncreate and infinite (DLW 4), it is love in its very *essence* (DLW 5). It is not limited to time or space (DLW 7), but infinitely transcends the highest human thought (DLW 7).

It is not possible to understand this love except in its proceeding, or manifestation. This manifestation is the *existere*. The term Swedenborg uses to describe the *existere* is 'wisdom'. One should not confuse 'wisdom' with book learning, or in any conventional sense of the word. In the book, Heaven and Hell, Swedenborg writes,

> It is believed in the world that those who have much knowledge, whether it be knowledge of the teachings of the church and the Word, or of the sciences, have a more interior and keener vision of truth than others, that is, are more intelligent and wise; and such have this opinion of themselves (HH 351).

He then proceeds to define true intelligence and wisdom as the ability to see and perceive 'what is good and true' (HH 351). God, because he is divine love itself, is better able than any living creature to perceive goodness, and thus he is wisdom itself.

For Swedenborg, the divine wisdom is the divine perception and consequent activity of the divine love. While love is powerful, it is invisible and needs to be expressed before it can be seen. For example, a man's love for his wife is invisible and unknown, unless he expresses it in word and deed. So too with God. Since his love is love itself, and because that love expresses itself perfectly, therefore his wisdom in its first proceeding is also perfect. Together love and its expression in wisdom make a perfect one. This initial paradigm is of great importance as Swedenborg unravels the mystery of the Trinity.

Swedenborg acknowledges that human minds are unable to grasp the perfection of divinity. In several passages he explains that the *esse* or being of God transcends human thought, is indescribable and incomprehensible (e.g. TCR 18). From revelation it is possible to truly understanding the divine being – albeit within the limitations of the human mind. It is therefore also possible to understand the divine manifestation of that being (AC 4687). Swedenborg grounded his insights into the nature of God on this basic premise. As orthodox scholars base the doctrine of the incarnate Christ on the pre-existent Word, so Swedenborg builds the rest of his teaching about God on this basis of transcendent, infinite love and wisdom, causing and expressing one another in perfect harmony. This is the very being of God, the core of his *existence*. The fact that it cannot be expressed in human terms means that in order for people to be able to experience God, God must accommodate himself to their reception.

Essence and Existence

The first accommodation of God is a derivative of the *esse* (being) and *existere* (manifestation), which Swedenborg terms *essence*[6] and *existence*[7]. The two bear a cause and effect relationship with each other identical to that of *esse* and *existere*. Thus the being and manifestation of God, being higher than the abilities of human thought, are revealed to thought in a lower manifestation.

> The reason for using the terms being (*esse*) and manifesting (*existere*) and not *essence* and *existence* is because a distinction must be made between being and *essence*, and consequently between manifestation and *existence*, as between prior and posterior, what is prior being more universal than what is posterior (TCR 21).

At first it would appear that Swedenborg is simply using words. However, the appearance of a universal, higher, thing in a lower is a feature of his theology. Human thoughts, for example, are higher than and more perfect, than the words describing them. Similarly, the soul is higher than the body. One should not think of 'higher' and 'lower' in spatial terms, but rather as cause and effect. God's love is the cause of things, his wisdom the way that end is carried into effect.

Swedenborg describes this system of relationships as 'discrete degrees', which he says, 'are like things prior and subsequent and final; or like end, cause and effect ... the prior is by itself; the subsequent by itself; and the final by itself; and yet taken together they make a one' (DLW 184). An ... example of discrete degrees in daily practice would be a person's thought, speech and action. The thought is within the speech, yet thought and speech are different things. In addition, the word used to describe an action is a different thing. When a person thinks of walking, says, 'I'll walk', and walks, three discrete degrees are present. The thought is higher, or within, often first in time, but being the goal certainly first in end. The word, drawn from that thought, corresponds and describes it. The action, the final enactment of both thought and word is the effect.

Discrete degrees, therefore, explain the relationship of one thing to another, no less so in God than anything else[8]. The *esse* and *existere*, which together is God as he is in himself, form the prior, the highest degree, unknowable to human minds. The *essence* and *existence* of God, are the same things, but on a lower plane in which they have been manifested to be at least intellectually understood by human beings. Swedenborg writes,

> [w]e have distinguished between the being of God and the *essence* of God, because there is a distinction between the infinity of God and the love of God, infinity being predicated of the being of God and love of the *essence* of God, for as was observed above, the being of God is more universal than the *essence* of God, and the infinity more universal than the love of God (TCR 36).

How then, does he describe the *essence* and *existence* of God? If one could reduce God to the very core of his being, one would find inexpressible divine love manifested in inexpressible divine wisdom (TCR 37). All things are created from this love, by means of this wisdom. Thus while God in his being is invisible, his quality begins to become visible on a lower plane within creation, for on this lower plane ineffable love can be expressed as good, and wisdom as truth (TCR 38).

Goodness reveals love. Swedenborg describes how from goodness in creation one can come to understand something about the nature of love,

> There are two things which make the *essence* of God, namely Love and Wisdom, and there are three things which make the *essence* of

his love, namely, to love others outside of itself, to desire to be one
with them, and to make them happy from itself. The same three
things also make the *essence* of His wisdom, because ... love and
wisdom make one in God, while love wills these things, wisdom
gives effect to them (TCR 43).

By this definition of the divine love, Swedenborg unveils his insight
into the very nature of God. On the highest plane, the core of God is
infinite love. On a lower plane that love takes the creative urge. It is the
nature of love to love someone other than oneself, otherwise there
would be a form of divine selfishness, so God created beings, who are,
to all extents and purposes separate, from himself, on whom he can
lavish love[9]. However, because love also requires a free response, he
created people in freedom to accept or reject him. In their acceptance,
he can be one with them and make them happy. In this way, the highest
things of God are revealed in his relationship to the human race.

The being of God can be understood in the goodness coming
from it. This infinite love is the source of all things, most particularly of
the human race, for as Swedenborg writes,

... the end of creation was an angelic heaven from the human race,
and consequently man himself, in whom God could dwell as in a
recipient of Himself. It was for this reason that people were created a
form of divine order (TCR 66).

God accomplished this from his love by means of his wisdom, or truth.
Just as wisdom should not be confused with book knowledge, so truth
in this sense should not be seen as anything other than the expression of
goodness, in the sense that all things created by God are a true
reflection of his love and goodness.

This, then, is Swedenborg's concept of God as he is in
himself. One could compare this with the substance of God referred to
in the Nicene Creed, for there it is stated that God is of one substance.
Swedenborg does not make this correlation, but it would follow that
any physical manifestation of God would draw its origins from this
highly philosophical description of the nature of God. It needs to be
stressed that in Swedenborg's mind this presentation of the Divine
cannot be divided. Understanding this basic premise about the nature of
God makes it possible to understand the presentation of God in Jesus
Christ, not as a separate person in the Trinity, but as the manifestation
of divinity at human level, for, as already observed, the Divine itself is
too high to be grasped by human minds. It must be drawn down, or

accommodated, to the human level. If God had not done this, no one could have known of him, resulting in his goal of a heaven from the human race failing.

The Successive Revelation of God

Intrinsic to Swedenborg's concept of a God of divine love manifesting himself as perfect and infinite wisdom, is the teaching that God's love moved him to create human beings who could receive and reciprocate his love. Creation has no other goal, with the physical universe, itself an expression of this infinite love acting through infinite wisdom, being the environment for the human being, created into the image and likeness of God.

The human capacity to perceive and understand God has passed through a series of evolutionary steps. Although Swedenborg lived in an age prior to the theory of evolution, an inkling of it appears in his works, for he writes that God never creates *ex nihilo* (DLW 283), for 'from absolute nothingness ... nothing is or can be made' (DLW 55). He writes,

> [e]veryone who thinks from clear reason sees also that all things have been created out of a Substance that is Substance in itself, for that is *esse* itself, out of which everything that is can take form; and since God alone is Substance in itself, and therefore *esse* itself, it is evident that from this source alone is the formation of all things (DLW 283).

God created things in degrees and phases, from inmost things to outmost. The pinnacle of creation is the human being, who created in his image and likeness, is able to receive and respond to him in spiritual freedom, and thus fulfil the essence of his love (TCR 43).

Freedom to respond to God is contingent upon knowledge of God. The internal dictate that there is a God and that he is one (TCR 8) only finds expression or recognition in the acquired knowledge of God. It follows that God cannot be known except through a revelation of himself to people. Just as children grow in their understanding of God, so the human race had to be perfected from creation to a point at which they could receive and respond to his presence. The ability to know is the determining factor of humanity, separating them from animals, for while animals can receive the presence of God, they cannot respond with faith and love, and therefore cannot be conjoined to God in the same way as people. Conjunction with God is only possible through the reciprocation of God's presence, and it is this that makes it possible for people to have eternal life, which is nothing else than conjunction with God (TCR 48, DP 123). In acts of wise love, God has consistently revealed himself to the human race, in different ways according to the ability of humanity to receive him. This revelation to the human race is an important facet in understanding Swedenborg's concept of God, for it is the means by which the invisible God, high above human understanding, is made visible and accommodated to people. Swedenborg describes how, prior to the advent, God revealed himself in different ways down the ages, each time presenting an image of himself to make it possible for people to know and respond to him. In this way salvation was possible to humanity before Christ was born.

Swedenborg calls each broad category of revelation a 'Church'. Prior to the incarnation there were three 'churches', each adapted to the state and needs of the people at that time. A 'church' in Swedenborg's terminology is a dispensation of the divine to meet the needs of humanity in a particular era of their development.

The Most Ancient Church

The first people conjoined to God were those of the Most Ancient Church. Eschewing a literal interpretation of the first eleven chapters of Genesis, he links this church to Adam in the Garden of Eden before the creation of Eve[10]. Adam was not an individual man, but a race or group of people very different from modern people. Almost infant like, and in true innocence, these people were receptive of God's love. Unpolluted by evil or sin, it was possible to reflect that love in their own lives. Their innocence is depicted by Adam and Eve naked in Eden, by the awareness of God, and by God speaking to Adam.

The *Arcana Coelestia* describes how these Most Ancient people worshipped the manifestation of God in human form. Since love is invisible, they saw God as the form of wisdom, which is the manifestation, or *existere*, of God. Because God is the origin of all things human, they worshipped this manifestation as a divine human being, establishing a principle that will follow throughout Swedenborg's work. The recognition of God as a person, as human, was not anthropomorphic, for these initial people saw themselves as images of God, rather than the other way around.

The people of the Most Ancient Church were intuitive and did not aspire to high theological explanations of the nature of God. That would come later in history. Rather they internalized God's love, reflecting it in a form of infantile wisdom. For them God's love was the prime motivator, all else was effect.

These original people were the ideal. God created humanity to be conjoined with him as an act of love made possible through wisdom. Had people remained in this initial state of innocence, they would have become more and more aware of the divine love, their lives becoming more perfect reflections of it (AC 2661) enabling them to see God more and more clearly (cf. AC 10355). But that was not to be.

The Most Ancient Church began to decline with the creation of Eve. In linking Eve to the fall of that Church, Swedenborg is not being anti-feminist in any way, for Adam represented a race of people, not an individual. Eve describes a time in the history of this church when the people began turning away from God's love and sought their own love, or 'proprium'[11]. A person's 'proprium', or own love, is, by definition dead and lifeless, for all life is from God. Its inertness is described by the bone taken from Adam's rib from which Eve was made. Swedenborg describes it thus,

> Man's proprium when viewed from heaven looks just like something bony, lifeless, and utterly misshapen, and so in itself something dead. But once it has received life from the Lord it appears as something having flesh. For man's proprium is something altogether dead, though it has the appearance to him of being something; indeed it appears to be everything. Whatever is living within him comes from the Lord's life; and if this were to leave him, he would fall down dead as a stone, for he is purely an organ of life, though the nature of the organ determines that of the life-affection (AC 149).

A person's own love is selfish, in direct opposition to the *essence* of God's love. With the appearance of selfishness and all its ramifications on the human scene, the people of the Most Ancient Church turned increasingly from God to themselves, giving in to the pursuit of loves and insights drawn from their senses rather than from God Himself – as depicted by the serpent beguiling Eve. This decline did not happen over night. The genealogies in early Genesis depict a generational decline in the Most Ancient Church, until eventually the people severed themselves from God completely.

At the time of the fall of the Most Ancient church,

... a promise was given concerning the Lord's coming into the world, who was to unite the human to the divine, and by means of this union was to join [to the divine] the human race that was abiding with him through faith grounded in love and charity (AC 2034).

The first prophecy, in Genesis 3, 15, comes in the wake of the fall of the Most Ancient Church. As the people turned to selfishness, they lost sight of the love of God and his wisdom. In the centuries to come, knowledge of God as he is in himself, would all but perish, leaving only the shell of an idea.

Swedenborg describes the decline of the Most Ancient Church as chronicled in the Bible stories of Genesis from the time of Adam and Eve to the flood. Each incident and list of genealogies speaks not of an individual person, but of states that that church passed through, each one a decline from the one before. As people increasingly became selfish, so they closed their minds to God until he vanished from their sight. Eventually a flood of pure evil and falsity swamped their minds, and the dispensation perished[12].

The distinguishing factor of the Most Ancient people was an intuitive grasp of the nature of God. They were moved by a love of God rather than by an understanding of his nature – much as children love their parents without understanding them. With the fall of the Most Ancient Church this ability to love God was extinguished, and since that time people have had no innate love of God, but come to it through an act of will based on an understanding of the nature of God.

The collapse of the Most Ancient Church required a new type of human being who was not motivated by intuition, but by the ability to think apart from feelings[13]. This type of person could be taught that there is a God and that he is one, making revelation more a revealing of God's manifestation, or *existere*, than of his love, or *esse*. Although it is possible to come to love God through his manifestation, still the love is more indirect. In this new dispensation the focus shifts from God's substance to form.

The collapse of the Most Ancient Church is described in the Bible as the flood, not a flood of water, but of evil and falsity (AC 659). Noah represents a group of people within the Most Ancient Church who could be used by God to form a nexus between one dispensation and the next. The Church raised up by 'Noah' is called the 'Ancient Church'.

The Ancient Church

The Ancient Church related to God through the intellect, rather than through the will, so recording and presenting doctrine was of primary importance to them. The infinite God could not reach merely human levels directly, as it had in the intuition of the Most Ancient Church, but he had to present himself in ways that could be grasped intellectually and still lead to an emotional response. Swedenborg describes a process of God's self revelation at this stage of human history, a process that would continue down the centuries to the last prophet before the advent.

The people of the Most Ancient Church perceived God in a human form, an image that God maintained in presenting himself to the intellect of the Ancient Church. Swedenborg describes the human form as the essential capacity to love and put that love into action, thus the *esse* and *existere* of God. Since these two things are the very being of God, it follows that human-ness originates in God and is impressed upon all things of creation. In the environment of this world, people recognize this form by comparing it with themselves, expanding it to include broader concepts. Hence countries are personified, and entities are often expressed in human terms, so the centre of a city becomes its heart, roads are its arteries and so on. All this is from an instinctual insight into the centrality of the human form.

As in the world, the primary characteristic of heaven is also the human form. Swedenborg reasons that since people were created into the image and likeness of God, it follows that humanity does not begin with people, but in God himself. By humanity one should think beyond merely the shape of the body to the abilities of the mind, primarily the ability to receive and reflect God's love and wisdom. These mental abilities in turn become the source of the body, for this is what makes it possible to practice love and wisdom in both heaven and on earth. Heaven is a collection of angels, each one in greater or lesser degrees reflecting God in such a way that heaven itself becomes an image and likeness of God. Since God is the very source of all things human, it follows then that as heaven reflects God, so it also reflects an ideal humanity.

God used the familiar human form to present himself to the intellectual capacities of the Ancient Church. Since he is the essence of humanity, this presentation did not require any change in God, but an adaptation of divinity to a level at which angels and people could receive it. Swedenborg describes this accommodation as God 'flowing across heaven' – or transflux – and in doing so limiting the presentation or manifestation of the divine until the angels could perceive it.

As God flowed across heaven, so he took on this image of his humanity, limiting himself to the characteristics and limitations first of heaven, and eventually of individual angels. Firstly he limited the expression of his love and wisdom to that of the angels in general, until he became visible to the angels themselves. In the book, Heaven and Hell, Swedenborg writes that when 'the Lord appears in heaven, which often occurs, he [appears] in the form of an angel, yet distinguished from angels by the divine shining through his face, since he is not there in person... but he is present by look' (HH 121). His 'look' is the transflux across heaven by which he presents himself to angelic view.

Prior to the advent, God could only present himself at angelic level by means of this transflux. People in the world, however, were too far removed to see even this. To bridge the gap, God extended his transflux as far as possible, by focusing on a willing angelic subject who made it possible for God to 'put on' an angelic body. Putting the angel's sense of self to sleep, and using the angel's body as his own, and by making it possible for a prophet to see or hear on the spiritual level, God was able to communicate the necessary revelatory truths to the people of this world.

In this in filled angelic form, God dictated to or showed visions to prophets, who wrote down exactly what they saw or heard, or practiced exactly the commands given to them, no matter how strange they may have been. In this way Divine truth was passed down to earth, and the concept of God, seldom understood by the prophets or the people, was preserved in a written document.

Swedenborg relates that there have been two such documents. The first, or Ancient Word[14], was the revelation to the people of the Ancient Church. Written entirely in parabolic form it served as the basis of that church. One important aspect of it was its Messianic prophecy, for from the time of the fall of the Most Ancient Church, God began preparing for the complete revelation of himself at human level (see also De Verbo 15).

The Ancient Church lasted from the time of Noah until that of Abraham. Like the Most Ancient Church before it, it went into decline, for from its knowledge of God people began making symbolic representations of the Divine. In time they focused more on the images themselves, until the overarching unity of God was forgotten, and idolatry took hold. Once again knowledge of God was submerged, and once again God prepared to enter this world himself, in human form, to set to right the errors of the time.

According to Swedenborg the Ancient Church spread across much of the world. Beginning in the Middle East it spread south into Africa, west into Europe and east to Asia. The commonality of many of the world's religious ideas, myths and forms can be traced back to it. Many of its corrupt, idolatrous forms continued down to the time of Christ and beyond, still influencing humanity in the heritage of the Greco-Roman philosophy in Europe and in the religious beliefs of Africa and Asia.

The slide into idolatry made it necessary for the final preparation for the advent, using the Israelites as a matrix within the Ancient Church. This preparation took some two thousand years, chronicled in the Old Testament. Crafted from events within their history, augmented by prophecies, God used the Old Testament to form a blueprint of his personal life on earth – later Christ would say that he had not come to destroy the Law, but to fulfill it (Matthew 5;17).

The Israelitish church

The Israelitish church was the third dispensation, or revelation, of God to the human race. Its point, however, was not so much to instruct about the nature of God as to provide a pattern of human behavior deeply symbolic of spiritual realities. Each detail of the Israelite sacrifices, for example, depicted something about God. By performing them exactly the ancient Israelites maintained a correspondential and mystical contact with God and heaven.

Ritualistic observances of this sort did not entail any high theological or doctrinal understanding of God, although these did evolve in later centuries, especially after the return from exile. However, there was an incipient Messianism, taking hold in early Genesis accounts, and developing over the centuries, becoming more explicit over time, until they informed the scholar that a Messiah would come, who would be born of a virgin in Bethlehem, and so on (Pendleton. NCL 1965, 497). Jews, and many Christians, question whether the Messianic prophecies were written as such, or whether the message was read backwards into them. This remains a subject of conjecture. Swedenborg, however, portrays these prophecies as a steady revelation of God's intention to be fully revealed on earth when the circumstances of both the spiritual and natural worlds were ready to receive him.

The overarching point of Swedenborg's chronicle of the history of the churches is to show how the infinite and invisible God accommodated himself to the needs of humankind. God did not at any point change in this process, but he presented himself differently to suit the needs of humanity at different ages of history. God in himself is immutable, for divine love cannot change. The presentation of this divine, however, can and does change, for example, in the Old Testament God is often presented as an angry parent, scolding and punishing his children. Yet the *essential* love of God is never angry, but in order to bring erring Israelites back into order, he allowed them to perceive him in this way (AC 3131, AC 3425, AC 588, AC 1408 et al).

A further *essential* established in pre-advent churches is the oneness of God. 'Hear, O Israel, The LORD our God, the LORD is one!' (Deut 6, 4), became the rallying cry of the Jews, and the foundation of Christian monotheism. Each presentation of God to the Ancient Church and the Israelites reinforced this teaching, in the face of the tendency to worship idols.

Jesus Christ

The history of the churches before the advent culminates in the birth of Jesus Christ, to whom Swedenborg refers as 'the Lord' (AC 14). In his treatment of Christ Swedenborg deviates substantially from orthodox Christianity. He is not willing, at any point, to consider that Christ is anything other than God in human form, and how this came about and the processes involved form a great deal of his theology.

For Swedenborg it was important to see Christ's being in two distinct sections, from birth to death, and from the resurrection onwards. Rejecting the Chalcedonian formula of the unchanging God, Swedenborg taught that Christ underwent a 'divinizing' process during his life in this world; so that in his resurrection he was fully divine. This process is called 'the glorification'. Once glorified, or made divine, Christ presents the divinity to human view, in a way people can see and worship. God understands humanity because there is nothing in human life that as Christ he did not experience.

Christ is the visible God, or to put it in another way, he is the super-eminent, infinite being of God, brought down to human level in the limited and finite world. In the process the *essence* of God does not change, but the manifestation is, once again, accommodated to human needs.

Like Servetus before him, Swedenborg is adamant that Christ is not a second Person in a trinity of Persons, but the Logos, or Word of God, in human form. As such there is no distinction between the pre-existent divine and the human manifestation, except in the period between Christ's birth and death, when the divine was covered with a human form taken on from Mary.

The Son from Eternity

Ecumenically accepted theology expresses a belief that Christ has been the Son of God from eternity. Swedenborg rejects this idea saying,

> It is believed at this day in the Christian Churches that God, the Creator of the universe, begot a Son from Eternity, who descended and assumed a human in order to redeem and save mankind. This, however, is erroneous, and cannot be upheld when it is considered that God is one, and that it is utterly opposed to reason to say that the one God begot a Son from Eternity, and that God the Father, together with the Son and the Holy Spirit, each of whom separately is God, is one God. This absurd belief is completely dissipated like a falling star in the air, when it is shown from the Word that Jehovah himself descended and became Man and also the Redeemer (TCR 82).

In another place in his writings, Swedenborg dismisses the idea of a Son born from Eternity as 'a paradox' (Ath. Cr. 24), or as an idea that 'immediately flees of its own accord and vanishes' (Ath. Cr. 32). Swedenborg held that the early Christian Church fathers created the idea of a Son from Eternity to explain the divinity of Jesus Christ, and to protect him from the teachings of Arius, who taught that he was a creature like an ordinary human being.

For Swedenborg the Logos, described in John's prologue, is both creative and redemptive. This concept lays much of the foundation of his theology, and he uses passages from the Old Testament to prove this assertion, many of them used by orthodox theologians to establish the doctrine of the Son from Eternity (for example, Psalm 2, 7 and Genesis 18). While Swedenborg rejects the traditional interpretation of these passages, he maintains that they do speak of Christ, but as a presentation of the undivided divine presented in human form, not as a Son born from Eternity, who is the second Person in a pre-existent

Trinity. For example, he describes Psalm 2 as a prophecy of the Lord to come (TCR 101).

Christ was not a Son born from Eternity, but is God himself manifested first as the creative wisdom of the divine *existere* and after creation as succession of revelations to the people of the various churches. Jesus Christ is simply the final presentation in the flesh of the God who prior to the advent presented himself by means of the transflux through heaven and in the form of an angel filled with the divine presence.

Thus Swedenborg is able to state that 'Jehovah of the Old Testament Word is the Lord himself' (AC 1736, AC 1815, AC 2921, TCR 30, 9Q2). Also,

> [t]he Lord has existed from eternity, this becomes clear from the fact that it was the Lord who spoke through the prophets, and that both for this reason and the fact that the divine truth came from him he was called the Word, which is spoken of in John (AC 3704).

Christ from eternity was the transflux through heaven (AC 6280), not as a separate person in the Trinity, but as an activity – or Divine proceeding as Swedenborg calls it – of the Divine itself (Ath. Cr. 62). Thus there was no pre-existent Christ as a person co-equal or co-eternal with the Father, but an activity of the infinite on the human level.

> Be it known, then, Swedenborg writes, that there is no Son from Eternity, but that the Lord is from eternity. When it is known what the Lord is ... it will be possible, and not before, to think with understanding of the Triune God (Lord 19, AC 1736).

Who is Jesus Christ?

Swedenborg contends that the divine has always manifested itself to humanity, in different ways down the ages, according to the ability of people to receive and respond to it. This manifestation is 'the Word of God' that people perceived in human form, called 'Christ' and which, according to the Gospel of John, 'became flesh and dwelt among us'.

The Word is basically synonymous with the divine *existere*, divine wisdom and divine truth. It is the creative form of the divine love, subsisting as a discrete degree of that love, and yet forming one, indivisible expression of it. In the book, *The Doctrine of the Lord*, Swedenborg writes,

> ... 'the Word' signifies divine truth or divine wisdom, and the Lord is divine truth itself, or divine wisdom itself... As therefore the Word was the divine wisdom [proceeding] from the divine love, it follows that it is Jehovah himself, thus the Lord by whom all things were made that are made, for all things have been created from divine love by means of divine wisdom (Lord 1).

When the people of this world had so separated themselves from this divine Word as to be incapable of genuine and meaningful contact with it, the Word took on a human form from Mary. Thus as regards his soul, Christ was the divine Word, as to his human he was merely human (Ath. Cr. 30), so that at his birth the divine human that had proceeded from the divine love, was born in time (AC 2803).

In the birth of Jesus Christ the self existent being of God took on an imperfect human form, which at the resurrection would be so united with him that the invisible God would become visible in the person of Christ (cf. AC 3938). This act would establish the presence of God in heaven and on earth. Swedenborg notes that, 'before the incarnation there was not any Divine Human except a representative one by means of some angel whom Jehovah the Lord filled with his spirit' (9Q6).

The human appearance of God, revealed to people from the creation of this world, was, in Christ, born in time (AC 2803). Thus the central point of Swedenborg's theology of the incarnation and subsequent glorification of Christ is the relationship of the divine and the body in Christ.

Swedenborg conceived of people as existing in three distinct degrees, the outermost being the body, with its senses and ability to live in this world. In itself the body is merely a machine, cast off at death and left behind. Yet without a body human *existence* cannot occur, for the body belongs to the rigidity and fixity of time and space. The memories accumulated from physical sensation and experience form the basis of spiritual life. Nevertheless, in itself, the body is merely a receptacle of higher, spiritual life.

The degree of a person imparting this spiritual life is the soul or the 'human internal' (AC 1999). In many ways the soul can be compared to a transformer, receiving life from God that is, because it comes from God, infinite and divine. As the soul receives this life it limits it, passing down to the lower levels of the person a life that is finite, a life on loan, so to speak, from God, but with all the appearance of being one's own.

This life, carrying the image and likeness of God with it, gives humans the image of the infinite *esse* and *existere*. From it people have the ability to love in a finite replication of the infinite love. They also have the power to manifest that love, first in thought and then in act. The soul, receiving these abilities from the Divine, does not do the loving, thinking or acting, but makes them possible.

To bridge the gap between soul and body, God provides the nexus of the mind. As an image of the soul, the mind is made up of a will and an understanding with the ability to look upwards to God and downwards to the world. The mind is formed progressively from birth to adulthood, and refined during life in this world and afterwards to eternity.

Central to Swedenborg's teachings on the mind, which constitute an entire psychology in themselves, is the element of free choice. The mind is formed by a combination of inner inherited tendencies towards evil, particularly towards selfishness, and counterbalancing states of goodness implanted during infancy, acquired knowledge and sense experience. The combinations of these things, fostered by the choices an individual makes, lead to a regular selection of certain behaviors, thought patterns and loves. As these are systematically favored and chosen, so the person gradually chooses a path leading either to heaven or hell.

The humanity of Jesus Christ included all these elements. Swedenborg writes,

> [n]ow since God came down, and since he is order itself ... it was necessary, in order for him to actually become man, that he should be conceived in the womb, be born, and that he should be educated, acquiring in due course the knowledge by which he might attain to intelligence and wisdom (TCR 89).

Christ's conception and birth

To keep to order, therefore, God had to clothe himself with a human body, yet the body, being matter, must begin in a soul. In the *True Christian Religion*, Swedenborg asks, 'Do you not know that the Lord, when in the world, had a soul like every other man? Whence had he that soul, but from God the Father?' (TCR 110). He maintains that the soul is implanted at conception by the father. Without this assertion his doctrine of the incarnation and glorification would be mere Arianism, and the humanity of Christ would be that of an adopted Son. However, by stating as often and as strongly as he does that the soul is the divine presence of the Father, inwardly as the motivating force of Christ; Swedenborg lays the foundation of the process of glorification. In Swedenborg's teaching,

> the soul is from the father and the body from the mother, for the soul is in the seed of the father, and this is clothed with a body in the mother; or what is the same, all that is spiritual in a person is from the father, and all that is material is from the mother (TCR 92, cf. Ath. Cr. 46).

He writes further that in the seed from which every one is conceived there is 'a graft, or offshoot of the father's soul in its fullness, within a kind of covering composed of natural elements' (TCR 103). The masculine seed, therefore, is a reproduction of the father's soul.

> This can happen thousands and thousands of times, because the soul is a spiritual substance, having no extension, but fullness. No part of it is taken away from it, but the whole is reproduced without any loss. This is why it is fully present in the tiniest of receptacles, the sperm, just as it is in the major organ, the body (CL 220)

Swedenborg describes how this image of the soul descends from the highest spiritual substances that form the male soul, through the mind, clothing itself with images of the loves, interests and dispositions of the man (CL 172, DP 277). This clothing of the spiritual source of life with the external elements of life is the means by which inclinations, particularly towards evil, are passed from one generation to the next, explaining why characteristics are common in families (CL 245).

As the reproduction of the soul passes through the mind, so it also passes through the body, there being clothed with the physical things of nature, until, with the spiritual substances so clothed, they can be transmitted during sexual intercourse to the woman (CL 183, TCR 110). As the ovum is fertilized, so the natural substances of the father combine with those of the mother. This process comes about and is directed by the living vessels that form the soul, which, now in the mothers womb, being to form its own body, gestating in utero until birth. The human being therefore lives on two levels, with a soul receiving life from God, and the body making it possible for that life to exist in the world. Swedenborg writes,

> [s]ince, then, a person is not life, but is a recipient of life, it follows that the conception of a person from the father is not a conception of life, but only a conception of the first and purest form capable of receiving life; and to this, as to a nucleus or starting point in the womb, are added successive substances and matters in forms adapted to the reception of life in their order and degree (DLW 6).

Or, to put it another way 'the soul is the *essence* itself of a person and the body is its form; and *essence* and form make one, like *esse* and *existere*, or life cause and effect' (TCR 111).

Christ was different from ordinary people in that his soul was not the finite human soul of humanity, but the infinite soul of God. An ordinary person receives the soul from the father, but this does not make a person the same as the father, for in the replication of the soul, the seed is separated from the father. The newly conceived person lives as a separate, integral person.

However, since the soul of God is divine love, clothed in and manifested by divine wisdom, and since divinity cannot be divided, it follows in Swedenborg's thought that the divine soul was passed down in fullness to Christ at conception. An ordinary human soul finites and limits the life flowing in from God, but the divine soul does no such thing. Thus Christ's soul had the ability to transmit divinity directly to the human. Swedenborg refers to this concept in the following passage,

> A mother cannot conceive a soul, for this is totally opposed to the order according to which every person is born; nor can God the Father implant a soul from himself and then withdraw from it, as every father in the world can, since God is his own divine *essence*, and this is one and indivisible; and because it is indivisible, it is himself. For this reason the Lord says that the Father and he are one... (TCR 110).

At conception, then, Christ had two elements, a divine soul from the father that, unlike an ordinary soul was not separated from the father (because God cannot be divided), and a human body. In the New Testament the divine soul connecting Christ with his divinity is called 'the Father' while the body presenting that soul in this world is called 'the Son' for the relationship of one to the other is of cause and effect, as is that of a father and his son. These operated and interacted in exactly the same way as an ordinary person's soul and body do, the soul imparting life (although a person's soul is merely a receptacle of life, while Christ's was life itself) and the body operating in this world (Ath. Cr. 46). In the case of Christ, as in that of each person, the soul and body do not commingle, for they exist on two different planes, spiritual and physical. In Christ's case the spiritual plane was divine, and thus the body contained the divine within its physicality. However, to all outward appearances, Christ was no different from any other person (cf. Luke 4).

One cannot separate the soul from the body as one cannot separate being, or *esse* from its manifestation, or *existere*. The physical body Christ took on from Mary played an important role in the process of glorification, making it possible for God to come down to human levels of *existence*.

Swedenborg's doctrine of the human of Christ needs to be seen on these two levels. First is the physical body itself. This he dismisses as a 'mere covering ... composed of material things belonging to the natural world' (TCR 103). After death this body is laid aside.

The importance of this physical body, however, is that it makes a person, including Christ, able to interact with the material world through the senses. Thus the body from Mary, which in every respect was exactly like anyone else's made it possible for the divine love and wisdom that was Christ's soul, to be communicated to the people of earth. Like our own, this body was passable, feeling pain, hunger and tiredness. Without it Christ's life in this world would have been pointless, for he would not have experienced the gamut of this natural world without it, and thus would not have descended to the outermost limits of creation, nor could salvation have been possible.

The second aspect of the human taken on from Mary, however, is more important. This is the mental or psychological aspect of the body. As stated earlier, the masculine soul descends through the spiritual, psychological and physical degrees of a father, so taking on all his characteristics, particularly inclinations towards evil. As that soul forms a body for itself in the mother's womb, so it draws to itself suitable things to form an external body for use in this world.

The physical substances of the seed draw other physical substances from the mother. The same is true on the psychological level. In this way the inclinations of the mother are attached to those of the father, the father's being more internal and spiritual in both mind and body, while the mother's are more external and physical, forming the outer aspects of both mind and body. Yet they come together and cohere to form one person who at birth is a spiritual, psychological and physical image of both parents, having both the physical and psychological characteristics of both parents.

Swedenborg notes that these characteristics are generally tendencies towards the evils favored by the parents. He sees the human race as intrinsically selfish since the fall of the human race, redeemed by the ever present love and wisdom of God[15]. He calls these inherited tendencies towards evil 'hereditary evil' (TCR 520), saying '[h]ereditary evil, my friend, comes from no other source but one's parents. And it is not real evil that one commits, but a tendency towards it' (TCR 521). Hereditary evil

> ... consists in willing and hence in thinking evil; hereditary evils begin in the will itself, and in the thought thence derived, and being the very conatus[16] or endeavor that is therein, and which adjoins itself even when the person is doing what is good... (AC 4317).

At birth hereditary evil lies dormant, awakened as the child's mind begins to grow and the inclinations towards selfishness and evil find suitable outlets. When a person permits these inclinations to erupt into behavior, the inclination of the will is changed into an actual evil, and the person must then repent and battle against the evil to bring it under control once again. Swedenborg teaches that hereditary evils are passed from generation to generation, inscribed on the father's seed and in the mother's being. These form a large part of the psychological aspects of the human being.

However, since Christ's soul was from the divine, he had no inclinations towards evil from that quarter, but since Mary was merely human, as tainted with heredity as anyone else, she passed this taint on to him whilst he was in the womb. Swedenborg notes that

> [t]o some it may come as a surprise to say that hereditary evil from the mother was present in the Lord ... but there can be no doubt that it was present. For no human being can possibly be born from another human being without deriving evil from him or her (AC 1573).

Swedenborg also points out that hereditary evil from the father is altogether different from that of the mother. The father's hereditary inclinations penetrate right to the soul, while the mother's belong only to the external coverings of the mind and body – those parts of us that

live in this world. Thus paternal heredity is permanent, while that from
the mother can be rooted out and changed, otherwise no one would
have any chance of true spiritual life or salvation (AC 1573).

This point is important in understanding Swedenborg's
teachings on the glorification, or how Christ's body, taken on from
Mary, identical to everyone's body, became divine. In Jesus Christ,
God himself was fully present as Christ's soul. There were no
blockages, barriers or filters such as ordinary human beings have, and
without which all people would be divine. Through this soul the divine
lived within Christ, guiding and motivating him with love and wisdom.

This divine soul, however, only lived in the higher reaches of
the Christ who walked this world, as a human's soul, exists within the
higher, invisible parts of one's being. As in the case of all people,
Christ's divine soul was connected to a lower, limited tainted human
body. The divine could not yet be fully present in the body, for the
hereditary inclinations towards evil, taken on from Mary, formed an
effective blockage to the descent of the divine. Thus the divine could
not yet be present in the world, for it was, in the person of Christ,
circumscribed by the hereditary weight of human inclinations.

During Christ's life, this humanity needed to be put into order
to make it possible for the divine to descend to the most external, or
physical levels of human life. The process required of Christ that he
battle against these inclinations, until, wholly removed, his human
could be completely in filled with divinity, and he would become a
divine human.

The Process of Glorification

At the moment of his birth, Christ had a divine soul and an
infant human body. His soteriological life lay ahead of him, for he had
to create a mind, or nexus, between the divine soul and human body, in
order that the invisible divine could become visible in him. Aside from
the miraculous nature of his conception, necessary for the divine soul to
clothe itself with a human body, the infant Christ was, on the human
level, no different from any ordinary person. Swedenborg writes,

> It is clear that the Lord was born like any other, though from a
> woman who was a virgin, and that he had sensory perception and
> bodily desires like any other, but that he differed from any other in
> that sensory perception and bodily desires were eventually united to
> celestial[17] things and made Divine (AC 1428).

Christ 'was born as any other is born' (AC 1444), and so 'received instruction as any other' (AC 1460). As an infant he had to learn to sit, to crawl and walk. He learned to speak, and as he grew up he assimilated the language, culture and religion of New Testament Judaism, including knowledge of the things of the Old Testament written as a blueprint for his own life. As he grew older, so he could see the errors of belief and practice from the insights derived from his soul. In this way he could see the issues and battle stretching out ahead of him. To all outside observation he was exactly like everyone else.

Swedenborg's spiritual experiences in the spiritual world convinced him that all people are held in connection with both heaven and hell (HH 291ff). Although people are unaware of it, they are constantly in company of both good and evil spirits[18].

> These spirits have no knowledge whatever that they are with man... The Lord exercises the greatest care that spirits may not know that they are with man; for if they knew it they would talk with him, and in that case evil spirits would destroy him (HH 292).

Spirits are attracted and repelled by a resonance between their loves and the person's. A person who loves goodness will attract spirits who love a similar goodness. Since evil is opposite to good, that person may also experience attacks from evil spirits who are repelled by that love. Consequently people are held by these spiritual associations in a state of equilibrium, between good and evil. This equilibrium allows humans to live in a state of spiritual freedom while in this world, giving people the freedom to choose between heaven and hell.

As Christ grew through his childhood, so both good and evil spirits were drawn to his human. Evil spirits were attracted by the incipient evil loves contained in the hereditary from Mary and brought to consciousness by the experiences of life. During his formative years Christ, as with each person, was exposed to external, cultural influences that stimulated this maternal heredity. As with all people, this stimulation attracted spirits from hell, who exacerbated the tendency. Swedenborg taught that all people experience this during their lives, and at that moment of temptation one makes choices about embracing or discarding the thing exciting their hereditary tendencies. In this way people create patterns in their lives leading directly to heaven or hell.

The difference between Christ and an ordinary person is that people cannot sense the presence of spirits in any way – their presence is an unconscious factor in our lives, and since the final destination in the spiritual world is not determined by the presence of these spirits, but by the reaction to them, in the actions one takes, it is not necessary for people to be aware of them. Christ, however, was aware of the spirits around him, as is apparent in the New Testament where evil spirits frequently address him by name (e.g. Luke 4, 34, 41; Mark 1, 34). So Swedenborg writes that 'he too had communities of spirits and angels around him, for it was his will that everything should be accomplished in keeping with order (AC 4075).

However, Christ's divine soul made it possible for him to regulate the kinds of evil spirits who were around him. Swedenborg notes that 'he chose for himself the kind of communities that would be of service, and changed them as seemed good to him' (AC 4075). By allowing evil spirits to be with him, he was able to bring them also under his control and put them into proper order in hell (AC 4075). During his life in this world he faced and overcame every single grouping of evil spirits, and thus extended his control over the whole of hell[19].

The process by which he brought order to hell is called 'temptation'. Most simply defined, '[t]emptations are nothing else than battles and wars against evils present within oneself, and so against the devil's crew who activate evils and endeavor to destroy the church and the member of the church' (AC 1659). Christ experienced the powers of hell as they attacked the weaknesses for evil within the human, inherited from Mary, especially the primary evil loves of selfishness and worldliness[20]. Yet because this humanity from Mary contributed his natural, conscious living self, he experienced temptations as coming from within himself, as people do when they experience temptation.

Temptations are an assault by hell on a good love. Christ's love, his reason for being in this world, was the salvation of the human race (AC 9937), a love higher than any love ordinary humans can experience. The hells attacked this love with continuous ferocity, inflicting anguish on Christ, and even reducing him to states of despair. Swedenborg describes these temptations in many places, and writes, that since

> ... the Lord underwent the most dreadful and cruelest temptations of all, it was inevitable that he too should be driven into feelings of despair ... even to the sweating of blood, and that he was at this time in a state of despair over the end in view and over the outcome (AC 1787).

Why did Christ allow himself to suffer and be tormented in this way? He had assumed a human according to order, taking on the limitations and heredity afflicting the human race. His goal was to put this human back into the order of creation, making it possible, in his case, for the divine to descend to human level, and for ordinary humans to 'take up their crosses' and follow him. The process, however, laid him open to attack from hell, but it also allowed him to enter fully into human life. By taking on hereditary evil, he was able to conquer that evil, put it into order, walk the path, so to speak, that he asks people to walk[21]. Yet he also had to feel this battle as his own. If as certainly he could have done, he had simply reduced hell to order by fiat, he would not have been any more present or visible on our level than before.

So Christ allowed the hells to attack him with all their vehemence and force. Swedenborg notes that,

> [t]he fact that the Lord's life from earliest childhood right through to the last hour of his life in the world consisted in constant temptation and constant victory is clear from many places in the Old Testament Word ... as well as his undergoing temptations right through to his death on the cross, and so to the last hour of his life in the world (AC 1690, see also AC 1812).

The crucifixion was the last and most severe of the temptations Christ endured (AC 2776), for on the cross the last of the limitations of humanity were overcome (AC 2818). Swedenborg insists that it is an error to believe that the crucifixion constituted salvation itself (AE 778, Ac 2776). In his view salvation was a process, beginning at Christ's birth with the taking on of the humanity from Mary, continued through the process of temptation and victory, and concluded at Golgotha when the final vestiges of the corrupt humanity were put off (TCR 95).

The states of temptation, however, must be balanced by Christ's continual victory over hell. In this he united the purified humanity with the Divine. When Christ was in a state of temptation, he fought hell with power derived from his divine soul, which Swedenborg identifies as the 'Father' in New Testament terminology (TCR 97).

As he fought against and rejected the inclinations towards evil inherited from Mary, Christ cleared, as it were, his humanity from the things that had blocked communication between the inner divine soul and the outer body. As the blockages were removed the divine could penetrate into those purified areas. This process, taking the whole of his life in this world, led to the total rejection of the corrupted humanity from Mary, and the full descent into the purified humanity of the divine.

This cleansing was not done all at once. States of temptation, or battle, alternated with states of victory. Swedenborg describes these as the states of 'exinanition' and 'glorification'. 'Exinanition' means 'emptying out', which took place during the process of temptation. In this state Christ humbled himself before his divine soul, or Father, 'for in it he prayed to the Father' as if a separate being (TCR 104). The illusion of separation comes from the sense in temptation that God is absent (TCR 105). Unless Christ had felt this separation, his temptations would not have been real.

However, once the temptation passed, he was filled with a perception of the Divine. Swedenborg calls this the state of 'glorification' or union between the human and the divine. He writes that Christ

> ... was in this state when he was transfigured before his three disciples, and also when he wrought miracles, and when he said that he and the Father are one, and that the Father is in him, and he in the Father that all things are his; and when the union was fully completed that he had power over all flesh (TCR 104).

The final victory was the resurrection, when, 'the Lord rose from the tomb with his whole body, leaving behind nothing; consequently he took with him from the tomb the natural human itself, complete from first things to last' (TCR 109).

Swedenborg sees this process entirely in soteriological terms. The human race, separated from God by its collapse into idolatry with all its attendant evils, could only be saved by Christ taking on an identical humanity, overcoming the evils and making that human divine. In the process he brought hell into order and reorganized heaven. As he did this, so he made it possible for the once invisible divinity of God to be visible in the Person of Jesus Christ (TCR 2). By walking this same path in their own lives, people go through the same process (TCR 105), drawing from Christ's power the power to make it possible for them to follow in his footsteps.

Swedenborg uses the term 'Divine Human' to describe the risen, victorious Christ, in whom the divine of the Father is fully present in the humanity of the 'Son', literally a soul within the body. So he writes,

> As therefore his soul was the very divine of the Father, it follows that his body, or human, must also have become divine, for where the one is divine the other must be too. In this way and in no other are the Father and Son one, and the Father in the Son, and the Son in the Father (Lord 29).

The Holy Spirit

Swedenborg's concept of the Divine Human, God visible in Christ, does not exclude the Holy Spirit. By rejecting the Nicene and Athanasian tri-personal Trinity, he points out that

> ... the Holy Spirit is not a God by itself, but when mentioned in the Word, it means the Divine Operation proceeding from the one omnipresent God (TCR 138).

After the glorification of Christ, the divine could be directly present in the world in a way not previously possible. God had no further need of a transflux through the heavens to infill angels who then carried his word to prophets. Now it was possible for God to be directly present with people as they read the Word, think about and live according to it. Similarly, he is present in every human impetus to goodness and every aversion from evil.

The Holy Spirit is the presence and activity of God in creation, proceeding from the infinite love, through the Divine Human, right down to the outermost levels of creation. For Swedenborg the terms 'Holy Spirit' and 'Divine Proceeding' are synonymous[22], both of which describe 'the extension of the divine into the universe' (Ath. Cr. 145). He compares this extension to the light and heat radiating from the sun (Ath. Cr. 127), saying,

> The holiness which radiates from the Lord has divine good and divine truth within it. These go forth from the Lord unceasingly and are the source of light which shines in the heavens and the source of light which shines in human minds. Consequently, they are the source of wisdom and intelligence, for these are present within that light. But the way in which anyone is affected by that light, or wisdom, or intelligence, depends on how he receives it (AC 4180).

In many places Swedenborg describes God as appearing in the spiritual world as a sun (especially DLW 83ff, and HH 116ff). This spiritual sun is not God himself (DLW 93), but is the first appearing of God to the vision of angels, so that sometimes God appears to angels in the sun of heaven, and sometimes outside of it as a man (DLW 97). The light and heat of that spiritual sun are the vehicles carrying God's love and wisdom to angels and human minds, the light carries wisdom, the heat love. This proceeding of the divine, and the subsequent extension to all things of the universe, is what Swedenborg calls 'the Holy Spirit'. By means of it all things were created and are held in their order. From it people and angels are able to think rationally and love in accordance with their choices.

While the origin of the Holy Spirit has been a debating point between Eastern and Western Christianity for centuries, Swedenborg side-steps the argument by linking the Holy Spirit firmly to the very core of God. As seen earlier, the *esse*, or being, of God, is divine love. Like all loves, this is invisible unless expre*ss*ed by its manifestation, or *existere*. Swedenborg calls this manifestation 'wisdom'. The action of this wisdom, as it proceeds from and manifests the divine love, is the Divine Proceeding, or *procedere*.

The Holy Spirit is best defined as the divine truth (TCR 139), for as that proceeds from God's love, so it brings the ends of that love into being. The divine truth is the revelation of love, and the proceeding is the activity of the truth. As such one cannot be separated from the other, for one cannot separate the source of an activity from the activity itself. Because the divine love, by definition, has always existed, it has always manifested itself as divine truth. The proceeding of this truth, therefore, was first the agent of creation, and secondly the means by which the divine has been revealed to the human race. The transflux of the divine through the heavens, whereby God revealed himself to people and angels, was this Divine Proceeding.

However, the Holy Spirit as understood in post-advent times is not the same thing. Prior to the advent the Spirit of God could be present in the heavens, and only indirectly through angels with people on earth. This all changed when Christ was glorified. The process of making his human divine meant that it was now possible for the divine to penetrate directly to the levels of human minds. Since the advent, the Holy Spirit, or Divine Proceeding from that glorified humanity, is directly present at mundane level. Swedenborg expressed the difference in the Divine Proceeding before and after glorification in a letter,

> The Spirit of God [in the Old Testament] and the Holy Spirit [in the
> New Testament] are two distinct things. The Spirit of God neither did
> nor could operate on people except imperceptibly, whereas the Holy
> Spirit, which proceeds solely from the Lord, operates on people
> perceptibly and enables him to comprehend spiritual things in a
> natural way, for the Lord has united the Divine Natural to the Divine
> Celestial and Divine Spiritual, and he operates from these two
> through that (9Q5).

The perceptible presence of the Holy Spirit is primarily
soteriological. If the Holy Spirit is divine truth proceeding from God,
and if that truth is the means, not only of manifesting the divine love,
but also of carrying it into action, it follows that divine truth is a
powerful action or activity. Swedenborg notes that 'the Holy Spirit is
the divine truth, and also the divine energy and operation proceeding
from the one God' (TCR 139)[23].

The energy, or power, of God in human lives, leads people
along the same path Christ himself walked. Swedenborg rejects the idea
of instantaneous salvation as a belief springing up from a separation of
the Trinity into three distinct persons. Christ himself, in the process of
glorification described the process by which sinful humans are led to
reconciliation, through repentance, reformation in which a person faces
temptations, seeming to fight from self, but in reality doing so from
God's power, now in the natural planes of life. Finally, as evils are
removed, the person is regenerated and given new loves in harmony
with those of heaven. Throughout this process there is the appearance
that the person acts from self, but the reality is that the impetus to
embark on this spiritual journey, the ability to fight evil, and the joys of
regeneration, all come from God. They are, in effect, the results of the
presence of the Holy Spirit. Thus Swedenborg writes,

> The Divine energy and operation, signified by the Holy Spirit, consist
> in general, in reformation and regeneration, and following upon
> these, renewal, vivification, sanctification and justification; and
> following upon these again, purification from evils, and remission of
> sins, and finally salvation (TCR 142).

The Holy Spirit, then, is present in every aspect of human life. 'without
ceasing renders effective those saving graces in every person, for they
are the steps to heaven, and the Lord wills the salvation of all people'
(TCR 142). The fact that some people embrace this presence of God

whilst others reject it, is evidence of God's gift of human freedom. All people are in the sphere of the Holy Spirit, but it only brings spiritual development and salvation to 'those who believe on him, and who adapt and prepare themselves to receive him' (TCR 142).

People experience the presence of the Holy Spirit in two ways, corresponding to the heat and light of heaven. The first activity of the Holy Spirit is to awaken in people a desire for salvation, and secondly to educate the mind to make it possible for people to reject falsity and embrace truth, intellectually and in the activities of life. Since the Holy Spirit is active in the lives of all people, it is not restricted only to Christians. God activates these principles in all those who are willing to be activated, leads them according to such truths as they have, and so draws all who are willing to be drawn into heaven.

Notes:

---

[1] The original Latin had eight volumes.

[2] I.e. the literal meaning of the Scriptures (Rose 1985, 40).

[3] Swedenborg attributes the origins of idolatry to the creation of images depicting attributes of God, and over time ascribing those attributes to the images themselves, which then came to be worshipped as gods (AC 1241).

[4] It is interesting to note that the Athanasian Creed uses the same example to stress the same argument.

[5] One should not confuse this with pantheism, however, for God in creating created substances derived from himself, but in which his divinity has been removed, and thus matter is formed. Matter comes from God, but is not God.

[6] Latin, essentia, the being or *essence* of a thing (Chambers, Murray).

[7] Latin, existentia, *existence*, coming forth, manifestation (Potts).

[8] Discrete degrees originated in God, between his invisible and visible, from being and manifestation, and so were impressed on creation and humanity which is an image and likeness of God.

[9] Note that this separateness is an appearance. Swedenborg teaches that all life originates in God, human beings being merely recipients of it. The appearance of self-life makes it possible for people to act in freedom and thus to accept or reject God. By making people in this way, God fulfilled the first object of his love.

[10] A description of the Most Ancient Church is expounded in volume I of the *Arcana Coelestia*.

[11] Swedenborg uses the term 'proprium' to describe a person's own love. It refers to the part of a person belonging to oneself apart from God. If one could abstract anything of God from a person, their own love, or proprium would be left.

[12] AC 660, 'That a flood means a deluge of evil and falsity is clear from ... the descendants of the Most Ancient Church being possessed with filthy desires and immersing doctrinal matters concerning faith in them ... This... annihilated all truth and good ... It was this that led to the death of the people who existed before the flood.'

[13] It is interesting to note the progression of human brain development. Neanderthals and earlier people had a poorly developed cerebral cavity, indicating poor reasoning ability. Cro-Magnon man marks a change to increased cerebral capacity. Could this be a cross over from the Most Ancient to a later Church?

[14] According to Swedenborg, this Ancient Word is lost. It is, however, referred to in the book of Numbers 21, 14, 15, and 21, 27. Further references to the Ancient Word may be found cited by David in 2 Samuel 1, 18 and Joshua in Joshua 10, 13 (TCR 265, SS 103, De Verbo 15). The Ancient Word was in wide usage in the Ancient Near East (TCR 279), and there are indications that it was spread widely, even to China (AR 11). The spread of the Ancient Word accounts for the many similarities in religious belief in many parts of the world (AE 1177).

[15] Swedenborg rejects the concept of original sin, holding that people inherit tendencies towards evil, but only condemn themselves to hell by realizing these inclinations in will, thought and deed.

[16] Conatus = striving, endeavor, impulse (Rose 1985).

[17] Swedenborg uses the term celestial to indicate things of love. Rose defines 'celestial' as 'supremely heavenly; having a quality of goodness and love, or the quality of loving the Lord' (Rose 1985). Thus the 'bodily desires ... eventually united to celestial' means Christ's bodily things would be united to his love, which Swedenborg defines as the love of saving the human race, thus, "The Lord's love was the love of saving the human race, which love was the *Esse* of His life, for this love was the Divine in Him" (AC 9937, see also AE 557, SE 5554, AC 8875).

[18] Spirits were once people in this world. At death people leave behind their physical bodies, but the mind continues to live in 'the World of Spirits' where the spirit is prepared for eternal life in either heaven or hell. Those who love evil tend towards hell, while those who love goodness, are prepared for heaven.

[19] Swedenborg rejects the idea of Satan saying 'there is no one devil to whom the hells are subject' (HH 544). Instead he teaches that Christ is God of heaven, and 'it is necessary that he who rules the one should rule the other, for unless the same Lord restrained the uprisings from the hells and checked the insanity there the equilibrium would perish and everything with it' (HH 536).

[20] Selfishness and worldliness (love of the world) are diametrically opposite to love of God and the neighbor (AC 4612, cf. TCR 661, AC 10584, AR 53, et al).

[21] Swedenborg writes, 'Anyone who thinks that the external can be brought into correspondence [with the internal] without the conflicts brought about by temptation is mistaken...' (AC 1717).

[22] 'The Holy Spirit is not any other than the Lord, and that to "go forth" and to "proceed" is nothing else than to enlighten and teach by the presence, which is according to the reception of the Lord' (Lord 46).

[23] 'et quoque divina virtus et operatio'. 'Virtus' is variously translated as 'ability' (Chambers/Murray), 'power' (Potts) and 'virtue'. In light of the dynamism of the Holy Spirit as the activity of God, the term 'power' seems most appropriate.

Chapter Ten

Swedenborg's Concept of the Trinity

Reviewing Swedenborg's idea of the nature of God makes it possible to come to an understanding of the Trinity as he conceived it. It is not sufficient to say that Swedenborg rejected the Nicene, Athanasian and Chalcedonian concepts of the nature of God without further explanation. Swedenborg was quintessentially a man of the enlightenment, and, while his Christology is based on Scripture, and his claimed observation in the Spiritual World, it also appeals to reason. He never accepted the idea that a teaching became acceptable because of its antiquity, or because a respected teacher had uttered the words, he was too aware of how in the scientific and medical fields people had been led astray for centuries by false assumptions about the human body. The same could apply to religion as well. His allegiance was solely to the Word of God, and while his spiritual experiences gave insight into it, still, he based his doctrine on Biblical passages. Yet, if God is the source of all rational things, then God, too, must be rational, and, in the spirit of the eighteenth century he wrote, 'now it is permitted to enter with the understanding into the mysteries of faith' (TCR 508).

Centuries of Christian scholarship had failed to adequately explain the Trinity because they began on the wrong foot, just as Galen had convinced medical science of his ideas, and Ptolemy the astronomers that the world was flat, and for hundreds of years observation proved those things, so the initial concept of the Trinity has blinded the eyes of theologians from Nicaea onwards. From his point of view, the failure of the church to understand the Trinity arose from a basic misunderstanding of God. Patristic fathers spoke of substance and person, without stopping to reflect on what the substance of God was, and how that could be manifested in person.

By examining the concept of God Swedenborg portrays in his teachings, it becomes clear why he recoiled from the orthodox trinity. His system is a steady eluctation of one state of God to the next, from the hidden, invisible God, unknowable to human minds, to the Divine Human, Jesus Christ, and in this the Trinity is revealed. A study of Swedenborg's God shows how he saw the Divine, invisible above human understanding, was revealed down the ages, until finally in the Person of the glorified Jesus Christ, the fullness of the Godhead is set forth bodily. The Holy Spirit is the activity of God in general and of Jesus Christ in particular in human life. Thus the Trinity is not a Trinity of Persons, but of Person, 'three essentials of one God, which make one, as soul, body and operation make on in one person' (TCR 166).

At Nicaea the Trinity was described in terms of Person, or hypostasis, to depict states of the divine substance (ousia) coming into manifestation. Each Person reflected some aspect of the Divine itself, the Father the creative, the Son the soteriological, and the Holy Spirit the active. The difficulty the church encountered was that this division of aspects of God tended to lead the mind into an actual division – one compounded by the separation of the humanity and divinity within the nature of Christ at Chalcedon. A further difficulty, at least in the Latin West, was the dual use of the term 'Person', which could mean a mask, or presentation, but could also mean a 'person' in the colloquial sense of the word. Thus the division of aspects of God, led to a division of Persons, who, in time took on the qualities of being three individual persons, in the face of protestations of oneness, and ultimately in the middle ages to the triumph of faith over reason.

For Swedenborg this was heresy. His firm monotheism rested on the idea of one God continually revealing himself to the human race, not as three Persons, but as one, for God is one. The revelation implied something hidden and something revealed a cause and an effect. He saw this clearly in the make up of people, for people, created into the image and likeness of God; also have a trine of soul, body and operation (DLW 231). This model fitted his concept of God perfectly, and, unlike Augustine who made a similar connection and yet withdrew from it, Swedenborg adopted it as the primary expression of the Trinity.

Soul, Body, Operation

Swedenborg asserted that the only way to explain or understand the Trinity is to see it in terms of one Person in God. The elements of this

Trinity fit the model of soul, body and operation, which, forming a trine while yet making a complete indivisible one, is universal. The clearest expression of this relationship outside of God is the human being, created into the image and likeness of God. As each person has a trinity of soul, mind and body within him or herself, so do the angels of heaven. Describing angels, Swedenborg writes:

> An angel ... is seen in human form; nevertheless there are three things with him which make one. There is the inward part of him which does not appear before people's eyes, there is the outward part which does appear, and there is the sphere of life belonging to his affections and thoughts, which flow out far and wide from him... These three make one angel (AC 9303).

Relative to people in this world, the invisible inward part is the soul, the visible the body and the sphere of life is the operation. There is no difference in the make up of an angel and a person in this world[1].

The trinity found in people and angels is reflected in all created things, for,

> ... in order that anything may be perfect, there must be a trine[2] in just order, one under another, and a communication between, and that this trine must constitute a one; no otherwise than as a pillar is a one, at the top of which is the capital, under this the smooth shaft, and under this again the pedestal. Such a trine is man, his highest part is the head, his middle part is the body, and his lowest the feet and soles (Coro 17).

The universality of a trinal form exists in all things because it first exists in God, and, as the trinal order of things in this world does not cause a single object to be three distinct things, so neither does the Trinity within God cause him to be three distinct Persons. Both people and angels are replicas, on a finite scale of the infinity of God, human love and wisdom coming into action, reflecting the divine. The human trinity is limited and finite, stemming from a human soul passed from father to child, a body taken on from the mother, and the resulting activity of both. The fact, however, that people are created into the image and likeness of God, makes it possible to understand the nature of the Divine Trinity through comparison. Because these essentials exist in people, it follows that 'everyone acknowledges that these three essentials, namely, soul, body and operation were and are in the Lord God the Savior' (TCR 167). The difference is that God is infinite, and people finite, but 'no one, not even an angel, can have an idea of the Infinite except from things that are finite' (AC 9303), and this makes it permissible to draw the comparison.

In saying these things, Swedenborg is not denying the Trinity, but simply restating it as a Trinity existing in Jesus Christ. He states categorically that

> ... in God Himself ... there is a Trinity, consisting of his Essential Divinity, Divine Humanity, and Divine Proceeding, which make one. And this Divine Trinity making One is the Lord (AC 9866).

If one considers the way Swedenborg describes the nature of God, the explanation of the Trinity becomes clear. As shown in the previous chapter, Swedenborg's definitions of God always indicate a Trinity.

Esse (Being)	Existere (Manifestation)	Procedere (Proceeding)
Love (the quality of being)	Wisdom (manifestation of love)	Use (the activity of love and wisdom)
Good	Truth	Use
Father	Son	Holy Spirit
Soul	Body	Operation

The structure of this thought focuses the whole of the Trinity into the oneness of an end/cause/effect relationship between one aspect and the next. Since Christ is the physical manifestation, after the glorification, that is, of the Divine itself, and since it is Christ as the Divine Human who is active in human affairs, Swedenborg asserts that the entire Trinity is concentrated in Christ. So he writes:

> ... the trine is in one Person; and ... the trine which is named in it is the Father, the Son, and the Holy Spirit, that this is in the Lord [i.e. the glorified Jesus Christ], in whom the inmost, which is the *esse* of life, is called the Father; the second, which is the *existere* of life thence, is the Son; and the third is the proceeding, and is called the Holy Spirit, and that such a union was effected by God the Father, by His coming in the world (LJP 89).

The divine love, or Christ's soul, is termed the Father, while Christ, as the divine truth is the Son. The relationship between Father and Son is that of being and manifestation. For Swedenborg this can be described as good presenting itself as truth. Truth, on the other hand, has no being unless it originates in goodness (AC 2803). By his life in this world, as he successively rejected the inherent limitations and inclinations towards evil inherited from Mary, Christ became a form of truth able to receive fully the divine love, which was his soul. Thus the divine truth became visible in Jesus Christ, and in doing so makes it possible for people to have a concept of God's love.

To understand this further, it is necessary to understand that for Swedenborg truth is nothing other than a presentation of goodness (AC 3704). However it is possible to distinguish between goodness and truth, to describe them as if they were two different things (AC 3704), and thus one can speak of a Father who is the originating divine good, and the Son who is the expressive divine truth (AC 7499, AC 8897). The distinction, however, is an appearance, much as the distinction between substance and form, for while one can speak of a ceramic cup, one cannot separate either the clay or the cup and still have the cup. The distinction is mental rather than real.

Part of the difficulty in seeing this oneness between Father and Son as soul and body is what while in the world Christ spoke to the Father as if he was a separate being. Swedenborg answers this when he describes a state of temptation, in which the merely human things from Mary, and the evil spirits exacerbating those things, plunged him into temptation. Explaining this he writes,

> It is well known from the Word, in the Gospels, that the Lord adored and prayed to Jehovah, His Father, and that He did so as though to Someone other than Himself, even though Jehovah was within Him. But the state that the Lord experienced at such times was the state of His humiliation (AC 1999).

In these times Christ thought with his human mind, and, the Divine seemed remote like another being. Swedenborg balances these times with the states expressing unity between Father and Son. After the glorification, when the body was fully glorified, that is, made divine, there was no longer any such separation, and the relationship of soul and body became clearer. Thus Christ's words as he looked forward to this state, 'he who hast seen me hath seen the Father ... Believe me that I am in the Father, and the Father in me' (John 14:9, 11).

The third aspect of the Trinity, the Holy Spirit, is the activity of truth flowing from the glorified Christ (AC 7499). As was shown in the previous chapter this is the result of the divine soul operating into and through the divine body. The Holy Spirit, or Divine Proceeding, is God's love acting through his wisdom to produce the effects of creation and salvation. In addition to these one can add the laws of Divine Providence, which Swedenborg describes in the book, *Divine Providence,* as 'the government of the Divine love and wisdom of Christ' (DP 1). The activity of God is universal, and yet is in most individual things, because all things stem from the Divine itself (DP 201, 202). Thus through the Holy Spirit God is able to be present with and affect each detail of creation and every aspect of human life.

However, he stresses that the 'Holy Spirit is not a God by itself, or singly; neither does it proceed from God through the Son as a Person from Persons, according to the doctrine at the present day' (Canons IV.1.1). According to Swedenborg's theology, there is no difference in real terms between the Divine itself and the Holy Spirit proceeding from it, for the Holy Spirit carries the essence of divinity down to levels at which people can receive and be affected by it.

The Trinity, therefore, rests in one Person, made visible in Jesus Christ. Swedenborg sums this up by stating that,

> ... within the Lord the entire Trinity is complete, that is to say, within him are Father, Son and Holy Spirit, and thus that there is one God, not three, who, though persons distinct from one another, are said to constitute one Deity (AC 6993[3]).

Turning to Scripture, Swedenborg uses the passage from the Gospel, '[All] power in heaven and on earth has been given to Me' (Matt. 28:18), to demonstrate his point. In explanation of this passage he writes:

> As regards all power in heaven and on earth being given to the Son of Man, it should be recognized that the Lord already had power over all things in heaven and on earth before He came into the world, for He was God from eternity and He was Jehovah (AC 1607).

That power, however, was focused on the level of the natural world, when Jesus was fully glorified and made divine.

Discrete Degrees

Swedenborg does not deny the Trinity, but expresses it in the oneness of God in the person of Jesus Christ. It would be simplistic to assume that he denies the differences between the aspects of God, for although these conspire to make one, still the soul is within the body, but is not the body, and the body is within but not the activity itself. Each exists within its own sphere.

To understand this Swedenborg introduces the concept of degrees, described earlier as the relationship of a higher and a lower state, much like end cause and effect. The doctrine of degrees runs throughout Swedenborg's teachings, and without an understanding of them, one is not able to understand his general principles (DLW 184).

All things are created in degrees, of which there are two distinct types, discrete[4] and continuous (DLW 184). Continuous degree are those of a 'gradual lessening or decreasing from grosser to finer, or from denser to rarer ... precisely like the gradations of light to shade, or of heat to cold' (DLW 184). They exist within the discrete degrees. Swedenborg writes that

> ... discrete degrees are entirely different, they are like things prior, subsequent and final, or like end, cause and effect. These degrees are called discrete, because the prior is by itself; the subsequent by itself; and the final by itself; and yet taken together they make one (DLW 184).

Each level of a discrete degree 'has a distinct existence[5]' (DLW 184), and each degree can be perfected by continuous degrees. The mind is a discrete degree above the body, for it is within the body, and operates into it. Yet the mind can be perfected to eternity without reference to the body – except insofar as any information needed in the mind for perfection must needs enter through the bodily senses. This perfection is a continuous degree. Similarly, the body, can be perfected apparently separately from the mind, for example through nutrition and exercise, thus different continuous degrees exist on each level.

Despite the appearance of separation, discrete degrees do not act independently of each other, for they make a single entity from inside out (DLW 189). The substance of the inmost, or highest degree is within the substance of the second or middle degree, which in turn is within the outermost, each acting as a soul to the body of the lower degree. If one compares these degrees to end, cause and effect, then it becomes clear that 'the end begets the cause, and, through the cause the effect, that the end may have form' (DLW 189). The unity of the degrees begins in the end, and is completed in the effect.

The effect, or outermost of these degrees is the 'complex, containant and base of the prior degrees' (DLW 209). Into it the whole force of the higher degrees is concentrated, where they take their form and give external expression of their existence. For Swedenborg this external is the total composite of all things prior, and as such the fullness or completeness of the higher things. Love and faith, for example, must find expression in works in order to truly exist, and unless they do, they 'are only like something airy which passes away, or like phantoms in air which perish; and they first become permanent in man and a part of his life, when he practices and does them' (DLW 216).

Further, this lowest degree, containing the fullness of the two higher degrees, is also the most complete, for it contains the substance of the first degree, the form of the second, and brings these into being in the activity of the third. Thus, the whole is caught up in the outermost degree and the whole acts as a one in harmony and power.

This concept of discrete degrees is crucial to understanding Swedenborg's reasoning behind the Trinity. Since he does not deny a Trinity, but expresses it in terms of an individual person, it follows that discrete and continuous degrees exist in God as well as in creation, with the difference that

> ... in the Lord the three degrees of height are infinite and uncreate, because the Lord is love itself and wisdom itself; and because the Lord is love itself and wisdom itself, he is also use itself. For love has use for its end, and brings forth use by means of wisdom, for without use love and wisdom have no boundary or end, that is no home of their own ... These three constitute the three degrees of height in subjects of life (DLW 230).

The degrees of height in God make it possible for the Trinity to exist. Love is the inmost or highest degree. It is God's being, and manifests itself as wisdom. Love and wisdom are intimately related, but they are not the same thing, although one is within the other, as substance is within form. The final degree is the operation or use of God, this is the effect, or lowest level, in which the love, expressed as wisdom is communicated. These degrees within God work together as a one, seamlessly presenting Him to the view of the human race, much as a person's mind, body, and operation present him or her to the view of others. The Trinity only comes to view in the Divine Human who is Jesus Christ. At all times, Swedenborg is insistent that the Trinity only exists in Christ, for he is the Divine Human, presenting God to human view, and acting in human lives.

The Trinity before Christ

Since Swedenborg so strongly asserts that the Trinity only exists in Christ, how does he explain the nature of God before the advent and glorification of Christ? He rejects the idea of a Trinity of Persons from eternity, calling this 'a Trinity of Gods' (TCR 172). He writes,

> In the Christian world at the present day a divine Trinity is acknowledged as existing before the creation of the world. It is based on the belief that Jehovah God from eternity begot a Son, and that the Holy Spirit then came forth from both, and that each of these three is a God by Himself or separately, since each person subsists from himself (TCR 170).

In the previous chapter, it was shown how Swedenborg rejected completely the 'Son from Eternity'. For him this is little different from tritheism (TCR 170, Canons 33). He quotes from the Athanasian Creed to give substance to his argument:

> There is one Person of the Father, another of the Son, and another of the Holy Ghost. The Father is God and Lord, the Son is God and Lord, and the Holy Ghost is God and Lord, nevertheless they are not three Gods and Lord, but one God and Lord; for as we are compelled by Christian verity to acknowledge each Person by himself to be God and Lord, so we are forbidden by the Catholic religion to say that there are three gods or three lords (TCR 172).

The only thing withholding the Church from believing in three Gods is the monotheistic ethic of the Christian Church. When the medieval scholastics allowed their reason to explore this matter, they arrived at the conclusion of three Gods, and, bound by the strictures of the church, held reason in abeyance to faith.

Rejecting the imagery of three Persons in the Trinity, Swedenborg recognizes only One (Canons 33).

Embracing a Trinity in the Person of Jesus Christ, Swedenborg side-steps the issues of tritheism, but is pressed to explain how the Trinity worked prior to the resurrection of Christ. He poses and answers the question himself.

> It has been said that one divine by itself is not possible, but that there must be a trine, and that this trine is one God in essence and in

Person. It may now be asked, what trine God had before the Lord took on the Human and made it Divine in the world? (AE 1112).

Answering his own question, he notes that God has always been a human, or at least in human form, for the essential qualities that make humanity, from which people recognize humanness in others, and so in God, comes from God (DLW 11). As was shown earlier, the essence of humanity rests in the trinity of soul, body and operation (TCR 166). It was also shown that these existed in God as *being, manifestation and proceeding*, or love, wisdom and use. These in themselves formed a trine, the most elemental aspect of the Trinity, for 'God without a trine is not possible' (AE 1112).

The trinity as it exists in Jesus Christ, however, did not exist at that point in a way that human beings could see or conceive of it. Prior to the advent, God was present in every part of creation through his love and wisdom – his presence being the Divine Proceeding, but he could not be present directly on the lowest levels of human life, that is at the level of thought drawn from the senses operating in this world, because human evil made this impossible by being unreceptive of the divine.

God has always presented himself to human beings. Before the fall of the Most Ancient Church, he could directly affect people's interior beings. After the fall, however, he could only be indirectly present, through the vision of angels filled with his spirit, through the writings of prophets, and indirectly through the sacrifices of ancient Israel. However, his presence was indirect. The trinal form of God, always present could not be seen.

Swedenborg writes that before the advent, God was present in heaven actually, but only potentially on earth (DLW 233). That potentiality changed, however, when he put on the humanity of Christ, including the corrupt natural inclinations inherited from Mary. For the first time, God could, in Christ, reach down to the lowest levels of human existence. In Christ's body he could fight the hells, reducing them to order, and so save the human race (TCR 2). Thus in Christ the divinity was able progressively to penetrate to the very boundaries of creation.

With the resurrection this state was made permanent, for in Christ the hidden divine soul was revealed and could be directly present with people in the glorified, or divine, body and mind of Jesus. In Christ the potential nature of God's presence on earth is realized and becomes an actual presence. The trinal order of God, then is fixed, in that the second essence, the manifestation or *existere*, the Word or Logos, was now perpetually in view of the people. So, he concludes, 'it was after creation that a Divine Trinity came into being, for then from the Father was born the Son, and from the Father by means of the Son proceeds the Holy called the Holy Spirit' (Canons 33).

The apparent paradox of a trine always existing in God, but the Trinity only after the incarnation and resurrection of Jesus Christ disappears. By denying a Trinity of Persons, Swedenborg denies the orthodox Trinity from eternity, and by focusing the revelation of God in Christ, he demonstrates how the fullness of God can only be revealed in the Son, not as a second person, but as the manifestation of God.

Reworking the Athanasian Creed

Swedenborg's concept of the nature of God and of the Trinity is radically different from the beliefs of the Christian Church in general. In his mind the divided Trinity established at Nicaea and confirmed in later Councils so impregnated the theology of the Christian world that few if any people stopped to reflect on it. Even the Reformation, which changed so much of Christian theology, stopped short of reexamining the central teachings of the nature of God. The concept of the Trinity did not change because 'few study into the differences of dogmas among the churches...' (BE 18). Even those who did study Scripture during the Reformation, and rectified many wrongs of the past, shied away from exploring the issue of the Trinity, as it was the underpinning of their new doctrines of salvation by faith alone and the imputation of the merit of Christ for the atonement of sin.

Swedenborg, in rejecting the Trinity of the past, presents a different answer to the questions of the nature of God, but is his theology inimical to standard Christianity? How do his teachings agree with or disagree with the orthodox? It is possible in his writings to trace this comparison, especially in relation to the Athanasian Creed[6], to which he refers frequently. He suggests that if one was to substitute Person in place of Persons, and think of God as one, the Athanasian Creed in its broad outlines would be in agreement with his own theology. The basic principals of the Creed, that God is one in three Persons, can be explained in such a way that they agree with Swedenborg. The key, however, is to see the Persons as attributes, soul, body and operation, of one Person, rather than as three distinct Persons.

If one examines the Athanasian Creed, step by step, using the principal of a Trinity in one Person instead of three Persons, one finds large areas of overlap.

One God

Swedenborg quotes the Athanasian Creed as stating, *That we worship one God in Trinity, and Trinity in unity.* He is willing to concede that Athanasius saw God as one (Ath. Cr. 8). This is borne out by the opening statement of ONE GOD. Here Swedenborg is in harmony, for to say anything different would be unthinkable, it would remove the church entirely from its Jewish roots, which were strictly monotheistic. Also the thrust of the earliest and most venerable of Patristic Fathers is that God is one.

The reality of the New Testament, however, is that it expresses this oneness in terms of a Trinity. Swedenborg notes that Athanasius 'assumed three persons in favor of their principle' (Ath. Cr. 8). This was an effort to express the Scriptural realities of Father, Son and Holy Spirit as aspects within that oneness. However, whilst Scripture speaks of this 'Trinity', it never uses the term 'Trinity', nor does it ever comment on the Father, Son and Holy Spirit as being three Persons derived from the same substance – that doctrine was derived by the Church Fathers. The weight of Biblical teaching is that God is one. The Prophecies speak of this one God being born into the world, and the Gospels preach that 'the Father and I are one'.

However, like Athanasius, Swedenborg is not reluctant to use the term 'Trinity', for it expresses the relationship of the different degrees within God. It is interesting to note his reason why Trinitarian terms are used in Scripture.

> ...in the Word the names Father, Son and Holy Spirit were used in order that people might acknowledge the Lord and also the Divine within Him. For mankind was in such thick darkness, as it also is at the present day, that it could not in any other way have acknowledged anything Divine in the Lord's Human, being wholly incomprehensible to them, it would have been entirely beyond belief (AC 6993).

The language itself, therefore, is an expression of all that is within Christ, yet used to protect those unable to grasp it from profanation. The truth of this statement is borne out by Arius who denied the divine within Christ, and by Athanasius, who, using the appearances of Trinity, restored this divinity to him. Swedenborg believed that in order to protect Christ from the Arian heresy that would eventually lead to denial of him, Christ allowed the Church to think in terms of three, because they did not understand the Word or the spiritual sense of the Word (Ath. Cr. 13,15). In a similar vein he writes in the *Doctrine of the Lord:*

> ...it was of Divine Permission that Christians at first received the doctrine of three Persons, provided that they at the same time received the idea that the Lord is God, infinite, almighty, and Jehovah. For unless they had received this too, it would have been all over with the Church (Lord 55).

The principle which makes the Athanasian Creed permissible, is that Christ is God in human form. This, of course, was at the forefront of the mind of those who wrote this Creed, and it shines through in many places in the Creed. For example, it says, 'The Godhead of the Father, of the Son, and of the Holy Spirit, is one and the same, the glory equal, and the majesty co-eternal'. Any Arian would understand this as a rejection of Arius teaching that Christ was a creature, and not of the same substance with the Father. In another place, the Creed states that 'there are not three infinites, nor three uncreates, but one uncreate and one infinite... and there are not three Almighties, but one Almighty... and there are not three Gods, but one God'.

The emphasis in the creed, then, is that there is one God in Trinity, and Trinity in unity. As such Swedenborg's thought is in keeping with it, for it allows an understanding of Christ as divine, although based on Scriptural ignorance (Ath. Cr. 13,15), and at the same defeating Arius.

Swedenborg further excuses this creed on the basis that it was written by 'simple folk' who 'understood everything in accordance with the literal import of the words' (Lord 55). If they had substituted the idea of Person instead of Persons, then the oneness of God would have been saved, whilst still allowing for a Trinity.

Three Persons

Having accepted the first basic premise of the Athanasian Creed, that God is one, Swedenborg turns his attention to the second, more contentious issue, the appearance of that one God. True to their era, the writers of the Athanasian Creed use the term 'Persons' to define the appearance of God. It is on this point that Swedenborg makes his stand, and yet, if one defined Person as he defines it, then even the statements made at this point are true, or so he held.

Swedenborg's difficulty with the Athanasian Creed is the use of the term 'Person', or in the Greek 'hypostases'. The immediate image of Person is that of a separate individual. Athanasius does not dispel this image by his description of the Persons, for the Creed affirms that 'there is one Person of the Father, another of the Son, and another of the Holy Spirit'. At the end of the Creed, the image of three Persons is exacerbated by the very literal image of the Son sitting 'on the right hand of the Father God Almighty'. This imagery implies a threeness, giving root to the later deterioration of the concept of the Trinity into three Gods. To the creed's credit from Swedenborg's point of view, it does indicate that they are 'one and the same, the glory equal, and the majesty co-eternal' – so that within the expression of separateness there is a restatement of the overarching teaching that God is one.

Swedenborg found this separation of the Divine essence into Persons hard to reconcile with the repeated emphasis that they are nevertheless one and the same. As was shown in an earlier chapter, he believed that there was a human tendency to honor one God with the lips, and acknowledge three in thought (TCR 7). Athanasius would have denied that three Persons equated to a plurality of Gods. He consistently insists that there is one God. For example he notes that

> ... the fact that there is one Universe only and not more is a conclusive proof that its Maker is one... if the one universe were made by a plurality of Gods, that would mean a weakness on the part of those who made it, because many contributed to a single result... if the universe had been made by a plurality of gods its movements would be diverse and inconsistent... Creation, then, being one, and the Universe one, and its order one, we must perceive that it's King and Artificer also is one (Athanasius. Contra Gentes 39).[7]

When Swedenborg contemplated the nature of the term 'Person' he described them as 'attributes[8] of one essence', which in turn make three Gods, 'and they call them three persons or three Gods from the three attributes' (Ath. Cr. 57). He claimed that by using the term in this way, the early Christians followed in the footsteps of the ancient Jews and Gentiles, both of whom made distinct Gods out of divine attributes (Ath. Cr. 57), which ultimately led to idolatry.

However, in the *True Christian Religion*, Swedenborg follows Athanasius' example of setting out the three attributes of the Divine, writing chapters on God the Creator, Christ the Redeemer, and the Holy Spirit. The difference, however, is that rather than leaving them seemingly separate, with the appearance of the Son seated on the Father's right hand, he sought to re-establish the unity of God in the Person of Christ Jesus Christ.

It is not wrong, therefore, to speak of three attributes or qualities of God. They exist. For Swedenborg, the problem with the Athanasian Creed is that instead of reuniting these qualities into a coherent form, it leaves them separate, as Persons, rather than components of one Person. The result, he maintained, is that the church 'has been based on the mental idea of three Gods, but on the lip confession of one God' (TCR 180).

In view of this, Swedenborg stresses over and over that, 'the Doctrine of the Athanasian Creed agrees with the truth, provided that by a Trinity of Persons is understood a Trinity of Person, and that this Trinity is in the Lord' (Lord 55). He then describes how in a Trinity of Person the Divine is the Father, the Divine Human the Son, and the proceeding Divine the Holy Spirit (Lord 57). To put it another way, when people think that the Divine is in Christ and the Holy Spirit proceeds from him, then they think of three in one Person (AC 10822).

When viewed from this perspective the Athanasian Creed agrees with Swedenborg's concept, so much so, that Swedenborg says,

> ... it is in complete harmony if only one God is acknowledged, so that there is no thought of three persons. If in accordance therewith the Creed of Athanasius is read, without allowing any other idea to enter, then full harmony is effected (Ath. Cr. 30).

Further, we are invited to

> [t]ake the idea that there is one person, with a Trinity in that Person, and you will see that the Creed of Athanasius will coincide and agree from beginning to end without any paradoxes or things that must be of faith although not understood (Ath. Cr. 110).

The Acceptable Athanasian Creed

Based on these two points of agreement (with adjustments), Swedenborg, demonstrates areas in which the Athanasian Creed, rightly understood, is in harmony with his own teaching. In the little book, *The Athanasian Creed*, he gives a list of areas where the Creed is acceptable, provided one regards the Trinity as being a Trinity of Person, not a Trinity of Persons.

Christ allowed Himself to be born.

The entire reason for writing the Athanasian Creed was to defend Christ's divinity, and this the Creed does well, stressing that 'such as the Father, such as the Son'. The first step in building a more complete idea of Christ is acceptance of his divinity and the fact that this divinity became human. To Swedenborg this is such an obvious fact it hardly needs to be said at all. But it was not obvious in the days of the Arian Controversy when Athanasius was Bishop of Alexandra.

The stress in the Creed of Christ's divinity is the first step to accepting him as God. It is also important to recognize the concept that this divinity could become human. Swedenborg's theology underpinning this is quite different from that of the Christian tradition. He speaks in many places of Christ's divine soul, implanted in Mary, clothing itself with a human body, taking on human weaknesses and inclinations towards evil, so that during his life in this world he had a dual nature, perfecting the human by expunging the evil through the process of glorification until the human was able to contain the Divine.

However, Christian theology, as opposed to Swedenborg's, is based on Paul's teaching that the advent entails Christ 'emptying' himself of divinity to take the form of a servant dying on the cross, as is described in Philippians 2:7-8. It should be pointed out that Paul uses this passage to cite humility and self-giving (Reid 1990:56), but it has become the explanation of how the Divine came to be man. This emptying of himself, known from the Greek word, kenosis (to empty), indicates a separation between the human and divine in Christ. As the idea grew, so it was assumed that the Son of God was the Word, or the Logos, through whom all things were made. After the fall of humanity, the only route to salvation was by means to this Logos, yet in its divine state it could not come to earth, nor could it taken on human sins, suffer and die.

Thus Christ had to empty himself of divinity to come to earth, and the man who was crucified, while having a divine nature - which would be so heavily contested at the Councils of Ephesus and Chalcedon - was in fact an ordinary man to outward appearances.

This, however, left open the question of his divinity. Arius, for example, exploited this idea to deny the divinity altogether. Perhaps unwittingly, Athanasius built into the Creed the concept that it was indeed the divine that was born into this world, not merely a man emptied of his divinity. He does this by stressing the oneness of the Trinity, while saying in the Creed,

> [f]urthermore, it is necessary for salvation that he believes rightly the incarnation of our Lord Jesus Christ. For the true faith is that we believe and confess that our Lord Jesus Christ, the son of God, is God and Man. God of the substance of the Father, begotten before the world, and man of the substance of the mother, born in the world.

Thus from Swedenborg's point of view, the Creed preserves the true relationship of the Divine within the Human, as a soul is within the body. This Swedenborg can agree with whole-heartedly.

The Divine of the Father took on a Human

The second point of agreement Swedenborg outlines, opens up a whole area of Christology and Trinitarian thought. Swedenborg points out that it is not really sufficient to say that the Divine put on a human when it entered the world (Ath. Cr. 30), because those who divide the Trinity into three separate Persons would argue that the Divine is the substance of God, and in the human form it is the Son of God, second of three Persons. To follow that line of argument would lead one to an affirmation contrary to the unity in Trinity.

However, he asserts that 'when it is said that the Divine of the Father put on the Human, the idea today in the Christian world is opposed' (Ath. Cr. 30). The opposition comes from the belief that Father and Son are separate beings. But he points out that the Creed insists that they are not, saying,

> [j]ust as the Father is infinite, eternal, uncreate, omnipotent, God the Lord, so is the Son, for no one of them is first or last, greatest or least, but are altogether equal (Ath. Cr. 30).

This equality, seen in the context of one Person, could be interpreted to mean sameness, for if one divine is equal to another, then they must be

242 Servetus, Swedenborg and the Nature of God

the same divine. It is perfectly permissible, then, to state that the Divine that assumed the Human was indeed the divine of the Father.

From this it is a small step to the statement of a Trinity in Person that the Father is within the Son, as a soul in the body. By reading the Athanasian Creed from Swedenborg's teachings, one can be led to this conclusion. However, before this conclusion can be fully established, there are several more steps to take into account.

The Rational Soul and Human Body.

The Creed states that Christ was 'perfect God and perfect man, consisting of a reasonable soul and a human body; equal to the Father as touching the Divine, and inferior to the Father as touching the Human'. This section of the Creed is difficult to understand, for the words are opaque. The term, 'reasonable soul' is especially difficult. Many have interpreted it to mean that Christ derived a soul from Mary, and it is therefore one of the points raised by critics against this Creed.

Swedenborg confirms that Christ was 'perfect God and perfect Man' (Ath. Cr. 30). He was 'perfect God' because he had a divine soul. The definition of 'perfect man', however, is harder. That Christ became a perfect man through the process of glorification is central to Swedenborg's doctrine. But in order to be glorified, in order to do the acts of redemption and bring people to salvation, required that he also take on our imperfections, the hereditary evils that would make it possible for the hells to draw close to him, to tempt him, and be defeated by him. From this sense, 'perfect man' needs to include those imperfections from Mary, and could perhaps mean that while Christ was 'perfect God' as to his soul, he was 'wholly and completely human' as to his life in this world.

The indications are that Athanasius did not mean that Christ assumed a human soul, but he needed some human soul to guide him through his life in this world. Swedenborg answered this dilemma in a way that Athanasius could not have begun to think of.

Beginning with the concept of the soul, Swedenborg notes that Christ indeed had a divine soul, passed from the Father, into Mary and thus became the source of his own life. This soul, because it was divine, was indivisible from the Father, which firstly meant that Christ was truly divine, even while in the body, and also made the glorification possible.

Secondly, however, Swedenborg introduces a concept to unravel the confusion left by Athanasius' 'reasonable soul', and that is the development of Christ's mind in this world. Many people have argued over Christ's mind, whether he was able to think like a human being. For example, Apollinaris in 362, contemporaneous with Athanasius, taught that Christ did not have a human mind, and that 'the Word himself has become flesh without having assumed a human mind changeable and enslaved to filthy thoughts' (Davis 1989:105). Swedenborg's point is that Christ did indeed have such a mind. From Mary he inherited inclinations to exactly all the 'filthy thoughts' people have. What Apollinaris missed was that from his divine soul Christ was able to rise above these things, to bring them into order, making it possible for people to do the same.

The development of Christ's mind is the key essential teaching of Swedenborg's teachings on the glorification. In the *Arcana Coelestia* he evolves this in the internal sense of the stories of Abraham, Isaac, Jacob and Joseph describing the process of how Christ's mind developed from infancy to rationality. Swedenborg believed that Christ actually took on the human, not only physically, but mentally, and brought it into order.

Swedenborg finds himself in agreement with Athanasius that Christ had a 'rational soul and a human body' – which he extends to include the mind. He bears in mind, however, that the rational soul was the divine, the Father, while the human body (and mind) was the vehicle for bringing that divinity into the world. Again, this leads him to the conclusion that there is one Person in the Trinity.

Christ's Soul

The issue of Christ's soul is deeply seated in the Athanasian Creed, and again if one thinks of the Trinity as a Trinity of Person, not Persons, as Swedenborg suggests, then it presents another area of agreement. If, as the Creed states, Christ was 'of the substance of the mother, born in the world', how could he be both 'Perfect man and perfect God'?

The answer lies in the statement in the Creed, that he is 'equal to the Father as touching the divine, and inferior to the Father as touching the Human, who although He be God and Man, yet He is not two but one Christ, one not by conversion of the Divine Essence into the Human, but by a taking of the Human Essence into the Divine'.

The only way to unravel this is to see the connection between human and divine in Christ. The human in the Person of Christ rests in his 'reasonable soul', or 'rational mind'. Yet, as Swedenborg point out, to

> ... believe that the Lord was perfect Man from the mother alone is quite contrary to all order and what is said. Is there not the image of the father in children equally with that of the mother? The very love or ruling affection of the Father stands out clearly in the grandchildren and families. In a word, there must be father and mother that man may be perfect man. How then is it to be believed that he was perfect Man from the Mother (Ath. Cr. 30).

As Swedenborg answers his own question, he returns to the image of the Trinity in one Person, then the Father, the originator and motivator, is the soul within the body. In the previous chapter we examined Swedenborg's doctrine of the implantation of the Soul into Christ. The soul from God, and so in all species, is a reproduction of the soul of the father. The first spiritual essences of life are gradually clothed with increasingly external garments until they are clothed with physical substances. When they are received by a wife, they initiate the process of growth in the ovum, and so life is transferred from one to the other, carrying all the qualities and essences of the father into the offspring.

Swedenborg held that the same principle is true for Christ as for any ordinary person. His soul, which is the divine life itself, stimulated the life in Mary's womb that would become Christ. But since the Divine is indivisible, by definition, so the soul within Christ was the same as the divine in the Father. On the basis of this he would consider his teaching in agreement with the Creed, which states quite clearly, that 'the Son is of the Father alone, not made nor created, but begotten'.

Thus Swedenborg would read the Creed as stating that Christ had a divine soul from the Father, making him equal to the Father. This was planted in a humanity, inferior to the Father, which Swedenborg would relate as the infirmity of the humanity from Mary, which when it was put off and glorified, made Christ both perfect God and perfect Man – or, in Swedenborg's terms, the Divine Human. Once again, he sees agreement with the Athanasian Creed.

One Christ

Following Swedenborg's reasoning, one can be led through the Athanasian Creed to the vitally important point that Christ is not of a dual nature, that is, not separately human and divine, but one. Athanasius could have a vague inkling of this when he said, for 'as the reasonable soul and body are one man, so God and Man are one Christ' (Ath. Cr. 30).

If one interprets that 'reasonable soul' as the glorified mind of Christ, made open and receptive to the Divine, then from Swedenborg's point of view this statement is also true, for the body, glorified and resurrected from the tomb is at one with the divine soul and divine mind. Christ is one. Once again Swedenborg sees an agreement between his teaching and the Athanasian Creed, and he makes the point that

> [f]rom these statements it is clear that, according to our creedal faith[9], the Divine and the Human in the Lord are together in one Person, and not that the Divine is outside the Human as many crazily imagine (Ath. Cr. 30).

The natures are not co-mingled.

For Swedenborg, the next stage in understanding Christ from the Athanasian Creed, is the caveat against the mingling of the human and divine in Christ. The Chalcedonian Formula addresses this point, that the human and divine natures in Christ are forever separate and distinct. This position led to the teaching that Christ has two natures that are joined together by the communicatio idiomatum (or hypostatic union).

Swedenborg indicates both a truth and a falsity in the Chalcedonian Formula. For him the truth is that the human and divine natures in Christ are indeed never mingled, while Christ lived in this world, for at that point his human would still have had impurities from Mary. He holds it as a falsity to say that they remain forever distinct and separate, for although the soul and body remain separate by a discrete degree, nevertheless one is within the other as a soul in the body, and together they act as a one.

In the Athanasian Creed the following point has relation to this:

> Although He be God and Man, yet He is not two but one Christ, one
> not by conversion of the Divine Essence to the Human, but by a
> taking of the Human Essence into the Divine. One altogether, not by
> confusion of essence, but by unity of Person.

Again, if one understands the Athanasian Creed to speak of a Trinity in
one Person, as Swedenborg suggests, this statement agrees with the
process of glorification in Christ. Through glorification Christ became
both God and Man, not, as Athanasius says, 'by conversion of the
Divine Essence to the Human, but by a taking of the Human Essence
into the Divine'. According to Swedenborg, the divine itself could not
become human at the natural level, for the natural was too riddled with
hereditary evil. So, through putting on the human from Mary, which
was indeed corrupted with hereditary evil, Christ was also able to put
off that evil, and unite the human essence with the Divine.

Following Swedenborg's thought, this could only be done if
there was one Person. If Father and Son were two distinct persons, or
hypostases, then the process does not work. The human of Christ would
have to be perfect, as it is commonly conceived that Christ at birth
was[10]. Then that perfect human could be united to the divine Word, or
Logos, and the dual natures in Christ ensue.

The Soul and the Body

The only conclusion that one can come to, then, is that the
relationship between Father and Son is not that of two Persons, but a
one of cause and an effect within one Person. Swedenborg writes:

> And so when the Divine takes to itself the Human, uniting Itself with
> the Human as soul and body, so that there is one united Person, then
> also the human participates in the Divine, namely, by becoming one
> [with it]. Thence also it can be confirmed that the Human, too, is
> Divine (Ath. Cr. 30).

Again, the Athanasian Creed expresses this doctrine. Firstly it says that
Christ is 'Perfect God and perfect man, consisting as reasonable soul
and a human body'. The same passage is repeated after the discussion
that while Christ is both God and man, he is 'one Christ' because the
human essence is taken up to the divine essence, concluding that
section by saying, 'for as the reasonable soul and body and one man, so
God and Man is one Christ.'

As we saw earlier, the term 'reasonable soul', for Swedenborg this represents the divine glorified mind, that is, the mind after the process of glorification. As such it represents the Divine penetrating down to human level, even to the very elements of the human body. Together the human and divine make one, as the mind or soul in each person live and acts within the body.

Since Swedenborg does not deny the Trinity, holding that there is a Trinity in Christ, but it is a Trinity of discrete degrees within one Person, rather than as three Persons representing one divine substance, he expects to find agreement with the Athanasian Creed. The points of agreement listed above are his own, and at each level, if he reads a Trinity of Person instead of Persons into the Trinity, and interprets it according to his overall teachings, then the agreement seems to be there.

Taking these points together, it becomes possible to see what Swedenborg means when he says that the Athanasian Creed agrees with Doctrine in every detail. However, the agreement only lasts as long as one is willing to concede Swedenborg's point on the Trinity in one Person. The paradigm does not hold if one believes that Father, Son and Holy Spirit exist as three Persons, or hypostases of the divine substance. Swedenborg believed that belief in three Persons in the Trinity 'tears asunder the unity of God', leading, as we are graphically told in the True Christian Religion, to the perversion of the whole Christian Church (TCR 177).

As seen in Chapter Two, Christian theology tried to explain the Trinity, until, exhausted, the scholars simply stated that a Trinity in three Persons must be believed because the Church has so stated. Thus the understanding of the Trinity closed down human understanding, stopped further research, punishing those, as it punished Michael Servetus in 1553, for reexamining the issue.

Swedenborg believed that as the original understanding of 'Persons' was defeated by the idea of three individual beings, so other teachings sprang up to further pollute the Church. One example is the belief in the nature of God, for

> ... it has been declared that God could beget a Son from eternity, and then cause a third God to proceed from Himself and the Son. Also that he could be angry with the human race, put them under a curse, and then be willing to show them mercy through the Son, by the Son's intercession and the remembrance of His cross (TCR 90).

This marked the extinction of the Christian Church in Swedenborg's mind, for as theology deteriorated, and salvation became a contract between individual Gods in the Trinity, so people lost sight of the true nature of God, not noticing that 'it is contrary to the Divine that God the Father alienated from himself the human race, and effected reconciliation through the blood of the Son' (Ath. Cr. 53).

He believed that carried to its logical conclusion, this error led to the destruction of all theology, for the idea of God enters all belief, and, if that idea is false, then everything else will be false. He wrote that as a result of the division of the Trinity into three Persons, 'a kind of insanity has pervaded the whole of theology and also the Christian Church' for people are 'so confused that they do not know whether there is one God or three; one is on their lips, but three in their minds, so that their minds and lips, or their thought and their speech are at variance. The result of this confusion is the denial that there is a God' (TCR 4).

His solution is simple, if instead of understanding Athanasius' Creed as referring to three Persons in Trinity, one understands the Trinity within one Person, then the whole of this problem is avoided. The Trinity existing within Christ reveals the inner divine, and thus Christ's statement to Philip, that 'He who as seen me has seen the Father, is true.' So also are Christ's words, that 'I and the Father are one'.

Notes:

---

[1] This fits with Swedenborg's contention that all angels were once people in this world, that at death only the physical body is rejected, while the essential spirit, with all that it contains, now clothed in a spiritual body, becomes an angel (or evil spirit) (AE 235, AE 985, DP 27, HH 314, HH 366, HH 415, LJ 18, AC 5053).

[2] 'Trine' and 'Trinity' are used interchangeably (Lord 46).

[3] Multiple references across Swedenborg's theological works attest to this belief, and since it is the basis of his belief, it forms an intrinsic part of the rest of his theology, having impact on the nature of salvation and the life after death.

[4] 'Discrete' means 'separate' – see DLW 184, Ager translation.

[5] Hi gradus sunt discreti, quia distincte existunt, ac intelliguntur per gradus altitudinis (DLW 184).

[6] All references to the Athanasian Creed in this chapter are from Swedenborg's version as contained in Appendix A.

[7] It is interesting to note that Swedenborg uses exactly the same argument, stating that 'unless God were one, the universe could not have been created and preserved' (TCR 13).

[8] Attributa.

[9] 'fidem nostram symbolicam' - throughout his teachings, Swedenborg, stresses that the Athanasian Creed is perfectly right if interpreted as being a faith in a Trinity in one Person, identifies it here as 'our Creedal Faith' - perhaps indicating that he considered his doctrine not so much a rejection of Christianity as a whole, but a reworking of false ideas. The inference is that not all things are rejected. This, however, has to be seen in the context of the many passages teaching that the Christian Church is dead.

[10] The doctrine of the Immaculate Conception teaches that Mary herself was born without original sin, and was therefore able to conceive the Lord in purity, and so prevent his being infected with original sin. His sinless human, could, therefore, be united to the divine Word.

Chapter Eleven

Servetus, Swedenborg and the Nature of God

A study of Servetus and Swedenborg shows their theology to be remarkably similar in more than a passing fashion. It was almost as if Servetus began the work, and Swedenborg, allowed the luxury of long life and respect amongst his contemporaries, finished it. In many cases the differences between the two are a matter of Swedenborg applying additional thought to a subject. One could speculate what Servetus would have written had he lived an extra twenty or thirty years – being only in his early forties when he was burnt at the stake. Would he, given time, have come up with the same concepts as Swedenborg? It is entirely possible, for the basic foundation of their theology is very similar, and the practical theology they drew from it shows a oneness of thought.

An instinctual claim, considering the similarities, is that Swedenborg read Servetus and modeled his theology after him, carrying it further than Servetus was able. However, this seems unlikely. Swedenborg lived two hundred years after Servetus, growing up in the conservative atmosphere of Lutheran Sweden. Searches of his studies at Uppsala University, of his libraries and collections, fail to show any connection with Servetus at all. Erik E. Sandstrom, curator of the Swedenborg Library in Bryn Athyn, Pennsylvania, having been asked to research Swedenborg's book lists, writes that 'I have found no trace of Servetus ... No bibliography of Swedenborg mentions Servetus' (Sandstrom 2000).

One should not be surprised at this. From the time of his burning, Servetus' books were systematically repressed across Europe, and only a handful of copies of the *Restitutio Christianismi* survived. An edition was published in London in 1723, but that was also repressed by the Church of England. It is extremely doubtful that Swedenborg would have encountered any of these, for at the time, as we have seen, his interest was philosophical, not theological. However, one cannot rule out as a fact that Swedenborg never encountered Servetus' theological thought, although it is highly unlikely.

That being the case, how does his theology come to bear so close a resemblance to Servetus? This subject is the focus of this chapter and the next. In this chapter we shall explore these similarities in detail – taking note of dissimilarities between the two men.

Historical Similarities

Although born nearly two hundred years apart, at opposite ends of the European continent, Servetus and Swedenborg share a surprisingly similar background which together with their education and interests may well have disposed them to a similar interpretation of the Scriptures. Similarity in thought may have led them to their similar conclusions.

Both men grew up in religious households. There is strong evidence that Servetus was destined for the Church, attending the University of Saragossa, where a liberal education equipped him with his theological knowledge, as well as the classics and scholastic philosophy. In addition he studied mathematics, astronomy and geography (Willis 1877:9). Although he seemed to break with the idea of the priesthood, studying law at the University of Toulouse, he kept his connection with the structures of the Roman Catholic Church in Spain by serving with de Quintana, confessor to the Emperor Charles V. It was in this capacity that he attended the Diet of Worms. Had he wished, it is almost certain that Servetus could have attained high and respected office in the Church.

Swedenborg's experience was similar but different. His exposure to religion came from living in a home headed by his outspoken episcopal father in which religious subjects were a frequent matter of conversation. The young Swedenborg was often included in these discussions, and early in life developed an interest in theology.

Yet he was, at all times, a layman. The weight of his interests lay in mechanics and science, in philosophy and physiology.

At eleven years old he was enrolled at Uppsala University. A curriculum from that period showed while religion was a principal field of study there were three other faculties, law, medicine and philosophy (Sigstedt 1952:9). The late seventeenth and early eighteen centuries – the time of Swedenborg's enrolment (1699 to 1709) were watershed years for the institution as the different faculties tried to shake off the stranglehold of the church and institute a more modern academic freedom to accommodate the desire for a higher education slowly developing amongst Sweden's nobility (Hubener 1988:288).

By 1700, only 55 per cent of the students, down from 70% in earlier decades, were destined for the priesthood (Sandstrom 2001). During this time, the academic offerings of the University indicated a change in thought.

> An interest in expanded knowledge and minute research was part of the liberal ideal. New theories and radical ideas made their way into the minds of students and faculty, sometimes struggling against the defenses and ignorance of extreme patriotism and religious orthodoxy (Hubener 1988:288).

These more secular subjects interested Swedenborg more than theology itself, while he came to embrace new theories and radical ideas in pursuit of a greater understanding of the mechanics of the natural world. He was enrolled in the Philosophy Department, focusing on philosophy, science, mathematics, and other such practical matters. He may also have studied law, 'since he took part in debates on that subject' (Sigstedt 1952:9).

While both Servetus and Swedenborg shared an interest in the natural sciences, the former was exposed to theology in a way Swedenborg was not. However, they shared a mutual interest in the physical sciences. Servetus was a 'natural philosopher whose eyes were open to the operation of spiritual law in natural things' (Odhner 1910:44). It is speculated that

> ... had Servetus been satisfied to remain in the service of merely natural science, he would no doubt be reckoned now as one of the greatest lights of learning in the sixteenth century. We can advance this claim without fear of contradiction, as it is now universally acknowledged that this Spanish physician was actually the first discoverer of the circulation of the blood through the lungs – a whole

century before Harvey more fully explained this process (Odhner 1910:45).

Much the same thing could be said about Swedenborg in the eighteenth century. Because of his turning to religion, his progress in scientific and anatomical fields has been largely overlooked by the scientific community who see him as a spiritual visionary. Like Servetus, Swedenborg was fascinated by the human body. Ever the scholar, in 1735 and 1736, he felt the need to improve his knowledge of anatomy and took an extended tour of Italy for this purpose. His notes on the brain fill one hundred and thirty closely written pages (Acton 1958:474). Swedenborg learned from other scholars, but also performed his own experiments. In his *Economy of the Animal Kingdom*, he writes, 'I admit that I have made use of the vigilant labors and the ocular evidences elaborated with great care by men pre-eminently worthy of credit, and have not drawn from my own store save in a few cases; but I have preferred to learn by sight rather than by touch (EAK 2:214).

It is somewhat indicative of Swedenborg's personality that while he believed he would excel at research, his own 'ego' would lead him a way from his true purpose of study, for

> ... to originate the whole series of inductive arguments from my particular discovery alone, and consequently to be incapacitated to view and comprehend the idea of universals in individuals and of individuals under universals ... I therefore laid aside my instruments, and restraining my desire for making observations, determined rather to rely on the researches of others than to trust my own (Swedenborg in Larsen 1988:490).

Swedenborg's studies in anatomy were thorough and comprehensive, but of a different quality than that of Servetus. Each was a man of his own era, coming at the subject from different perspectives, influenced by different philosophies, but they shared in common an ideal of the physical body as an example of the wonder of creation and an image of God.

This similarity in scientific knowledge is echoed in another personality similarity, both sought to share their discoveries and insights with the world. Both were prolific authors. For many years Servetus made his living by overseeing works through the press, adding to them his own quality. Perhaps his version of Pagnini's Bible is the best example of this, although his additions to Ptolemy came to haunt

him at his trial in Geneva – Calvin would not accept his statements that
the Holy Land was a wasteland. Servetus' greatest contributions to
human thought, however, are his theological treatises, which although
they have attracted much opprobrium, have challenged orthodox
Christian thought.

Similarly, Swedenborg also sought to question and re-educate,
and, because he lived in a different era, was free to express his opinions
in a way denied to Servetus. His first major publication, the *Daedalus
Hyperboreus* (the Northern Daedalus), was published shortly after his
return from his Grand Tour of Europe in 1715 (Acton 1958:92). As a
scientific journal it caught the eye of King Charles XII of Sweden,
launching Swedenborg in an association with the Swedish royal family
that would last his lifetime.

The difference between the two men lies in longevity.
Servetus was executed while still a comparatively young man. His
theological output was three major works. Swedenborg, however,
living to the age of eighty four, in an era of great intellectual freedom,
wrote a range of theological works, which, in English, fill thirty
volumes. It is interesting to wonder how much more Servetus would
have written, and what direction his thoughts would have taken, had he
been allowed to live.

Both men, however, were communicators of their interests. As
these lay in theology, so other similarities between them came to the
fore. One primary one, which influences both their religious writings, is
an interest in the language of the Bible itself. Servetus lamented that
Hebrew 'cannot be kept up in our translations' (Anon 1724:42). He is
quoted as writing that,

> [t]hey who are ignorant of the Hebrew language and history are only
> too apt to overlook the historical and literal sense of the Sacred
> Scripture; the consequence of which is that they vainly and foolishly
> expend themselves in hunting after recondite and mystical meanings
> in the text where nothing of the kind exists (Servetus in Willis
> 1877:141).

Swedenborg shared his sentiments. While he studied Latin and
Greek at Uppsala, he was also exposed to Hebrew (Sigstedt 1952:10).
His real interest in the language, however, came after his 'call' in 1744,
when he realized that 'a thorough study of Scripture requires a
knowledge of the Hebrew language, it may have been just at this time
that he took up the study of Hebrew, for in his diary are found various

notes in that language' (Sigstedt 1952:215). Over the years Hebrew became increasingly important. In his book, *Heaven and Hell*, he writes that the Hebrew language coincides in some respects to angelic language (HH 237). Elsewhere he observes that the Hebrew language contained the very essence of heaven (AC 618) and that the very shape of the letters indicates secret things of love and wisdom (SS 90, TCR 241).

Their similar interest in ancient languages, especially Hebrew leads to a certain similarity in their interpretation of the Scriptures, as will become apparent later on in this chapter. Both of them saw a difference between the words used, and the deeper underlying meaning of those words, and this distinction would inform their theology, adding immeasurably to their concept of God.

Finally, both Servetus and Swedenborg believed that they had been called by God to reform the Christian Church. It was this sense of calling that led the young Servetus to break first with the Roman Catholic Church and later with the Protestants. He articulated it by writing and publishing the books that would eventually claim his life. Swedenborg's experience, as we have seen, was somewhat different. Firstly he was much older, in his fifty-sixth year. Secondly he was in no personal or imminent danger because of his ideas. However, he felt no less called by God to reform the church.

The elements of their call are remarkably similar. Both believed that Christianity had alienated itself from its true message, sharing a common belief that the early Christian Church had not looked to a Trinity of Persons, but had articulated a belief in one God. The fall of the church can be traced to the council of Nicaea in 325, when the substance of God was divided into three hypostases. They shared the idea that only a radically new approach to the doctrine of the Trinity could restore the Church.

Swedenborg goes further than Servetus in outlining the fall of the Christian Church, perhaps because he had more time in which to elaborate on its demise. He taught that the division of the Trinity at Nicaea caused a 'sort of frenzy' to invade 'not only all theology, but the church ... it is called a frenzy because men's minds have been made so demented by it as not to know whether there is one God or three' (TCR 4). The loss of clarity over the nature of God, led to the consummation of the church (Coronis 12). It gave rise to lists of heresiarchs, beginning with Simon the Magician, and ending with Calvin, Melancthon and Luther (TCR 378).

Only a full reworking of the Trinity could restore the Church to its pre-Nicene glory. It is in the working out of this restoration that Servetus and Swedenborg are most similar. From the theological underpinnings of their thought to the outcomes based on a revised view of the trinity, one finds a tremendous overlap. How this is accounted for, in the absence of any evidence that Swedenborg was consciously aware of Servetus, will be explored in the next chapter. For the present it is enough to consider these similarities in more depth and detail.

Concept of the Bible

Before considering their similarities of concept in the nature of God, it is useful to note the similarities in their interpretation of the Bible. Friedman notes that 'the contours of Servetus' system can be determined through an examination of the function of Scripture in his thought' (Friedman 1978:27). This is equally true of Swedenborg. The Bible was their common source, and both being students of the Hebrew language, both studied more deeply than the mere words on a page. Both Servetus and Swedenborg saw the Bible as written in types, or to put it into Swedenborg's terminology, the Bible has an 'internal sense', which describes the things of heaven by means of correspondential terms.

For Servetus, the Bible contains a two-fold sense. He expressed this philosophy of the Scriptures in his introduction to *Pagnini's Polyglot Bible*, where he noted that 'there is a two fold face in the Scripture' (Anon 1724:43). The first face is the Hebrew and Jewish context of the Bible, and thus 'the Bible [must] be understood within its own historical, philological and philosophical context' (Friedman 1978:28). Thus David was a king of Israel, no more, no less. Similarly, the virgin who shall conceive and bear a child, refers not to Mary, but to the conception of Hezekiah. According to Servetus, 'everything in the Jewish Church took place by means of representatives' (Odhner 1910:50), which formed a shadow in which God was presented to the world, and from which he was worshipped.

> I say that the worship of God was a shadow, and God was never truly worshipped in the law because even as God can not be seen, so also he can not be worshipped, apart from Christ ... Previously he was worshipped not in truth but in a shadow, in a temple of stone, a tabernacle of wood, where the darkness of the glory of the Lord appeared (Dia. 1.5).

The second face of Scripture is the light in that darkness, the hidden reference to Christ within the letter of the Bible that can only be revealed in the Christian era, for from within one sees all things as a type of Christ. Thus Servetus writes, that in the Bible that 'Christ was there typified and prefigured; for in all the law were anticipated the mysteries and types of things to come, which we can also call shadows' (Dia. 1:2). The things written on the page, therefore, are true stories and prophecies of the Christ to come, but they are told by means of types, shrouded in shadow. Thus Abraham, Isaac, Moses and David, are all types of Christ. However, the things written about them, especially in the prophets, were written to be understood according to the context of their time. It is true that as prophecies they may be referring to the coming Christ, but it is also true that 'you must bear in mind that all things that are written of Christ took place in Judea, and in the Hebrew tongue' (Tr. 1:19).

The ancient Jew had no idea that the prophecies were about anything other than the mundane things of his or her life. The stories of David spoke to the ancient Jew about David, since they had no experience of Christ, yet to the Christian who has such experience, David can be seen as a type of Christ. From him one can come to understand Christ himself. As this is true of David, so it is true of the entire Old Testament. The Bible, therefore, is an archetype[1] expressing God in terms of this world, especially in history, within which 'Christ was typified and pre-figured' (Dia. 1.2). To understand God, one must not, however, read back preconceived ideas, superimposing them on the shadows, but allow the truth to speak from within the shadows, revealing the nature of God to humanity. In one passage, Servetus refers to Peter Lombard, who claimed to see the doctrine of the Tri-Personal Trinity written on every page of Scripture. To him, this is reading a concept back into a place where it should not be. In response to the Lombard he writes, 'to me not merely the syllables, but all the letters, and the mouths of babes and sucklings, nay the very stones, cry out, One God the Father, and his Christ, the Lord Jesus Christ' (Tr. 40).

If one looks past the shadows, and does not superimpose later ideas onto the Bible, then the truth will shine forth. This is Servetus' approach. Over and again he challenges the preconceived ideas as they are read into Scripture, trying to get to the very heart of what the writer was saying, and then, from that, showing how it is a type of Christ.

This approach to exegesis is similar to that of Swedenborg. He too held that there was more to the Bible than is immediately apparent. He too claims that the Bible was written to accommodate the spiritual development of people at different times. Thus the Word for the Ancient

Church, which he says is lost, was written in purely symbolic forms, or correspondences. The Word of the Jewish Church, or the Old Testament, was written to appeal to the understanding of the ancient Jew, in which the images of an angry, vindictive God, so common in the Old Testament, are a clothing of the true nature of God, put on to keep the Israelites in order.

Within the letter of the Bible, hidden from human eyes, is an angelic sense (TCR 193). Swedenborg writes,

> [t]he Word of the Old Testament contains heavenly arcana, with every single detail focusing on the Lord, His heaven, the Church, faith and what belongs to faith; but no one grasps this from the letter (AC 1).

The Bible has this spiritual sense because it originates in God, and descends to the natural world. On its way it passes through the different levels of heaven, being adapted at each level to the understanding of the angels there. Finally the truth reaches the natural world, where, clothed in the history and prophecies of the Old Testament, it is adapted to the perception of human beings (TCR 193). Nothing is lost in this descent of truth. Each degree of truth is external to the one before it, so that as the truth passes from God to man, it is progressively covered in more and more external layers of truth, while still containing the inner and higher levels of truth. In this way the highest truths, those dealing with the subject of God himself, are hidden and protected from people who, through their more external nature, would be prone to profaning them.

Much of Swedenborg's theological works outline the inner meaning of the Old and New Testaments. By using a system of correspondential meanings, he claims that the Bible is a parable, which explored, reveals levels of spiritual truth. The spiritual sense closest to the stories themselves is the 'historical' outline of the progress of the 'churches' or dispensations of God's presence in this world[2]. On a higher plane, however, lies a second degree of truth, one referring primarily to human regeneration. The level of the internal sense, containing a great deal of deep psychology, speaks to universal human conditions, about evil and salvation from it. Within this sense, as a wheel within a wheel, the Bible speaks about God, for 'that universal Holy Scripture has been written solely about the Lord' (Lord 7). Swedenborg's concept of the Bible can be schematically represented as follows:

God	The existere or manifestation of God as Divine Wisdom or truth
The Celestial Sense	Speaks of God, his glorification, providence, etc.
The Spiritual Sense	Speaks of human regeneration, evil and salvation
The Natural Sense	Speaks of the history of the Churches – human responses to God
The Literal Sense	Speaks of the History of the Jews as a containant of all the above degrees of meaning

Each degree of truth lies within the other, and thus one story, or even a word, contains all the inner meanings, connecting the reader of the literal story to the heavens, and through them to God himself.

Seen from this point of view, Swedenborg agrees with Servetus that every part of the Old and New Testaments sets forth a type of Christ, for Christ is the visible manifestation of God, the only way people can know God. Even though this is not clearly evident to the reader of the literal Bible, still those inner types are present, and the Bible, in Servetus' terms, becomes 'a shadow of God'.

Swedenborg developed this theme very fully in the Arcana Coelestia. For example, Abraham, whom he never doubts lived and walked in this world in flesh and blood, is, nevertheless, a type of Christ as an infant, responding to the first call of the Divine within. The birth of Ishmael describes how Christ 'increased in wisdom and stature, and in favor with God and man' (Luke 2:52). More concerned with the mental processes taking place – which he outlines in clinical form – Swedenborg links Ishmael to the change in mental abilities that takes place between childhood and adulthood. However, as Ishmael was not to inherit Abraham's household (at least in the Judeo-Christian tradition), Isaac represents Christ as a young man in the first flush of truly mature adult ability. While each of these speak of different stages of the Church, and the process of development applies to ordinary humans, for Swedenborg the most important aspect is that they are types of Christ, showing His development from infancy to adulthood, and the attendant levels of maturity, spiritual growth, temptation and victory he passed through in the process of glorification.

The major difference between Servetus and Swedenborg then, is that Servetus stated with biblical references that the Bible is a type of Christ. His use of Biblical passages to support and underscore his opinion, however, kept him much on the same literal plane. Swedenborg, taking a very similar standpoint, moves onto a different plain by opening up the literal stories to show a higher meaning. It could be argued that while Servetus drew his inspiration entirely from the Bible, Swedenborg looked beyond the written page to his own spiritual experiences for insight.

Neither Servetus nor Swedenborg felt it insulting to the Old and New Testament to think of them as shadows, or as containing an inner meaning. Servetus writes, apologizing for describing the literal sense of the Bible 'a shadow', that 'it is from necessity that I have been forced to use this expression, because I could find no other term by which to signify this divine mystery. Nor would I suggest that the Word is a shadow that is past and remains no more' (quoted in Odhner 1910:51). To him the shadow of the Bible does not disparage it because it sets forth Christ, pre-existent within it (Restitutio 202). Swedenborg holding much the same idea, states that the literal sense of the Bible is the 'basis, containant and support of its spiritual and celestial sense' (TCR 210), and therefore in it rests the whole force of Divine Truth 'in its fullness, its holiness and its power' (TCR 214).

The full force of this power for both men comes in the explanation of the nature of God. The whole of Swedenborg's theology of the Bible can be summed up by a statement made by Servetus that 'the whole secret of the Word was the glorification of this Man' (Restitutio 579)[3]. Although they lived two centuries apart and there is no evidence that Swedenborg was ever exposed to the writings of Michael Servetus, the theology of the two men resulting from this very similar belief in the nature of the Bible, led to a very similar concept of the nature of God.

Nicaea

Servetus was convinced that nothing outside of the Scriptures could be held as binding on the conscience of the Church. 'For that reason he set the fall of the Church at the Council of Nicaea' (Bainton in Becker 1953:30). The root of his rejection of the Nicene Creed lay in its expression of the Trinity in three distinct Persons. He noted that the Bible never uses the term Trinity, nor does it treat of Father, Son and Holy Spirit as Persons. He saw this as a theological interpretation of the Biblical descriptions of God, arrived at through a failure to properly understand the nature of types presented in the Old Testament. 'All that came after [Nicaea] was to his mind corruption and the scholastic authors were subjected to the strictures of one common condemnation' (Bainton in Becker 1953:30).

The Trinitarian formula resulting from Nicaea was the root cause of the Church's troubles, for it obscured the face of the Savior (Beilby 1936:216), by presenting an impossible concept of God (Willis 1877:55).

> Infinitely great, he (Servetus) writes, has been the injury brought upon the Christian Church by this doctrine of Tritheism. Innumerable heresies and monstrous notions have sprung from it, and within the Church it has given birth to the most marvelous doctrines and thousands of inexplicable hair-splitting and unreasonable problems (Servetus quoted in Beilby 1936:218).

He believed that the reign of the antichrist began in the fourth century, if not sooner (Anon 1724:65), ushered in by the Arian denial of Christ's divinity, and fixed by the Nicene Council.

Swedenborg takes a very similar path, stating that 'the Trinity as defined by the Council of Nicaea and by Athanasius caused a faith to arise which has perverted the whole Christian Church' (TCR 177). The perversion arose because of the failure of the Church to acknowledge the unity of God in the Trinity, stressing rather the threeness of God in unity, and 'hence have founded a church in the mind upon the idea of three Gods, and in the mouth upon the confession of one God' (Ath. Cr. 75). The result has been a separation of humanity from God to the point at which people have no idea of anything divine left in Christ's human nature.

Swedenborg's resounding indictment of the Church comes from his total rejection of the Trinity as enunciated at Nicaea. As was shown earlier in the chapter on Swedenborg's Concept of the Trinity, he was not an anti-Trinitarian, for he wrote that a Trinity did indeed exist. His point however, is a Trinity of Person, not of Persons, which exists in Jesus Christ as soul, body and operation. By separating these into distinct persons who have forever been separate was, to Swedenborg, anathema, for it destroyed the basis of human interaction with God, and plunged the human mind into spiritual darkness. While he does not use the term 'antichrist' as Servetus does, the effects are the same, for the human being is reduced to spiritual impotence, and denied the use of the very faculties that make him or her human.

Deprived of the basic assumptions of orthodox Christianity by their rejection of the Nicene and Athanasian Creeds, and consequently of all subsequent theological development, both Servetus and Swedenborg began to reconstruct the understanding of the nature of God anew. Their source was the Bible. Servetus, the trained theologian looked back to the patristic Fathers, while Swedenborg looked to his spiritual experiences. The result was a remarkably similar body of doctrine.

The Idea of God

The greatest difficulty in outlining the overlaps in the theological systems of Servetus and Swedenborg is the difference in their approach. Servetus' writing does not follow a clearly defined or even overtly logical order, and his points are often obscured by attention to Biblical and patristic detail. Swedenborg, on the other hand, presents his thesis very logically, especially in the *True Christian Religion*. Any reading of the two authors shows a marked similarity in their work, although the expression of this varies. In following the similarities around the nature of God, we will follow Swedenborg's model of presentation in the *True Christian Religion* in which he presents chapters on the three main aspects of God, God the Creator, the Lord the Redeemer, and the Holy Spirit. At the end of dealing with these aspects of God, he then unites them in an explanation of the Trinity.

God the Creator

Servetus defines God as he is in himself, in grand terms. The Father, he says, is 'immeasurably inaccessible, incomprehensible, light invisible[4]' (Restitutio 704). In himself, God is unknown and unknowable, except to say that he is the source and creator of all things. Servetus writes that 'before the creation of the world God was not light, nor Word, nor Spirit, but something else ineffable; and all these are words of dispensation' (Dia. 1:4)

He then explains that God could not be light, because light can only shine in creation, and not before (Dia. 1.4). The same is true of the Word, for creation came into being when God spoke the Word. Nor was he spirit, for the spirit, being the activity of the Word, could not exist prior to it. Thus God in Servetian terms cannot be defined by anything belonging to the body, but only by the fact that he actuates all things, causing them to exist (Dia. II).

Beyond this there is little else to say about God as he is in himself, prior to creation. One cannot know God except by the Word, and until the Word was spoken, little can be said about the unseen, unknowable God. One cannot ascribe to him a 'nature' for 'nature' describes 'that which is inborn from any being from birth, and is characteristic ... But God in himself has no Nature nor origin such as his Son has. No kind of Nature was appropriate to God, but something else ineffable' (Dia. II.3).

However, Servetus is adamant about one aspect of God, he is one, complete and indivisible. This concept has immense ramifications in Servetus' theology of the Trinity, and in his Christology.

Swedenborg, as was shown earlier in the chapter on his concept of God, concurs to some degree with Servetus, but takes a different approach, for there are certain things that can be said of God, all of which, when extrapolated in human terms, confirm the point that in himself, God is ineffable.

He makes several points about the nature of God prior to creation. First is the fact that the term 'before' implies time, and since time only came into being at creation, and since God, by definition is not bound to time. To him, 'prior to creation' is an concept that appears to make sense to human reason, but in reality has no reason. Thus, 'he is the same since the world was created as before; and as before creation there were in God and in His sight no spaces and no times, but only since, and as He is always the same, so is He in space without space and in time without time' (TCR 30).

It is not possible to say that God was in either time or space before or after creation (Canons 34), for the essence of God never changes. As was shown earlier, Swedenborg's idea of the nature of God is that as to his being, or *esse* he is pure love, manifesting itself as wisdom, or *existere*. This inner relationship of essences within God did not change in creation, but became manifest. Love is always invisible, and can only be seen through a manifestation, through wisdom or truth. Creation was this expression, and in it, one is able to see God's wisdom or truth. Thus Swedenborg writes 'before creation God was Love itself and Wisdom itself, and He was these two exerting themselves to perform services' (TCR 67). Therefore, 'the Divine Truth, which before creation was in Jehovah[5], and after creation was from Jehovah, and finally was the Divine Human which Jehovah took to Himself in time; for it is said that "the Word became flesh", that is became Man' (Canons 16).

Thus Swedenborg goes further than Servetus in describing God before creation. Servetus' ineffable terms are given a new meaning in Swedenborg's system, for rather than speaking simply of the divine qualities of indivisibility and inscrutability, Swedenborg attaches to these ideas more reflective of human qualities, love and wisdom, although in God himself these are ineffable, far surpassing anything we can experience, but at least giving a dim image of the nature of God.

The two are, however, in absolute agreement in their statement of the oneness of God, before, during and after creation. Swedenborg's words could have been said by either of them when he says, 'the truth is that, from eternity or before creation, there were not three Persons each one of Whom was God; thus there were not three Infinites, three Uncreates, three Immeasurable, Eternal, Omnipotent Beings, but One' (Canons 33).

It was this one God who spoke the Word by which the universe was created, and which in time was born as a man in this world. For both Servetus and Swedenborg, God could reveal himself in creation and to humanity, but could not be divided into three distinct Persons. In both their systems, this God is the Father, the divine substance, from which Christ is the manifestation, one within the other, as a soul within a body.

While Servetus does not define the substance of God in specific terms, Swedenborg does. Servetus never separates the substance of God from its expression in Christ (Dia. 1.5). He understands substance and nature to be properties in Christ, rather than in God himself, for

> [n]o human reason can attribute to God any name of Substance or Nature, for he exists outside of Substance and Nature; but when about to create the world, he created in himself Substance in the likeness of the things of this world, and this was the Word, and the light and cause of all nature (Dia. 1:6).

Swedenborg's concept is very similar, except that he describes the prior 'substance' of God as love, the manifestation of which is truth. Thus Christ as the Word is the manifestation of substance of God, or divine love, in no way separate, or separable from the originating substance. One should not understand this as meaning substance in any physical sense of the word, however. Divine love is infinitely higher and prior to mere substance. In Christ, God has a divine substantial element, but as was shown in an earlier chapter, there is a discrete degree between the being of God and Christ the manifestation of this being, much as there is a distinction between the soul and the body. One could not say that the soul has substance in any physical form, but the potential of substance. The body, on the other hand, does have substance, although it only comes into being at the instigation of the soul[6]. The soul within actuates the body, causing it to act. Since humans are created into the image and likeness of God, and since the soul and body cannot be separated and maintain integrity, so the substance of love and form of wisdom in God cannot be separated. 'Both can therefore be predicated of God,' Swedenborg writes, 'on condition that he is the sole, very and prime substance and form' (TCR 20). The Divine, therefore, does not have substance in itself, but the ability to project substance from himself by giving form to his divine loves.

God created the spiritual and physical worlds by expressing this substance of love through wisdom, or the Word, limiting and finiting it until it took on the material form, emptied of its divine origins, and yet able to both reflect, and in the human being, receive them. Swedenborg argues that everyone

> ... who thinks from clear reason sees that the universe was not created out of nothing, for he sees that not anything can be made out of nothing; and since nothing is nothing, and to make anything out of nothing is a contradiction, and a contradiction is contrary to the light of truth, which is from Divine Wisdom (DLW 283, see also DLW 55, DP 1).

Therefore, he argues, God 'created the universe and all things thereof from himself' (DLW 282), 'out of things created and finited, and so formed that the Divine can be within them (DLW 4).

Servetus and Swedenborg, therefore, have similar views on the nature of God as he is in himself, although Servetus did not articulate it in the same philosophical terms favored by Swedenborg. Their ideas coincide again on the subject of Christ, the visible presentation of the invisible Divine.

The Word prior to the Advent

For both Servetus and Swedenborg, Christ is the Word of God, the human form of the Divine. Both men stand opposed to the orthodox Christian view that Christ is a Son from Eternity, the second Person in the Trinity, but the creative manifestation of the Divine itself, the only way in which the ineffable Divine can be set forth and known. In Servetus' works, this Word is termed 'Christ', and as Bainton notes, an

... ambiguity enters, in that the term Christ is applied both to the man Jesus, the Son, and also to the pre-existent Logos or Word. The reason may well be that for Servetus the man Jesus became so identified with the Word that thereafter no distinction could be drawn (Bainton 1953:49).

Bainton has no need of tentativeness in asserting his point. Servetus saw no distinction, other than the physical body, between the Word spoken by God, and Jesus Christ the man. He argues this cogently in the Dialogues,

> [i]n order to prove that the Word is Christ himself, I was saying the Logos and Elohim were the same thing (Dia. 1.2) ... The invisible God, as he was before the creation of the world, is altogether incomprehensible and unimaginable to us, and by the mere good-pleasure of his will he determined to create the world and to express himself to us ... (Dia. 1.3).

These passages indicate the full identification Servetus makes between Christ and the Word. It was Christ, who was the Word, who created, who was incarnated, who redeemed the human race.

Swedenborg has a very similar view. He does not use the term 'Christ' in his writings, preferring the inclusive 'Lord' (AC 14), which contains the complete Trinity. Thus he speaks of 'the Lord' creating, indicating his point that God created from his love by means of his wisdom (DP 3). He does not separate out the various functions of God in terms of creation, for wisdom would not be able to create without the instigation of love, and love would not come into expression except by means of wisdom. It is superfluous to speak, then, of Christ before the incarnation, unless one connects him with the Word itself.

The role of the Word in creation finds its fulfillment in the creation of people, into the image and likeness of God. Servetus indicates that God created humans in order to reveal himself to them (Dia. 1.3), while Swedenborg, elaborating on this theme teaches that humans were created in order that God might have subjects able to receive his love and wisdom and be blessed by it (TCR 43). In both cases, the rationale is the same, a revelation of God to the creation, and although Servetus makes no mention of, if God is truly love in form, then reception of that love must be heaven.

This is only possible in Christ, for he is the only aspect of God we can know on our earthly level. The question could be raised of how

Christ could have revealed God to humanity prior to the advent? Again, Servetus and Swedenborg have developed a very similar theology on this topic. Before the incarnation, people experienced God by means of angels. Servetus writes that 'Christ, in the shape of angels, also shined in our hearts, that we might be enlightened to know him' (Dia. 1.4). These angels were a 'shadow of the true representation [of God] to come' (Dia.1.6), and elaborating on this, he writes:

> ... in the angels there was a mystery of the Christ to come, there was the name of God, which dwelt in the angel. That is, it was God himself, who then manifested himself through the angels under the person of Christ, and obscurely. If you wish to trace this ministry of the angels further, you should know that the angels were created for our sakes, and minister to us, and good angels guard us, even as bad ones tempt us. And the ministry of angels began in man, as God was at that time to be manifested to man through them (Dia. 1.6).

While Swedenborg's theology on this subject is almost identical, there are some points of divergence. He would be more inclined to use the term 'Lord' in preference to 'Christ', the latter indicating the incarnate God. However, since Servetus makes no distinction between incarnate and pre-incarnate, both being the Word, and since Swedenborg makes a similar point, the difference in terminology can be overlooked as a minor discrepancy.

Far more important is the similarity in their view that God revealed himself before the incarnation by means of angels. Swedenborg, elaborating more than Servetus, describes how an angels' sense of self was made quiescent and an accommodated form of divinity flowed in from God. As the angel spoke, so it truly was God, using the angels' form, who spoke through him. In this way the will of God was communicated to the people of this world. Three such in filled angels presented themselves to Abraham, and on another occasion was the source of the voice at the burning bush, and on Mount Sinai (HH 254, AC 1745).

Swedenborg calls this presence of God through angels 'mediate' presence, which came to an end at the incarnation, when the Word, putting on a human form, became 'immediately' present in Jesus Christ. From that time onwards, there has been no need for God to infill an angel in order to communicate with people, for he is now directly present in the natural world, and can illuminate human minds by means of the Word (TCR 109).

In spite of Swedenborg's elaboration on the subject, the theology of God's presence before incarnation is remarkably similar for both men. One fundamental difference lies in an understanding of the nature of angels, for Servetus believed that 'angels were created for our sakes' (Dia. 1.6), implying a belief in harmony with the Christian world, that angels are a separate creation to men. Swedenborg, however, is adamant that angels are not a separate creation, but are people who, loving God, turning from evil and doing good, after death enter heaven and are angels (HH 311). The source of angels aside, however, they agree that prior to the incarnation, God used the angels to make his will known to the people of this earth.

The Incarnation

Just as God created people in order to manifest himself to them, and, Swedenborg would add, to bless them, so manifestation could be perfected. Mediate revelation, by means of angels, only presented God to human minds in shadows, in types. The true glory of God remained hidden like the sun on an overcast day. Under such circumstances it was not surprising that people misunderstood God, and turned from him. The histories and prophecies of the Old Testament bear abundant witness to the decline of human ability to perceive God. Angelic representations of God grew scarcer – at the time of John the Baptist, there had been no prophet in Israel for four hundred years[7]. Redemption and salvation could only be accomplished by a full revelation of God.

Again, Servetus and Swedenborg follow a parallel path in their ideas of the incarnation. Both rejected the notion of a 'Son from eternity', and both believed that Christ was the incarnation of the Word itself, and that without this revelation it is impossible to have any true concept of God. Servetus sums this up when he asks,

> [f]or what can man conceive with regard to God   unless he has rendered himself visible? Much rather is he hidden. The mind fails in thinking of God for he is incomprehensible... God transcends all things and exceeds all intellect and mind ... If one reflects upon light or anything else known to us, one plainly observes that God is not light but above light, he is not essence but above essence, he is not spirit, but above spirit. He is above everything that can be conceived. The true knowledge of God is that which teaches not what he is but that which he is not. No one knows God unless one knows the way in which God has made himself manifest (Bainton 1953:132).

Both Servetus and Swedenborg strove to understand the incarnation of God. They agree that Christ was the bodily expression of the Word of God, and in him 'that deity is plainly said to be' (Dia. 1.7). But how did this come about? In trying to answer this, they both touched on that great imponderable of Christology, how Christ could be both man and God. The end result of their theology is much the same, Christ is God in human form, the invisible rendered visible in him. Sharing a rejection of the concept of a pre-existent Second Person in the Trinity as an entity within itself, and the Chalcedonian formula of two distinct natures in Christ, both men tried to articulate how the Divine itself could descend into a human form in such a way that the divinity was preserved and reflected in human terms, and the humanity likewise was preserved and reflected in divine terms. Servetus notes that 'those who make a sharp demarcation between humanity and divinity do not understand the nature of humanity which is of such a character that God can communicate to it divinity' (Bainton 1953:47).

The relationship of divine and human in Christ cannot be seen in terms of either a degradation of divinity, nor an exaltation of humanity (Bainton 1953:47), for divinity and humanity are not mutually exclusive (Bainton 1953:48). Swedenborg would agree to this, with his principle that all humanity begins in God and is reflected in creation. Since God is human in a divine sense, that is, the essence of humanity, there is no reason why he could not present himself in human form to the people of this earth.

Servetus answers the question of how God could be man with his trilogy of statements, 'I shall admit these three things, first, this man is Jesus Christ, second, he is the Son of God; third, he is God' (Tr. I.2). This is the crux of both men's arguments. To understand the incarnation and subsequent revelation of God, and in Swedenborg's terms, to understand redemption, one must begin with the man. Servetus argues in the first book of the *Trinitatus*[8] that Christ was a man. A human being in every sense of the word – he walked and talked in the world as we do, suffered and died as we do.

While Servetus demonstrates from Scripture that Christ was a man (Bainton 1953:46), Swedenborg goes further. Christ was a man by birth, for although his soul was divine, his body was no different from anyone else's. Humanity, however, is not simply a factor of the body. Swedenborg describes how the Word took on not only the flesh from Mary, but also her hereditary inclinations towards evil[9]. For Swedenborg Christ's purification from these hereditary evils was the entire point of the incarnation. Flesh allows people to live in this world, but flesh in itself is lifeless, deriving all its motivation and direction from the mind. If the mind is corrupt, then the flesh will act in corrupt ways, but if the mind is pure, then the flesh acts in pure ways. By taking on this human mind, corrupted by generations of accumulated tendencies towards evil, Christ took on the fullness of human life. Thus Christ is a man in every sense of the word, not only physically, but mentally. Redemption was achieved by the consistent rejection of his corrupt mental state – including battling with the spirits attracted to perverse human loves and thoughts. Thus the 'flesh' allowed Christ to enter also into the life of the human being in terms of spiritual struggles and battles.

Since both Servetus and Swedenborg reject the *communicatio idiomatum* the manhood of Jesus Christ is not divorced from his divinity, it is not a parallel nature within him. Servetus held that a division of humanity and divinity in Christ led to a disparagement of the humanity, saying, 'you seem to call him a man by way of contempt' (Dia. 1:10). That contempt is misplaced, however, for the man Christ was the vehicle of salvation

> ... it was fitting that to men a man be given as Savior, expressly on account of his spirit. We therefore glorify the Nature of Christ, and of his flesh, and of his body, exalted unto God; nor is there in this any confusion or plurality of beings, but one sole being, one hypostasis or one substance, one thing formed of heavenly seed planted in the earth and coalescing into one substance (Dia. 2.4).

What distinguishes Christ from ordinary people, for both Servetus and Swedenborg, is the fact that while he was a man, Christ was also the Son of God. Servetus defends his declaration by appeal to the New Testament, for example, the miracles Christ performed lead one to 'conclude that he is the Son of God' (Tr. 1.9). However, Christ is the Son of God 'for he was not begotten of the seed of Mary ... but instead the almighty power of the Word of God overshadowed Mary, the Holy Spirit acting within her' and she conceived (Tr. 1:9), and asks, 'what is the offspring begotten and conceived in her, which comes from the Holy Spirit, from which he [the angel Gabriel] concludes that the son whom she brings forth will be the Savior, Immanuel? ... He shall be called the Son of God for the reason that the power of God is instead of the seed of man' (Tr. 1.9).

Thus the man Jesus, a man in every sense, was the Son of God because his conception was from God (Dia. 2.1). He was not a son in the sense of being a separate Person, for as Servetus says, the angel did not say 'he shall be called the Son of the first Person' (Tr. 1.9), but in the sense that as one person derives his life from his parents, so Christ drew his from God himself. However, God's life is not divisible, and his life above heaven, as it is in himself, is necessarily the same life in Christ. The man, therefore, was the Son of God.

Swedenborg would have concurred with this logic and carried it further. The soul, he taught, carries from Father to Son, and since God, through the Holy Spirit – which he understood to be the activity of God – impregnated Mary, the soul of the man Jesus was necessarily Divine, making Christ the Son of God. The soul, he writes,

> ... is the inmost man; consequently, [it] is the man from head to foot. Thence it is, according to the ancients, that the soul is in the whole, and in every part thereof; and that in whatever part the soul does not dwell inmostly, there man has no life. From this union it is, that all things of the soul belong to the body, and all things of the body belong to the soul ... Thus they are one (Invitation 13).

In Swedenborgian terms, therefore, one can think of Christ on two distinct levels[10], internally, that is, in relation to his soul, he is divine, the same divine that has always been, that created, that appeared in the form of angels. In his external he is man, encased in flesh, corrupted in mind by hereditary evil from Mary. This duality in the person of Christ is the source for Swedenborg's doctrine of the glorification, whereby Christ redeemed the human race, united his humanity to his divinity, and is now fully visible to human minds. He did this by systematically fighting against his hereditary evil – since he never gave in to its pressure, he never committed any sin – and rejected it As the humanity from Mary was purified, so the Divine which was his soul and which could be present in all things except evil, became present, first in his mind, his love and thoughts, and eventually, after the resurrection in the body itself.

The conclusion for both Servetus and Swedenborg, therefore, is the same, Christ was a man, he was the Son of God, and since this did not imply any separation from the Divine, it follows that he was God. For each of them this complete association of the Divine to the human described a revelation of the divine as it is at human level. Christ as the incarnation of the second Person of the Trinity would have failed to do that in their minds, for there would always have been a distinction between the Divine as it existed in the Father and in the Son. Yet by expressing Christ as the full revelation of God in one Person, with the

Divine as his soul, not as a separate being, he put the entirety of God on view.

This full association of the human and divine in Christ, making man God, cannot come about without some sort of process. In this Servetus and Swedenborg have a general agreement, but some distinctly different concepts. Both agree that there was no such thing as the *communicatio idiomatum* (Dia. 1.7), while Swedenborg labels the hypostatic union as irrational:

> Again, I ask, What is the hypostatic union? If you reply that it is a union as between two persons, a superior and an inferior, you are irrational; for thus you might make God the Savior two persons, as you make God three; but if you say that it is a personal union like that of soul and body, you say rightly, and this is in harmony with your doctrine (TCR 137).

The question of how the human was subordinated to the divine, however, is one of those areas in which Servetus had no real answer. His solution, outlined at the end of the *Trinitatus* was a 'blending' of God and man. Referring to the Patristic Fathers, he writes:

> The older writers say that man was blended, rather than united, with God. But even if you say that man was united with God, or God united with man, or that a kind of deity was united with Christ, I shall not condemn you... And this is the view of Irenaeus[11] and also of Tertullian[12] who say that the change was made from the Word to flesh, and that along with this a kind of Deity was blended and united with the man, because God in Christ is just this (Tr. 7.5).

He explains this blending as a passing over of the qualities of the Word into man, who is now God, so that as those qualities are embedded in the man, the man becomes God, and as those qualities are implanted in the man, so 'God made himself visible according to the likeness of Christ... Christ was then with God in power, in the Word and in Person' (Tr. 7.7).

Thus Servetus could reason, from Biblical passages that Christ was a man, was the Son of God and was God, but he could not explain how this happened. Swedenborg, however, following much the same line of reasoning, makes it abundantly clear in his writings.

In following Swedenborg's reasoning, one needs to be careful of the use of the concept of blending or mingling. God, always divine is above the time and spatial elements of this world, and never mingles with them (TCR 30). Had the Father, the divine soul, 'mingled' with the body from Mary, it would have resulted in a confusion of divinity with merely human hereditary evils. Such an outcome is, of course, unthinkable. Swedenborg uses the concept of glorification in place of this.

God is present in the human, not by a mingling, but by purification and replacement. The divine could only 'descend' into the human to the degree that Christ had fought against his inherited inclinations towards evil and overcome them. As the crucifixion, which Swedenborg sees as the last and greatest of Christ's temptations, the last human impediment, the flesh itself, was enabled to receive fully the divine presence. There is not, therefore, any mingling of human and divine, by the human facilitating the descent of the Divine to human level.

On the surface Swedenborg's concept of the Divine Human looks like a mingling, and it may be that this is what Servetus was attempting to say when he refers to the Fathers as saying 'the change was made from the Word to flesh, and that along with this a kind of Deity was blended and united with the man, because God in Christ is just this (Tr. 7.5) – a statement as true in Swedenborg's terminology as in Servetus'.

It would not have been possible for Servetus to explain his 'blending' in Swedenborgian terms as he was lacking the essential components of Swedenborg's thought. In the first place he did not have a concept of hereditary evil passed from Mary to Christ. This meant that he could not see the need for the cycle of temptation and victory characterizing Christ's life in this world. In Swedenborg's theology, temptation was a mechanism for rejecting the corrupt human and allowing the divine to descend into the body.

Secondly, without knowing about the process of temptation, he could have not understood how the process of glorification worked. He could say that the Divine and human were mingled, but could not explain it – something he freely admits,

> [g]reat and ineffable is the mystery, that that flesh is the same as our own, and that by its own nature it has a divine substance; that it was conceived in the womb of a virgin, and born from the substance of God; that it was brought forth after the likeness of us, coming forth from God even from everlasting; that Christ was made from a woman, born of Mary, and was at the same time born and begotten of the substance of God; and as no one can declare his generations, so no one knoweth who the Son is, save the Father (Dia. 2.2).

Yet it was precisely to unravel this mystery that Swedenborg propounded his doctrine of the glorification, of the divine soul clothed in a human body, making Christ at once Son of God and man from Mary, who became the visible God.

It is as if Servetus began a series of ideas, of interpretations of the Bible, and Swedenborg finished them, giving them shape and form, expressing them not only in the language of the Bible, but of enlightenment philosophy and science. Servetus says that Christ was man, Swedenborg explains why, not only in physical terms but in psychological ones. Servetus defends Christ as the Son of God, Swedenborg explains how this came to be, and what it means. Finally, as both agree that Christ is God, Servetus shows how and Swedenborg why. The two theologies match step for step.

The Holy Spirit

The third chapter in Swedenborg's *True Christian Religion* deals with the subject of the Holy Spirit. Here again, the ideas and concepts are almost identical. Since both men reject the Trinitarian formulation of Three Persons in one Substance, the Holy Spirit cannot be a 'Person' in its own right. Servetus writes:

> The doctrine of the Holy Spirit as a third separate being lands us in practical tritheism no better than atheism, even though the unity of God be insisted on ... The Holy Spirit as a third person of the Godhead is unknown in Scripture. It is not a separate being, but an activity of God himself (Tr. I Argument).

Swedenborg notes that clerics in the next life 'receive instruction at first about the Divine Trinity, and particularly about the Holy Spirit, that it is not a God by itself, but that the Divine operation proceeding from the one and omnipresent God is ... the Holy Spirit' (TCR 138).

The Holy Spirit is the activity of God, flowing into and affecting people's lives, 'a kind of in-working or in-breathing of the power of God' (Tr. I.40). This inflowing is called 'the Holy Spirit', for God is a spirit[13], and his presence is his spirit acting in people. Swedenborg shares a very similar point of view. He describes the Holy Spirit as the 'divine energy and operation proceeding from the one God in whom is the Divine Trinity' (TCR 139), and carrying the idea further, identifies this as the divine truth proceeding from the glorified Christ – the same truth that created the world, now acting as a force in human redemption.

In reading Servetus one should be cautious of his terminology describing the Holy Spirit. Having expressed his rejection of the Holy Spirit as a separate Person in the Trinity, he still uses the term 'Person' to describe it. In Book I of the *Trinitatus* he writes that 'since I am unwilling to misuse the word Persons, I shall call them the first being, the second being, the third being, for in the Scriptures I find no other name for them, and what is properly to be thought of the Persons I shall say later on' (Tr. I:30). Later on he does indeed return to the subject saying that

> ... in Scripture the outward form and appearance of a man is called his person ... But apart from the Scriptures, the meaning of the word *persona* is in itself so well known to the Latins that some devil must have suggested to them to invent mathematical Persons, and to thrust their imaginary and metaphysical beings upon us as Persons (Tr. I.51).

Servetus rejects the numeracy of the term Persons, preferring Tertullian's term, *disposition* which does not imply a number of beings, but the appearance of beings. This consideration need to be borne in mind in the opening argument of Book II, where speaking of the Holy Spirit, he says 'God's Spirit, which is a person of the Godhead. It proceeds from the Son, not as a separate being but as a ministering spirit. It is holy, one of the three persons in the Godhead, and sanctifies us by dwelling within us' (Tr. II Argument).

A cursory reading of the above passage could confuse the reader who, having been told in Book I that the Holy Spirit is not a Person, is told in Book II that he is. However, Servetus has not changed his mind on the nature of the Holy Spirit – it is not a numerical person, but the activity of God in human life.

Swedenborg allows for no such ambiguity. Rejecting the use of the term Persons in relation to the Trinity, he uses the word 'Divine Proceeding' to describe this presence of God. He defines the Holy Spirit as 'the Holy which proceeds from the Lord (AC 6788). As was shown earlier, this 'holy' is the Divine truth (TCR 140).

Thus even though the terminology used between the two men differs, and Servetus' terms are at times confusing, the essential concept of the Holy Spirit is very similar. In light of their similar beliefs about the nature of God, this similarity is to be expected, for if one denies the three Persons of the Trinity, then the working model of the nature of God must be different. Should one state, as both Servetus and Swedenborg do, that God is one, and that Jesus Christ is the manifestation of that God, then it follows that the Holy Spirit must needs be the operation of that manifestation. According to this model of the Trinity, the three aspects, or elements of God make a oneness, conforming to the image of soul, body and operation in the human being.

The Trinity

Swedenborg's chapter on the Holy Spirit in the *True Christian Religion* ends with a treatment of the nature of the Trinity. It is not surprising that the commonality of ideas about the nature of God, find fullness of expression in their ideas of the Trinity. Odhner writes of Servetus:

> That which above all characterizes and distinguishes the Theology of Servetus from the doctrines of his contemporaries, and that in which above all else he approaches most closely to the 'Universal Theology'[14] of the New Church, is his doctrine concerning the Lord and the Trinity in him (Odhner 1910:65).

For both Servetus and Swedenborg, the redefinition of the understanding of Father, Son and Holy Spirit, leads to redefining the Trinity. Both have been accused of rejecting a Trinity completely, but this is not the case. Their shared image of Christ as the manifestation and representation of the Divine Father, or soul, acting as the Holy Spirit, leads to a Trinity composed not of numerical Persons, but states of the Godhead within the person of Christ. Their rejection, therefore, is less one of a denial of three 'dispositions' of God, as Servetus terms them, or three 'beings', but one of three distinct, co-equal Persons, each a God in his own right.

Servetus dismisses this belief contemptuously as an emblem of derision in the Muslim and Jewish world (Tr. I.59), calling it a 'most burning plague... brought upon us by the Greeks' (Tr. I.60). Swedenborg's dismissal is equally strong, for in his view, this doctrine led to the perversion and destruction of the Christian Church (TCR 177).

To fill the gap left by dismissing the Tri-personal Trinity, Servetus and Swedenborg propose very similar theories of how the Trinity works. Father, Son and Holy Spirit are not distinct hypostases of the Divine Substance, for they claim that this would lead to a Tri-theism. Instead, Christ is the single hypostasis of the Divine Substance, the Father, and the Holy Spirit the activity of that substance, acting through the person of Christ. In this way, God is one and undivided.

However, neither man rejects the notion of the Trinity if it is seen in this form. God, as he speaks the Word, is the Father. While Servetus does not define this unknowable element of God, Swedenborg does, God is the divine Love. The Word, the means by which God revealed himself and created, when put into human form, is Christ. Yet the Word proceeds at all times from the Father, there can be no disconnection from him. The Word acting is the Holy Spirit, present in human life. Each of these together make one God, and yet each of them is God on a different plane or level. Swedenborg's doctrine of discrete degrees outlines this the best, for while each degree is distinct from the others, nevertheless, they are in a prior/posterior or cause and effect relationship with each other. At no point, for example, does he confuse divine love with the Word, or the Word with the activity. Yet together they make a perfect one.

While Servetus did not have a theological principle of discrete degrees, he does seem to allude to them in speaking of the nature of the Trinity. For example, in the *Dialogues* he writes, 'as Christ has a certain difference from God, so also does his Spirit, whose distinction arises from the distinction of Christ; because the Spirit is the Spirit of Christ, and as the Word became flesh, so the Spirit of the Word became the Spirit of the flesh of Christ' (Dia. 1.12). Had he had a notion of discrete degrees, he could have written that Christ is a more external degree of God, and the Holy Spirit an even more external degree, and yet each degree is drawn from and derives its being from the one before, and expresses itself in the one after. Swedenborg, in developing the idea of degrees, speaks of these aspects of God as 'distinctly one' (DLW 14, DLW 21), indicating that they have perceivable, but not real differences. The doctrine of discrete degrees makes it possible for one thing to take on a certain reality on different planes, whilst retaining the integrity of the whole, and this is what Servetus seems to be trying to say.

Their idea of God coincides, therefore, on all levels. It is true that Servetus did not have the freedom to elaborate his theology as Swedenborg did, and perhaps if he had had the time, the gaps between the two would have closed. These differences, however, are more mechanical, explaining how the Trinity works, rather than conceptual. Thus it almost appears as if Swedenborg finished the work Servetus started.

The Consequences of this Belief

Similarity in a primary doctrine leads to similarity in secondary teachings. The teachings of a church can be traced back to its primary concept of God. For example, the doctrine of the vicarious atonement is, by definition, an expression of a Tri-Personal Trinity. Since Servetus and Swedenborg reject this model of the Trinity, these teachings become untenable, and must be replaced with others in accordance with their united Trinity in the Person of Jesus Christ.

For both men, the grand finale of the subject of the incarnation is that in Christ God became man, and returned to being God. The focus of spiritual life, therefore, is Christ, in whom is the Divine Trinity of Father, Son and Holy Spirit. Thus Servetus writes of Christ,

> ... he is now God in the same place and in the same way as before ... the Christ himself is now by his resurrection raised to so great glory that he would not now say, 'the Father is greater than I' ... but now the glory of the Father has been obtained, this causal glory ceases. And neither is he less, nor the Father greater. Nor is there any other power of God than the Son himself, whom Paul thus calls 'the power of God'[15] (Dia. 2.6).

Swedenborg concurs that in the resurrected and glorified Jesus Christ, there is all power:

> The Lord alone has all power, and he exercises it through divine truth that proceeds from him. But that this may be more clearly perceived it shall be shown:
> 1.   that the Lord has infinite power.
> 2.   that the Lord has this power from himself through his divine truth.
> 3.   that all power is together in ultimates, and therefore that the Lord has infinite power from things first through ultimates (AE 726).

This power is the source of their theology, and its specific applications to human life, and especially to soteriology. It needs to be borne in mind, however, that they wrote in two different milieus. For Servetus, the issues of the Reformation were immediate. While it is not known if he met Martin Luther, he was at the Diet of Worms. He personally knew Oecolampadius and Calvin, the latter tragically, was exposed to their thoughts and ideas. Thus Servetus dealt with the cutting edge of the Reformation. By the time Swedenborg wrote his theology, in the third quarter of the eighteenth century, that cutting edge was pretty blunt. The innovations of the Reformation had settled down to the orthodoxy of the Enlightenment era. In sophisticated circles, deism, naturalism and atheism were all gaining ground.

This difference in milieu accounts for some of the differences in their writing, but their commitment to Christ as the all-powerful manifestation of God, led to a rejection of the two major articles of the Reformation, faith alone and predestination. In addition, Swedenborg rejected the developments in theology in the eighteenth century – although these fall outside the scope of this chapter.

Rejection of faith alone

The basic tenet of the Reformation is the belief, articulated by Martin Luther, that one is saved by faith alone. As Servetus and Swedenborg conceived this faith, however, it indicates a Trinity divided into three Persons, for the Father, alienated from the world, sent his Son, who made satisfaction for human sins. Those who believe in this satisfaction are saved by their belief, and the Father and Son together send the Holy Spirit to reconcile the sinner to God (Faith 38).

> Almost in the very words of Swedenborg, Servetus condemns the reformers for their fundamental ...doctrine of salvation by faith alone. Faith, he admits, does indeed save a man, but not faith alone, especially not the faith of the Lutherans, or of any church that has divided the Godhead into three Persons, and Christ into two natures (Odhner 1910:58).

They held that the division of the Godhead obscured the nature of God, and as Servetus writes, 'to believe is supposed to be sufficient for salvation; but what follows is to believe aught which cannot be understood' (Restitutio 288), and again, 'no one can have faith in that of which he has no knowledge whatsoever' (Restitutio 300).

Swedenborg says much the same thing. He defines faith as 'an internal acknowledgement of truth' (Faith 1), saying that at

> ... the present day the term faith is taken to mean the mere thought that the thing is so because the church so teaches, and because it is not evident to the understanding[16]. For we are told to believe, and not to doubt, and if we say that we do not comprehend, we are told that

this is just the reason for believing. So that the faith of the present day is a faith in the unknown, and may be called blind faith, and as it is something that someone has said, in somebody else, it is a faith of hearsay. It will be seen presently that this is not spiritual faith (Faith 1).

The main article of religious belief obscuring faith, according to Servetus and Swedenborg, is the misunderstanding of the nature of God. The Nicene and Chalcedonian formulas confuse the mind, creating images of a God who is both one and three. As we have seen earlier, both men claim that this leaves the believer with a mixed message, resolved by a statement of one God, with thought of three. Similarly, Christ himself, simultaneously God and man, is a dual character, who in history is distorted either towards the human side, as by the Antiochene school, or the divine side by the Alexandrian. Thus the nature of Christ, instead of being a unifying factor in the church, has contributed to factions and divisions. Both hold the solution of the *communicatio idiomatum* in disdain.

Thus people are left in a situation in which they can have no faith, for the principle of God is destroyed. However, Servetus and Swedenborg offer a solution. One is not saved by faith alone, but by an imitation of Christ, for he was born a man, making his starting point the same as ours, yet he was also a Son of God. People are not sons by nature as Christ was, but sons by adoption. People become 'Sons of God' by learning and living by the teachings of Christ, thereby submitting themselves to God. Christ became God, something not possible for ordinary people, but through submission, people become images and likenesses of God. This is the final object of faith, to lead people to become images of God, and since he is a God of love and wisdom, to lead people into the practice of those things in their own lives.

An alternative to salvation through vicarious atonement is the double predestination offered by Calvin. Although he described predestination in a cautious and gingerly way, Calvin believed that God alone was the author of salvation, regardless of the state of the individual per se. In his *Institutes* he writes that 'no one who wishes to be thought religious dares simply to deny predestination, by which God adopts some to hope of life and sentences others to eternal death' (Bouwsma 1988:172). Those elected to heaven are given every advantage by God to prepare them, but those destined to hell are effectively blocked. Elaborating this Calvin writes that as

> ... God by the effectual working of his call to the elect perfects the
> salvation to which by his eternal plan he has destined them, so he has
> his judgements against the reprobate, by which he executes his plan
> for them. What of those, then, whom he created for dishonor in life
> and destruction in death, to become the instruments of his wrath and
> examples of his severity? That they may come to their end, he
> sometimes deprives them of the capacity to hear his word; at other
> times he blinds and stuns them by the preaching of it (Bouwsma
> 1988:172).

Calvin's double predestination runs contrary to both Servetus'
and Swedenborg's ideas of salvation because it is opposed to their
understanding of the nature of God. Their God, essentially love clothed
in wisdom, reaches into human hearts, but at all times respects and
preserves spiritual freedom. Servetus describes God as 'freedom itself,
since he is infinitely superior to all external and compelling influences.
And as God is freedom itself, so he grants to man to will freely and act
freely, within certain limits (Odhner 1910:61, Restitutio 54).

In a similar vein, Swedenborg writes that,

> ... without free will in spiritual matters man would have nothing by
> which the Lord could link himself to him; yet without a reciprocal
> link there could be no reformation or regeneration, and consequently
> salvation would be impossible. It is an irrefutable consequence that
> without a reciprocal link of man with the Lord and of the Lord with
> man, there could be no imputation (TCR 485).

Calvin's system contains a denial of the nature of Christ as the
salvation of all men, for if some people were predestined to hell, Christ
could not have saved them. In his own right, he thought it 'terrible that,
as Scripture compelled him to believe, only a small number, out of an
incalculable multitude, should obtain salvation' (Bouwsma 1988:173).
In spite of this, he demanded that people not question the teaching, as it
would lead to an abyss, a labyrinth from which no one could be led out
(Bouwsma 1988:173), thus making the acts of God inscrutable and
unintelligible, drawing a curtain over salvation.

Servetus and Swedenborg saw different teachings about God
in the New Testament. For Servetus, predestination was a travesty of
divine justice (Odhner 1910:61), while for Swedenborg it is hurtful and
cruel (TCR 486), criminal (TCR 487) and unnatural (TCR 488). The
alternative offered by Servetus and Swedenborg, is, as one would

expect, remarkably similar, an exercise of human freedom to walk the path of Christ in repentance, reformation and final regeneration. Salvation comes as an effect of the human being opening his or her mind to receive the Holy Spirit, or the presence and activity of God within them, which can only be done by willfully turning from evil and embracing goodness. Faith plays a vital role in instructing and leading the individual in this process. Charity, or love of goodness, keeps one constant, and the external manifestation of faith and charity in good works, seals the process, giving it a tangible reality. Thus the individual becomes an image and likeness of God.

Notes:

[1] 'ut in archetypo mundo vere lucentes' (Restitutio 137).

[2] As shown earlier, these were the most ancient, the ancient, the Jewish, Christian and the New Church that he claims will arise in response to the restoration of the Trinity and the revelation of the inner meaning of the Bible.

[3] Totum Verbi arcanum erat hujus Hominis glorificatio (Restitutio 579).

[4] Erat Deus pater, immensitas inaccesssibilis, incomprehensibilis, lux invisibilis (Restitutio 704).

[5] Swedenborg uses 'Jehovah' in this context to refer to God himself.

[6] Swedenborg states that the soul, at conception, clothes itself with a material body, 'Every person starts from the soul, which is the true essence of the seed. This not only initiates but also produces one after the other the bodily structures; and later on it initiates the products of the soul and the body working together, what are called its activities' (TCR 166, see also TCR 82, NJHD 286, AC 10125, AC 10076).

[7] The prophecy of Malachi is dated at approximately 430BC.

[8] Exactly the same argument is used in the opening of the *Restitutio*.

[9] Swedenborg rejects original sin in favor of inherited tendencies towards evil which, when they are acted out in life, become sins.

[10] As Servetus would say, 'according to the flesh he is man; and in the spirit he is God' (Tr. 1.14).

[11] Against Heretics V.i.3.

[12] Against Praxean xxvii.

[13] Here Servetus refers to John 4:24, 'God is Spirit, and those who worship Him must worship in spirit and truth.'

[14] I.e. Swedenborg's *True Christian Religion* which is subtitled, '*the universal theology of the New Church.*'

[15] 1Cor 1.24).

[16] Compare this to the statement attributed to Tertullian, credo quia absurdum.

Chapter Twelve

Common Sources and Roots

It is fascinating that Swedenborg had no apparent knowledge of Servetus. During the two hundred years separating them theologians of Europe suppressed Servetus' books, making it unlikely that Swedenborg read them. There is no evidence that he did. It is also interesting to bear in mind that prior to 1744; Swedenborg had little more than a passing interest in theological studies. Certainly, as a practicing Christian, he included concepts of God in his scientific and philosophical work, but his interest was scholarly, and there is no evidence that dogma as such appealed to him in any way. Certainly, he would have been exposed to some theology during his years at Uppsala[1] and through his contacts with his father, brothers-in-law and other clerical friends and relatives. Nevertheless, Swedenborg left many notebooks and outlines of his studies that indicate little or no interest in the doctrines of formal religion, and no evidence of any interest in Servetus.

This being as it may, it follows that there must be some explanation for the similarity and overlap between the two theological systems. Since Servetus is open and clear about labeling his sources, it is possible to make a direct study of them. The early Patristic Fathers, particularly Ignatius, Irenaeus and Tertullian were a profound influence. He also understood the other major theologians of the Patristic and Scholastic eras. Indeed, using the understanding of theology gained from the early Fathers, he held the later developments of Christianity up to ridicule, and attempted to show, from his own in-depth study of the Old and New Testaments, that the Fathers were right, and those who followed were wrong.

Swedenborg, however, does no such thing. His theology, he asserts, is a revelation from God, saying,

> ... the Lord has been pleased to show Himself to me, and to send me to teach the doctrines of the New Church meant by the New Jerusalem in the Book of Revelation. For this purpose He has opened up the inner levels of my mind and spirit. This has allowed me to associate with angels in the spiritual world and at the same time with human beings in the natural world, something I have now experienced for twenty-five years[2] (CL 1).

He makes similar claims in other books of his theological writings[3]. He did not see the rewriting of Christian theology as an enterprise to be based on reading and studying the works of others, for in his opinion, these had either not gone far enough in developing doctrine, or they had failed to explain it accurately. For him a completely new beginning had to be made in the light of heaven. His claims to spiritual enlightenment, however, should not block either his theology, or in the search for its source and roots in this world. Swedenborg could not have acted in a vacuum. Many of the general principles he elaborates in his works have their roots in the works of earlier people. There are echoes between the Patristic Fathers and himself, although, as in the case of the similarity between his theology and that of Servetus, Swedenborg often elaborates a concept, introducing new factors to the ancient equations, until his product goes further in explaining the mysteries of Christianity than the early writers dreamed of doing.

Swedenborg looked back on Christianity from the perspective of the enlightenment. His milieu was not the foundation era of the Church fathers. He was in no personal danger for his beliefs in the way that either Ignatius or Augustine were. He was also not hidebound by the medieval mysticism of the scholastics. Unlike Servetus, he had no Inquisition or Calvin to take him to task. Breathing the freer air of the enlightenment, he drew on a far more secular basis for his theology. The foundations of Christianity were being questioned in his level of academia. Science was the new buzzword. The age of reason was in its full glory. As a scientist and philosopher, with a penchant for mechanics, Swedenborg was interested in how theology worked, and, in places where, in his mind, it did not work, how it could be restated in such a way that, for him, appealed to the rational senses and worked.

It seems anachronistic, from a modern point of view, that someone with such a scientific bent would approach theology from a mystical point of view – but his mysticism only served as an entrée to the subject. Once he had opened the doors of theology through his spiritual experiences, he brought forth the full power of his intellect, and, reading the Bible afresh, he saw things differently from almost everyone, except Servetus.

As was shown in the previous chapter, Servetus and Swedenborg shared the belief that the church underwent a dramatic change at the time of Nicaea. Prior to that time, they believed that the church had not yet been subverted to a belief in three Persons in a Trinity, who, although they were said to be one, acted as if distinct. They held that in the early church it was still possible to think and say 'one God' simultaneously, something lost to the church after 325 AD. Since they share a common belief in the unity of the Trinity, expressed in the Person of Jesus Christ, it follows that their common sources must lie in the Patristic Era. Although their treatment of this subject matter differs, the result is remarkably similar. The difference in treatment lies in how Servetus uses the Fathers to support and underpin his conclusions drawn from reading the Bible. Swedenborg, not truly interested in the Fathers in general, nevertheless thinks in paradigms very similar to theirs, couching and explaining the ideas in terms of his own rationalistic approach to theology. Yet despite these differences, the result between Swedenborg, Servetus, and the early Fathers is much the same.

One of the essential aspects of Pre-Nicene theology is the concept that all history and revelation prior to the advent found full expression in Christ – he was the recapitulation of history. In him the Godhead dwells bodily. Osborn (1997, 84) notes that 'all early Christian theologians believed that history had a purpose and that it was summed up in Christ'. The essence of the recapitulation paradigm is that in Christ the monarchy of God exists (Osborn 1997, 120), and from this it is but a small step to Servetus' one God revealed in the man Jesus Christ, and Swedenborg's Trinity in the Person of Jesus Christ. Servetus does not have as complete a view of history as Swedenborg does, but sees Christ as the fulfillment of the past. Swedenborg, as was shown in the first chapter on his theology, traces three 'churches' prior to the advent, each contingent on a presentation of God to the human race. In each, the prophecy of the coming Christ takes a central point, in response to the fall of the first, or Most Ancient Church. These prophecies are completed in Christ, who, in his glorified human, made it possible for the invisible God to be visible and present at human level. Thus, Swedenborg writes,

So when the Word had been wholly falsified and adulterated by the Jewish nation, and, as it were, made of no effect, it pleased the Lord to descend from heaven, and to come as the Word, and fulfill it, and thereby to restore and re-establish it, and give light once more to the inhabitants of the earth, according to the words of the Lord, *The people that sit in darkness saw a great light, and to them that sit in the land and shadow of death, to them did the light spring up* (Isa. 9, 8, Matt. 4, 16 – TCR 270).

The recapitulation paradigm, contained in the words 'fulfill', 'restore' and 're-establish' when related to the advent of Christ echoed in the theology of both Servetus and Swedenborg, is the first common ground these two men find with the Pre-Nicene Church. It provides the framework for their approach to the Trinity. For neither of them saw the progression from Christ as the recapitulation of God's presence with humanity to Christ as second Person of the Trinity as a normal nor desirable progression of doctrine. For Christ to be the fulfillment of all history meant a closer bond between him and the Father than is always apparent in the Nicene expression of the Trinity, for in the recapitulation model, it is possible to see Christ as the natural extension or expression of God without necessarily having to be a separate entity. According to this model, God is one, revealed in Christ, acting through the Holy Spirit. Neither Servetus nor Swedenborg believed that there was necessarily a need for the church to progress to the Trinitarian formula, but could have elaborated on patristic concepts without that outcome[4].

Servetus and Swedenborg came to the recapitulation doctrine independently, Servetus first in time, Swedenborg two hundred years later, although he was oblivious to Servetus' writings. Since countless other theologians have visited and reviewed the history of Christian dogma without reaching these conclusions, there had to be some motivation within the body of Patristic writing that lead both these men, separately, to such a firm conviction. The answer lies in the earliest systematized statements of the Christian faith.

Since Swedenborg makes few direct references to the Patristic Fathers, and since his theology is similar to that of Servetus, it makes sense to examine again the theologians that most clearly influenced Servetus, to see if they would have had the same effect on Swedenborg. By doing this, it could be possible to establish, at least some likelihood that Swedenborg was exposed to them.

The three primary theologians of the early church to whom Servetus refers are Ignatius, Irenaeus, and Tertullian. Their impact on his theology was explored in the chapter on his sources. Swedenborg does not refer to either Ignatius or Irenaeus. As a result, it must be assumed that his knowledge or interest in them was not sufficient for them to make an impact on his theology, although their contribution to Servetus' thought was not inconsiderable. For the purposes of this study, however, they must be discarded as not being part of the common ground between Servetus and Swedenborg, except as illustrations of Swedenborg's view that prior to Nicaea people did not separate Father from Son.

Swedenborg also makes only a few passing remarks about Tertullian[5], each in his pre-theological works, and each of those times, in the context of a quotation by another philosopher[6]. These fleeting references, however, indicate that he had at least a passing acquaintance with Tertullian, if not in the original form, then in references by others. A case can be made, however, for reading Tertullian in relation to Swedenborg's theology, that there are significant echoes in Swedenborg's writings. These are very similar to those found in Servetus' work, and it may well be that both find common seminal ground in Tertullian's work.

Tertullian

Tertullian's theology on the nature of God, and his Christology, was outlined in Chapter Two, especially as it is defined in the work *Against Praxean*. In many ways he shared many common characteristics with both Servetus and Swedenborg. He was opposed to any teachings going against the faith as he understood it, and his motivation to set the misunderstanding of his contemporaries to rights is reflected down the centuries by both Servetus and Swedenborg. Servetus, riding the crest of the Reformation, sought to reform the most fundamental doctrine of the Church, the Trinity. As such he stood in opposition to those who did not recognize his version of the Trinity, labeling the medieval scholastics as 'philosophers', while deriding both Luther and Calvin as misguided. Swedenborg, too, took a similar stance. For him those external to Christianity were the increasing numbers of naturalistic and materialistic philosophers of his own time, while those within the church espoused the doctrine of faith alone anchored in a Trinity of Persons, which he abominated. The common denominator for all three men was one of rejection and a desire to restate the doctrines of the church.

Tertullian wrote in a time before Christianity assumed the role of the favored religion of the Roman Empire, in the days when state sponsored persecution and responsive martyrdom colored theology. A convert to Christianity himself, he wrote both for Christians and non-Christians alike, with the intention of setting the doctrine into an orderly and coherent form (Bray 1979 Preface). As the earliest writer of documented systematic theology, he devised the language, in Latin, of the Trinity and Christology that is still in service to the Western Church (Stead 1970, 46). In the West, his influence has left an indelible mark on the history of the church (Bray 1979, 1).

Tertullian's theological writings differ from those of both Ignatius and Irenaeus. Ignatius wrote letters, within which his concept of the Trinity shines very dimly and is never clearly stated. Irenaeus, in his treatise *Against Heretics* deals with a specific issue, Gnosticism, with the result that his doctrine of the Trinity is scattered throughout the volume. It is not brought together in a complete and coherent form as Tertullian does in *Against Praxean*. In addressing the subject, Tertullian attempts to set into order 'the different realities known through reason and faith' (Danielou 1977, 343), a task shared by both Servetus and Swedenborg. While his clearest definition of the nature of the Trinity is set out in *Against Praxean*, Tertullian establishes a continuity of thought, and a uniformity of expression across all his writing.

In addition, Tertullian was greatly influenced by materialistic Stoicism (Wiles1966, 15), while Irenaeus was a Platonist (Norris 1966, 68). While 'the African was doubtless acquainted with the great Adversus Haereses; and if so, one can be sure that he read it with no little sympathy, since the doctrines of the sort which it attacked were a familiar problem to him', it does not follow that he followed Irenaeus blindly. Tertullian is somewhat of a new strain in Christianity (Norris 1966, 81).

Tertullian's exposition of the Trinity in his Treatise against Praxean showed an orderliness of thought that both Servetus and Swedenborg believed were necessary to understand the nature of God. Servetus readily accuses the scholastics of confusion – although, as has been noted, his own writings are often confusing, while Swedenborg equates order with God himself, and held that the order of the universe, and thought, are reflections of God.

For Tertullian the most effective way of promoting orthodox Christianity was in the refutation of what Danielou (1977, 344) calls 'the various deformations of that faith'. In doing this, he forged a completely original understanding of theology (Danielou 1977, 344). Again, Tertullian shares a similar spirit with both Servetus and Swedenborg. The former rejected the entirety of Christian teaching on the nature of the Trinity, and, in doing so, sought to give form to a new understanding. Swedenborg, also alienated from orthodoxy, sought to redefine the Trinity without denying its existence.

For Servetus and Swedenborg, the early church epitomized the purity of doctrinal thought, and if Tertullian was the first Latin to express this thought in coherent form, then it follows that much of their thoughts may well be based in his works. It is interesting to note that although Tertullian did provide much of the framework of theological thought, still his works fell into disfavor as the effects of the Nicene and Chalcedonian Councils permeated the Church.

The church stopped reading his work for 'his writings contained little of value which by that time could not be found elsewhere' (Bray 1979, 11), consequently the Monarchical nature of his understanding of the Trinity also was lost. His stress on the oneness of God, revealed in Christ, was edged out by Christ as second Person in the Trinity of Persons, existing from eternity. The external factors, for example, his intransigence on certain moral and ethical principles, are cited as the reason for his disfavor, but in the main, the whole of Tertullian's theology was at odds with the Post Nicene orthodoxy.

General interest in his work revived somewhat in the late Middle Ages, coinciding with the increased religious fervor in Western Europe. The reformers found him to be of great use in describing the role of the church, using it in to underpin their opposition to Rome (Bray 1979, 12). The Roman Catholic studied him to support the Church's claims to orthodoxy. In this way, he was studied at universities, and so Servetus was exposed to him, although his interest became more focused on the nature of God than of the Church. Among the church related teachings that were of interest to the Reformed scholars, were, of course, his ideas on the economy and monarchy of God, and it was this latter field of study that arrested Servetus' attention, contributing tremendously to his rejection of the orthodox Trinity in favor of his own.

Swedenborg, following later, reflected that the Reformation was important as it made possible the return of the Bible to the people. He writes,

> ... the Word, which is in the possession of the Protestant and Reformed churches, enlightens by spiritual communication all nations and peoples; also ... the Lord provides that there shall always be on earth a church where the Word is read, and thereby the Lord is made known. Therefore, when the Papists had almost wholly rejected the Word, by the Lord's Divine Providence, the Reformation took place, whereby the Word was drawn as it were from concealment and brought into use (TCR 270).

As the structure of the medieval Church was 'shaken to its foundation' so the works of the Patristic Fathers took on new importance (Bray 1979, 11). Swedenborg may well have seen Tertullian's presentation of the Trinity as an alternative presentation of the dogma to begin a new epoch in Christian history. However, only Servetus seems to have drawn from him the same kind of dogmatic philosophy as he espoused in his own writings.

What then did Servetus and possible Swedenborg, draw from Tertullian that was essential to their understanding of the Trinity and the nature of God?

The Rule of Faith

Tertullian's concept of God is encapsulated in his Rule of Faith, which

> ... prescribes the belief that there is only one God, and that He is none other than the Creator of the world, who produced all things out of nothing[7] through his own Word, first of all sent forth; that this Word is called his Son, [and] under the name of God, was seen in divers manners by the patriarchs, heard at all times in the prophets, at last brought down by the Spirit and Power of the Father into the Virgin Mary, was made flesh in her womb, and being born of her, went forth as Jesus Christ ... having been crucified, he rose again on the third day [then] having ascended into the heavens, he sat at the right hand of the Father, sent instead of himself the Power of the Holy Spirit to lead such as believe ... (Prescription XIII).

The utter simplicity of this statement lies at the heart of all Christian beliefs, and, as it stands, unites Servetus and Swedenborg with the whole of the Christian tradition. The difficulty Christianity has traditionally faced has been how to express the inherent relationships within this formula. There is no doubt that there is a God and that he is one, the Creator of the world. Without this belief, Christianity would cease to be monotheistic. More difficult to express, however, is the connection of the Word, the Son, with the Father. Since the Nicene Council, the Son has come to be regarded as a 'Son from Eternity', always coexisting with God. However, as was shown earlier, both Servetus and Swedenborg denied this, holding instead that the Son was the enfleshment of the Word of God proceeding from the mouth of God. This too is what Tertullian appears to be saying when he writes that the Word, first sent forth to create was 'at last brought down ... into the Virgin Mary ... [and] went forth as Jesus Christ'.

It is this perception of the relationship of the Father and Son, so often expressed by Tertullian as the Son proceeding from the Father as the Word, that finds expression in Servetus' formula that Christ is 'man, Son of God, God'. Tertullian's high Christology describing the descent of the Word to the flesh finds its reciprocal echo in Servetus' low Christology from man to God. Servetus arrives at this Christology largely through the thoughts of Tertullian, although he finds supporting evidence in other patristic writers, for example, Origen who wrote,

> We worship one God, the Father and the Son ... We worship, therefore, the Father of Truth and the Son, who is the Truth, and these, while they are two, considered as person or subsistence, are one in unity of thought, in harmony, and in identity of will. So entirely are they one that he who has seen the Son ...has seen in him who is the image of God, God himself (contra Celsus VIII XII).

Although Origen expresses similar ideas to those of Tertullian, Servetus bases his thought more fully on Tertullian. He begins his argument on the nature of God by drawing on Tertullian to establish that Jesus was a man (Prax. XXVIII), and that the name 'Christ' was given as an indication of his relationship to the Father (Marc. IV. XXVIII), which made him Son of God, and indeed, because God cannot be divided, it made him God (Marc. IV. XVIII). For Servetus this meant that 'according to the flesh he is man; and in the spirit he is God' (Tr. 1.14). Thus both the high and low Christologies lead to the oneness or monarchy of God.

If God is one, then how does that oneness find expression in the Father, Son, and Holy Spirit? For Servetus the issue of the Trinity lies in Tertullian's teaching concerning the progressive revelation of God as a series of dispositions[8] of the divine, for Tertullian wrote that he believes 'that there is one only God, but under the following disposition, or economy, as it is called, that this one only God has also a Son, His Word, who proceeded from himself, by whom all things were made' (Prax II).

It is this disposition that 'distributes the Unity into a Trinity, placing in their order the three – the Father, the Son and the Holy Spirit, three however, not in condition, but in degree' (Prax. II). This distribution, therefore, neither separates nor changes the oneness of God. For Tertullian, this explains how God is both one and three. The relationship is a matter of degree, of one dispensation proceeding from the one prior, descending into Jesus Christ who is the invisible God made visible (Prax. 14, Osborn 1997, 128).

Drawing his idea from *Against Praxean* Servetus repeats this idea in the *Trinitatus*,

> There are three wonderful dispositions of God, in each of which his divinity shines forth; and from this you might very well understand a Trinity. For the Father is the whole substance and the one God from whom these degrees and presentations proceed (Tr. 1.41).

The unity of God, therefore, is not divided by the three separate persons each of whom is God, but is the one God presented in three apparently distinct forms, conveniently labeled *Father, Son,* and *Holy Spirit.* The degrees within God could be more accurately termed substance, form and use, in which the Father is the substance, Christ is the form, and the Holy Spirit the use. The three make a complete one, indivisible and united. Servetus bases his concept of the Trinity firmly on this point. He was unwilling to use either the term 'Trinity' or 'Persons', on the grounds that they were not Biblical, and yet he was compelled to say that as God made himself visible in the Person of Christ, 'Christ was then with God in power, in the Word and in Person' (Tr. 7.7). Thus Christ was the dispensation of God, revealed to make human salvation possible.

There is no doubt that without Tertullian to guide him, Servetus would have been unable to erect the theological edifice as he did. Accepting Tertullian's point that Christ was indeed the dispensation of God, he also accepted the way in which this

dispensation came about. Tertullian describes a progressive unfolding
of God, for God spoke the Word, and that Word became flesh. There is
no distinction between the speaker and the Word, or between the Word
and the flesh, and thus Christ preserves the monarchy intact, in him
dwells the fullness of the Godhead bodily.

However, Tertullian did use terms that future generations
would use to defend the Tri-personal Trinity, particularly 'substance'
and 'Person'. These were important in explaining the rationale, the
economy, of this presentation of the Divine in Christ, as well as
explaining how they interrelated. Creation was only possible because
God spoke the Word, salvation was only possible because that Word
became flesh. 'God reconciles mankind because on the cross Father and
Son are distinct' (Osborn 1997, 121). Servetus marks that distinction by
focusing on the manhood of Christ, a humanity that was reconcilable
with the Father in the process of salvation. However, he lacks the terms
and thus the mechanism of explaining how this reconciliation took
place through the degrees of dispensation – although he is not an
adoptionist, for the man Christ is the incarnation of the Word. He uses
the model of Tertullian's economy to express his own, arriving at
Tertullian's point that 'Trinity has to do with the internal disposition of
the Godhead' (Osborn 1997, 121).

As one cannot doubt the influence Tertullian's theology had
on Servetus, it is less clear how much he affected Swedenborg's
thoughts. The echoes, however, are very strong.

Tertullian and Swedenborg

Swedenborg follows both Tertullian and Servetus in his
expression of one God, and largely in the way in which God rendered
himself visible first through the Word and then through the incarnation.
In harmony with both earlier men, he too describes a progressive
dispensation in which the substance of the Father is revealed in the
form of the Son and acts as the Holy Spirit. For him, the Trinity exists,
not as three Persons, but in the Person of Christ as soul, body, and
operation.

Swedenborg, however, finds similarity with Tertullian in ways
that Servetus either could not or did not. Servetus spoke of the
relationship of Father, Son, and Holy Spirit as dispensations of the
divine, a progressive rendering visible of God himself. He developed
those ideas with the same precision and clarity as Swedenborg whose

doctrine of discrete degrees could very well have grown out of the distinctions of the relative disposition of aspects within God as given by Tertullian, but he did not have the precision of terminology to express them. Servetus had no written concept of the process of discrete degrees, and how one could be within another, nor did he have an idea of continuous degrees, in which something is perfected at its own level. For him the dispensation of God into Persons was a more static relationship, rather than the dynamic inter-dimensional relationship described by Swedenborg's system of degrees.

Danielou notes that one of the most original features of Tertullian's theological system is his system of categories[9] (Danielou 1977, 344). Tertullian

> ...stated more clearly than any other early Christian writer the central significance of relative disposition. God was one God, but Father and Son were mutually necessary to each other and never identical. Identity would destroy them; their difference was the ground of their unity (Osborn 1997, 134).

For Tertullian, the Father, or source, spoke the Word. The Word thus came from God, was God, but had the appearance of an existence of its own, yet not of its own. The Word's own existence was the creative act outside of God, and yet it was not possible for the Word to perform the work of creation separate from God. One can think of voice and speaker, differentiate between the two, and yet not separate them. This was Tertullian's relative disposition, and it resounds strongly with certain concepts key to Swedenborg's explanation of the Trinity.

In speaking of the divine *esse* as the being of the Divine, Swedenborg notes that this *esse* (being) can be expressed and thus takes form – the *existere*. The relationship between these is exactly the same as Tertullian's idea of God and the spoken Word, for one comes from the other as an expression. Treated separately, the *esse* and *existere* appear to be different things, and yet, as the former is the source of the latter, that difference is merely illusion. The *esse* and *existere,* 'are one in such a way that they may be distinguished in thought but not in operation, and because they may be distinguished in thought though not in operation, it is said that they are one distinctly' (DLW 14).

Swedenborg then compares this distinction to the soul and body, which, although they appear to be different, yet are one within the other, co-operating to make a single individual, or as the similarity between thought and speech (Osborn 1997, 121). They are *distinctly one*[10]. For Swedenborg the key to the riddle of the Trinity lies in these terms and the relationship between them. This concept of 'distinctly one' is quite similar to Tertullian's usage of the terms 'substance' and 'person' relative to God.

Substance

Tertullian's use of the term *substantia* – substance – is elusive (Osborn 1997, 131), and very elastic (Stead 1985, 55). The fact that he uses the term over three hundred times does not make it easier to define (Danielou 1977, 345). Generally, the term refers to 'stuff' or 'material' (Osborn 1997, 132). Tertullian believed that all reality was made of some substance, 'even spiritual beings which are invisible to man have a body or form which makes them visible to God, who is himself a corpus[11]' (Stead 1985, 59). This concrete idea of substance can be summed up as that which

> ...points to the concrete ground which permanently underlies individual realities and persists throughout the variety of qualities, actions and changing elements. *Substantia*, in other words, is what determines the fundamental characteristics of things, and their level in the scale of realities (Danielou 1977, 346).

Tertullian's use of *substantia* in this concrete form is a throwback to his pre-Christian Stoicism, in which 'spirit was not something immaterial, only a more refined form of matter' (Wiles 1966, 15). However, Tertullian uses the term in other ways as well, for example substance can be material, but it can also be mental, and indeed, there is a substance of the soul itself (Danielou 1977, 346). However, substance is the unitive element of a thing (Osborn 1997, 133).

In God the divine substance is the Divine stuff of which God is 'made', and the term might also mean the way in which he exists, and the way in which he exhibits himself (Stead 1985, 62). One cannot separate out the stuff of God from God, and still be left with God, in much the same way as one cannot separate the substance of a person from his or her mind, body or action. Together they make a one because they are derived from the same substance.

The broadness of these definitions of *substantia* provides fertile ground for theological speculation. However, it echoes with many of the ideas held in Swedenborg's concept of the *esse* of God that forms the *substantia* of the one God. This 'one God[12] is Substance itself and form itself, and angels and men are substances and forms from him, and so far as they are in him and he in them are images and likenesses of him' (TCR 20). The substance of God, for Swedenborg, is the indefinable divine *esse* or divine love, and this is the ground permanently underlying the reality of God, persisting in every detail of his revelation of himself to people. Thus divine love forms the 'stuff' from which the discrete degrees of God, which form the Trinity, are formed.

Swedenborg also notes that 'degrees of height are homogeneous[13]' (DLW 189), and because of this, 'the first degree is the all in everything of the subsequent degrees' (DLW 195). Thus the Divine love is the first and highest degree of God, perfect in every way, expressing itself as substance in the lower degrees. The system of discrete degrees only works if each degree is an expression of some common, homogeneous, entity, be it physical, mental, spiritual or divine. Thus the substance of God, which is the first degree of God, since there is nothing prior to it, must be present in each and every subsequent degree. Tertullian's elastic and elusive term, *substantia*, therefore, finds an echo in Swedenborg's description of the discrete degrees that form the Trinity.

Person

Substance has little meaning unless it is put into form, as Swedenborg says, 'unless a substance is a form it is a figment of the reason' (TCR 20). Wood has little value until it is fashioned into a chair or table. So too, in trying to understand the nature of god, one needs to take cognizance of his substance, and then attempt to articulate that substance in ways accessible to human minds. To do this, Tertullian developed the term '*person*', probably the first author to do so (Danielou 1977, 364). Like '*substance*' this latter term is almost equally difficult to define.

The Person is a manifestation of the substance and, as Osborn points out, it is not a substantive thing in its own right (Osborn 1997, 137). As we saw in an earlier chapter, Tertullian's use of 'Person' should not be confused with an 'individual', which unfortunately is a frequent mistake; for example, Wolfson devolves the term Person down to the level of individual Persons, for 'three members of the Trinity are taken by Tertullian ... to mean three real individuals' (Wolfson 1977, 327). This is in spite of Tertullian's characterization of the three Persons as 'degrees and forms' (Prax. II). He also noted that people fall into error when they assume that the numerical order of the Trinity to be divisive in any way (Prax. III), which is implied in the phrase 'three real individuals'. The explanation of Person lies in his concept of the progressive revelation of God. Each step of that progression, called a Person, is simply another step towards full disclosure of the nature of God.

In this use of Person as a manifestation of substance, Tertullian covers very similar ground to that covered by Swedenborg, and while Tertullian puts his concepts into more ambiguous terms that could lead to interpretations of the persons as 'individuals', Swedenborg uses his paradigm of discrete degrees to explain the relationship in a way which avoids this.

If the substance of God, the divine *esse* or love makes up the first degree, then should his model work, it is the homogenous substance informing every other level or aspect of God's manifestation. In Trinitarian terms, this is the Father, for it is the source of all things and on this level can be called the first Person of the Trinity.

However, as Tertullian points out, God in his own right is invisible, and reflects only by means of the Word. Initially the Word was the vehicle of creation and in time was born into the world as Jesus Christ. At no point is Christ separated from the Father, but is like a tree trunk growing out of a root. This is the second Person, not a second individual, but rather the second manifestation of God, the visible face of the invisible God.

For Swedenborg the manifestation of the *existere* or divine wisdom as an expression of the divine love is a discrete degree below the *esse*. Being 'distinctly one' this lower expression of love shows a different form of God for it makes the invisible divine love visible, showing us in a lower way what he is in himself, for here we have the spoken word, and indeed, the incarnate Word.

The discrete degree between substance and form, between love and wisdom is perfected as a continuous degree. Thus, the Word of God that creates becomes the same Word speaking to the prophets and is revealed through angels. In time, the Word takes on the flesh of the incarnation and God is fully revealed to humanity in the person of Jesus Christ. In this way, there is a perfecting of how God could reveal himself. In broad terms, one can label these two degrees as Father and

Son, the Father the source or origin, the substance itself and the Son the expression, the derivative external. Together, in Swedenborg's terms, they relate to each other as soul to body. The relationship between Father and Son is one of discrete degrees, one from another. The economy resulting leads to human salvation, and this forms the third and final degree, the Holy Spirit. For Tertullian, as for Servetus and Swedenborg, the Holy Spirit is the activity of God, the working out of the divine economy in human lives. He refers to the Holy Spirit as a Person in the same way as he refers to the Son, a Person in the sense of the final manifestation of God to humanity, the fruit of the tree, or the lake resulting of water flowing from a fountain and through a river.

Tertullian's concept of progressive dispensation, therefore, fits extraordinarily well with Swedenborg's idea of discrete degrees. Because the substance of God, that which makes God, which caused him to create, which prompted him to save the human race, is in all the other degrees, it leads to a revelation of this in Christ, and in the work of the Holy Spirit.

Could Tertullian have influenced Swedenborg?

The similarities of the two approaches lead one to question whether Tertullian could have influenced Swedenborg as he no doubt influenced Servetus. Yet apart from a few sketchy, second hand references to Tertullian, mainly on the subject of the soul, Swedenborg does not refer to him. The complementarity of Tertullian's progressive Trinity, and Swedenborg's discrete degrees, however, indicates that they followed similar paths. We are lead to ask if Tertullian used any concept of degrees in his own writings that could have triggered a sympathetic response from Swedenborg.

To begin we need to consider two things,

1. Tertullian's main concern is to arrive at a correct formulation of the data concerning the Trinity implicit in Scripture in order to counter the incorrect formulations made by Praxean (Danielou 1977, 363).

2. Tertullian's problem is to demonstrate that there can be number in God without jeopardizing the unity of the divine substance (Danielou 1977, 363).

Both Servetus and Swedenborg shared the latter of these goals with Tertullian, except in their case the objective was to rescue the Trinity from the essentially Tri-theistic state they understood it to have reached. To achieve his end, Tertullian makes use of categories, *status*, *census* and *gradus* to explain the relationship of the different qualities and aspects of divinity that make up the Trinity (Danielou 1977, 361), and it is in the use of these terms that one finds the greatest concord with Swedenborg's ideas as they are articulated in the doctrine of discrete degrees.

There can be little doubt that for Tertullian some notion of degrees was essential to his explanation of the Trinity, which he describes as 'flowing down from the Father through intertwined and connected steps[14], [which] does not at all disturb the Monarchy; and it at the same time guards the state of the Economy' (Prax. VIII).

The key word in this description is steps – *gradus* – the exact word Swedenborg uses to define degrees. While translator Holmes translates the word as 'steps', Evans (Evans 1948, 140) uses the term 'degrees', and it would appear that Tertullian has a similar concept to Swedenborg's discrete degrees when he uses the term. Unfortunately, Tertullian does not systematize his concept of degrees; they are inferred from the words he uses, often separately and in other contexts. To more fully appreciate Tertullian's concept of degrees, one needs to take an overview of the three terms he uses to describe the relational qualities of one thing to another, *census, status* and *gradus*.

The term *census* describes the category to which something belongs and how it relates to its origins. The original meaning of the term is 'to register', being a list of persons or things belonging to one category because they all go back to the same origin (Danielou 1977, 348). Tertullian uses the term to express the underlying substances in a series of things, for example, of Adam to the human race. Adam is the first 'substance', and his essence is found in all subsequent human beings. Another example is the church originating with the Apostles. The love and faith of the Apostles laid the basis for the spread and development of the church, and thus informs all the churches springing from it. A final example is the soul's substance vivified by the breath of God from which the body and indeed the whole person lives (Danielou 1977, 349).

This notion of an original substance that defines all the subsequent manifestations of it is closely allied to Swedenborg's statement that discrete degrees are of an homogenous nature, for as the *census* determines families or categories of things, so the basic substance in the first degree of a series of discrete degrees, determines the resulting degrees. Thus, the *census* forms the basic criterion for all the following degrees. It is from an idea very similar to this that Swedenborg's doctrine of degrees takes root, for every substance must first exist as a substance in its own right, then manifest itself and finally fulfill the role demanded by the substance. In other words, it is the 'end' in an end/cause/effect relationship.

It is interesting to note, however, that Tertullian does not use the term *census* as part of his Trinitarian vocabulary[15], because the category implies some source of origin, and, of course, God has no origin. The concept, however, is important, because although God himself has no origin, the things flowing from Him, which make up the Trinity, have their origin in him. Thus, the unspoken term takes on an importance when seen in that light.

The second term important to Tertullian's system of degrees is *status*, which 'refers to the whole complex of properties which characterize a given reality (*substantia*) and enable us to define its relation to other realities' (Danielou 1977, 352). The *status* of anything defines its characteristics placing it in relation to its origin, or *census*. It allows one to think beyond the general category to the individual particulars derived from it.

This has great ramifications for his understanding of the Trinity. For Tertullian, the *status* or properties of God are the same for each person of the Trinity because they come from the same *census*. The underlying substance of God has the same properties in every manifestation of God. This provides the unitive element that makes it possible for the different persons of God to remain as one God.

In Swedenborg's system of degrees, *status* likewise would be an essential element in each of the degrees of God, for example, God's infinity and eternity. The divine love, which is God's substance and forms the highest or first degree of God, is reflected within the manifestation of God, which is the divine wisdom, which in turn is the second degree. Likewise, the third degree, the use or activity of God, is merely an expression of this divine love, made possible by means of the divine wisdom. Each of these degrees, arising from the divine *census* or original substance, would share in the *status* proper to that substance, thus each is infinite and eternal.

The third term Tertullian uses, and the one which has the most direct connotations when compared to Swedenborg's theology of degrees, is *gradus*. This is the 'heart of Tertullian's logical method'

(Danielou 1977, 356), for it describes the establishment of an order in the reality of things. Danielou points out that '*Gradus* always points to a progressive series ... but it also has more precise implications, indicating the organic bond between the various data in the series (Danielou 1977, 356).

The progressive series of various *statu* includes a causal relationship between one and the following step (Wolfson 1970, 330). It is a concept that Tertullian uses in different ways, for example to express the different states of life (Danielou 1977, 356), or the progression from goodness to rational thought to justice. It implies that there is an order imposed on all things, so that the first of any series of things be they thoughts or actions, or material things, begin at a certain point, and then progress, by orderly steps to the conclusion.

Degrees, therefore, hold all things in their connection,

> When the third degree is linked to the second and the second to the first, then the third degree is linked to the first by going through the second. It is by ordinance of nature that every kind of thinking without exception derives its classification (*census*) from its origin (Danielou 1977, 358).

This concept of degrees is very similar to Swedenborg's idea of discrete degrees. As was shown earlier, discrete degrees are a series of derivative states drawn from on original state. The quality of the first degree, similar to Tertullian's *census* and *status*, which provide the substance and quality of the subsequent degrees, is expressed in the lower degrees. The *census* holds them together; the *gradus* makes it possible for it to function on different levels.

Tertullian applied his concept of *gradus* to Christ in two ways, explicitly in describing his genealogy from Jesse (de carne XXI), but more importantly, implicitly in describing the progression from God to Word to incarnation in Christ. His example in Prax. VIII,

> For God sent forth the Word, as the Paraclete also declares, just as the root puts forth the tree, and the fountain the river, and the sun the ray. For these are emanations[16] of the substances from which they proceed ... every original offspring is a parent, and everything which issues from the origin is an offspring (Prax. VIII).

The *census* of God is present on each level of God sending out his Word, and the qualities, or *status* of divinity applies as much to the

Word as to God. The difference between them, however, is one of *gradus*, for God is the origin, the root, the fountain, and the Word is the effect, the tree, and the river. Thus there exists within God a series of degrees marking his descend from invisible to visible creator. It is on the basis of this argument that Tertullian advocates the monarchy of God, and yet speaks of three Persons. Each person is a degree of God, and yet they remain God for they all belong to the same category of God, and each has his qualities. There is little significant difference between this understanding and Swedenborg's expression of the oneness of God as soul, body and operation. Each degree is 'distinctly one' from the other degrees, they all draw from the same homogenous source, and thus have the same essential characteristics, and yet each is different on its own level or degree, able to carry out specific functions at that level.

These then are the 'intertwined and connected steps', the degrees by which the Trinity is derived from the Father. This makes it possible to express, as Tertullian, Servetus and Swedenborg each do, a concept of the monarchy, and yet protect the Biblical declaration of Father, Son and Holy Spirit. Within this model, each 'Person' of the Trinity does indeed have a distinct individuality, but, as in the case of mind, body and operation, these cannot be truly separated. They are to use Swedenborg's term, 'distinctly one'.

While it is not definitively possible to state that Swedenborg, like Servetus, was influenced by Tertullian, it is possible to say that there are amazing similarities between the underlying structures of their doctrine. Swedenborg paid service to these similarities by his assertion that the Pre-Nicene Fathers more accurately approximated the truth, only to have it undermined by the outcome of Arianism and Nicaea. Even then, he is more than willing to concede that the Athanasian Creed is an acceptable portrayal of the nature of God, if instead of a Trinity of Persons, one understood a Trinity of Person.

The Testimony of the Soul

There is one further thread in Tertullian's writing that may have been influential in forming Swedenborg's thought, the nature and impact of the soul. At first glance, this might seem removed from the subject of the Trinity, and indeed, Tertullian does not speak of the soul as part of the economy of God. However, the concept of the soul is central to Swedenborg's argument about the relationship of Father to the Son, and secondly as part of God's revelation of his monarchy to humanity.

In *De Anima*, Tertullian describes the origin of the soul in Biblical terms, as God breathing the breath of life into Adam, and he became a living soul (anima III). Thus the soul has an origin, it is a created thing within a person (anima IV). From these points, Tertullian concludes that the soul has a corporeal quality to it. To make his point he calls on the Stoics who,

> ... while declaring almost in our own terms that the soul is a spiritual essence (inasmuch as breath and spirit are in their nature very near akin to each other), will yet have no difficulty in persuading [us] that the soul is a corporeal substance (Anima IV).

The soul's corpus comes from the fact that it is generated with the body, and is, like the body, 'susceptible of likeness and unlikeness' (anima IV), meaning that each person's soul is individual and differentiated from that of any other individual. The close connection of the soul and the body means that

> ...the soul certainly sympathizes with the body, and shares in its pain, whenever it is injured by bruises, and wounds and sores, the body, too suffers with the soul, and is united with it whenever it is afflicted with anxiety, distress, or love ... the soul, therefore is corporeal from this inter-communion of susceptibility (Anima IV).

By corporeal, however, Tertullian is not speaking of something physical. The soul is not an organ of the body. He continues his description of the corporeal soul, showing that really it is within the body, it is 'a spiritual essence' that can be compared to breath and spirit (Anima V). However, it is the soul that is 'endued with a body' (Anima V), which it puts off at death. The soul is corporeal in that it relates to the body, and yet does not belong to the body (Anima VI).

Tertullian's doctrine of the soul finds echoes in Swedenborg's work, and indeed this is the one verifiable area in which Tertullian's teachings did form a part of Swedenborg's studies. In Swedenborg's *Notebook* spanning the period 1740 and 1741 he collected extracts from various philosophical writers, he refers to Tertullian three times of which the one below deals with the subject of the soul. He notes that

Tertullian believed the soul to be the body, and this for no other reason than that he could not think of it as incorporeal, and therefore was afraid it would be nothing if it were not body. [Nor was he able to conceive of God in any other way. But being an astute man, when the truth appeared, he was sometimes conquered even against his own opinion[17]. For how could he speak more truth than where in a certain passage, he declares that every thing corporeal is capable of suffering? (Notebook 20).

In his pre-theological period, Swedenborg thought of the soul as a physical entity – a corpus far more material than Tertullian's description. Much of his anatomical research was focused on finding the soul. In his theological writing, however, the soul is the receptacle of life from the divine, symbolized by God breathing into Adam's nostrils. At conception, the soul, passed from Father to offspring, begins the process of clothing itself with a body, and thus the soul is 'endued with a body' by means of which it is able to live in this world. There is no part of the body separate from the soul, for it is the receptacle receiving the life force of God enabling people to live.

The similarity of Swedenborg's concept of the soul with the teaching of Tertullian was recognized in his own lifetime. In 1767, F.C. Oetinger, 'a learned German prelate ... who was extremely enthusiastic about Swedenborg' (Toksvig 1948, 333) proposed to Swedenborg that he [Oetinger] was

...thinking of a book wherein I shall show that through you god intends again to bring out the ideas of the church fathers, as, for instance, Tertullian's concerning the soul, concerning the state after death with a removal of the popish idea of purgatory. Write me what you think of this. (Oetinger. December 16th 1767).

Thus again, there is a closeness between Tertullian and Swedenborg in their basic concept of the soul. However, it is not until Swedenborg explains his teaching on the incarnation of Christ, and of how Christ received divine life directly, through an infinite soul that this doctrine really comes into its own. For Swedenborg the essence of the incarnation is his notion of the soul, and should that idea by lost, then his entire structure of glorification and salvation comes to grief.

One teaching about the soul in which Tertullian and Swedenborg closely coincide, deals with the recognition of the soul of God. Tertullian says that 'the knowledge of God is given to the soul from the beginning' (Marc. I.X.1-3). In the Apology, Tertullian describes how the soul, laboring

> ... under the oppressive bondage of the body, ... led astray by depraving customs, ... enervated by lusts and passions, ... in slavery to false gods, yet whenever the soul comes to itself, as out of a surfeit, or a sleep, or a sickness, and attains something of its natural soundness, its speaks of God... O noble testimony of the soul by nature Christian, then, too, in using such words as these, it looks not to the Capitol but to the heaven. It knows that there is the throne of the living God, as from Him and from thence itself came down (Apology XVII).

For Tertullian the soul is naturally Christian, testifying at all times to the universal God and the climax of his dispensation in Christ. Swedenborg makes the same point in his *True Christian Religion*, when he writes that 'there is a general feeling emanating from God and flowing into men's souls that there is a God, and that he is one' (TCR 8). Thus God influences people, predisposes them, so to speak, to believe in him, in his monarchy. He explains that the

> ... reason why there is a feeling that God is one emanating from God and entering men's' souls is that everything divine, both understood universally and in particular, is God; and because everything Divine holds together as a single unit, it must inevitably inspire a person with the idea of one God. This feeling is strengthened day by day, as a person is lifted by God into the light of heaven. For angels, in the light they enjoy, cannot force themselves to say 'Gods'. For this reason too when they are speaking the end of every sentence finishes on a single note. This is entirely due to this feeling that God is one entering their souls (TCR 8).

The testimony of the soul for both Tertullian and Swedenborg is that the soul acts as a vehicle for God's oneness to enter into their minds, unconsciously perhaps, but increasingly as the person is receptive to this teaching. Both men teach that even though the soul is Christian in essence, still a person has to become a Christian, 'Christians are made, not born' (Apology XVIII). Faith, freely chosen, is the recognition of the one God, granted by creation to the soul, and through education to the conscious mind.

Could it be, then, that the common sources behind Servetus and Swedenborg was Tertullian? As we have seen earlier, Servetus bases much of his concept of the Trinity on the Treatises Against Praxean and Marcion. His sources are clearly footnoted, and it is possible to trace his work back to them in considerable degree. It is true that Ignatius and Irenaeus, and others of the patristic era also influenced him. Swedenborg, on the other hand, claims his theology is a revelation from heaven, and makes no direct references to any of the patristic Fathers. It is much harder to trace the sources of his theology, at least in terms of its connection with other theologies in this world.

However, as both Servetus and Swedenborg indicate that the Patristic Church taught the truth about the nature of God. The Fathers, they held, were not influenced by the later Trinitarian and Christological disputes that so colored the history of theology. It follows then, that the doctrine of the early church would resonate with both. Which indeed they do. There is considerable common ground between Swedenborg and Tertullian – although it must be admitted, there are differences, arising largely from their use of different terms. Also Swedenborg, bringing an eighteenth century reason to the questions at hand, plus a highly developed mechanical and scientific mind, attempts to unravel the issues and put them into a scientifically sound framework.

While one cannot say for certain, and point to specific references tying the three together, there is a case to be made for saying that Servetus and Swedenborg found common ground in the early Christian Church. They traversed the same general area, Servetus from his perspective, and Swedenborg from his, and came to similar conclusions. What led them to these conclusions, when countless other scholars have traveled the same path, read the same books, and come to other results, is a matter of conjecture.

One possible answer is that both Servetus and Swedenborg rejected the Nicene Trinity and Chalcedonian Christology. Their idea of the nature of God is different from the standard. Both came to this in their own way, Servetus when he read the Bible and found nothing of a Trinity there, and was unwilling, in the light of the current nature of the church to accept its explanations unopposed. For him it was simple, the Bible does not speak of a Trinity or Persons, of substances or hypostasis. It speaks of God, Christ, the Son of God, and the Holy Spirit. His attempt to understand the God of the New Testament led him to the Patristic Fathers, and there, in Pre-Nicene theology he found his answer. God is one, he is expressed as one and acts as one. The Trinity is not of three Persons, but complete and present in Jesus Christ. He could not have come to this conclusion without Tertullian's theology to guide him, but also he would not have seen this in Tertullian unless he had cast aside the spectacles imposed by Nicaea, which caused others to read back into Tertullian the concepts of Nicaea.

Similarly, Swedenborg, growing up in a religious household, and a philosophic believer all his life, found it necessary to understand and explain the nature of God. He was prompted to do this by his spiritual experiences, and, laying aside his anatomical research, he delved into the Bible, seeking answers. Like Servetus, he could not accept the traditional theology. For him it was neither Biblical, nor did it make sense, and so, using his spiritual experiences and the enormous powers of his intellect, he set the Nicene Trinity aside and began again. By defining and giving a name to the divine substance, he was able to explain its relationship to the Word, and how that Word could be conceived in the Virgin, and born. From this he develops his doctrine of Christ's glorification and human salvation. As a backdrop to this, he developed the doctrine of discrete degrees, explaining the relationship of one thing to another, and finally, the relationship of Father, Son and Holy Spirit in the Trinity.

There are many echoes of Tertullian's work in Swedenborg's mind, and from his notebook it is clear that he had had some exposure to the Father. Beyond that, however, it is all conjecture, although it is amazing how three such different people, living in different eras could read and interpret the scriptures, and end with such overlapping theology.

Notes:

---

[1] All students were required to attend a lecture course in theology (Acton 1958, 13).

[2] *Conjugial Love* was published in 1768. Thus the 'twenty five years' would mark the beginning of Swedenborg's spiritual experiences at 1743.

[3] E.g. AC 5, TCR 779, DP 135, AE 1183, SE 1647.

[4] Some scholars believe that Tertullian's influence triumphed at Nicaea (Osborn 1997, 116), although Danielou (1977, 365) links Tertullian's theology of Christ too closely with the creation of the universe, a connection only disentangled after Nicaea, and therefore Tertullian's teachings did not triumph at that council.

[5] Note Book passage numbers 20, 204, 287.

[6] He refers to references to Tertullian made by Augustine, Grotius and Malebranch.

[7] 'Tertullian does not dispute that the world may have been made from something, but insists that this something from which it was made is divine wisdom' (Danielou 1977, 367).

[8] Or economies (Prax. II).

[9] It is possible that Tertullian was introduced to the idea of categories through reading Aristotle (Stead 1975, 49), although the Stoics had their own system of logic and categories (Stead 1985, 54). Generally Tertullian does not speak respectfully of Aristotle, 'Unhappy Aristotle! Who invented for these men dialectics, the art of building up and pulling down, and art so evasive in its propositions, so far fetched in its conjectures, so harsh in its arguments... From all these, when the apostle would restrain us, he expressly names philosophy as that which he would have us be on our guard against ... What indeed has Athens to do with Jerusalem?' (Heretics VII.)

[10] Distincte unum – a term Swedenborg uses (DLW 14, 17, 22, 34, 223 and DP 4) to express the idea that levels of co-dependent existence appear separate, and yet are part of a whole.

[11] Swedenborg espouses a very similar concept. People, he says, do not know 'that the body lives not from itself, but from its spirit, and that a man's spirit is his essential affection, and his spiritual body is nothing else than his affection in human form, and in such a form it appears after death' (HH 521). This spiritual body, invisible to people, makes spirits visible to each other.

[12] That is, the esse or being of God, which is Divine Love (cf. TCR 19)

[13] ... quod gradus altitudinis sint homogenei ... (DLW 189).

[14] ... ita trinitatas per consertos et connexos gradus a patre decurrens (Evans 1948, 97).

[15] Although the term census was used by the Romans to categories their gods into genealogical systems, and it might have been for this reason that Tertullian avoided using the word in connection with God (Danielou 1977, 351).

[16] προβολαι - emanations.

[17] Swedenborg's brackets.

Chapter Thirteen

Conclusion

We have examined the considerable similarities in the theology of Michael Servetus and Emanuel Swedenborg, similarities even more interesting because of the unlikelihood that Swedenborg was ever exposed to Servetus' theology. The previous chapter was an attempt to trace common sources between the two men. Servetus, trained in theology, draws heavily on the Patristic Fathers, liberally annotating his work with their references, particularly to Tertullian, whose thought, as outlined in the work, *Against Praxean*, forms the basis of his theology. Swedenborg, on the other hand, attests that he never read any theology before his spiritual experiences, although his notebook indicates some exposure to early Christian writers, including Tertullian. The essence of his theology, however, is a rejection of much of orthodox Christianity's conclusions. He claimed that his doctrine came from revelation alone.

However, Swedenborg speaks highly of the Apostolic Church, and a comparison of his work with that of Tertullian shows considerable areas of overlap. Both men use a recapitulation paradigm to account for the incarnation. In addition, their expression of how the Logos became the Son is remarkably similar; especially as both lead back to the Monarchical nature of God. Significant also is the similarity in the concept of degrees to explain the relationship of the Trinity.

Considering this, the questions raised in the introduction to this study become relevant. In view of the previous chapter, one has to assume that if there is a connection between Servetus and Swedenborg, it must have come through several sources.

Conclusion

The first is a similarity of mind. The history of the two men shows several areas of commonality, for although they came from different historical eras, and opposite ends of the European Continent, they were both well studied in the science of their day. Both had scientific, philosophic, and medical interests, both have been accorded important discoveries. In short, they shared many interests. Most important of these, however, was their commitment to God. For Servetus, theological expression of this came early, for Swedenborg in middle life, yet both brought a scientific analysis to bear on the dogmas of the Church. The result was that they both rejected these dogmas as not sustainable in the light of the Old and New Testaments, especially when read and interpreted in the original Hebrew and Greek.

A second similarity is the study of the early Church. Both concluded that the Church deviated from her earlier understanding of the nature of God at the time of Nicaea. Until that time, heretical opinions could be met and overcome with the emphasis on the one God, who recapitulates history in the person of Christ. In their eyes, the Nicene Symbol broke the patristic mould, making it possible to view the Persons of the Trinity as distinct entities rather than as the presence and activity of one God. All subsequent doctrine, arising from the Nicene Council, was thus tainted, and, in Swedenborg's view, led the Church into progressively deeper darkness, which could only be dispelled with the restoration of an understanding of the Trinity, and so of God, more in keeping with that of the Early Church. Servetus and Swedenborg, then, ally themselves closely with the Early Christian Church, especially as espoused by Tertullian.

Most historians view the development of the Church as a steady progression in understanding the nature of God. According to this paradigm, the early Fathers had a true, yet simple concept of the Trinity, which needed to be fleshed out and expressed in order to answer the questions leveled by philosophic opponents. One outcome of this was the Nicene Creed, which, drawing on the concepts of substance and Person, presented a Platonic idea of the nature of God – of a higher, perfect substance, manifested in the distinct forms of Father, Son and Holy Spirit. Many considered this an advance in the understanding of God, and the history of Christianity has been shaped by it.

So powerful has the hold of this theology been on the Church that when people rejected these theses of the Church, they are labeled 'heretics', for they go against the stream of the common understanding. The history of Christianity is littered with the ideas, and corpses, of those who chose this path. Servetus and Swedenborg are no different. Both are labeled as heretics, Servetus lost his life because of it, and Swedenborg has been relegated to obscurity, his ideas ignored by the mainstream of the Church. This rejection of their teachings, moreover, took place in the last five hundred years, which leads one to ask if these men had lived in the time of Tertullian, in Pre-Nicene times, would they have been considered heretics?

The answer, based on the similarities of their doctrine to Tertullian, and other Patristic Fathers, is 'no'. They shared too much in common with the Pre-Nicene Church to have earned that label. However, by the time of their own eras, the dogmas of the Trinity were firmly entrenched in Christian thought, along with centuries of penalties heaped upon those who questioned those doctrines. The Council of Nicaea provided a new set of spectacles through which the church for centuries to come would view the nature of Christ. Any deviation from this was considered heresy, and since Servetus and Swedenborg departed from the accepted doctrine, the label is applied to them as well.

The Catholic Encyclopedia in its entry on 'heresy' defines heresy as follows,

> The right Christian faith consists in giving one's voluntary assent to Christ in all that truly belongs to his teaching. There are, therefore, two ways of deviating from Christianity, the one by refusing to believe in Christ Himself, which is the way of infidelity, common to Pagans and Jews; the other by restricting belief to certain points of Christ's doctrine selected and fashioned at pleasure, which is the way of heretics.

Considering this definition, it is not clear whether Servetus and Swedenborg should be considered heretics, for they gave voluntary assent to Christ's teaching, and did not 'restrict belief to certain points … selected and fashioned at pleasure'. A study of their works shows the contrary to be true. Both men were deeply committed to Christ in their personal lives, in fact, much of Swedenborg's philosophical writing are an exploration of science in an attempt to explain how God created and are present in creation. He asserted that one cannot be a true philosopher by denying God. However, it is interesting that when these men were tried by courts in their own times, both were labeled, Servetus as an atheist, and Swedenborg as a Socinian[1], charges that cannot be sustained in the light of their teaching.

Similarly, study of their theological works shows a commitment to studying the Old and New Testaments carefully and fully to come to an understanding of the nature of God. Opponents would argue that they 'selected and fashioned [their doctrine] at pleasure', yet, historians demonstrate that this is the only way to make sense out of any mass of detail (Elton 1969, 108, Carr 1961, 29). Both men studied the Bible extensively, in its own language, and both came up with a different answer to that offered by the Church. It is the conclusions they drew, therefore, not the process they followed, and that has led theologians to label them as heretics.   The   Catholic Encyclopedia continues its article on heresy by introducing the role of the Church in the determination that 'believer accepts the whole deposit as proposed by the Church; the heretic accepts only such parts of it as commend themselves to his own approval'.

The point of the Nicene Council was to create a creed binding on the whole of the Christian world. Once that Creed was accepted, further councils could elaborate it on, but it could not be rejected, for the Church had decided, and the Emperor defended, the integrity of this Creed. Anyone who wished to be a part of the Church was required to accept this Creed and its successors, in fullness. It is 'the whole deposit as proposed by the Church'. Thus subjection of the understanding to the Church became the criteria for orthodoxy, which lead, as was shown in Chapter Two, to a steady withdrawal of reason from faith. Increasingly discrimination and persecution of those who did not agree accompanied this withdrawal.

As the Church developed its hold on doctrine, the intellectual freedom of people to examine the Bible and come to independent conclusions was proportionately limited. Again the Catholic Encyclopedia gives insights into this,

> But what authority is to lay down the law as to what is or is not essential? It is certainly not the authority of individuals. By entering a society, whichever it may be, the individual gives up part of his individuality to be merged into the community. And that part is precisely his private judgment on the essentials, if he resumes his liberty, he *ipso facto* separates himself form his church.

In the era after the Council of Nicaea, as Christianity extended its role as the official Church of the Roman Empire, people entered the Church at baptism which took place at birth, with no rational consent – this is one of the reasons why Servetus was so strongly opposed to paedobaptism. This initiation meant that that person had lost his or her freedom to exercise judgment in matters of faith. The Church would define those for him or her.

This concept governed the Church from the time of Constantine onwards. It is true that adherence to orthodoxy as opposed to individual interpretation of the Bible was espoused prior to Nicaea – as indeed Arius was silenced for his views – the penalties for heresy climbed dramatically after 325 AD. Constantine changed the scenario by bringing the issue of the state to bear on the picture. Thus the Catholic Encyclopedia notes,

> Under the purely ecclesiastical discipline no temporal punishment could be inflicted on the obstinate heretic, except the damage which might arise to his personal dignity through being deprived of all intercourse with his former brethren. But under the Christian emperors rigorous measures were enforced against the goods and persons of heretics.

Beginning with Constantine, then, in direct response to the creation of the Nicene Creed, a system was put into place that remained so in the Christian world. Both Servetus and Swedenborg thought independently of the Church, they rejected the Nicene Creed, at least as it is usually understood, and interpreted the Bible according to their own reading. This was sufficient for the Church in their respective times to brand them as heretics, and bring upon them the wrath, not only of the Church, but also of the state. Servetus paid this price in full, Swedenborg, living in more theologically liberal times, was not in personal danger, but was nevertheless branded a heretic and ignored.

The laws enshrined in the Roman Empire against heretics became progressively more draconian. In 380 the Emperors Valentinian and Theodosius passed a law demanding adherence to Christianity alone, as defined by the Church at the time,

> We command that those persons who follow this rule (lex) shall embrace the name of Catholic Christians. The rest, however, whom We adjudge demented and insane, shall sustain the infamy of heretical dogmas, their meeting places shall not receive the name of churches, and they shall be smitten first by divine vengeance and secondly by the retribution of our own initiative, which We shall assume in accordance with the Divine Judgment (Cod. Theod. 16.1,2 in Hillar 1997, 50).

Over a period of time, new laws were passed making heresy a crime, expropriating their property, forbidding them from being re-baptized or holding services (Hillar 1997, 54). By 382 the death penalty was applied to heretics, 'though seldom executed in the time of the Christian emperors of Rome' (CE). The result of this was two-fold, firstly independent inquiry into matters of doctrine was forbidden except along lines strictly defined by the Church. The second was that 'the terms Catholic and citizen became synonymous (Hillar 1997, 57). If one was to be a Catholic or a citizen of the Roman Empire, one could not question the Church, particularly on matters of the Trinity. Stepping outside the ecclesiastically defined dogmas made a person an outlaw, to be hunted down and punished.

This may seem like ancient history in the case of Servetus and Swedenborg, yet both of them in Protestant countries, faced the results of centuries of this type of thinking – with few, if anyone, comparing their theology to the pre-Nicene Patristic theologies, to a time esteemed by most in the church, when, ironically, neither would have been considered heretics. As the Roman Empire gave way to the Germanic kingdoms the intolerance of the Emperors was enshrined in the Medieval Church. St. Thomas Aquinas noted that 'if anyone were obstinately to deny [the matters of faith] after they had been defined by the authority of the universal Church, he would be deemed a heretic' (Aquinas[2]), and his solution for these people, is death. Aquinas wrote,

> With regard to heretics, two points must be observed, one, on their own side, the other, on the side of the Church. On their own side there is the sin, whereby they deserve not only to be separated from the Church by excommunication, but also to be severed from the world by death. For it is a much graver matter to corrupt the faith that quickens the soul than to forge money, which supports temporal life. Wherefore, if forgers of money and other evil doers are forthwith condemned to death by the secular authority, much more reason is there for heretics, as soon as they are convicted of heresy, to be not only excommunicated but even put to death (Aquinas[3]).

It did not take long for this confirmation of the ancient Roman Christian codes to become fully established in Medieval Europe in the form of the Inquisition, charged with maintaining the purity of the Church, authorized to use torture and the death penalty to enforce it. By 1240 the medieval pattern was set. The Church determined the heresy, the civil authority 'was obligated to perform an execution almost immediately' (Hillar 1997, 123). The stake became the most popular way of dealing with obstinate heretics.

Little changed as the Middle Ages gave way to the Reformation. Protestantism, while at risk from the Catholics, was by no means any more tolerant of those who stepped beyond the parameters of defined dogma. With few exceptions, indeed, possibly with only the exception of Servetus, the Reformers were not willing to re-examine or restate the essentials of the Nicene Trinity. The orthodoxy had been too deeply ingrained, too harshly enforced, for most people in the sixteenth century to even begin to consider questioning it. Instead, Luther, Calvin and the others incorporated that concept of the Trinity into their own theological systems until it became as much of an integral part of it as it had been in the Catholic Church.

Thus when Servetus questioned the Nicene Trinity his work was tentatively well received until his readers began to grasp the radical departure from tradition he was proposing. He was committing the sin of thinking independently on spiritual subjects, rather than accepting 'the whole deposit as proposed by the Church' as defined by the Catholic Encyclopedia. It is not surprising then, that when his identity became known; he was seized by the French Inquisition, and held on charges of heresy.

While one could argue that Servetus would not have been considered a heretic in the Early Church, there is no doubt that he was so considered by his contemporaries, and indeed, in the present as well. In his book, *Michael Servetus, a case in total heresy*, historian Jerome Friedman notes that Servetus' model of God 'threatened the structure of Christian belief as it had developed for over one thousand years' (Friedman 1978, 61). It was inevitable that this threat would result in charges of heresy and ultimately death.

When Servetus published the *Errors of the Trinity*, and the *Dialogues on the Trinity*, he encountered such opposition that he was forced to change his name and live incognito for the next twenty years. However, while writing the *Restitutio*, he re-established contact with Jean Calvin in Geneva. In 1553, Calvin received a copy of the *Restitutio*, probably sent to him by means of the publisher, Frelon, in Lyon (Willis 1877, 231).

> It is not difficult to imagine the alarm that must at once have taken possession of Calvin's mind when he saw the errors, the heresies, the blasphemies, as he regarded them, which in bygone years he had

vainly sought to combat, now confided to the printed page and ready to be thrown broadcast on the world (Willis 1877, 233).

It is true that Calvin had challenged the Roman Catholic Church, breaking away from it completely. Yet he had not at any point questioned the authority of the ancient Councils to define the nature of God. His understanding of the Trinity and Christology was not only completely orthodox, but formed the basis of his own interpretations of theology. His reaction to the *Restitutio*, then, was identical to that of any Roman Catholic of his time. He determined to shut Servetus down, to brand him a heretic in name, with the consequences of the stake to follow.

At Calvin's instigation the machinery designed over a thousand years to deal with a heretic rumbled into place in France. Without a miracle, Servetus would be found guilty of heresy and burned at the stake. However, whether it was a miracle or not, the French Inquisition was to be cheated of their justice. On his third night of imprisonment, Servetus scaled a garden wall in his prison and escaped (Bainton 1953, 162, cf. Willis 1877, 263). Although a hunt was mounted, the fugitive made his way out of the immediate area.

The story of the tragic events that took place after Servetus fled France has been recounted in Chapter Three. Captured in Switzerland he was tried for heresy in Geneva, found guilty, and burned at the stake. This proved not so much that he was a heretic, but that the Church at that time still adhered to the age-old formulas declaring that only the Church has the right to determine doctrine. Should one, as Servetus did, take that right upon himself, then, the full power of both church and secular authority conspired against him.

This still leaves one with the question of whether Servetus was a heretic. Before answering that question let us turn to Swedenborg's experience, and his branding as a heretic. Servetus' death left many troubled and uneasy – he became, 'even in his own day, a potent symbol of religious intolerance' (Pettegee 1990, 40). By the mid-seventeenth century the convulsions of religious intolerance that had plunged Europe into protracted war were beginning to fade. By the mid-eighteenth century, Western Europe had taken a vastly different stand. It was in this milieu that Swedenborg wrote and published his books. It is true that he could only publish them in England or Holland, where the press was free and religious censorship all but forgotten, while in his own country, Sweden, stricter, more medieval restraints were still in force. However, even in countries where more traditionalist attitudes held sway, his books were read and discussed. Swedenborg enjoyed fame withheld by circumstances from Servetus.

It was with some surprise, then, that Swedenborg, at the end of his life, found himself embroiled in a heresy trial. The major difference with Servetus' experience was that Swedenborg himself was never on trial, he never had to address a judge, nor submit himself to any secular authority. Certainly he was not burned at the stake. Much more in tune with the eighteenth century, the ideas were on trial, not the man. Even so, Swedenborg describes this trial as 'the most important and most solemn that has been before any council during the last seventeen hundred years' (Odhner 1910, 153).

The Gothenburg Trial, as it is called, erupted in the Swedish city of Gothenburg in 1768, although its roots go back to August 1765, when Swedenborg, stayed in that city en route to Holland to publish the *Apocalypse Revealed*. Waiting for favorable winds before sailing, he spent several days there. During that time he met the main role players in the trial that would take place three years later.

Swedenborg was a man of substance in Swedish society, well known for his philosophic and scientific work and more recently, for his theological writings. Once the people of Gothenburg knew he was there, they invited him to participate in the life of the city. 'One man who invited him was a professor who lectured in the Gymnasium – a Lector of Eloquence, Johan Rosen' (Acton 1960, 14)[4]. Rosen was deeply impressed by and interested in Swedenborg's writings. He became a lifelong reader and champion of them, incorporating them into his university lectures.

A second person of importance who was introduced to Swedenborg by Rosen was Dr. Gabriel A. Beyer, Professor of Greek and Theology at Gothenburg Gymnasium[5]. He had read something by Swedenborg, but put it aside without interest. However, once he met the man, his interest was sparked. After Swedenborg had left for Holland, Beyer procured several more books, studying them deeply. In 1766 he wrote to Swedenborg of his reactions to reading these books,

> I will not speak of the pleasure they have often given me, of how the glorious truths are beginning to shine forth, and how, were not my official duties and daily circumstances in the way, following my desire, I would not stop until I had been through all the writings, and read them over again (Acton 1955, 608).

At the same time he began compiling his 'Index Initialis' to these writings (Odhner 1910[a], 222). Thus he became a lifelong friend and supporter of Swedenborg. In 1768 and the years following, the axe was to fall, so to speak, not on Swedenborg himself, but on these two friends and their right to introduce Swedenborgian theology into the University.

During that stay in Gothenburg in 1765 Swedenborg met two other men who were to play a crucial role in this trial, Bishop Erik Lamberg[6], and the Dean of the Consistory of Gothenburg, Dean Ekebom[7]. Both were very friendly with Swedenborg and gave every appearance of being receptive to his teachings. 'in fact, both gentlemen made such a pleasant impression that for some time afterwards Swedenborg always wished to be remembered to Lamberg and Ekebom when writing to Beyer' (Acton 1960, 15).

In this way the main characters in the Gothenburg Trial were present some three years before the crisis came to a head. They were deeply involved with each other, for each was a member of the Consistory, or governing body of the diocese of Gothenburg, and it was to this body that complaints against Swedenborgianism were leveled. Each city or diocese in Sweden had a Consistory, in which the bishop was simply one among equals. Every question was decided by a majority vote (Acton 1960, 16). In Gothenburg the Consistory consisted of eight members plus the bishop. These included Ekebom, Rosen and Beyer. Meeting weekly they had many diocesan problems to deal with.

> During the twenty years between 1755 and 1775 no fewer than 137 clergymen were charged with various offences. This included more than half the clergymen in the diocese. There seems to have been considerable rivalry and hostility among the clergy, indeed among the Consistory itself (Rose 1968, 457).[8]

Even though religion was heavily controlled in eighteen-century Sweden, Swedenborg's ideas were becoming known amongst the intelligentsia. When the *Apocalypse Revealed* was published in Holland, Swedenborg sent copies to Beyer with instructions to disperse as follows,

> ... 1 for himself, 1 for the Bishop, 1 for the Dean[9], 1 for Dr. Rosen, 1 for the Burgomeister, Herr Petterson, 1 for the library, and the 2 remaining copies the Herr Doctor can hand out to his friends (Swedenborg. Letter to Dr. Beyer. April 8th 1766. Acton 1955, 610).

In addition to this, at the same time, he also sent 'a complete set of the *Arcana Coelestia* to Bishop Lamberg' (Acton 1960, 15). There was, therefore, no attempt by Swedenborg to conceal his ideas. On the contrary, on the basis of his contacts in Gothenburg in 1765 he fully expected a friendly response. Certainly Beyer and Rosen were so taken with Swedenborg's writings that they put Swedenborgian doctrine into their university lectures, and in 1766 Beyer published, with permission of the Consistory, as series of sermons based on Swedenborg for use by Lutheran pastors[10] (Acton 1960, 15). The result was that 'soon there was quite a circle of interested men, including some of the wealthy directors of the East India Company and some of the merchants in the town' (Acton 1960, 16)[11].

However, not all readers of Swedenborg's writings were impressed. A German theologian, Ernesti wrote a review of the *Apocalypse Revealed*, with 'some very invidious criticisms' (Acton 1960, 16). In April Rosen published this review, with notes of his own, and several pages of quotations of the *Apocalypse Revealed* in defense of Swedenborg. It was at this point that the events leading to the Gothenburg Trial began,

> In September 1768, a few months after this article had appeared, a man from the country arrived in Gothenburg, who proved afterwards, with others, to be the leading cause of all the trouble that followed. His name was Aurell. He was a lawyer who seems to have had a special enmity against the Gothenburg Consistory, but his enmity was also directed against Beyer (Acton 1960, 16).

Aurell asked the Consistory to explain whether they believed Swedenborg's works were orthodox or not. In the ensuring discussion the extent of the headway these ideas were making became apparent, which led to one of the priests, Kollinus' 'to address a formal letter to the Consistory ... asking to examine these writings' (Acton 1960, 17). The task was delegated to look into this matter.

Beyer did not report back to the Consistory on this matter until February 1769, when he reported that

> ... Swedenborg was a learned man, with works scattered in all the learned libraries ... both abroad and in Sweden; and the universities, he said, would surely have complained about them had they been heretical. However, he welcomed any examination of these books;

but he considered that the Consistory members were too busy to
engage in a studied examination (Acton 1960, 41).

Three weeks after this response, Dean Ekebom presented some notes to
the Consistory 'in which he admitted that he had not read
Swedenborg's works ... but, on the basis of conversation with
Swedenborg himself, he declared the works heretical in the highest
degree' (Acton 1960, 20). He compared Swedenborg's writings with
those of Socinius, who denied the divinity of Christ (Acton 1960, 20).
In the light, however, of his own admittance of ignorance of these
works, the rest of the Consistory was reluctant to similarly condemn
Swedenborg, with the result that battle lines were drawn between
Rosen and Beyer on the one side and Ekebom on the other.

Bishop Lamberg, after carefully considering his options
decided to take the side of orthodoxy and sided with Ekebom – he too
admitted to never having read Swedenborg, but would take Ekebom's
word on the heresy (Acton 1960, 21) but was all to ready, with
Ekebom, to label Swedenborg a Socinian[12]. This demonstrated the level
of the accusations made against Swedenborg. Commenting on this
later, Count Anders von Hopken[13] wrote that 'Bishop Lamberg accuses
Swedenborg of Socinianism. Has he read Swedenborg? Does he know
what Socinianism is? I doubt it' (Odhner 1898, 107). Lamberg also
asserted in a published letter that Swedenborg's writings were 'quite
sufficiently tinged with Mohammedanism (sic)' (Odhner 1910[b], 158).
Under Lamberg's leadership it was decided to refer the matter of
Swedenborg's heresy to the Diet (Acton 1960, 21).

In the meantime Swedenborg knew nothing at all about these
events in Gothenburg, for he was in Amsterdam at the time (Acton
1960, 21). When the news reached him, however, he was indignant. On
April 15[th.] 1769 he wrote a response sent under a covering note to Dr.
Beyer, in which he asked that his letter be published. He also
threatened that

> Should the Herr Doctor and Dean not take his Reflections back and
> wholly repudiate them, I insist that, just as the Opinions of the Royal
> Council, the Courts of Appeal, and the Colleges are printed, the same
> should be done with the Dean's Opinion and my answer; and then I
> can institute a criminal suit with regard to it (Acton 1955, 665).

In his response to Dean Ekebom, he referred to the Dean's
accusation of Socinianism as 'an accursed blasphemy and lie, for
Socinianism means the denial of the divinity of our Lord Jesus Christ,

and yet it is his divinity that is principally affirmed and proved in this New Church doctrine' (Acton 1955, 668).

When Swedenborg's response was read in the Consistory in April 1769, Ekebom was irate, and the matter became suffused with personal anger and recriminations, and both Rosen and Beyer came under personal attack. They were accused of subverting the Lutheran Church by including Swedenborgian dogma in their lectures. Aurell, who had precipitated this crisis, procured some notes, in Latin, from Dr. Beyer's students, read them to the Consistory and asked permission to publish them as evidence of Swedenborg's heresy. This was denied.

However, in May 1769, the first sequence of published minutes of Consistory meetings, as they pertained to Swedenborg, was published, and the matter became a more public affair. At about the same time, Dr. Beyer became the Rector of the Gymnasium, with the duty of presenting theology classes to the entire student body. He took the tack of

> ... proving by quotations from the modern theologians, and also the early Christian Fathers, that there is an inner and deeper sense to Scripture. He does not mention a word about Swedenborg, but all in the Consistory knew very well that it was Swedenborg's doctrine that was being set forth. Beyer wished to show that the doctrine of Swedenborg was simply the doctrine of enlightened theologians in the Christian world (Acton 1960, 23).

At this point, Dean Ekebom tried to silence Beyer completely (Acton 1960, 23).

All the events in 1769 were preliminary to the heated persecution, which began in the second half of the year. Leaders of the Consistory, who, by their own admittance had not read Swedenborg, declared him a heretic, and set into motion the full machinery to silence those who taught him. The institutions of the Inquisition and burning at the stake may have fallen away, but the age-old custom of strict, unquestioning adherence to orthodox faith, remained as strong as ever.

The publication of the Consistory minutes 'had produced so great an effect that Swedenborgianism became the talk of the town. Rumors arrived from France to the effect that Swedenborg had 'made a little disturbance in Paris' (Acton 1960, 54). The intent was to discredit Swedenborg personally, and by that means to discredit his theology. Swedenborg arrived back in Stockholm at about this time, and, hearing of the rumors in Gothenburg, wrote to Dr. Beyer, describing his reception there,

> Not until this month did I arrive here in Stockholm, and I found both high and low very pleased and favorable, and I was then at once invited to a meal with His Royal Highness, with whom and the Crown Princess I had quite a talk. Since this, I also ate with members of the Privy Council. I have talked with the most prominent men in the House and also with the Bishops ... (Acton 1955, 691).

Swedenborg then continued in this letter to mention people by names, and to defend his doctrine of the Trinity. He also gave Beyer permission to print and publish this letter, to counteract the rumors generated in Gothenburg (Acton 1960, 55). The implication was that through his connections at Court, Swedenborg was beyond reproach, and that those who attacked him or his doctrines, should be wary. However, as Acton points out, Swedenborg was deceived, as those with whom he dined may have regarded him in high esteem, but they did not so regard his writings (Acton 1960, 55).

The exercise of printing this letter increased, rather than decreased the tension. Beyer had published it without censorship or permission, and so had broken the law. The result of this publication of the issues which had up to now been debated in the Gothenburg Consistory was now public knowledge. People had to take a stand. Rosen and Beyer defended the letter, and found themselves isolated from sympathetic colleagues in the Consistory. The Consistory decided to confiscate every unsold copy, but only four were found. In addition, specific Bishops, mentioned by name in the letter, were embarrassed.

The matter therefore was referred to the Chancellor of Justice, 'to be dealt with as recommended by the King' (Acton 1960, 57). It is interesting to note that in the consequent reaction, it was Beyer, and not Swedenborg who was censured. Up to this point, Dr. Beyer had assumed that the Councilors of State and the Bishops were on his side.

Both Beyer and Rosen offered to stop teaching Swedenborg's religion publicly (Acton 1960, 58). However the covering letter from the Consistory to the Chancellor 'was a dangerous letter, designed to undermine every effect anticipated to be produced by Beyer's letter' (Acton 1960, 58). It was designed to reflect him in a poor light, and to deflect any blame for the spread of Swedenborgianism in the Diocese of Gothenburg from themselves.

At this time, the students and the Gymnasium in Gothenburg began to heckle Beyer during his lectures, adding the charge of incompetence to the other of heresy. Rumors began to circulate that

Beyer and Rosen were to be exiled from Sweden. This, however, proved to be false.

On March 9th 1770, the Royal Council met. Both the King and Swedenborg were present. Acton writes,

> I have no doubt that the king was friendly to Swedenborg, and friendly, if not sympathetic to his writings... He attended the first meeting of the Council, which was occupied with reading the documents – including Beyer's oration, itself one hour and a half in length – and which took a whole day (Acton 1960, 59).

As the Councilors listened to the arguments back and forth, weighing up the differences between Swedenborg's theology and the Lutheran doctrines, the distinctions between the two became clear. 'Some of the Councilors were so concerned that they did not favor even arguing with the two Lectors, but wanted action at once' (Acton 1960, 59). It was recommended that Swedenborg's doctrines be declared heretical, while Beyer and Rosen should be prosecuted for teaching them (Acton 1960, 60). Swedenborg was forbidden to import his works into Sweden.

By May 1770, the Council's decision was complete, and a letter was sent to the Gothenburg Consistory. The letter began with an admission that

> ... there is much good in Swedenborg, yet, on the whole the writings are against our Confession, and are therefore rejected by the King as heretical. The Consistory must use care in spreading these doctrines... (Acton 1960, 60).

The Royal Letter was read aloud in the Gothenburg Consistory – Beyer and Rosen being humiliated by being forced, by Bishop Lamberg, to stand during the proceedings. Again they promised not to teach Swedenborgianism publicly, nevertheless, both were deposed from their teaching positions at the Gymnasium. Neither, however, stopped propagating Swedenborg's teachings. As a result, they were again summonsed before the Royal Court of Justice on charges of heresy.

In this court case, Beyer and Rosen asserted 'that they could not be tried for heresy until the Uppsala Faculty had declared that Swedenborg's works were heretical' (Acton 1960, 63). The court agreed, and the matter was referred to Uppsala, and, at this point interest in the matter abruptly ceased. Uppsala never did return a report. Beyer and Rosen returned to Gothenburg, and it is certain that they held 'classes for private people' interested in Swedenborg (Acton 1960, 63).

Rosen died in 1773, and, with no report from Uppsala, the case stagnated until, in 1778 the Court asked the king for permission to dismiss it (Acton 1960, 63).

So ends the heresy case against Swedenborg's doctrines. It is interesting to note the similarities and differences between the Gothenburg Trial and Servetus' trial two hundred years before. In both cases the theology itself was on the stand, in each case it was compared to the orthodox dogma determined by the Church over a thousand years. In each case, the new doctrine was branded heretical and rejected by those who had neither read nor studied it in any detail at all, but for whom the superficial dissimilarities with the received doctrine was sufficient. One important difference between the two is that Swedenborg himself was not on trial, his life was never in danger. Church and state in Sweden instead targeted his followers, and they bore the brunt of the attack.

In the final analysis, Servetus lost his life because Calvin chose to enact the historical laws calling for the death penalty of heretics. Beyer and Rosen were more lucky, due mostly to the change in European culture, in the Royal letter to the Consistory, it is noted that 'His Majesty, from a tender regard for their welfare, is not yet willing to proceed against them according to the civil laws, but hopes they may yet be brought to repentance' (Odhner 1910[a], 625). Thus the penalties against heresies were still in place, and only the kings 'tender regard' preserved Beyer and Rosen from Servetus' fate. Had this trial taken place a hundred and fifty years before, they would no doubt have shared it.

This consideration brings us back to the question, asked at the beginning of this book, were Servetus and Swedenborg heretics. The answer depends on how one defines heresy, and in what era one so defines it. Since both men looked back to, and drew inspiration from the Early Church, one would have been hard pressed to label them as heretics in the period of the Church prior to 325 AD. Certainly Servetus bases his theology heavily on Tertullian, who as one of the Fathers of the Church greatly influenced Christian theology.

Many historians see in Tertullian's thought the beginning of the Nicene Trinity, and his introduction of specific terms, such as 'substance' and 'Person' point in that direction. Yet he does not separate the 'persons' of the Godhead into the individual's they became in subsequent centuries. The terminology of Nicaea can be traced back to him, but it might also be argued that Servetus' different interpretation of the same material was an equally valid alternative approach. Perhaps it is possible, that had Arius not entered the Church scene in the early fourth century, then Nicaea would not have become necessary, and thus the history of the Trinity may have evolved more along the lines which Servetus envisioned.

Had this happened, Swedenborg, whose theology again, bears striking resemblance to Servetus', would have been more orthodox than heterodox, and he too would not have been called a heretic. But these events did not happen. Tertullian's thought did fuel the Nicene Council. The Trinity of Persons became the orthodox Christian expression of God, and the state united with the Church to enforce it. Under those circumstances, Servetus and Swedenborg found themselves beyond the pale of Christian theology. As such they were labeled heretics. Servetus died, and Swedenborg was relegated to obscurity.

However, as the world changed at the Nicene Council, so it is changing again. In the twentieth century the concepts of the Trinity and Christology have been questioned again and again. More often than not scholars reaffirm the traditional understanding of the nature of God, but questions raise awareness, and awareness stimulates people to new studies. Who knows, in five hundred years time, Servetus and Swedenborg may be hailed as men who broke the hegemony of the past, set the intellect free from the imposed shackles of faith, and reopened once again, those age old Christological questions, who is Jesus, how is he divine, and how is he human?

Notes,

---

[1] One who denies the distinction between Father and Son in the Trinity.
[2] Aquinas, SMT SS Q [11] A3 para 1.1.
[3] Aquinas. SMT SS Q[11] A3 body para. 1.2.
[4] Rosen was born 1726 the son of a Lutheran clergyman. Studied at Gothenburg, Uppsala and Lund. He received a master's degree in 1748 and received Doctor of Theology (date unknown). In 1759 appointed Professor of Eloquence (Rhetoric) and Latin poetry. Edited a number of journals, and founded 'the present Royal Society of Science and Literature in Gothenburg' (Odhner 1910, 156).
[5] Beyer studied at Gothenburg. Completed a Master of Philosophy at Lund in 1775, was appointed to the Consistory of Gothenburg in 1748, became professor of Greek in 1752 and Doctor of Theology 1762 (Odhner 1910, 156).
[6] Lamberg. Born 1719. Studied at Gothenburg and Uppsala. Appointed Royal Chaplain in 1753 and Bishop of Gothenburg in 1760 (Odhner 1910, 157).

---

[7] Ekebom was born in 1716. Studied at Gothenburg, Uppsala and Lund. Ordained in 1747. Appointed Arch-Dean of Gothenburg and vice president of the Consistory in 1761 (Odhner 1910, 158).

[8] Records from the time list these offences as, fighting, drunkenness, immorality, forgery, avarice, 'vicious life', burglary and theft in church. Approximately 54% of the clergy were brought to court for various offences (Odhner 1910, 155).

[9] Lamberg and Ekebom.

[10] The full title in English is, New Attempts at an edifying Explanation of the Gospel Texts for Sundays and Holy Days (Acton 1955, 621).

[11] A society called the 'Philanthropic Society' was formed in Gothenburg at this time. It was the first such group dedicated to the study of Swedenborg's writings in the world (Odhner 1910a, 223).

[12] Bishop Lamberg wrote tot he Gothenburg Consistory on December 4th 1769, in which he says, 'Socinianism manifests itself so clearly there that no one except the merest idiot in polemics can dare deny it' (Odhner 1898, 107).

[13] Count Anders von Hopken, twice Prime Minister of Sweden, Chancellor of the University of Uppsala, founder of the Swedish Academy of Sciences (Odhner 1898, 107).

Appendix A

Swedenborg's Version of the Athanasian Creed

The Creed is as follows:

Whosoever will be saved, before all things it is necessary that he hold the Catholic (other authorities say, Christian) Faith; which faith, except every one do keep whole and undefiled, without doubt he shall perish everlastingly. And the Catholic (others say, Christian) Faith is this:

That we worship one God in Trinity, and the Trinity in Unity, neither confounding the persons, nor dividing the substance (others say, essence).

For there is one person of the Father, another of the Son, and another of the Holy Spirit; but the Godhead of the Father, of the Son, and of the Holy Spirit, is all one, the glory equal, the majesty coeternal.

Such as the Father is, such is the Son, and such is the Holy Spirit.

The Father uncreate, the Son uncreate, and the Holy Spirit uncreate.

The Father incomprehensible (infinitus), the Son incomprehensible (infinitus), and the Holy Spirit incomprehensible (infinitus).

The Father eternal, the Son eternal, and the Holy Spirit eternal: and yet there are not three eternals, but One Eternal: as also there are not three incomprehensibles (infiniti), nor three uncreates but one uncreate, and one incomprehensible (infinitus).

So likewise the Father is almighty, the Son almighty, and the Holy Spirit almighty and yet there are not three Almighties, but One Almighty.

So the Father is God, the Son is God, and the Holy Spirit is God and yet there are not three gods, but One God. So likewise the Father is Lord, the Son Lord, and the Holy Spirit Lord; and yet not three lords, but One Lord.

For like as we are compelled by the Christian verity to acknowledge every person by himself to be God and Lord, so are we forbidden by the Catholic Religion to say there be three gods or three lords (others say, still we cannot, according to the Christian faith, mention three gods or three lords).

The Father is made of none, neither created, nor begotten (natus): the Son is of the Father alone, not made, nor created, but begotten (natus): the Holy Spirit is of the Father and of the Son, neither made, nor created, nor begotten (natus), but proceeding. So there is one Father, not three Fathers; one Son, not three Sons; one Holy Spirit, not three Holy Spirits.

And in this Trinity none is afore or after another none is greater or less than another; but the whole three persons are coeternal together, and coequal. So that in all things, as is aforesaid, the Unity in Trinity and the Trinity in Unity is to be worshiped (others say, three persons in one Godhead, and one God in three persons, is to be worshiped). He therefore that will be saved, must thus think of the Trinity.

Furthermore, it is necessary to everlasting salvation that he also believe rightly the incarnation of our Lord Jesus Christ (others say, that he firmly believes that our Lord is very Man).

For the right faith is that we believe and confess that our Lord Jesus Christ, the Son of God, is God and Man; God of the substance (or essence; others, nature) of the Father, begotten before the worlds; and Man of the substance (others say, nature) of his mother, born in the world; perfect God, and perfect Man, of a reasonable soul and human flesh (corpore) subsisting; equal to the Father as touching his Godhead, and inferior to the Father as touching his manhood.

Who although he be God and Man, yet he is not two, but one Christ; one, not by conversion of the Godhead into flesh (corpus) but by taking of the manhood into God (others say, He is one, yet not that the Godhead was transmuted into manhood, but the Godhead took up the Manhood to itself); one altogether, not by confusion (others say, commingling) of substance, but by unity of person (others say, He is altogether one, not that the two natures are commixed, but he is one person).

For as the reasonable soul and flesh (corpus) is one man, so God and man is one Christ, Who suffered for our salvation, descended into hell, rose again the third day from the dead.

He ascended into heaven, He sitteth on the right hand of the Father, God Almighty, from whence He shall come to judge the quick and the dead.

At whose coming all men shall rise again with their bodies, and shall give account for their own works. And they that have done good shall go into life everlasting, and they that have done evil into everlasting fire.

(Lord 56)

Appendix B

References to Classical Sources in the Trinitatus

Author	Book	Reference in Tr.
Aristotle	De Anima	1.45; 1.46
	Anal Poster	1.46

References to Patristic Sources in the Trinitatus and Dialogues

Author	Book	Reference in Tr.
Augustine	De Trinitate	1.38; 1.57; 1.56
	De Haeres	1.55
	Joannis Evang	1.33
Aetius		1.55
Basil the Great	Adv. Eunomium	1.57; 1.33
Clement	Homily	2.9; 7.10
Clement	Recognitions	1.41; 1.3; 1.20
Cyprian	Ep ad Magnum	1.34
	Test. Ad. Judaeos	4.6
Ignatius	Ep ad Ephesus	7.11
	Ep Ad. Magnesians	7.11; 1.48
	Ep Ad Phila	1.26
	Ep ad Polycarp	7.11
	Ep ad Smyrnians	7.11
	Ep Ad Tarsenses	1.48
	Ep. Ad Trallianos	1.11; 7.11
Irenaeus	Adv. Haeres	1.48; 1.56; 1.59; 2.4;

Appendices

		2.5; 2.6; 2.7; 7.1; 7.5; 7.11
John of Damascus	De fide orthodoxa	1.56
Lactantius	Divine Institutes	1.47
Macedonius		1.55
Origen	Contra Celsum	1.33
Tertullian	Adv. Hermogenem	2.4
Tertullian	Adv. Marcion	1.3; 1.4
Tertullian	Adv. Praxeas	1.2; 1.3; 1.33; 3.17; 3.19; 7.5
Tertullian	Adv. Valent	1.56; 2.5; 3.22; 7.1

References to Medieval Sources in the Trinitatus and Dialogues

Author	Book	Reference in Tr.
Gregory Nazianzen	Fifth Theological Oration de Spiritu Sancto	1.57
John Major	Sentences	1.30
Hilary of Poiters	De Trinitate	1.35; 1.43

Moses Maimonides	Guide for the Perplexed		3.4
Occam, William	Questiones Decisiones	et	1.58
Peter Lombard	Sentences		1:38; 1:40.; 1.58; 1.58
Richard of St. Victor	De Trinitate		1.44
Strabo, Walafrid	Glossa Ordinaria		1.36
Valla, Laurentius	In Novum Testamentum		3.6

Appendix C

Main Works of Emanuel Swedenborg

Opera Poetica	1700 - 1740	Uppsala
Camena Borea (The Northern Muse)	1715	Griefswalde
Daedalus Hyperboreus (The Northern Inventor)	1716-1718	Uppsala
Motion and Position of the Earth and the Planets	1719	Skara
Height of Water	1719	Uppsala
Prodomus Principiorum Rerum Naturalium (Chemistry)	1721	Amsterdam
Miscellaneous Observations	1721	Leipzig
Philosophical and Mineralogical Works: Volume one – Principia Volume two – On Iron Volume three – On Copper	1734	Dresden and Leipzig
On the Infinite	1734	Dresden and Leipzig
The Cerebrum	1738-1740	Manuscript only
Economy of the Animal Kingdom	1740-1741	London and Amsterdam
The Fibre	1741	Manuscript only
The Rational Psychology	1742	Manuscript only
The Brain	1743-1744	Manuscript only
The Animal Kingdom Parts I and II	1744	London
The Journal of Dreams	1744	Manuscript only
Part III	1745	London
Parts IV and V	1745	Manuscript only
The Worship and Love of God	1745	London
The Word Explained	1746-1747	Manuscript only
The Spiritual Diary	1747-1765	Manuscript only
Arcana Coelestia	1749-1756	London
Earths in the Universe	1758	London

Heaven and Hell	1758	London
The Last Judgement	1758	London
The New Jerusalem and Its Heavenly Doctrines	1758	London
The White Horse	1758	London
The Apocalypse Explained	1759	Manuscript only
The Athanasian Creed	1760	Manuscript only
The Internal Sense of the Prophets and Psalms	1761	Manuscript only
Doctrine of the Lord	1763	Amsterdam
Doctrine of the Sacred Scripture	1763	Amsterdam
Doctrine of Life	1763	Amsterdam
Doctrine of Faith	1763	Amsterdam
Continuation of the Last Judgement	1763	Amsterdam
Divine Love and Wisdom	1763	Amsterdam
Divine Providence	1764	Amsterdam
Apocalypse Revealed	1766	Amsterdam
Conjugial Love	1768	Amsterdam
A Brief Exposition of the Doctrine of the New Church	1769	Amsterdam
Intercourse of the Soul and the Body	1769	London
The True Christian Religion	1771	Amsterdam

Bibliography

Primary Sources

Acton, Alfred, ed. 1948. *The Letters and Memorials of Emanuel Swedenborg.* Volume One. Bryn Athyn, PA. Swedenborg Scientific Association.

Acton, Alfred, ed. 1955. *The Letters and Memorials of Emanuel Swedenborg.* Volume Two. Bryn Athyn, PA. Swedenborg Scientific Association.

Aquinas, Thomas. 1947. *The Summa Theologica of St. Thomas Aquinas.* 2nd rev. ed., translated by the Fathers of the English Dominical Province. [s.l.] Benziger Bros. 1947.

Athanasius. 1887. Contra Gentes, in *A Select Library of Nicene and Post Nicene Fathers of the Christian Church. Second Series 4,* translated by Archibald Robertson. Edinburgh: T and T Clark.

Augustine. 1872. De Trinitatus, in *A Select Library of Nicene and Post Nicene Fathers of the Christian Church. First Series 3,* translated by A. W. Haddon. Edinburgh: T and T Clark.

Cyril. *Letter to the Monks of Egypt,* in McGuckin, John A. 1994. St. Cyril of Alexandria. The Christological controversy, its history, theology and texts. Leiden: E.J. Brill.

Ignatius. 1980. Epistle to the Ephesians, in *Early Christian Writings. The Apostolic Fathers,* translated by Maxwell Staniforth. Harmondsworth: Penguin.

Ignatius. 1980. Epistle to the Magnesians, in *Early Christian Writings. The Apostolic Fathers,* translated by Maxwell Staniforth. Harmondsworth: Penguin.

Ignatius. 1980. Epistle to the Trallians, in *Early Christian Writings.* *The Apostolic Fathers,* translated by Maxwell Staniforth. Harmondsworth: Penguin.

Ignatius. 1980. Epistle to the Romans, in *Early Christian Writings. The Apostolic Fathers,* translated by Maxwell Staniforth. Harmondsworth: Penguin.

Ignatius. 1980. Epistle to the Philadelphians, in *Early Christian Writings. The Apostolic Fathers,* translated by Maxwell Staniforth. Harmondsworth: Penguin.

Ignatius. 1980. Epistle to the Smyrnians, in *Early Christian Writings.* *The Apostolic Fathers,* translated by Maxwell Staniforth. Harmondsworth: Penguin.

Ignatius. 1980. Epistle to Polycarp, in *Early Christian Writings. The Apostolic Fathers,* translated by Maxwell Staniforth. Harmondsworth: Penguin.

Jung-Stilling, J.H. 1841. Testimony of Dr. Johann Heinrich Jung-Stilling, Professor of the Universities of Heidelberg and Marburg, respecting Swedenborg's intercourse with the spiritual world, in *Documents concerning the life and character of Emanuel Swedenborg, collected by Dr. J.F.L. Tafel of Tubingen,* edited by I.H. Smithson. Manchester: Joseph Hayward.

Origen. 1872. Contra Celsus, in *The Writings of Origen,* translated by Frederick Crombie. Edinburgh: T and T Clark.

Oetinger, F.C. 1955. Letter to Swedenborg. December 16th, in *The Letters and Memorials of Emanuel Swedenborg.* Volume Two. Bryn Athyn, PA. Swedenborg Scientific Association.

Sandstrom, Erik E. 2000. Letter to A. Dibb. 22nd June.

Sandstrom. Erik E. 2001. Letter to A. Dibb. 22nd June.

Servetus, Michael. 1969. *On the Errors of the Trinity: Seven Books.* Translated by Earl Morse Wilbur. Harvard Theological Studies XVI. New York: Krause Reprint Co.

Serveuts, Michael. 1969. *Dialogues on the Trinity. In two books.* Translated by Earl Morse Wilbur. Harvard Theological Studies XVI. New York: Krause Reprint Co.

Servetus, Michael. 1553. *Christianismi Restitutio.* Frankfort-am-Main: Graphisher Betrieb Heinz Saamer.

Tertullian. 1868. Against Marcion, in *Ante-Nicene Christian Library 7,* Translated by Peter Holmes. Edinburgh: T and T Clark.

Tertullian. 1868. Against Praxean, in *Ante-Nicene Christian Library 7,* Translated by Peter Holmes. Edinburgh: T and T Clark.

Tertullian. 1868. The Apology, in *Ante-Nicene Christian Library 7,* Translated by Peter Holmes. Edinburgh: T and T Clark.

Tertullian. 1868. Prescription Against Heretics, in *Ante-Nicene Christian Library 7,* Translated by Peter Holmes. Edinburgh: T and T Clark.

Tertullian. 1868. The Soul, in *Ante-Nicene Christian Library 7,* Translated by Peter Holmes. Edinburgh: T and T Clark.

Swedenborg's Philosophical Works

Swedenborg, Emanuel. 1931. *A Philosopher's Note Book. Excerpts from philosophical writers and from the Sacred Scriptures on a variety of philosophical subjects, together with some reflections and sundry notes and memoranda.* Translated by Alfred Acton. Philadelphia: Swedenborg Scientific Association.

Swedenborg, Emanuel. 1843. *The Animal Kingdom, considered anatomically, physically, and philosophically.* Translated by J.J.G. Wilkinson. London: W. Newberry.

Swedenborg, Emanuel. 1955. *The Economy of the Animal Kingdom, considered anatomically, physically and philosophically.* Translated by Augustus Clissold. New York: The New Church Press.

Swedenborg, Emanuel. 1928. *The History of Creation, as given by Moses.* Translated by Alfred Acton. Bryn Athyn, PA. The Academy of the New Church.

Swedenborg, Emanuel. 1847. *The Infinite and Final Cause of Creation, also the mechanism of the operation of the soul and body.* Translated by J.J.G. Wilkinson. London: The Swedenborg Society.

Swedenborg, Emanuel. 1845. *The Principia; or , the first principles of natural things, being new attempts toward a philosophical explanation of the elementary world.* Translated by Augustus Clissold. London: W. Newberry.

Swedenborg, Emanuel. 1977. *Journal of Dreams.* Edited by W.R. Woofenden. New York: Swedenborg Foundation, Inc.

Swedenborg, Emanuel. 1950. *Rational Psychology.* Translated by N.H. Rogers and Alfred Acton. Philadelphia: Swedenborg Scientific Association.

Swedenborg, Emanuel. 1948. Letter to Benzelius. August, in *The Letters and Memorials of Emanuel Swedenborg.* Volume One. Bryn Athyn, PA. Swedenborg Scientific Association.

Swedenborg, Emanuel. 1948. Letter to Benzelius. September 14th, in *The Letters and Memorials of Emanuel Swedenborg.* Volume One. Bryn Athyn, PA. Swedenborg Scientific Association.

Swedenborg, Emanuel. 1948. Letter to Benzelius. September 8th, in *The Letters and Memorials of Emanuel Swedenborg.* Volume One. Bryn Athyn, PA. Swedenborg Scientific Association.

Swedenborg, Emanuel. 1948. Letter to Benzelius. May 26th, in *The Letters and Memorials of Emanuel Swedenborg.* Volume One. Bryn Athyn, PA. Swedenborg Scientific Association.

Swedenborg, Emanuel. 1955. Letter to Oetinger. September 23rd, in *The Letters and Memorials of Emanuel Swedenborg*. Volume Two. Bryn Athyn, PA. Swedenborg Scientific Association.

Swedenborg, Emanuel. 1955. Letter to Beyer. February, in *The Letters and Memorials of Emanuel Swedenborg*. Volume Two. Bryn Athyn, PA. Swedenborg Scientific Association.

Swedenborg, Emanuel. 1955. Letter to Beyer. April 23rd, in *The Letters and Memorials of Emanuel Swedenborg*. Volume Two. Bryn Athyn, PA. Swedenborg Scientific Association.

Swedenborg, Emanuel. 1955. Letter to Mr. Hartley. August 5th, in *The Letters and Memorials of Emanuel Swedenborg*. Volume Two. Bryn Athyn, PA. Swedenborg Scientific Association.

Swedenborg, Emanuel. 1955. Letter to Dr. Beyer. November 14th, in *The Letters and Memorials of Emanuel Swedenborg*. Volume Two. Bryn Athyn, PA. Swedenborg Scientific Association.

Swedenborg, Emanuel. 1955. Letter to Count von Hopkin. November 17th, in *The Letters and Memorials of Emanuel Swedenborg*. Volume Two. Bryn Athyn, PA. Swedenborg Scientific Association.

Swedenborg, Emanuel. 1955. Letter to The King of Sweden. May 25th, in *The Letters and Memorials of Emanuel Swedenborg*. Volume Two. Bryn Athyn, PA. Swedenborg Scientific Association.

Swedenborg, Emanuel. 1955. Note Against Ernesti, in *The Letters and Memorials of Emanuel Swedenborg*. Volume Two. Bryn Athyn, PA. Swedenborg Scientific Association.

Swedenborg's Theological Works

Swedenborg, Emanuel. 1969. *Angelic Wisdom concerning the Divine Love and the Divine Wisdom*, translated by J.C. Ager. New York: Swedenborg Foundation.

Swedenborg, Emanuel. 1949. *Angelic Wisdom concerning the Divine Providence*, translated by William Dick and E.J. Pulsford. London: Swedenborg Society.

Swedenborg, Emanuel. 1983. *Arcana Coelestia, principally a revelation of the inner or spiritual sense of Genesis and Exodus*, translated by John Elliot. London: Swedenborg Society.

Swedenborg, Emanuel. 1971. *Heaven and Its Wonders and Hell, from things seen and heard*, translated by John Whitehead. New York: Swedenborg Foundation.

Swedenborg, Emanuel. 1968. *The Apocalypse Revealed, wherein are disclosed the arcane there foretold which have hitherto remained concealed*, translated by John Whitehead. New York: Swedenborg Foundation.

Swedenborg, Emanuel. 1954. *The Athanasian Creed*, translated by Doris Harley. London: Swedenborg Society.

Swedenborg, Emanuel. 1970. *A Brief Exposition of the Doctrine of the New Church, which is meant by 'The New Jerusalem' in the Apocalypse*, translated by John Whitehead. New York: Swedenborg Foundation.

Swedenborg, Emanuel. 1969. *The Canons of the New Church, or the entire theology of the New Church*, translated by John Whitehead. New York: Swedenborg Foundation.

Swedenborg, Emanuel. 1996. *The Delights of Wisdom on the subject of Conjugial Love followed by the gross pleasures of folly on the subject of scoratory* love, translated by John Chadwick. London: Swedenborg Society.

Swedenborg, Emanuel. 1969. *The Coronis, or Appendix to the True Christian Religion*, translated by John Whitehead. New York: Swedenborg Foundation.

Swedenborg, Emanuel. 1969. *De Verbo, concerning the Sacred Scripture of the Word of the Lord from Experience*, translated by John Whitehead. New York: Swedenborg Foundation.

Swedenborg, Emanuel. 1971. *The Doctrine of the New Jerusalem concerning Faith*, translated by John Faulkner Potts. New York: Swedenborg Foundation.

Swedenborg, Emanuel. 1971. *The Doctrine of the New Jerusalem concerning the Holy Scripture*, translated by John Faulkner Potts. New York: Swedenborg Foundation.

Swedenborg, Emanuel. 1971. *The Doctrine of the New Jerusalem concerning the Lord*, translated by John Faulkner Potts. New York: Swedenborg Foundation.

Swedenborg, Emanuel. 1969. *An Ecclesiastical History of the New Church*, translated by John Whitehead. New York: Swedenborg Foundation.

Swedenborg, Emanuel. 1969. *Invitation to the New Church*, translated by John Whitehead. New York: Swedenborg Foundation.

Swedenborg, Emanuel. 1970. *The Last Judgment and Babylon Destroyed*, translated by John Whitehead. New York: Swedenborg Foundation.

Swedenborg, Emanuel. 1970. *The Last Judgment (Posthumous)*, translated by John Whitehead. New York: Swedenborg Foundation.

Swedenborg, Emanuel. 1971. *Nine Questions chiefly relating to the Lord, the Trinity and the Holy Spirit*, translated by John Faulker Potts. New York: Swedenborg Foundation.

Swedenborg, Emanuel. 1977. *The Spiritual Diary. Records and Notes made by Emanuel Swedenborg between 1746 and 1765 from his experiences in the spiritual world*, translated by W.H. Acton. London: Swedenborg Society.

Swedenborg, Emanuel. 1950. *The True Christian Religion*. *Containing the universal theology of the New Church foretold by the Lord in Daniel vii:13,14 and in the Revelation xxi:1.2*, translated by William Dick. London: Swedenborg Society.

Swedenborg, Emanuel. 1928. *The Word of the Old Testament Explained*, translated by Alfred Acton. Bryn Athyn, PA: Academy of the New Church.

Secondary Sources

Acton, Alfred. 1939. Discarding Anonymity. *New Church Life*, 193 – 198.

Acton, Alfred. 1958. *The Life of Emanuel Swedenborg*. Unpublished manuscript. Bryn Athyn, PA: The Academy of the New Church.

Acton, Alfred. 1960. The Gothenburg Trial. *New Church Life*, 14-24, 53-64.

Anonymous. 1724. *An Impartial History of Michael Servetus, burnt alive at Geneva for heresy*. London: printed for Aaron Ward.

Anonymous. 1883. Catalogue of Swedenborg's Library. *New Church Life, 183*.

Bainton, Roland H. 1953. *Hunted Heretic: the life and death of Michael Servetus 1511 - 1553*. Boston: The Beacon Press.

Bainton, Roland H. 1953. Michael Servetus and the Trinitarian Speculation of the Middle Ages, in *Autour de Michel Servet et de Sebastian Castellion,* edited by B. Becker. Haarlem: H.D. Tjeenk Willink & Zoon N.V.

Barnes, Timothy D. 1993. *Athanasius and Constantius - theology and politics and the Constantinian Empire*. Cambridge, MA.:Harvard University Press.

Beaver, R. Pierce et al eds. 1982. *The World's Religions*. Cape Town: Struik Christian Books.

Becker. B. ed. 1953. *Autour de Michel Servet et de Sebastien Castellion.* Haarlem: H.D. Tjeenk Willink & Zoon N.V.

Beilby, Rev. Arthur Edgar. 1936. *Arthur Edgar Beilby. His Book, being a collection of Essays, Addresses and Reviews.* Ed. Hall, Rev. Charles A. London: New Church Press, Ltd.

Bettenson, Henry. Ed. 1981. *Documents of the Christian Church.* Oxford: Oxford University Press.

Bouwsma, William James. 1988. *John Calvin. A sixteenth century portrait.* New York: Oxford University Press.

Bray, Gerald Lewis. 1979. *Holiness and the Will of God: perspectives on the theology of Tertullian.* London: Marshall, Morgan and Scott.

Caldwell, W.B. 1926. Swedenborg's Early Ideas of the Lord. *New Church Life*: 236 – 241.

Caldwell, W.B. 1925. Swedenborg's Inspiration. Notes on two features of his preparation. *New Church Life,* 41-47.

Carr, E.H. *What is History?* London: Penguin Books.

Casey, Maurice. 1982. Chronology and the development of Pauline Christology, in *Paul and Paulinism, essays in honour of C.K. Barrett,* edited by M.D. Hooker and S.G. Wilson. London:SPCK.

Catholic Encyclopedia, The. 1910. S.v. 'Heresy'. New York: Robert Appleton Company.

Chadwick, Henry. 1977. *The Early Church.* Harmondsworth: Pelican Books.

Culpepper, R.A. and Black, C.C., eds. 1996. *Exploring the Gospel of John, in honour of D. Moody.* Louisville: Westminster John Knox Press.

Danielou, Jean. 1977. *The Origins of Christiantiy*, translated by David Smith and John Austin Baker. London: Darton, Longman and Todd.

Davis, Leo Donald. 1983. *The First Seven Ecumenical Councils (325 - 787)*. *Their history and theology.* Collegeville, Minnesota: The Liturgical Press.

de Lacy, Douglas R. 1976. Image and Incarnation in Pauline Christology - A Search for Origins. *Tyndale Bulletin* 1979. Vol. 30:3-28.

Drane, John W. 1994. Patterns of Evangelisation in Paul and Jesus: a way forward in the Jesus-Paul debate? In *Jesus of Nazareth: Lord and Christ. Essays on the Historical Jesus and New Testament Christology*, edited by Joel B. Green and Max Turner. Grand Rapids: William B. Eerdmans Publishing Company.

Dunn, James D.G. 1980. *Christology in the Making. A New Testament inquiry into the Origins of the Doctrine of the Incarnation.* London: SCM Press.

Dunn, James D.G. 1994. The Making of Christology - Evolution or Unfolding. In *Jesus of Nazareth: Lord and Christ. Essays on the Historical Jesus and New Testament Christology*, edited by Joel B. Green and Max Turner. Grand Rapids: William B. Eerdmans Publishing Company.

Durant Will. 1953. *The Renaissance. A history of Civilization in Italy from 1304 - 1576 A.D.* New York: Simon and Schuster.

Edwards, Ruth B. 1994. The Christological Basis of Johannine Footwashing, in *Jesus of Nazareth: Lord and Christ. Essays on the Historical Jesus and New Testament Christology*, edited by Joel B. Green and Max Turner. Grand Rapids: William B. Eerdmans.

Ellis, E.Earle. 1994. Deity Christology in Mark 14:58, in *Jesus of Nazareth: Lord and Christ. Essays on the Historical Jesus and New Testament Christology*, edited by Joel B. Green and Max Turner. Grand Rapids: William B. Eerdmans Publishing Company.

Elton, G.R. 1969. *The Practice of History,* London and Glasgow: Collins.

Estep, William R. 1986. *Renaissance and Reformation.* Grand Rapids, MI.: William B. Eerdmans Publishing Company.

Evans, Ernest. Tr. 1948. *Q Septimii Florentis Tertulliani, Adversus Praxean Liber. Tertullian's Treatise against Praxean. The text edited, with an introduction, translation and commentary.* London: SPCK.

Fee, Gordon D. 1994. Christology and Pneumatology in Romans 8:9-11 - and elsewhere; some reflections on Paul as a Trinitarian, in *Jesus of Nazareth: Lord and Christ. Essays on the Historical Jesus and New Testament Christology,* edited by Joel B. Green and Max Turner. Grand Rapids: William B. Eerdmans Publishing Company.

Friedman, Jerome. 1978. *Michael Servetus: a case study in total heresy.* Geneva: Libraire Droz.

Gasque, W. Ward, and Martin, Ralph P. eds. 1970. *Apostolic History and the Gospel. Biblical and Historical Essays presented to F.F. Bruce on his 60th Birthday.* Exeter: Paternoster Press.

Garret, James Leo Jr. 1974. A Reappraisal of Chalcedon. *Review and Expositor.*

Green, Joel B. and Turner, Max, eds. 1994. *Jesus of Nazareth: Lord and Christ. Essays on the Historical Jesus and the New Testament Christology.* Grand Rapids: William B. Eerdmans.

Grillmeier, Aloys. 1975. *Christ in Christian Tradition. Volume One. From Apostolic Age to Chalcedon (451).* Bowden, John. Tr. Oxford: AR Mowbray and Co. Ltd.

Gwatkin, Henry Melvill. 1900. *Studies of Arianism.* 2nd Ed. Cambridge: Deighton Bell and Co.

Gwatkin, Henry Melvill. 1927. *Early Church History to AD 313.* London: Macmillan and Co. Ltd.

Hartin, P.J. 1985. A community in crises. The christology of the Johannine community as the point at issue. *Neotestimentica.* 19 (75) 37-49.

Hillar, Marian. 1997. *The Case of Michael Servetus (1511 – 1553); the turning point in the struggle for freedom of conscience.* Lampeter: the Edwin Mellen Press.

Hooker, M.D. and Wilson, S.G. eds. 1982. *Paul and Paulinism, essays in honour of C.K. Barrett.* London: SPCK.

Hubener, Anja. 1988. Academic Uppsala, in *Emanuel Swedenborg, A Continuing Vision, a pictorial biography and anthology of essays and poety,* edited by Larsen et al. New York: Swedenborg Foundation.

Jedin, Hubert and Dolan, John. Eds. 1980. *The Imperial Church from Constantine to the Early Middle Ages,* by Baus, Karl; Beck, Hans-Georg; Ewig, Eugen; Vogt, Hermann Josef. Biggs, Anselm, translator. London: Burns & Oates.

Jones. W.T. 1969. *Kant and the Nineteenth Century; a history of Western Philosophy.* 2nd ed. New York: Harcourt and Brace Jovanovich.

Keck, Leander E. 1986. Toward the renewal of New Testament Christology. *New Testament Studies,* 32:362 - 377.

Larson, Robin et al, eds. 1988. *Emanuel Swedenborg, A Continuing Vision, a pictorial biography and anthology of essays and poety.* New York: Swedenborg Foundation.

Larson, Stephen. 1988. The Soul and the Abyss of Nature, in *Emanuel Swedenborg, A Continuing Vision, a pictorial biography and anthology of essays and poety,* edited by Larsen et al. New York: Swedenborg Foundation.

Latourette, Kenneth Scott. 1975. *A History of Christianity. Volume 1: to AD 1500.* New York: Harper Collins.

Latourette. Kenneth Scott. 1975. *A History of Christianity. Volume II: AD 1500 - AD 1975.* New York: Harper Collins.

Liturgy and Hymnal for use of the General Church of the New Jerusalem. 1966. Bryn Athyn, PA.: General Church of the New Jerusalem.

Loader, W.R.G. 1984. The Central Structure of Johannine Christology. *New Testament Studies,* 30:188-216.

Mackall, Leonard L. 1919. *Servetus Notes.* New York: Osler Anniversary Volumes II.

McGuckin, John A. 1994. *St. Cyril of Alexandria. The Christological Controversy, its history, theology and texts.* Leiden: E.J. Brill.

Muddiman, John. 1984. Adam, the type of the One to come. *Theology,* 1987:101-110.

Nickelsburg. 1993. Jews and Christians in the First Century; the struggle over identity. *Neotestimentica,* 27:365 – 390.

Noble, Samuel. 1886. *An Appeal in behalf of the views of the eternal world and state, and the doctrines of faith and life, held by the body of Christians who believe that A New Church is signified (in the Revelation Chap. XXI) by the New Jerusalem; embracing answers to all principal objections.* 11th edition. London: James Speirs.

Norris, R.A. 1963. *Manhood and Christ, a study in the Christology of Theodore of Mopsuestia.* Oxford: Clarendon Press.

Norris, R.A. 1966. *God and World in Early Christian Theology. A study in Justin Martyr, Irenaeus, Tertullian and Origen.* London: Adam and Charles Black.

O'Collins, Gerald, S.J. 1995. *Christology A biblical, historical and systematic study of Jesus Christ.* New York: Oxford University Press.

Odhner, Carl Theophilus. 1898. Some New Documents concerning Swedenborg. *New Church Life,* 107 – 108.

Odhner, Carl Theophilus. 1900. The Lord's Personal Manifestation to Swedenborg. *New Church Life,* 1 – 10.

Odhner, Carl Theophilus. 1910. *Michael Servetus: His life and teachings.* Philadelphia: J.B. Lippincott Co.

Odhner, Carl Theophilus. 1910[a]. The Gothenburg Trial, an analysis of documents. *New Church Life,* 221 – 239, 618 – 620, 742 – 753.

Odhner, Carl Theophilus. 1910[b]. The Gothenburg Trial, a review. *New Church Life,* 153 – 164.

Odhner, Carl Theophilus. 1914. The Origin of the Report that Swedenborg was Insane. *New Church Life,* 235.

Osborn, Erik. 1997. *Tertullian, First Theologian of the West.* Cambridge: Cambridge University Press.

Osborne, Grant R. 1994. Structure and Christology in Mark 1:21-45, in *Jesus of Nazareth: Lord and Christ. Essays on the Historical Jesus and New Testament Christology,* edited by Joel B. Green and Max Turner. Grand Rapids: William B. Eerdmans Publishing Company.

Osler, William. 1909. *Michael Servetus.* London: Oxford University Press.

Painter, John. 1983. Christology and the Fourth Gospel. A Study of the Prologue. *Australian Biblical Review* (31) 45-62.

Pelikan, Jaroslav. 1985. *Jesus Through the Centuries. His place in the history of culture.* New York: Harper and Row.

Pendleton, Charles R. 1906. Swedenborg in the Dawn of the New Dispensation. *New Church Life.* 497.

Pendleton, Willard D. 1965. The Messianic Prophecy and its Fulfillment. *New Church Life.* 497.

Pettegree, Andrew. 1990. Michael Servetus and the Limits of Tolerance. *History Today* (40) 40 - 45.

Pettersen, Alwyn.1995. *Athanasisus.* London: Geoffrey Chapman.

Reid, Jennings B. 1990. *Jesus, God's emptiness, God's fullness: The Christology of St. Paul.* Mahwah, New Jersey: Paulist Press.

Retzius, Gustaf. 1903. Emanuel Swedenborg as an Anatomist and Physiologist. The opening address at the Congress of Anatomists, Heidleberg, May 29th 1903. *New Church Life.* 565 – 577.

Rose, Donald. 1968. Two Hundred Years Ago. *New Church Life.* 159 – 161, 419 – 420.

Rose, Frank. 1985. *Words in Swedenborg, and their meanings in modern English.* Bryn Athyn, PA: General Church Press.

Schweizer E. 1982. Paul's Christology and Gnosticism in *Paul and Paulinism, essays in honour of C.K. Barrett,* edited by M.D. Hooker and S.G. Wilson. London: SPCK.

Shelley, Bruce L. 1982. *Church History in Plain Language.* Dallas: Word Publishing.

Sigstedt, Cyriel Odhner. 1981. *The Swedenborg Epic. The Life and Works of Emanuel Swedenborg.* London: The Swedenborg Society.

Smith, T.C. 1974. The Christology of the Fourth Gospel. *Review and Expositor.* 19-29.

Smithson, I.H. ed. 1841. *Documents concerning the life and character of Emanuel Swedenborg, collected by Dr. J.F.L. Tafel of Tubingen.* Manchester: Joseph Hayward.

Sproston, W.E. 1985. `Is not this Jesus, the Son of Joseph...?' (John 6:42). Johannine Christology as a Challenge to Faith. *Journal for the study of the New Testament.* (24) 77-97.

Staniforth, Maxwell. Tr. 1980. *Early Christian Writings. The Apostolic Fathers.* Harmondsworth: Penguin Books.

Stead, Christopher. 1985. *Substance and Illusion in the Church Fathers.* London: Variorum Reprints.

Stead, Christopher. 1994. Arius in Modern Research. *Journal of Theological Studies,* 45:24 – 36.

Stroh, Alfred. 1904. Swedenborg's Earliest Publication. *New Church Life,* 359 – 360.

Stroh, Alfred. 1907. Research Word on Swedenborgiana at Stockholm and Uppsala. *New Church Life.* 346 – 349.

Stroh, Alfred. 1909. Outlines of Swedenborg's early life, with a brief account of the origin and first development of his philosophy. *New Church Life,* 689 – 702.

Tafel, R.L. ed. 1875. *Documents Concerning the Life and Character of Emanuel Swedenborg.* London: Swedenborg Society.

Thompson, Marianne Meye. 1996. The Historical Jesus and Johannine Christ, in *Exploring the Gospel of John, in honour of D. Moody Smith,* edited by R.A. Culpepper, and C.C. Black. Louisville: Westminster John Knox Press.

Thrall, Margaret E. 1970. The origin of Pauline Christology, in *Apostolic History and the Gospel. Biblical and Historical Essays presented to F.F. Bruce on his 60th Birthday,* edited by W.Ward Gasque, and Ralph P. Martin. Exeter: The Paternoster Press.

Toksvig, Signe. 1948. *Emanuel Swedenborg, scientist and mystic.* New Haven: Yale University Press.

Trobridge, George. 1968. *Swedenborg, Life and Teaching.* New York: Swedenborg Foundation.

Wadkins, Timothy H. 1983. A Recipe for Intolerance: a study of the reasons behind John Calvin's approval of punishment for heresy. *Journal of the Evangelical Theological Society* (26) 431 - 441.

Webster's New World Dictionary of the American Language. 1960. Cleveland and New York: World Publishing Company.

Wiles, Maurice. 1966. *The Christian Fathers.* London: Hodder and Stoughton.

Williams, Rowan. 1987. *Arius - heresy and tradition.* London: Darton, Longman and Todd.

Willis, R. 1877. Servetus and Calvin. *A study of an important epoch in the early history of the reformation.* London: Henry S. King and Co.

Wolfson, Harry Austryn. 1970. *The Philosophy of the Church Fathers.* Volume I. Faith, Trinity, Incarnation. Cambridge, Mass.: Harvard University Press.

Young, Frances M. 1983. *From Nicaea to Chalcedon.* London: SCM Press Ltd.

11773831R00221

Printed in Germany
by Amazon Distribution
GmbH, Leipzig